-Gone Riding-

Dom Giles

Cardiff Libraries
www.cardiff.gov.uk/libraries

Llyfrgelloedd Caerdydd
www.caerdydd.gov.uk/llyfrgelloedd

Pen Press

First published in Great Britain by Pen Press

All paper used in the printing of this book has been made from wood grown in managed, sustainable forests.

ISBN: 978-1-78003-720-2

Printed and bound in the UK
Pen Press is an imprint of
Indepenpress Publishing Limited
25 Eastern Place
Brighton
BN2 1GJ

A catalogue record of this book is available from
the British Library

Cover design by Fil Schiannini

For Mum and Dad.

I hope I would have made you proud.

THANKS

I'd like to start by thanking my sponsors, but I didn't have any so I can't. However, it would be fair to say that without my wife's support the whole thing might never have happened. Tracy encouraged me to get on with it, supporting my crazy adventure but was also willing to tell me I was being stupid when I was. She did her fair share of editing too!

A special thank you must go to Grant and Susan Johnson of Horizons Unlimited (www.horizonsunlimited.com). Their website is full of useful information and has a forum dedicated to adventure travel. I used it to ask lots of questions and was always pleasantly surprised by the helpful responses I got. The annual bike rally they hold afforded me the chance to ask questions in person and chat with like-minded travellers; it's always good to know you're not alone. Thank you to everyone who helped me and answered my queries.

Special thanks must also be reserved for Sam Manicom. Reading his travel books fuelled my enthusiasm to do my own trip and his help and advice, once I'd decided to write a book, has been invaluable. And, of course, to my editor, Paul Blezard, who seemed to enjoy (perhaps a little too much) pointing out my idiocies, both grammar and motorcycle related. His forthright, honest and blunt style has made my story immeasurably better. Also, thanks to Fil Schiannini, who kindly designed the book cover, and Nigel Lea, who created the maps.

On the road there were many people who helped me. Nevil, David and Jill, Jim, Chrissy and Alan, Daryll and Angela, Tom, Pat and Chris, all deserve special mention. It was a pleasure riding with you all and I hope we'll meet again sometime. Thanks to Trent for finally replying to my emails, Norman for your help and accommodation and Lerato for being an inspiration.

Thanks also to The Ted Simon Foundation, especially Iain Harper, Geoff Thomas and Helen Lloyd, and to Damien Fauchot, Norman Magowan and Bernard Smith. You may have thought you only helped a little – it was appreciated a lot. I found writing harder than I thought I would and I needed the support, advice and encouragement you all gave.

And finally, thanks to Heidi. I probably couldn't have done it without you.

CONTENTS

WHY?   ix

PROLOGUE   Don't Cry For Me Argentina   xi

PART ONE
NORTH AND CENTRAL AMERICA

Chapter 1   Homefries Or Grits?   3

Chapter 2   Crazy Dogs   15

Chapter 3   Fires And Friends   26

Chapter 4   Ursus Arctos Horribilis   37

Chapter 5   Looking For America   51

Chapter 6   Finding America   62

Chapter 7   Up And Down Like A Yoyo   76

Chapter 8   Can Lightning Strike Twice?   87

Chapter 9   Leaving Las Vegas   97

Chapter 10   A Changing State Of Mind   107

Chapter 11   On A Dark Desert Highway   120

Chapter 12   Two-Up and Heading For The Hills   133

Chapter 13   A Mayan Odyssey   145

Chapter 14   Sandinistas And Sloths   157

Chapter 15   Panama Here We Come!   173

PART TWO
SOUTHERN AND EASTERN AFRICA

Chapter 16   The Sani Pass, South Africa   191

Chapter 17   Getting A South African Education   193

Chapter 18   How High Can You Get?   205

Chapter 19   Motorcycle Safari   218

Chapter 20   The Kingdom In The Sky   233

Chapter 21   Into Namibia   244

Chapter 22   Sand   253

Chapter 23   Waving At The Locals   265

Chapter 24   The Smoke That Thunders   275

Chapter 25   Great Stone Houses   289

Chapter 26   From Harare To Malawi   296

Chapter 27   Splitting Up   305

Chapter 28   The End Of The Road   313

EPILOGUE   Why Not?   323

WHY?

"Why give up your job and travel half way around the world by motorcycle?"

This was the question people asked, over and over again; and even when they didn't say it out loud I could see it in their eyes. "Because I've always wanted to" never seemed a mature enough response. But there is something inside me that always yearns to see what's around the corner; what's out there on this unique planet we all share. Perhaps growing up on the small island of Jersey had instilled in me a desire to see the wider world and wander around it.

I always knew that I wanted to travel and soon after starting my teaching career in West London, I moved to a school in Argentina in 1995 where I also met my future wife, Tracy. I bought a motorcycle and spent the holidays exploring Argentina, Chile, Uruguay, Brazil and Paraguay. This is where I developed a taste for two-wheeled adventure. From Argentina we spent the next ten years teaching in Colombia, The Falkland Islands, Ethiopia and Dubai. Throughout that whole time I indulged my passion for travelling, but no longer from the seat of a motorcycle.

We returned to live in the UK in 2007. I found a good job in a good school and everything was, well, good. But three years of 'good' gave me itchy feet; and this time I was determined to travel by motorcycle. Tracy didn't want to do a whole year but was more than happy to take some sabbatical time to travel with me for parts of the journey. I'd also stumbled across www.horizonsunlimited.com, an overland adventure motorcycle website which gave me all the advice and confidence I needed to plan my trip. I began to realise that ordinary people can accomplish their dreams of long distance travel; it wasn't just reserved for super-humans and film stars. I decided to take the plunge – soon.

And then my father died. My mother had died in 2005 after a short illness but my dad didn't give us any warning at all. The day after returning from a holiday in April 2009 I got a phone call to say he was dead. He had gone to bed the night before and just didn't wake up. And that was the final wake-up call I needed. "Why do it?" had become "If not now, when?"

Not being one to rush a decision, I spent over a year planning where I wanted to go and how I would do it and designed a route which included places Tracy wanted to visit. I'd always wanted to go to Alaska so that seemed like a good place to start. I'd got to the age of forty without ever going to the US or Canada, despite being an experienced traveller, so my plan was to explore North America before heading into Central America. I'd spent four years living in South America so although it made sense geographically to go from Panama to Colombia, as many travellers do, I decided to miss out South America and instead try to head from Panama to Africa. I am drawn to large open spaces and the thought of riding a motorcycle around southern Africa was thrilling.

I didn't just want to ride around the world. I also wanted to do some volunteering along the way and spent a long time researching various projects before settling on two conservation projects: a turtle project in Baja California, Mexico and a sloth sanctuary in Costa Rica. In addition, I made arrangements to work with township children in Cape Town.

I'd prepared all these plans but still hadn't put my money where my mouth was and resigned my job. And then, on holiday over Christmas 2009, in Kerala, India, I turned to Tracy and said, "That's it. I'm going. I've been going on about this for long enough. I either need to do this or shut up about it. It may well end in disaster; it will most certainly cost us a lot of money, but what is life for? So what if I don't really know much about motorcycles? I'll learn along the way and when I break down I'll deal with it. I want to do this on a bike. It will give me the freedom to go where I want but won't cut me off from what I'm seeing. It'll make the journey exciting, unpredictable and unforgettable. And you can join me for the bits you want to see. What do you say?"

Tracy turned her head and said, "What? Sorry, I had my iPod on. What did you say?"

The feeling that I was doing the right thing didn't diminish over the rest of my holiday and I returned to the UK excited and alive to the idea that I was about to make my dream come true. I will never forget the look on the face of my Head Teacher when I went into his office one January morning to tell him that I was resigning as I had a plan to ride a motorcycle around the world. He hid it well, and said all the right things, but I could tell that behind the words of support and encouragement he was silently screaming out that question that everyone asked, but which I still didn't have a reply for: *"Why?!"*

I hope this book will go some way to providing an answer.

PROLOGUE

DON'T CRY FOR ME ARGENTINA

"There must be more to life than sitting wondering if there is more to life."
(Anon.)

It wasn't even my idea. I enjoyed travelling and also happened to have a full motorcycle licence, but I'd never thought about putting the two together. In February 1995 I was a young Secondary school history teacher, two and a half years into my career at a challenging comprehensive school in west London. It was tough, stressful work and so when an opportunity arose to teach in an international school in glamorous and far-away Buenos Aires, I was happy to take it.

My friend Justin gave me a copy of Ted Simon's *Jupiter's Travels* as a leaving present. I had no idea who Ted Simon was and at that time I hadn't ridden a bike for several years. In fact, I'm not even sure Justin knew I could ride a bike; in hindsight it was a strange gift. I started reading the book on the flight from Heathrow and by the time we landed I was hooked. Simon had spent four years riding around the world on a motorcycle in the mid-1970s and I found his story captivating. So it's all Justin's fault. It's always good to have friends to blame things on and I blame it on him.

But not just him. Reading *Jupiter's Travels* planted a small seed which lay germinating in the back of my mind as I settled into life in Argentina but I also blame Gwen and Maggie for their part in nurturing that seed. Gwen was my great aunt who had left me £2000 in her will and Maggie was a fellow teacher who suggested that I should spend it on a motorcycle. Buenos Aires, it must be said, is not the most likely place to prompt the thought: "What a great place to ride a motorcycle." It's a massive, noisy, polluted South American city with chaotic traffic. I was, however, young and adventurous, or at least impetuous. I popped out one day after school and bought myself a Honda 250 something-or-other. To my eternal shame, I can't even remember which model it was. It was black.

I don't think, at that stage, I had any idea what I was going to do with this bike except ride it around Buenos Aires and out on to the flat, boring, monotonous plains or *pampas* that surround the capital – but there we were – I had a bike. Maggie had a bike too and we went out at weekends to explore the flat, boring, monotonous pampas together. The most exciting trip we did was to a nondescript dusty town famous for being the birthplace of Eva Peron. We went, hoping and expecting, to find some sort of museum or memorial, but there was neither; although strangely there were lots of posters of Evita (as she was known) on the main road heading back towards town. I remember commenting to Maggie that Eva Peron looked strikingly like Madonna. Six months later, the film *Evita* was released.

I also blame Trent. Because that would probably have been that – weekend trips out on to the flat, boring, monotonous pampas – if it hadn't been for Trent. Trent was an American Primary school teacher and keen cyclist with whom I shared a flat. He was planning to cycle back to the USA from Tierra del Fuego (at the southern tip of Argentina) and his enthusiasm for long distance, solo two-wheeled travel was contagious. When he suggested I spend the summer biking around Patagonia, I couldn't think of a good reason not to. After all, I had a bike and I'd read *Jupiter's Travels*, what was stopping me?

But if I was going to do this I needed more ccs beneath me, having neither the time nor frankly the fitness to rely merely on my own muscle power like Trent. I hunted around lots of Buenos Aires bike shops but couldn't find anything that suited until quite by chance, on the way back from one of my boring days out on the pampas, I saw a big Honda sign. I pulled into the shop forecourt and immediately my eyes rested on a huge, shiny bike in the window. Surely that would be big enough for the job? I spoke to the shop owner, part-exchanged my Honda 250, left a deposit and went home to write in my diary, "I've found it, the big trail bike that will take me to Patagonia. I've just bought a brand new Honda Translap 600." It was several days before I realised it was actually called a Transalp not a 'Translap', but a little motorcycle ignorance shouldn't get in the way of a big trip; a maxim that was to become my motto.

By now it was early November and I had four weeks left of term before the summer holidays and in those four weeks I had to cover 600 miles so I could get the first service done. This was where those flat, boring, monotonous pampas came into their own; every weekend I was out clocking up the miles. On one occasion I was stopped by the Argentine police who wanted to have a look at the bike but as soon as they saw my UK passport the conversation quickly changed. By now I was used to this and although it was harmless enough, it was predictable how almost every conversation I seemed to have with an Argentine male revolved around what I came to call 'The three M's': Maradona and his 'hand of God' (which put England out of the 1986 World Cup); Las Malvinas (the Falkland Islands) and how they are Argentine; and Mujeres (women) and how Argentina has the most beautiful women in the world. This line of questioning, especially from the police, was always difficult for me to handle. First, obviously Maradona was a cheat and it's hard to see how anyone can get past that. Second, The Falklands are British and definitely aren't going to belong to Argentina any time soon. And anyway, what annoyed me was not that people argued that the Falklands *should* be Argentine, but insisted they *were* Argentine. You can't just re-write the geo-political world map how you want it. And third, whilst I might be willing to admit that many Argentine women are very beautiful, it was too often the kind of beauty associated with anorexic supermodels. The story at my school was that the plumbing in the girls' toilets had to be regularly changed as the post lunchtime rush led to erosion of the pipes due to stomach acid. I had to sit at lunch with a table of eight teenage girls for two years. I can attest to the fact that they did not eat much and that the conversation revolved around diets, food, diets, supermodels and diets. Rumour had it that Argentina in general, and Buenos Aires in particular, had more psychiatrists and plastic surgeons per head than anywhere else in the world. Obviously I'm not stupid and I didn't mention any of these reservations to the police. I just agreed with them. They had guns.

So, that's how it all began, by accident, in Argentina and through no fault of my own. I had, needless to say, a fantastic ten weeks riding down to Tierra del Fuego and back again up Route 40. At the bottom of Argentina, on Tierra del Fuego, I stopped for the obligatory photo next to the sign telling me I'd made it to the bottom of the continent. I could go no further south. However, if I headed north Alaska was only 17,848km away. That was too far to go in one summer holiday but, it made me think.

I met Trent in Chile who, by then, had cycled a thousand miles through the remote wilderness of Patagonia and was having an amazing time. We climbed a volcano together, went hiking in a national park and spent a memorable night lost in the wilderness sleeping rough in a chicken shed. As I left him in Pucon and headed back to Buenos Aires and work, I was envious of his spirit of adventure and freedom to carry on northward towards the United States. Months later I heard that he had made it all the way up Chile and then had his bicycle stolen on the Peru border. Although devastated by the experience, he wasn't bitter or resentful, and it hadn't diminished his love of travelling. He knew, one day, he would get to continue his big trip. I completely understood what he meant. When I got back to work I knew that I had a big trip in me and that one day I would do it, but life, and work, got in the way. It was another fifteen years before I found myself, aged 42, on a plane heading for Alaska and this time I had no one to blame but myself.

PART ONE

North and Central America

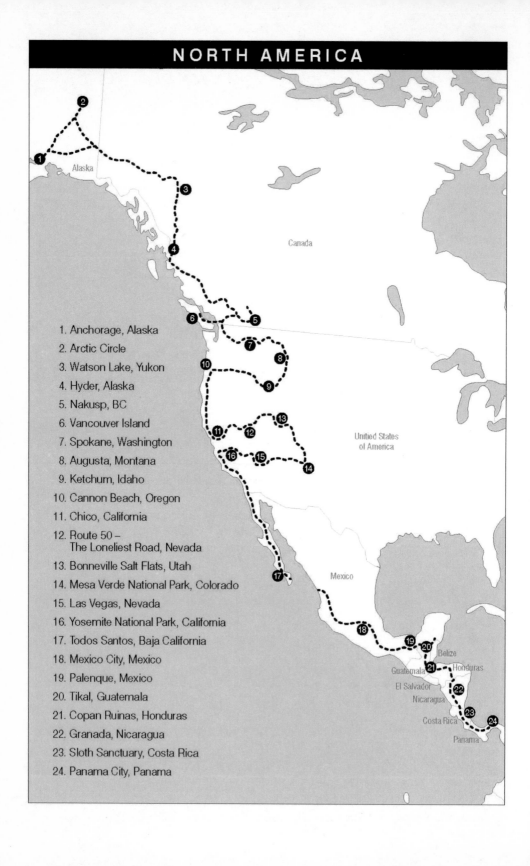

NORTH AMERICA

Alaska

Canada

United States
of America

Mexico

Belize

Guatemala   Honduras

El Salvador

Nicaragua

Costa Rica

Panama

1. Anchorage, Alaska

2. Arctic Circle

3. Watson Lake, Yukon

4. Hyder, Alaska

5. Nakusp, BC

6. Vancouver Island

7. Spokane, Washington

8. Augusta, Montana

9. Ketchum, Idaho

10. Cannon Beach, Oregon

11. Chico, California

12. Route 50 –
    The Loneliest Road, Nevada

13. Bonneville Salt Flats, Utah

14. Mesa Verde National Park, Colorado

15. Las Vegas, Nevada

16. Yosemite National Park, California

17. Todos Santos, Baja California

18. Mexico City, Mexico

19. Palenque, Mexico

20. Tikal, Guatemala

21. Copan Ruinas, Honduras

22. Granada, Nicaragua

23. Sloth Sanctuary, Costa Rica

24. Panama City, Panama

CHAPTER 1

HOMEFRIES OR GRITS?

"I have wandered all my life and I have also travelled; the difference between the two being this, that we wander for distraction, but we travel for fulfilment."

(Hilaire Belloc)

Alaska. It's just one of those places you have to go to, isn't it? It's there at the top end of the North American continent just screaming out to be visited. How can anyone look at a map of the western hemisphere and not say "Wow, look at Alaska. It's so huge and so far away. I wonder what it's like?" That and a craving to know what a place that could elect Sarah Palin as Governor would be like, led me to choose Alaska as my starting point. So let's start by getting the facts and figures out of the way. As Michelle Shocked sings in 'Anchored down in Anchorage' Alaska is 'the largest state in the union.' It's more than twice the size of Texas (but don't remind a Texan) and if it were a country it would be, geographically, the 19th largest in the world (between Mongolia and Peru; the UK is 79th). Its population hovers (or is that shivers?) around the 700,000 mark, making it the least densely populated state in the USA and, again, if it were a country, third in the world: one person per square mile. Only Greenland and The Falkland Islands have a lower population density. But what intrigued and amazed me is that a hundred years ago Alaska's population came in at a mere 60,000. With less than 10% of today's population it must have been a very lonely place.

These thoughts, however, weren't going through my mind as the plane landed in a rainy Anchorage in July 2010; I was much more worried about US customs and immigration. A UK citizen can normally apply for the visa-waiver programme but only if you have a return rather than, like me, a one-way ticket. I had to go to the US Embassy in London and be interviewed for my visa. I explained that I had given up my job and was flying to Alaska so I could ride a motorcycle down through North America and on to Panama. I didn't mention that I was then planning to go on to Africa. I didn't want to freak her out too much: the woman behind the bullet-proof glass window was already looking at me as if I were insane. I'd come to recognise that expression from people when I mentioned my plans but I didn't expect it from someone who worked at the visa section of the US Embassy and must surely have come across the odd traveller before. She asked me if I had any proof that I had the funds to finance the trip. I didn't.

"But sir," (I just hate it when people call me 'sir' when what they really mean is 'git') "You are here to convince me that you are going to be doing what you say you are going to be doing. Do you not have any bank statements or anything?"

I wanted to scream. I had thought this was all going to be a formality. It had never really crossed my mind that I would have to convince her of anything. I wanted to shout but I knew she had the power to say no to my visa application and I'd already bought the bike in Alaska and my flight ticket.

"Look," I said. (Not a good start I know, but a much better four-letter word than the one I had in my head.) "I've had this lifelong dream to ride a motorcycle down the Americas. I gave up my job to do this and, of course, I have the funds to do it. It doesn't cost that much anyway. I have a wife and a house in the UK. I'm not going to give all that up to become an illegal immigrant in the US."

"It says on your forms that you are a school teacher. They don't get paid much do they? How can you afford to do this?"

Through gritted teeth I replied, "My grandmother died and left me some money."

She looked at me, long and hard, seemingly unconvinced, but eventually she acquiesced and granted me a visa. And I thought getting into some Central American countries would be hard!

So as I approached immigration in Anchorage I fully expected to be stopped and strip-searched. How dare someone come to America on a one-way ticket with his life savings and a motorcycle. He must be a terrorist.

"Morning, sir. Can I see your passport?"

"Good morning. Here you are," I replied.

"Here for shooting?"

"Er, pardon?"

"Are you here shooting, or fishing?"

"Er, no. I'm riding a motorcycle."

"OK, that's unusual. Most people come here to shoot."

And that was it. I was through customs, although it seemed it would have been more conventional if I'd had a gun with me instead of a crash helmet. Welcome to America.

I found a payphone and called up Motoquest. This was the Anchorage-based motorcycle dealer who'd sold me the bike over the internet. I'd been in regular contact with Nicole from Motoquest for a few months, paying for the bike and ordering a few extras as I was only allowed 20 kilos of luggage on the plane. I dialled the number and someone called Phil answered.

"Hi, my name's Dom and I hope you've got a BMW 1200GS waiting for me," I jested.

Silence.

"Nicole will know who I am," I added.

Silence.

"Erm. I'm from the UK and I bought a bike from you. Over the internet. I've paid for it and everything."

"Nicole doesn't work for us anymore," Phil replied in a very deep, deadpan voice. I'm sure the silence that followed only lasted for a couple of seconds but it felt like hours. "But don't worry, Dom," Phil eventually added in a chirpier voice, "We know who you are and I'm on my way to get you." I could tell Phil was a real joker!

Motoquest was situated next to a Harley-Davidson shop not far from the airport. The bike shop owned a patch of grass out the back and I was allowed to camp there for free. Phil dropped me off and said he would return first thing in the morning when the office opened and we could take a look at the bike and do all the paperwork. Excitedly, I put my tent up in the drizzle, trying to keep everything as dry as possible, but in a way I didn't really care. I was here, in Alaska; they'd let me into the country and just a few yards away in the Motoquest shed, I had a bike waiting to take me all the way down to Panama.

Across the road from where I was camping there was a 'diner' mentioned in the Lonely Planet as "Alaska at its best; lots to look at – totems, stuffed bears and a gurgling stream – and big portions." And they were right. However, as a vegetarian I was limited to eating omelette and potatoes. I'd never been to the United States before and it all felt a little surreal, like being in a film (or is that a movie?). Diners for me, were associated with Nicholas Cage films; I hadn't thought that they might actually exist. It was all so familiar and yet so strange. The waitress was friendly, bubbly and loud and kept saying, "You got it!" every time I asked for something. For the first time in my life I became conscious of my own accent and began to feel as if I was talking in a very posh voice.

When the food came it was huge, bland and should have had a health warning attached to it. I was given a four-egg omelette and a field full of fried potatoes. But I didn't really care. I was here. They'd let me in. The bike I had paid for existed (even if Nicole had mysteriously disappeared); all was in order and the following morning Phil and I would take care of the paperwork and my trip would really begin. After eating my first all-American meal, I walked back over to the Harley campground in the rain. (That rain had started just as I landed and didn't let up for the next three days.) It was 11 pm but still light, and I was wet, jet-lagged and full of too much egg and potato but I was happy. Day one complete. Bring it on!

The following morning, before Motoquest opened, I walked back over to *Gwennie's Old Alaska Restaurant*. I hadn't bought any food to cook yet, and although I knew I couldn't afford to eat out every day for a year it was still raining and, after all, I was celebrating my first full day. I asked for toast and scrambled egg. At least vegetarians are catered for at breakfast everywhere. After giving me a huge variety of breads to choose from (what is sour bread?) I was asked if I wanted homefries or grits? Too ashamed/polite to ask what grits were, I opted for homefries. I ended up getting exactly what I had the night before, the eggs were more omelette than scrambled and the homefries were sliced, fried potatoes. If this was to continue I was bound to have a heart attack before I'd even left Alaska.

I also noticed that I hadn't even been in the country 24 hours and I'd begun to talk like the locals. I asked if I could 'get' some coffee and then, where the 'restroom' was. I'm sure I've read somewhere that this kind of behaviour – adopting local colloquialisms, accents or dialects – is a sign of emotional intelligence, but to me it almost felt as if I was taking the mickey.

After my 'cawffeeee and eggs,' I met Phil and we went to the Anchorage vehicle registration office. It took less than ten minutes to get the bike signed over to me. I had to show my passport, hand over about $40 and register the bike using the Motoquest office as an address. It was as simple as that. I'd pre-arranged insurance with a large American insurance company online before leaving the UK and we then drove to their Anchorage office and in no time I had valid bike insurance which would cover me for a year. I was assured that when I left America for Mexico a quick email to them would result in a refund for the months I hadn't used. I was hugely impressed with the efficient, friendly service I was receiving and I was back at Motoquest before lunchtime ready to hit the road.

The final thing I needed to do was to chat to Mike, the mechanic. I made a quip about Mike Rutherford and the band Genesis which was followed by an awkward silence – the first of many cultural mix-ups I was to encounter this side of the pond. As I was to learn, Brits and Americans might speak the same language but we don't necessarily share the same cultural references. But it didn't matter – there, in a corner of the garage was my bike, looking very much like the photos I'd been sent (which was reassuring). Several months previously I'd been looking online to see if I could buy a bike State side and I'd found Motoquest, which runs escorted bike trips and also rent out bikes. I'd emailed them in the hope that they might have an ex-rental bike for sale. They'd written back saying they had one – a BMW R1200GS complete with panniers, tank bag, heated grips and crash bars. They had also been very honest about the fact that she had been well used.

Mike introduced me to a slightly battered and bruised blue 2006 BMW R1200GS with 46,500 miles on the clock. I'd paid $8,000 which I thought was a good deal; certainly cheaper than the equivalent bike would have been in the UK and I didn't have to pay to ship her over.

There were several small scratches on the midnight blue paintwork and what remained of a large Velcro pad which presumably once attached a tank bag to the tank. The bash plate under the engine had clearly done its job, several times over and the front of the engine casing was caked in a white, salty solution which looked as if it was starting to eat into the metal. Mike said it was something and nothing. The stainless steel downpipes were also totally caked in a muddy brown paste that clearly wasn't going to come off easily. The two Touratech panniers both looked in good order although the left one had a slight dent towards the bottom but made up for it by having an England sticker on the back. The bike certainly looked 'used' but as long as she worked and was mechanically sound, I didn't mind too much what she looked like.

Mike assured me that the bike was in good working order despite a warning light flashing red and constantly saying 'brake failure'. There are no official BMW dealers in Alaska so the bike couldn't be hooked up to a computer and rebooted or whatever it is they do to the electronics to sort them out. Normally on a GS the brake warning light goes out as soon as the brakes are engaged and the anti-lock braking system is automatically checked. But this bike wasn't like normal GS bikes and the warning light stayed on – constantly. Mike assured me that it was just a glitch, the ABS brakes worked, it was just that the sign wouldn't turn off. I wasn't really sure what ABS was so I wasn't really in a position to tell if Mike was right or not.

The computer didn't recognise the gear ratios properly either, so when she was actually in neutral the computer said she was in first gear. I was going to have to ride all the way down to the 'Lower 48' (as Alaskans call the rest of the mainland USA) like this until I could find a BMW dealership with the necessary computer equipment to re-configure the electrics. But Mike said it would be OK and who was I to argue with a mechanic?

*

On my second day in Alaska, in the afternoon rain, I rode my bike for the first time. Everyone should remember their first time and mine was through the wet afternoon traffic out of town to a shopping mall to buy some waterproofs. I also needed to get a few camping things and had a scary trip around an Anchorage camping store. Millets it was not. All I really wanted was a penknife, but I could have bought a gun, a stuffed animal, or even a crossbow. There was a whole row of products for hunters to wear to attract wild animals. I was worried that my fellow shoppers might be able to sniff out my vegetarianism. I needed some cover. I lingered at the gun section for a few minutes in case I was being watched, trying to beef up my manly credentials. Then I went to find some pepper spray.

All the literature I'd read had told me that the number one threat to campers this far north was bears. Be they grizzly or brown they would rip your throat out as you slept and the only defence you could muster came in a small can, a little like a mini fire extinguisher. It was hard to imagine, stood in a large store on the edge of Anchorage, that camping could be so dangerous. I'd done a lot of camping in my time and had never felt threatened by anything. But out here bears are a real and present danger and should be taken seriously. $40 was a lot of money for something I really didn't think I was going to need. On the other hand, it wasn't much if it was going to save my life.

When I got back to the Harley campsite it was clear that I had a neighbour and beside this second tent was a UK-registered bike, a KTM 990 Adventure. I found the owner sheltering from the perpetual rain in the Motoquest workshop. Errol had set out from New York three months earlier and had been in Alaska for a few days. He'd had a few problems with sprockets and had been waiting for parts but was keen to get back on the road as he had to get across Canada in just three weeks. We had a beer and a chat in Gwennie's bar. Errol was a friendly guy who kindly passed on a few helpful tips. He had a glint in his eye that spoke of someone who'd been on the road for a while. I'm not sure what Errol did for a living back in the UK but now he was a fully paid-up member of the adventure motorcycle community. He lived and breathed it and when I met him in Alaska he was right in the middle of his adventure. I got the feeling he was fully alive, enjoying every minute of his experience. The contrast with me couldn't have been starker. I hadn't even started, I had no experiences to call upon and had only questions, not answers. I wondered how long it would take for me to feel the way Errol did. The thought thrilled me.

Between beers I went to the bar for a refill. "So, you're not from these parts then?" the barman asked. Obviously my accent had given me away.

"No, I'm from England."

"So, you're from England – what's it like there? Is it like Alaska? Do they all speak the same language?"

'Of course we speak the same fucking language you idiot, it's called English,' I thought to myself, as I mumbled something much more polite. But then I got to thinking. Actually we don't all speak English. Later that evening, I turned to my new best friend, Google. While 95% of the United Kingdom's population speak English as their sole UK language, the UK actually has several native languages. Whilst not necessarily a first language, 20% of the population of Wales speak

Welsh, 1% of Scots speak Gaelic, 7% of people in Northern Ireland speak Irish Gaelic. Two to three thousand people speak Cornish, although the last native speaker of Cornish died in 1893. Not to mention the over one hundred other languages spoken by people across the country every day. So really, it wasn't that stupid a question after all.

Interesting as that was, it would probably have been too much information for the barman. I just said, yes we all speak English; it's a lovely country and he should go and visit. It's hard to sum up a whole country in one sentence. I remember meeting someone in my youth who'd been to China and I stupidly said, "China, wow, what's it like?" How I ever expected him to answer that, I just don't know. This is, however, a perennial problem for the traveller. After coming home from a long trip abroad people ask, "So, how was it?" But before you've even finished the first sentence you can see their eyes beginning to glaze over. The best answer would have to be 'Go and see for yourself.'

Back in the bar Errol gave me some advice on how to avoid bears, which I would heed, and a recommendation which I would ignore. He had found that McDonald's was brilliant for wi-fi and, as he pointed out, the golden arches are everywhere; they're easy to spot, reliable and fast (I think he was referring to the wi-fi but it stands for the food as well). I had never been into a McDonald's because I'm boycotting them. I disapprove of the way they treat their workers and of the environmental damage they cause. It's a whole McLibel thing. I know I'm not having much of an impact on them as they seem to be doing quite well as a company without my custom, operating as they do in 119 countries, serving over 65 million people every day. But after 40 years of never going into one I didn't want to compromise my stand just for some free wi-fi.

Errol set off for Canada the next morning and I thanked him for his advice and wished him well. I wondered how many other people I'd meet, chat to and leave in such a short space of time; one of the inevitable consequences of this sort of travel I supposed. As Errol headed east for Canada I took my first real ride on the BMW: 125 miles south to Seward on one of America's top ten roads (according to my Alaska guide book). As soon as I left Anchorage the clouds disappeared and I saw the Alaskan sun for the first time. One hundred and twenty-five miles of pine forests, mountains topped with snow, twisty roads and azure blue lakes – and a moose, just munching the lilies, as moose do. My first real trip on the bike and it felt great. All the parts of the BMW seemed to work in harmony with each other and with me, and it just felt right.

I got back to Anchorage (which was still under a rain cloud) and said goodbye to the guys at Motoquest. They had been great at helping me out and telling me where to shop for stuff. Phil had made it easy for me to get the bike registered and on the road. Mike the mechanic had set the bike up, he'd put in fresh oil and serviced the engine. The tyres, Avon Distanzia, weren't brand new but were in fairly good condition. He even gave me a spare inner tube and some tyre irons to take with me. I knew the bike had tubeless tyres but I'd read that it didn't do any harm to carry a spare inner tube just in case. In fact one of the reasons I'd opted for a GS was because it was tubeless; I was bound to get a flat somewhere and was much happier plugging a tyre from the outside rather than having to take the wheel out then lever the tyre off just to get at the innertube to patch it. I'd been on a one-day adventure motorcycle maintenance course in Wales before setting off for Alaska and one of the things we'd done was plug a punctured tubeless tyre so I'd at least had some practice at that whereas I'd never actually changed a tyre, or patched a motorcycle innertube, in my life. I put Mike's tyre irons in the pannier, hoping to hell I'd never see them again.

*

The following morning (still in rain) I left Anchorage and headed north for Fairbanks. Excited by the prospect of what lay ahead and thrilled to be on my way, I bombed up the highway stopping only to fill the tank and made it up to Fairbanks in under six hours. My trip had finally begun and I was in such a mad rush just to get somewhere – anywhere – that I didn't really take much in. That evening, I wrote in my diary: *Wed 28th July – Great day. Rode 350 miles north to Fairbanks and then ate waffles with blueberries and drank root beer.* Simple pleasures, but perhaps the best thing about Fairbanks was that the sun had come out. And this far north it stayed out. The days were warm and balmy and the nights cool but hardly dark. Fairbanks is situated at 64 degrees north, the same as Reykjavik, the capital of Iceland. On my first night camping in Fairbanks, I was reading my book (*The Redbreast* by Jo Nesbo) in my tent without a torch at 11 p.m. Very disconcerting.

The one thing I did take note of on my way up to Fairbanks was that my bike didn't have a tail rack. I'd stuffed the metal Touratech panniers and slung a big grey waterproof bag across the passenger seat but since my wife was due to fly out to join me in Canada for a while I knew I needed to free up that seat space. I wondered if there might be somewhere in Fairbanks where I could get a rack.

Whilst planning this trip I'd discovered an incredibly useful website and online forum called Horizons Unlimited (HU). Run by and for adventure bikers (which I proudly now was!) HU was full of useful information and a very friendly discussion forum where, it seemed, every question was answered speedily, helpfully and accurately. I logged on (at a gas station, not a McDonald's) and asked if anyone knew of a motorcycle dealer this far north. By the time I got to Fairbanks, a few hours later, my post had been answered. I was pointed in the direction of a man called Dan who lived in the hills behind the city. Slightly concerned about what I would find, I headed for Dan's.

Dan Armstrong and his son live in a large two-storey cabin in a pine forest. Dan had a huge, long grey beard and looked exactly like the kind of person who should be living in a cabin in Alaska. When I arrived, there were two other motorcycles already there getting their tyres (or rather tires) changed. Unbeknownst to me when I started my trip, everyone who comes up here on a bike is heading for the Dalton Highway: a 400 mile road from Fairbanks north to Prudhoe Bay (also known as Deadhorse, and the road made famous in the TV programme 'Ice road truckers'). It's one of the most northerly roads in the world and was built in the 1970s as a supply line for the oil industry. The Dalton is a Mecca for bikers but the road is only partly paved and where it isn't, it's constantly being repaired. It was described to me as, "like riding on snot and marbles." On the HU website I'd read of a biker who'd started his trip in Anchorage and headed up the Dalton, where he crashed and broke his thumb. Trip over. I also knew that Italian adventure biker, Italo Barazzutti, had crashed there in June on his Honda Goldwing and he's a professional, who's ridden to Mongolia in the past. He'd started his most recent trip in Argentina and had made it all the way up to Alaska. He was still in hospital. If he could crash on the Dalton what chance did I have?

Anyway, I wasn't there to get new tyres, or ride the Dalton, I just wanted a tail rack and amazingly, Dan had one. His son had a 1200GS and had changed his tail rack for a new larger one. He'd kept the original.

"Your bike would have had a tail rack. Someone's taken it off," Dan informed me.

"Yeah. I didn't really notice in Anchorage. I was just so excited about the whole thing I didn't really take note."

I had to wait as bike after bike turned up for a 'pit stop' tyre change. All in all I was there for three hours and eight other bikes turned up, all with tales of the Dalton. They were all Americans and mainly on BMW GSs; some heading up, some returning. The ones who had been up to Deadhorse were pumped with adrenaline and clearly chuffed to bits that they'd done it. Those heading north were full of excitement. The atmosphere was contagious.

All these bikers had come up to Alaska especially for this and I could see how thrilled they all were. This was their trip of a lifetime. Mine had just begun. The Dalton had come too soon in my adventure to take the risk – or at least too soon to try the whole 400 miles of it. But after three hours of meeting excited bikers, I was starting to change my mind. Apparently the Dalton was in quite good condition as far as the Arctic Circle. I had to at least try riding it that far and decided to give it a go in the morning. I was going up the Dalton!

*

Under a beautifully warm sun, the paved road out of Fairbanks was just glorious. Far away from polluting cities, life seems in sharper focus: colours more vivid, smells more defined, sounds more distinct. The two-lane highway I was riding up was bordered with vibrant green spruce and pine trees which smelt as fresh as, well, an Arctic meadow.

After about an hour the tarmac ran out as I passed a sign informing me that I was now on the Dalton Highway. Initially the road was quite bad with deep potholes and loose gravel and for the first ten miles I wondered if this was worth it, but I'd also heard that they keep the first section in poor condition on purpose to dissuade people from using it in 'unsuitable vehicles'.

Once I'd made it through that tricky section the surface suddenly became smoother. A well-graded earthen road swept me up and over the rolling hills of northern Alaska. To my left I could see for miles and miles as the low scrub afforded me a wonderful Arctic vista of rolling hills and rocky outcrops; very little of the vegetation at this latitude grows more than a foot high. On my right I was confronted with a huge metal pipeline!

The Trans-Alaska Pipeline snakes for 800 miles from Prudhoe Bay in the north to Valdez in the south where 700,000 barrels per day are pumped onto ships. There are 42 US gallons in a barrel so that's nearly 30 million gallons a day or more than 110 million litres. It takes, on average, twelve days for the oil to make this journey.

It amazed me that the pipeline was so close to the road, and so unprotected. I realise that it's hard to protect 800 miles of pipeline in such an environment but it carries a huge amount of oil and is surely an easy target for someone (and there's always someone) who might want to disrupt America. With that thought going through my head I continued up the highway wondering whether a simple gunshot could pierce the pipeline. Later, I read on Wikipedia... *The pipe is resistant to gunshots and has resisted them on several occasions, but on October 4, 2001, a drunken gunman named Daniel Carson Lewis shot a hole into a weld causing the second-largest mainline oil spill in pipeline history. Approximately 6,144 barrels leaked from the pipeline. In 2002 Lewis was found guilty of criminal mischief, assault, drunk driving, oil pollution, and misconduct. He was sentenced to 16 years in jail and ordered to repay the $17 million clean-up costs.*

How, I ask you, is someone supposed to repay $17 million? I also love that phrase, 'criminal mischief'. He wasn't a dangerous drunken vandal, he was, as Brian's mum declared in *The Life of Brian*, "a very naughty boy".

I knew that the Arctic Circle was situated at mile 115 on the Dalton Highway and, helpfully, every mile was marked with a large milepost, but as I drew nearer I started to think, what is the Arctic Circle? I mean what does it denote? Why is it there? God, can I really be this thick? I'm aiming to get myself and my bike to the circle but I have no idea why. I knew that the tropics of Cancer and Capricorn

12

mark the most northerly and southerly overhead points of the sun. Stand at the Tropic of Cancer for example and you will have the sun directly overhead on the 21st June; the sun will not go any further north. Six months later the sun is directly over Capricorn. On 21st March and September the sun is directly over the Equator. But what did the Arctic Circle denote? Come on, Dom, use your brain! Why on earth are you heading here if you don't even know what it signifies? If there was a signpost in Alaska that said, "Come here, just because I said so," would you go to it? Probably, it would make for a great photo!

I'd always been a little suspicious of trips that had definitive start and end points: that whole 'Alaska to Ushuaia' or 'Cape to Cairo' thing. It might look and sound neat, beautifully packaged and bookended but it seems to be focusing more on the destinations than the journey. The English anthropologist E. E. Evans-Pritchard said: "History is not a succession of events, it is the links between them," and I think the same can be said about travelling. It shouldn't be about where you start and where you finish as much as about what happens in between. My trip, as planned, was never about getting from Alaska to Panama or even Nairobi. Obviously every trip has to start and finish but I knew the journey lay in the links in between.

I knew that what I was doing had been done, in one way or another, a thousand times before, but this was my own version of the mid-life crisis road trip. I would be riding solo for much of the time, but Tracy, my wife, would be joining me for sections of the route. I also wouldn't just be riding a motorcycle. I was keen to find out more about the environments through which I was travelling and to that end I'd arranged to stop and volunteer on two different conservation projects in Central America, and one in Africa.

That's why, at the time, I'd christened my trip and blog 'thedomwayround'. It was supposed to be a nod and a wink towards Ewan McGregor and Charley Boorman's Long Way Round and Long Way Down adventures and all the hoopla that had been created as a result. I enjoyed watching their programmes and they'd certainly brought adventure motorcycling to a new and wider audience but I'd been thinking about and planning this trip for well over ten years and I was going to do it my way. I was going where my whims took me. And yet, here I was, heading for the Arctic Circle with no idea why. What a muppet!

As I got closer to milepost 115 I eventually worked out what I was getting closer to. The Arctic Circle had to be solar in nature (it was a global circle what else could it be?) so there was only really one logical explanation. If you stand at the Arctic Circle on June 21st you will get twenty-four hours of daylight. The imaginary line marks the southerly limit of the twenty-four hour polar day (or in winter polar night), so the Arctic and Antarctic Circles denote the extremity of the sun's rays. I was trying to ride a motorcycle and understand astronomy at the same time. Neither comes naturally to me.

Somehow, having demystified it, it seemed less of an important milestone to reach. Which was just as well since I did, in fact, miss it.

I'd been concentrating so much on working out what the Arctic Circle represents that I'd forgotten to keep an eye out for it. The next milepost read 121. Ooops, I'd gone six miles too far. I pulled over into the next lay-by and switched off the engine. It's a bit of a cliché but the silence really was deafening. How often do we hear real silence? It seldom happens in our everyday lives and when it does it can be rather bewildering.

Although I could see for miles in every direction I really couldn't hear a thing. I was alone with my bike, several miles north of the Arctic Circle and… nothing. Just nothing. I knew that on this trip there would be moments of real discovery: moments of elation, panic, amazement, shock and awe. Standing in the vastness of the Arctic, surrounded by everything and nothing, almost drowning in the enormity of it all, I was experiencing one of those moments.

Gathering myself together I walked around a bit, listening to the absurdly loud sound of my own footsteps. Then, remembering that bears lived here, I rushed back to the bike; somehow standing next to her felt safer. But I did make a mental note to make sure that in future the expensive bear pepper spray that I'd bought in Anchorage would be best stored in my tank bag and not in my locked pannier.

I took out my phone and thought about either phoning or texting Tracy. But it just didn't seem right. With the click of a few buttons I could whisk myself away from this wonderful isolation and hear a familiar voice. But I just felt it would ruin the experience, cheapen it even. There would, no doubt, be times when I would be grateful to have a phone with me, but not now. This was not one of those times. This was my time; my experience, which I just couldn't share with anyone else. This was truly one of those 'Hamlet cigar' moments.

But what next? This was a pivotal moment in my whole trip. I'd made it to (or rather past) the Arctic Circle. I was now going to turn around and head south to Panama and then on to Africa. Me, this bike and all my gear would be riding through the USA, on to Mexico, then the jungles of Central America, the Namibian desert, Zimbabwe and on to Kenya. I could hardly believe it and to be honest, I was slightly overcome by it all. The more I thought about it the more frightened I became. I felt a wave of self-doubt wash over me. I couldn't do this. I didn't know how to do this. What the hell was I doing? Out there on the tundra, all alone, I suddenly felt very, very small.

I jumped back on the bike, turned her around to face south and screamed into my helmet:

"Panama here I come!"

CHAPTER 2

CRAZY DOGS

"One's destination is never a place, but a new way of seeing things."

(Henry Miller)

I was heading down the Alaskan highway and then onto the Richardson highway aiming for a place called Paxson. It was less than two hundred miles from Fairbanks and although I'd only been on this bike a few days I was fairly sure I could cover that mileage without running out of petrol. I couldn't cover it without eating however and I pulled into a service station for some food. (It would be a few more weeks before I went totally 'native' and started calling them 'gas' stations.) Alaska seems to be a major destination for American bikers and you don't have to wait long in a petrol station before a new friend on a shiny bike shows up. Surprisingly, this guy wasn't on a Harley or a BMW. Dan was from Florida and was riding a Ducati Multistrada 1100. He had started in May on a Kawasaki but didn't like it so he bought a brand new $20,000 Ducati in Phoenix, Arizona. He too had been to see the other Dan at Cycleworks in Anchorage but discovered that a tyre change was impossible without a special Ducati tool to remove the special wheel nut from the single-sided swinging arm. He'd ordered one from the 'Lower 48' and was just riding around until it arrived. We had a good chat but Dan certainly wasn't counting the pennies and I soon got the feeling that unlike me, he wouldn't be looking for a campsite later in the day so I watched as he mounted his bike and rode off.

Fuelled up with calories rather than gas I mounted my steed and headed south for Paxson. I climbed the 3000 ft Isabel Pass almost having to pinch myself at what I was doing. The bike was purring like a kitten and the beautifully smooth road wound its way through the stunning landscape. Arctic meadows stretched into the distance sprinkled with small lakes and ponds while the snow-capped mountains on the horizon framed the whole picture perfectly. Even though it was early August, vivid yellow and purple spring flowers lit up the foreground. All I wished for was a couple of moose and perhaps a bear. I didn't have a care in the world and, to my surprise, I found myself singing out loud into my helmet. So, this is what riding a motorcycle around the world was like! Why hadn't I done it years ago?

Then I looked down at my control panel. The little gremlin of doom who lives somewhere inside my head was telling me something wasn't right. I looked at my dials. Speed and revs were OK. The red brake warning light was flashing but that was always on and Mike the mechanic had told me not to worry about it. It had been easy to nod my head, chuckle, and say something manly like, "Yeah, no worries mate," in the workshop in Anchorage, but now, out in the middle of nowhere, it was a little more disconcerting. Oil temperature looked fine. That just left the fuel gauge – it had been sitting at 'don't worry mate we've got loads left' around the half full mark for ages but now it had dropped alarmingly quickly to a quarter. It had never been that low before. I had assumed that on a big expensive BMW the fuel gauge would drop, much like a car does, slowly and accurately, giving the rider plenty of warning that the juice was getting low. I now had less than a quarter of a tank. I didn't even know how many litres were in a tank. I had a Haynes manual and a small BMW 1200GS owner's manual but I'd been so excited about getting on the road I hadn't bothered to actually look at them yet. A quick mental calculation inside my helmet told me that I'd done about one hundred and twenty miles since Fairbanks where I'd filled up, so I should have at least one hundred miles of fuel; in which case I should have more than a quarter of a tank.

I passed a sign that said 'Paxson 80 miles', followed by one that said 'Watch out for bears'. Then I remembered that Alaska has a system of pre-payment for petrol. (I stumbled across one petrol pump that had a sign on it saying "*Must pre pay do 2 drive ofs*") First you pay then you fill. That might be all right for car owners who can go into the store and pay say $50 and stick it in their large tanks, but for bikers it's different. You have to guess how many litres you can fit in, and that morning I must have underestimated. So although I was fairly sure I could get a good 200 miles out of a full tank, the last fuelling hadn't actually been a tankful.

Not knowing whether I would make it to the next petrol station changed everything. The bike was no longer purring, it was guzzling fuel at an alarming rate; the beautiful smooth road now resembled a scene from an American movie where a hitch-hiker gets picked up by a trucker and brutally murdered; the Arctic meadow had become barren, dark and eerie and the snow-capped mountains looked as if they belonged in Mordor. The last thing I wanted to see now was a bloody bear. (No prizes for guessing that I still hadn't managed to take my pepper spray out of the locked pannier.) I'd stopped singing.

This went on for what seemed like ages. There were no more signs telling me how far it was to Paxson. I slowed to 55 mph to reduce my fuel consumption. I thought about Dan on his lovely shiny red Ducati. 'Next time I meet a biker at a petrol station,' I thought, 'I'm going to leave first!' Then a new light came on which illuminated a petrol pump symbol and below it, on the digital display, the number 50 was now showing. It didn't take a genius to work out that the GS was telling me I had fifty miles of fuel left.

And so the countdown began: 50, 40, 30. I slowed to 50 mph and subconsciously decided that it would help to grip the handlebars extremely tightly and tense my whole body. There were still no signs telling me how far away I was from Paxson but I guess-timated that it was about thirty to forty miles away and my bike was telling me I probably wouldn't make it. The road ahead climbed a little and swerved to the left and as I banked around the corner I saw a movement in the boggy meadow off to my right. About thirty metres away a huge male moose, resplendent with velvety horns, was wallowing (do moose wallow?) in the water. What an awesome sight. The optimistic, adventurous side of my brain told me to slow down, stop and enjoy the experience. The negative, cautious, safe side told me to carry on. I'd be wasting petrol by pulling over and stopping and there would surely be other moose as I travelled south. I listened to the negative and carried on.

The counter went down to single figures and as if that wasn't bad enough, it started to rain. Just an hour before I had been in biking heaven wondering why I hadn't decided to do something like this years ago. Now I was running out of fuel, getting cold, wet and miserable; Paxson was nowhere in sight and I was down to my last few miles. Somewhere in the back of my un-mechanical mind I was trying to remember whether it was actually dangerous to run out of fuel. I was fairly sure that for either a petrol or diesel engine it was fatal to run out. But I couldn't remember which. Why don't they teach you stuff like this at school? (I have since learnt that diesels can be more difficult to re-start if run dry, but it's certainly not 'fatal'!)

And then I was down to zero. My BMW computer was telling me I had run out of fuel but the engine was telling me I hadn't. There was nothing behind me for a long way: any traffic would be visible for miles with its lights on in the increasingly gloomy rain. My mirrors were telling me I was on my own.

I carried on with an impending sense of doom. There wasn't much else I could do. Almost in a trance I motored on at 50 mph waiting for the engine to splutter and die. I must have been running on zero for ten miles before I finally saw the lights of Paxson in the distance. With a huge sense of relief I saw a sign for a petrol station and pulled onto the forecourt. I put over nineteen litres into my twenty litre tank. The sun came out and suddenly the road seemed busy with friendly traffic heading in both directions. I sat down for a drink and a think. Ted Simon had started *Jupiter's Travels* with a story of him running out of fuel and just sitting at the side of the road waiting to see what happened. He'd been on the road for years by this point and was totally at home with being at the mercy of the gods. He always managed to see every setback and problem as an opportunity and believed that a breakdown led to an adventure. I suppose he was right, but I'd been on the road for days not years and hadn't quite got myself into the Zen state of mind yet. I was still worried about 'getting it wrong' or 'doing the wrong thing' but really, what was I worrying about? What would have happened if I had run out of petrol? I would have waited for the first car to stop and give me a lift to Paxson and a whole new adventure would have opened up to me. Running out of juice is a problem if you're on the way to work, but I wasn't. I was on the road; I was having a motorcycle adventure; I wasn't on a timetable or schedule and I could do anything and be anywhere. So what if I ran out petrol? Slightly embarrassing, yes, but hardly the disaster I had been turning it into in my head. Unfortunately I never did get to see another moose.

*

I hadn't just come to Paxson to get fuel. It was also the eastern edge of the Great Denali Highway, a one hundred and thirty mile gravel road heading west from Paxson towards Denali National Park. My guidebook refers to it as, "one of Alaska's most stunning rides." It's only open from about mid-May to October due to snow and even then the gravel surface keeps tourists to a trickle. The Lonely Planet also talks about 'wash-boarding', hairpin bends, slow going and flat tyres.

With trepidation I pulled out of the petrol station to take a look. I was heading for a campground which was only about twenty miles down the road. This was only the second time I'd been off-road on this bike and my previous off-road riding experience was non-existent. I wanted to explore and experience Alaska at its best but wasn't sure what I, or the bike, was capable of. Well, that's not strictly true. I was pretty sure that the bike was capable of dealing with most things – it was me I was unsure of. I tend towards the cautious side of things and one of the reasons for doing this whole trip was to push myself, stretch my boundaries and take myself out of my comfort zone. That all sounds well and good, but when riding a big heavy motorcycle on rough ground in the middle of nowhere with little mechanical knowledge and even less common sense there's a fine line between pushing oneself and falling over.

Fortunately the road wasn't too bad; just standard gravel, not very deep and only a few potholes. Standing up on the footpegs, carving a path through the glorious countryside I was beginning to get the hang of this off-road malarkey. I was actually enjoying the experience.

Tangle Lakes campground was set in trees, right next to the lake and was a wonderful place to stop. It was popular with anglers and there were several huge RVs spread out around the camp. (Recreation Vehicles – huge American motor-homes, often sixty feet long). I managed to find a relatively flat spot to pitch my tent right next to a designated campfire pit. I was beginning to get into my camp set up routine by now and it only took me twenty minutes to erect the tent and sort all my stuff out. But as it was early evening, and wouldn't get dark for hours, if ever, I decided to take the bike for a ride further up the highway (I *was* getting brave!). The plan was to get back by sunset, have some food and possibly a fire to round off the day. Security is always an issue when camping alone and I had to decide what to do with my expensive and important gear. Often I'd just leave it in my tent cunningly hidden under my sleeping bag (no one would ever think of looking there!) but as I was riding off for a few hours I decided to take my passport, wallet, laptop and camera with me.

The road west just got better and better; not the quality of the surface but the views. As the highway worked its way up and over the passes, I was rewarded with breathtaking vistas of meadows, rivers and mountains. Then on the horizon I spotted a small group of cattle moving parallel to the road. No, not cattle, too weird for cattle. Moose? No, it was reindeer. How fantastic. I rode for over an hour getting just over half way down the highway before turning around and heading back with regret. I don't remember seeing another vehicle at all. This place was 'Scotland on steroids'!

On my way out I'd passed a sign that said 'Crazy Dog Kennels' next to a small bridge. As I came back to that spot I read the sign in more detail. It was a dog-yard for unwanted sled dogs and they offered tours. I passed by. I had no knowledge of or interest in sled dogs, why would I want to stop? Then I got to thinking. Why was I on this trip? Wasn't it partly to see new cultures, experience new things? The very fact that I didn't know anything about sled dogs was surely the very reason I should stop. I swung the bike round (well to be honest there was a lot of gravel in the road so I slowly shuffled the bike around) headed back to Crazy Dog and pulled into the empty car park.

I spent an absolutely fascinating two hours there. John Schandelmeirer and his wife Zoya DeNure showed me round and couldn't have been more helpful. (Some might say they were happy for the company.) They painstakingly took me thorough the whole sled-dog racing thing explaining how they train the dogs, and most importantly how they rescue these particular dogs and look after them. John is a two times winner of the Yukon Quest, an annual 1000 miles dog sled race which runs between Whitehorse in the Yukon, Canada and Fairbanks, Alaska. By the end of the two hours there wasn't much I didn't know about sled dogs. I thanked them both for their time and friendliness, left a hefty donation in the gift shop and was just about to leave when I remembered something.

"John, it's a long shot but you don't happen to know someone called Trent do you?"

John looked at me blankly.

"It's just that years ago, in Argentina, I shared a flat with an American school teacher. I managed to track him down, before coming to The States, on a sled dog racing website but I have no idea where he lives. His name is Trent Herbst."

"No, no I don't think so."

"Never mind. Like I said, I don't really know if he's involved in sled dog racing or anything. If you knew him you'd remember him. He has a huge ginger beard."

"Wait," piped up Zoya. "I think I know who you mean. He's a Primary school teacher from Wisconsin right? Long blond hair and a ginger beard? I know Trent, kinda. I wouldn't say I was his friend and I would have no idea how you could get in touch with him but we've met a few times at races."

I didn't know what to say then and there was a slightly awkward silence. There we were: complete strangers in the middle of Alaska with something in common but nothing else to say about it. It all felt a little weird. I asked them to pass on my best wishes to Trent should they bump into him over the winter and left my details with them so he could contact me.

I'd made a few cursory attempts to contact Trent before my trip had started but meeting John and Zoya gave me new hope. Perhaps I could find him and meet up again. That would be so cool – seventeen years after we'd travelled in Patagonia together – to meet up again, with me on my big bike trip.

I rode back to the campsite with a huge smile on my face. Not just because I was thinking of Trent but also because I'd had the most amazing day. So much had happened in one day I could hardly take it all in. All I wanted to do now was get back, boil up some pasta, maybe have a little camp fire and go to bed. I noticed that there were a few more vehicles in the campground as I rode down the dusty gravel path. But where was my tent? I couldn't see it. All I could see was a big pickup truck and a crowd of people where my tent should be. As I passed the truck, I spied my tent dwarfed as it was by the vehicle. When I had left, I had been at least thirty metres away from anyone else, now I had neighbours or rather, tenants. There was a group of people right outside my tent – lighting a fire in my fire pit.

"Excuse me," I muttered. "This is my tent here."

They all looked at me but no one spoke.

"Sorry, I'm camping here." I wasn't sure what else to say. This is my fire pit? Get away from my tent? It seems churlish to be arguing over space in Alaska, which has an abundance of the stuff but I really didn't want to share my campsite with a drunken group of anglers.

"Do you have to do that here?" Is all I could come up with.

"We want to eat," one of them managed to say in what I can only describe as drunken poor English. At this stage it wasn't clear if he was a really drunk North American struggling to speak his native tongue or a mildly drunk second language speaker.

"Can you not go somewhere else?" I asked, immediately aware that the sentence structure might be difficult for either a drunken local or foreigner to interpret.

"We want to cook our fish." Or more accurately: "We wan tooo cuck fshhhhhh."

"Look, I wanted to camp here on my own. Don't you think you could go over there?"

I pointed up the path at nothing in particular but hoped it would give them a way out. As a vegetarian I really can't stand the smell of fish but I was going to hold this particular piece of information in reserve. I felt it wasn't going to be a winner.

They seemed to be chatting to themselves and I still couldn't tell if it was English or not. One of them came over and said something that could either have been "Yes, you are right. It was incredibly inconsiderate of us and we will, forthwith, be removing ourselves from your vicinity;" or "We're going but we'll be back in the night to gut you like a fish." Either way, they left. That night I slept within grasping distance of my pepper spray.

*

The next few days were a blur of riding fast and long, trying to cover as much ground as I could before having to leave Alaska. It seemed ridiculous, at the beginning of a trip like this, to be thinking of time and moving on but I had to get to southern Canada by the middle of August to attend a motorcycle rally, and to meet Tracy, who was flying out for a three-week holiday. The wide, open, inviting roads, fresh northern air and exhilarating scenery of Alaska are a motorcyclist's dream and I was caught in its spell as I rode to McCarthy in Wrangell-St. Elisa National Park in glorious sunshine and then on to Valdez.

Reading a lot of adventure motorcycle travel books you can hardly fail to notice how often the weather is mentioned. If you don't ride a motorcycle you might think this is just some British quirk and nothing unusual; if you do ride a bike you'll know differently. A slight change in the weather can make the difference between an excellent day's riding and a downright miserable one. To be caught out all day in drizzle or freezing cold isn't much fun and of course poor weather means poor views and generally a depressing day. I faced such a day on my trip down to Valdez.

Valdez, to me, meant *Exxon Valdez*. In 1989 the oil tanker, leaving Valdez for 'the Lower 48' hit a reef and spilled between ten and thirty million US gallons of crude oil. This resulted in the death of around 250,000 seabirds, nearly 3,000 sea otters, 300 harbour seals, 250 bald eagles and up to 22 killer whales. The Captain, Joe Hazelwood, was accused of being drunk at the time of the accident but was acquitted on all felony charges; however, he was convicted of a misdemeanour charge of negligent discharge of oil, fined $50,000, and sentenced to 1,000 hours of community service. Although he did the service, paid the fine and apologised to the people of Alaska for the spill, he always denied it was his fault. Investigative reporter Greg Palast supports Hazelwood's contention, assigning considerable blame to Exxon itself. Hazelwood, allegedly had a serious drinking problem, which Exxon knew about but they let him continue to skipper their vessels. It appears he had been drinking on the day in question but had not been on deck at the time of the accident. Palast writes, *"Forget the drunken skipper fable. As to Captain Joe Hazelwood, he was below decks, sleeping off his bender. At the helm, the third mate would never have collided with Bligh Reef had he looked at his Raycas radar. But the radar was not turned on. In fact, the tanker's radar was left broken and disabled for more than a year before the disaster, and Exxon management knew it. It was (in Exxon's view) just too expensive to fix and operate."*

I read this with surprise when I was in Valdez because although I hadn't really taken a huge interest in the details of the disaster at the time I, like many people I'm sure, had the feeling that it was the captain's fault. It's interesting how accusations quickly become historical accuracy regardless of the truth. I was also under the assumption that Exxon had cleared up the mess and paid for it. Wasn't that what we'd been told? Well, that doesn't appear to be the whole truth either if Palast is to be believed. Initially a federal jury in Alaska awarded $5 billion in punitive damages in 1994. A federal judge later reduced the punitive damages to $4.5 billion, and the appeals court further cut it to $2.5 billion. In 2008, twenty years after the spill, the US Supreme court cut this to $507.5 million. Still a lot of money? According to *The Washington Post* in 2007, Exxon Mobil set a new record for profits by a US corporation, earning $40 billion. The company's sales, more than $404 billion, exceeded the gross domestic product of 120 countries. In plain English, Exxon earned more than $1,287 of profit for every second of 2007.

So, Daniel Carson Lewis gets 16 years for shooting at the pipeline and Exxon get a fine they'd barely notice paying. It's hard not to be cynical about this. I vowed to add Exxon Mobil to my list of multinational companies I was boycotting. It wouldn't, of course, make a blind bit of difference to anyone but every time I rode past a McDonald's or an Exxon Mobil petrol station I could feel the warm glow of self-righteousness deep in my soul.

Needless to say on the surface it looks as if the oil spill has been cleared up but even twenty years on, many fish stocks have yet to return to their pre-Valdez disaster levels; hardly a cheery thought on a cloudy and decidedly cool day in Valdez. I was sat in a Mexican restaurant having a surprisingly tasty burrito, mulling over what to do next. It was only early afternoon and the thought of staying in Valdez was not a pleasant one. My guidebook refers to the place as, "still one of Alaska's prettiest spots," and I could hardly disagree more. I crossed out that sentence and scribbled: "A cold dump of an industrial port, reeking of fish and oil." I looked at my map. I had to go all the way back to Anchorage to pick up a few bits and bobs from The Motorcycle Shop and if I left soon I could, surely, get to Palmer, which was a stone's throw from Anchorage, by early evening. I left Valdez fairly confident that I would never return.

However, there had been one good reason for going to Valdez. The Richardson Highway had been a spectacular mountain route into town and, as the weather cleared a little, was equally stunning heading in the other direction. The road climbed up and out of The Sound and past a magnificent glacier. Wildflowers sprinkled the wayside as the road snaked its way up and down and round the natural contours of the landscape. The sun had come out again and all was good in my world once more. For about ten minutes. Then I started to get a funny feeling in the pit of my stomach. Not a poetic funny feeling, associated with the glorious countryside and wonderful views; not a physiological funny feeling associated with being at one with my machine. No, this was a biological funny feeling and it had Mexican burrito written all over it. I knew I had to stop and eagerly looked for the next turn off or rest place in which to pull over. My stomach was telling me I didn't have much time but I wasn't inclined to just stop on the hard shoulder. I'd heard that America was quite strict on its road laws and I didn't know how serious an offence stopping on the hard shoulder was. The last thing I needed was a gun-toting highway patrol officer telling me to come out of the bushes with my hands up.

It had only taken a few minutes for my stomach to change from 'contented' to 'hostile'. I had to get off the bike. I pulled into a lay-by which was, thankfully, devoid of huge RVs and screaming children. I hurriedly turned the engine off, kicked the side-stand down and prepared to dismount. Unfortunately there is only one way to get off a motorcycle and it involves unclenching your buttocks. Let's just say that the delayed dismount provoked a premature discharge. I rushed towards the bushes, not even thinking about bears, still wearing my helmet and heavy Hein Gericke textile jacket. Crouched in the undergrowth I just had to laugh. This, I thought, wasn't going to be mentioned on my blog.

But my body had made a serious point. I'd been running around Alaska like a mad thing not eating properly and not looking after myself. This couldn't continue. I was travelling on my own and needed to take care of myself; this was just a little friendly reminder of that fact. However, this little episode had one positive outcome: my luggage had been lightened by one pair of underpants!

I rode four hundred and forty miles that day, heading all the way back to Palmer. I arrived there exhausted, slightly dehydrated and in a mild state of shock. I wasn't used to riding a motorcycle for so long and that day I'd been in the saddle for over ten hours. I'd covered five hundred miles in the previous two days and the day before that I totalled four hundred miles getting up to the Arctic

Circle and back. This was too much too soon. I'd only been on the road a week and I'd already ridden two thousand miles. I needed to slow down and enjoy the ride. The problem was that the roads in Alaska are excellent and the distances between places are huge, so it was hard not to ride all day, especially as it didn't get dark until at least ten in the evening.

Over a large pizza in a local diner in town I had a long hard talk with myself. I would slow down, eat less junk food, cover fewer miles and take in the scenery a little more. I wasn't going to do four hundred miles again. That was a promise.

The following day I picked up a few spare parts in Anchorage and then headed east for Canada. I covered three hundred and ninety-five miles.

My last night in Alaska was spent in Tok at the Thompson's Eagle Claw Motorcycle Park. Famous in adventure motorcycle circles, the Thompsons run this 'off the grid' campsite for overland bikers (mainly Americans on Harleys). There is no electricity or running water, but for $10 a night what do you want? I arrived and set up and then sat down with the Thompsons and two other bikers for the evening. We were fed blueberry cake and the conversation revolved around hunting. I ate the cake but didn't really join in the conversation much. They knew I was British and, I guess, didn't expect me to. Mr Thompson went into some detail about how to skin a rabbit properly and both Mike (from Ohio) and Dan (from Minnesota) occasionally added some detail. I smiled politely and hid my discomfort behind my accent.

Then the conversation inevitably turned to motorcycles. This was more of a problem for me. It was OK for me to be naïve about hunting and how to skin a rabbit, I'm British. But I *was* riding a motorcycle, even if it was a BMW, so surely I could keep up with talk of camshafts and calipers? I tried my best but failed miserably. Obviously when three or four men (Mrs Thompson had disappeared by now – I think she'd gone to skin a rabbit) are gathered together near machinery they need to not only talk about it, but go and stand next to it. So off we went, first standing next to Mike's bike. (At this point I should mention exactly what kind of bike Mike had. I could lie and say I'd forgotten but to be honest even standing next to it in the fading light of a glorious Alaskan evening I couldn't tell. It looked, to me, like a Harley type thing but it could have been anything.) Next we moved on to Dan's Honda Shadow (see I do know some things!). A Shadow is very low to the ground and this one had a huge windscreen on the front. Necessary, I guess, if you're riding with an open-face helmet. I expected Dan's bike, like mine, to be covered in dead flies and such but it was shiny and looked almost new. As I couldn't really join in the conversation about how subtly different Dan's Shadow was to Mike's bike, I said, "Oh, it looks very clean."

All three of them looked at me as if I'd just come out of the closet and propositioned them. Thank God they didn't know I was a vegetarian as well. "It's important to keep your bike clean," Dan eventually said. "Look, I have an excellent windshield cleaner I use to keep it clean." At which point he rummaged around in his tent and came out with an orange coloured litre bottle. "Let me show you."

We walked over to my Boxer. (By now I knew that a BMW flat twin is sometimes called a Boxer, and a Harley was a Hog, I just needed to make sure I got them the right way round.) My whole bike was covered in squashed flies and was very, very dirty. I hadn't cleaned it once yet and although I'd only been on the road a week it had picked up a lot of crap along the way. Dan took one look at the screen and insisted on giving it a good clean. He must have spent fifteen minutes on that alone. It was all rather embarrassing, standing there watching someone else cleaning my bike. But then I started to get worried. Dan was using a citrus-based, orange smelling substance to clean my bike, which was sitting a few feet from my tent. Wouldn't that attract bears? What's the point of making sure there's nothing smelly in my tent, if right outside I've parked up a huge 250 kg orange?

Yet again, I went to sleep that night clutching my pepper spray.

CHAPTER 3

FIRES AND FRIENDS

"I'm kinda disappointed that Canada isn't like the South Park movie said it was."

(Joel Madden)

Border crossings. My guess would be that along with flat tyres this is one of the biggest worries adventure bikers have. They are notoriously dodgy (borders not bikers), and the potential for being ripped off is huge, but my first could hardly have been easier. To start with there wasn't even an exit. Perhaps the USA doesn't recognise Canada as a separate country, or maybe they just assume that everyone who goes into Canada will eventually return to the US. Either way, there was no departure gate from Alaska. I only knew I was at the border when I saw a huge building in front of me with a sign saying: 'Welcome to Canada' next to a conspicuously large maple leaf flag. I rode up to the border kiosk, lifted my flip-front lid and smiled at the customs official. I didn't even get off the bike. It was like paying a toll to cross a bridge or join a motorway.

"Can I see your passport, sir?"

"Certainly."

"Do you have any contraband, sir?"

"No."

"Any guns, tobacco, alcohol?"

"No."

"Are you travelling all the way through Canada on that motorcycle?"

"Yes, down to Panama actually." I thought this might impress her and I never tired of saying it. It didn't.

"Where's your wife?"

I thought this was a strange question but things were going so well that at this point I decided to inject a little humour into the proceedings. I spun my head around as if I were looking at the pillion seat and said:

"Oh my God, she was there this morning!"

The border guard looked at me with an expression half way between pity and embarrassment.

"Sorry. No, my wife is in the UK. But she is flying out to join me in the Rockies." Not sure why I added that bit. I began to fear she'd decide I was best contained in Alaska. But with a "Have a good day," she handed my passport over and that was that.

So, country number two: civilised, polite, friendly Canada.

After about two hours on the road heading south I pulled into a roadside café. I'd heard about this place from a couple of bikers back in Alaska. It was run by a French Canadian couple and they baked their own bread; a real oasis of French pâtisserie cooking in the middle of the massive Yukon. Alaska had been fast food and 'Cawffeeee'; Canada started with crêpes and a cup of tea.

The bike was running well; I had plenty of petrol in the tank, I'd eaten and the sun was out. I left the French bakery without a care in the world. I was heading down Route 1, the Alaska Highway, through Yukon. Canada is made up of ten provinces and three territories – Yukon is one of the territories. It's reasonably small by Canadian standards but bloody huge for me, being twice the size of the UK but with a population of just 33,000 (about 22,000 of whom live in Whitehorse, the state capital). That's just astounding. This land is so big – and silent. Whenever I stopped the bike for a break, all I could hear was silence. There was very little traffic on the road and it was easy to pull up at a rest stop, look out at miles and miles of rolling hills and hear absolutely nothing. This continued for day after day as I made my way south. The paved road meanders its way round and up and over the undulating hills; hills covered in pine trees, nothing but pine trees. (Well, I supposed there were bears as well but I still hadn't actually seen any yet.)

What little traffic there was all seemed to be travelling at roughly the same speed, so overtaking something, or being overtaken, was a rare event. Occasionally RVs would rumble past heading north with their kitchen sink but generally it appeared as if I had the whole world to myself. It only took me three days to ride a thousand miles south to Watson Lake but for those three days I saw a lot of country, very few people and even less evidence of people. Of course I was riding down a manmade road and there were the occasional settlements and signs of life, but it brought home to me how, in our everyday lives, we rarely get away from signs of civilisation. I was getting lost in the enormity of it all. Being alone, on a bike, surrounded by the vastness of nature, I was humbled by how small and insignificant I was. Riding for hours and seeing nothing but nature and then looking at a map and seeing how huge Yukon was made me aware of how large the natural world is. I'd read somewhere that we could fit the population of the whole world on the Isle of Wight, and although a little research pointed out to me that this was no longer the case (we would now need two Isles of Wight) it does help put things into context. There are seven billion of us, using up resources, and there are fewer and fewer places unscarred by human contact, but you wouldn't know that travelling through Yukon. Here was just the loneliness of the road, the deafening silence and the vastness of the natural world.

At Watson Lake I stumbled across a rather bizarre site: signposts. Not just a few local signposts but thousands upon thousands of signposts pointing to the four corners of the globe and more besides. There were ordinary signposts indicating how far it was to New York or London and more idiosyncratic signs telling me that the Brown family from Arkansas had been here in June '08. Signs made out of hubcaps, dustbin lids, dinner plates and anything else that could have something written on it and then nailed to a post. In fact most of them seemed to be car license plates, which begs the question: are the police stopping hundreds of cars on the Alaska highway for only having one license plate? I must admit I found it all a little depressing. I was on the trip of a lifetime. I felt like I was the first and only person ever to have given up his job, bought a motorcycle and ridden around the world; I was unique, original, special. The last thing I wanted, was to be reminded that in fact, thousands of people had already been here.

The 'Signpost Forest' as it has become known, has its origins back in World War Two when the Japanese attacked Pearl Harbor in December 1941. (And, according to the literature in the tourist centre in Watson Lake that was the catalyst for the *beginning* of the war! As a History teacher I was pretty sure that the war had started in September 1939.) Anyway, America was worried about a Japanese land assault and knew that overland links between the 'Lower 48' states and Alaska were not good. So plans were hastily put together to construct what became known as the Alaska Highway. In 1942 a US Engineer working on the road, Carl Lindley, decided to erect a sign stating that he was 2,835 miles from home in Illinois. This struck me as rather a strange thing to do. If I were homesick the last thing I would want is a big sign telling me how far from home I was.

Others have been adding to Lindley's 1942 erection ever since and there are now over 65,000 signs. There's a great photo of Mr Lindley on the official website, taken when he returned to the scene of his 'crime' half a century later, in 1992. He's got an expression on his face that looks like, "What have I done?" I was intrigued to read that while it took nearly 50 years for the first 10,000 signs to be added, the remaining 55,000 came in only the last two decades; a quirky reflection of the recent growth of tourism in Yukon.

Apart from the sign forest, Watson Lake had one other tourist attraction: The Northern Lights Show. I was hoping my $10 would buy me an in-depth explanation of the science behind the *Aurora Borealis*. It didn't. Instead, I got a long explanation of what the First Nations People (previously known as 'Red Indians' or 'Natives') thought about the lights and how they reflected the moods of the gods. The whole show bent over backwards to be politically correct and even referred to the science behind the explanation of the lights as 'a theory'. I was rather disappointed by the experience except for one entertaining moment when a French Canadian tourist in front of me in the queue tried to pay for her admission with a mixture of Canadian and UK money. She argued that they should accept UK money as it has the Queen on it. Priceless!

From Watson Lake, there are two routes south. East takes you along the infamous ALCAN (Alaska-Canadian Highway, number 97), the route favoured by most Americans. Like Route 66, the ALCAN seems to be seared into the brains of American road trippers and the road is (apparently) frequented by RVs and bikers alike. Head west a few miles and then south from Watson Lake, and you can take the much quieter Stewart-Cassiar Highway (Route 37). Only fully paved in the last few years, the Stewart-Cassiar seemingly hasn't even earned its own abbreviation yet (I'm going to run with the STEWCASS). Hardly any RVs ply this route (yet) because it has only recently been paved and RVs like to stick together. Their occupants never actually get out of their huge mobile homes, except to hook up to the electricity supply, but they do like to stick together on the roads.

For me it was a no-brainer: the STEWCASS. However, when I passed the turn-off on my way into Watson Lake the STEWCASS was shut because of a forest fire. I asked at the roadblock if any traffic was getting through and was told to come back in the morning at 9 am when a convoy would be leaving. I was going to join a convoy! Cool!

I spent the night in a large campground just outside Watson Lake. But with the constant threat of bears in this part of the world, camping in Canada was different. Bears are hungry, inquisitive animals and campers have to be careful that they don't attract them by leaving any smelly food lying around. For a large animal, with reasonably poor eyesight but excellent smell, which normally eats worms, berries, nuts, leaves and insects, a discarded peanut butter sandwich is too good to pass up. The advice is to make sure all food (and indeed anything that might smell interesting – which includes such items as toothpaste and soap) is kept well away from the tent. Many campgrounds supply bear-proof lockers or ropes for hanging food up in the trees. Of course people with cars could keep their food in the vehicle but a quick search on YouTube will show you what a hungry bear can do to the roof of a car. I didn't want to leave anything in my panniers in case they got destroyed. Perhaps I was being a little paranoid but I'd also read that a diligent camper doesn't even clean his teeth before going to sleep!

So, I'd got myself into a regime every night whereby I'd eat early, carefully wash up and make sure all my equipment was kept in special sealed bags and either stored away in the bear-proof containers supplied or simply left outside on the floor away from my tent and bike. I didn't clean my teeth or wash in the evening. Perhaps I was being overly careful but as I had no frame of reference I felt it was better to be overly safe than ripped to shreds and very, very sorry.

Statistically, I knew bear attacks were uncommon. In the last century, there were only forty deaths in North America caused by black bears. A person is over three hundred times more likely to die from a lightning strike than to be killed by a black bear. (More on that later!) But these are just statistics and statistics can be misleading. If I were on holiday in New York City I wouldn't be worried about bears, but I was camping, alone, every night, in bear country.

So, every night I went through the same process, dutifully keeping anything that smelt interesting out of my tent, and making sure I had my pepper spray to hand. I had little faith that the pepper spray would actually do me much good if I was woken in the middle of the night by a hungry bear ripping through my tent but it was my 'comfort blanket'. I was just glad I'd forked out the $40 for it in Anchorage. It seemed like a lot of money at the time. Not now.

The following morning, glad to be alive but desperate to clean my teeth, I would emerge from my tent, relieved to see that once again my bike hadn't been ripped apart and my bags of food were exactly where I had left them. I wondered how far away the nearest bear was?

Now where was that convoy? Already at 8.30 am there must have been fifty vehicles gathered together. There were about twenty other bikers at the front of the queue; a really eclectic mix. I'd already seen plenty of other motorcyclists on the road, and noticed that Harleys were popular while BMWs were quite rare but this group really brought home how different we all were. There were Kawasaki KLR 650s, various Harleys, a BMW 800, a Honda Africa Twin with an Irish flag on the front and many more.

Now, I'm actually quite a shy guy and one of the things I hoped to achieve through this trip was to deal with this shyness. I know I should have spoken to the Irish guy but I just didn't know what to say.

"Hi, I'm British and you're Irish."?

While I was trying to muster up something to say, another biker came over to me. "Hey, how's it going?"

Damn, I could have thought of that line. However this enthusiastic American greeting really threw me. He was saying it as if we knew each other. But how could we? So I just said, "Good, good. How are you?"

Somehow my British accent sounded very reserved.

"We're good. How's your trip going?"

Why had this guy suddenly started to refer to himself in the plural? Again, unsure what to say I replied, "I'm looking forward to going through this fire in a convoy. Sounds really exciting."

"Yeah, but we're surprised to see you here so soon."

This was getting weird. Should I run with it or ask what the heck he was talking about?

"Sorry?" (Typical middle of the road answer.)

"I thought you'd stay in Alaska a little longer. We're only here as we have to get back to Frisco."

"I'm sorry, you've lost me?"

"Didn't we hook up in Anchorage? I'm sure we met you in Anchorage. Hey, Bill!" he called to the guy who was crouching down next to a very old bike, which quite bizarrely had two huge Moose antlers tied to the back. "Bill, isn't this the British guy we met in Anchorage?"

I have no idea what the bike was but I think the antlers were moose

Eventually the penny dropped. This was Bill and Chris. I'd met them (very briefly, in my defence) on my second day in Alaska. They'd pulled up at the Harley place, where I was camping. It was all coming back to me now. One of them was on a 1960s 'something' and the other on a very old Indian which they'd rebuilt. They'd ridden up from San Francisco, touched base at Anchorage and were heading back home, all within a three-week period. Chris had lost his leather jacket on the way up ("I'd tied it to the back of my bike and it must have blown off.") and was riding the whole way in just a woolly jumper. They seemed like some sort of weird mix of the characters in the book *Zen and the Art of Motorcycle Maintenance* and the Anthony Hopkins film *The World's Fastest Indian*.

I was just about to explain that it was all coming back to me when a car with flashing lights turned up and everyone started to return to the RVs. The convoy was on! I told Bill I'd catch him up with him later, screwed my earplugs in, replaced my helmet and got on my bike. I never got the chance to find the Irish guy.

And then we were off. A lead car followed by twenty motorcycles, then dozens of other vehicles, all heading for a forest fire. For the first few miles everything looked normal: trees, nothing but trees. Riding down from Alaska, I was used to seeing thick forests of pine trees on both sides of the road but after about twenty miles I could sense a change, via my nostrils. First, just a whiff, then a more powerful aroma of smoke. It became quite strong and I began to wonder if this could actually be dangerous. How much smoke inhalation can a biker take? The RVs and cars could shut their windows and turn the AC on. We were stuck out in the 'fresh' air. I wondered what I would have done if I'd been on my own. I'd never ridden through a forest fire before and had no idea what was safe and what was reckless. But, 'safety in numbers' and all that, and blind faith in the notion that someone was in charge and they knew what they were doing, calmed my nerves.

And then I could see it. Not huge walls of fire but huge swathes of land where once mighty trees stood, now all burnt to a cinder. Tree stumps at the side of the road were still smouldering and occasionally we'd pass some trees that were still alight. The smell was almost overpowering and I was grateful I could lift my flip-front lid. Somehow I felt I was able to gulp in more fresh air with an open lid. It was all quite eerie and humbling. Again, nature was showing me what it could do and how we, as humans, were pretty much extraneous to its goings on. We passed a group of fire fighters: ten men and a truck in the wilderness. This fire, though not huge by Canadian standards, covered hundreds and hundreds of square miles. These ten men were doing their best but it really was a token gesture.

Of course, as a Brit, all this was really exciting, but Canadians are used to forest fires. I was staggered to discover that British Columbia alone has, on average, 2,000 forest fires a year, with a peak of over 3,000 in 2009. In that year alone over 240,000 hectares of land was consumed. (One hectare is two and a half acres; 100 metres square, so about twice the size of a football pitch.) Most forest fires are natural, caused by lightning, but an alarming number (40% on average) are apparently caused by people. I couldn't get my head around these figures. Occasionally, in the summer in the UK, on a slow news day, we hear of a forest fire in Canada or America – usually when it's threatening a rich neighbourhood. I had no idea it was this common. I guess that's why I'm travelling – to learn stuff. I later discovered the fire I was passing through had destroyed over one hundred hectares. Two hundred football pitches and it probably only got a small mention in British Columbia's media.

Although I hadn't started at the very front of the convoy I soon found myself there. As the paved road turned to gravel, I passed the Harley Davidson bikers with ease. Their bikes are just not set up to cope with anything other than pure American asphalt and I found it quite amusing how they would overtake me on the tarmac but fall back embarrassingly quickly as soon as there was a sniff of gravel. I was also amused by their attire. They really lived up to the caricature: stylish boots, blue jeans, leather jacket, neck-tie and a small open-faced helmet, none of which would help you as you skidded down that lovely American asphalt at even fifty miles per hour. Sometimes the helmets were so small they looked more like the kippah or yarmulke worn by devout Jews. These minimalist 'helmets' were designed more for nominal law abidance than head protection. Again, something I couldn't really understand. What makes you more concerned about fashion than saving your life? (No doubt those Hog riders would have said, "It's all about freedom. Man!")

All of this gear seemed to be worn without the slightest hint of irony. And then there were the accessories. The girlfriends on the back (all Harleys seem to come supplied with a small female pillion), typically would have no protective clothing at all. A pair of boots, jeans and top designed solely for fashion not protection and the ubiquitous backpack designed to look like a squashed sheep or dog or something. I've always taken motorcycle protective clothing seriously (which, I like to think, is partly why I'm still here). I fully expected my heavy-duty textile jacket to become burdensome and stiflingly hot at times on this trip but I had vowed never to take it off when riding. I'd rather be hot than cool, if you see what I mean. Sweat washes off, whereas 'road rash' is exceedingly painful, and a skin graft is forever.

Continually passing and being passed by two or three Harleys on the Stewart-Cassiar Highway, got me thinking. I could feel another Wikipedia moment was due next time I could log on... On average ten US bikers die on the roads every day. That seems a shocking number, but then again the USA is big. More research... I know it's not always fair to compare the UK with the USA but the UK figures for motorcycle fatalities are under two per day. When you factor in that the US population is five times the size (and assuming a similar proportion of the population ride) it's closer than I thought it would be. That did slightly dent my argument about the importance of protective clothing. Perhaps I needed to look into motorcycle injuries rather than deaths but decided I'd wait until my trip was over. It made for depressing reading.

Possibly the most famous UK motorcycle fatality was T.E. Lawrence (Lawrence of Arabia). He died in 1935 near Wareham in Dorset, in South West England. He was riding a Brough Superior SS100 (to me that sounded more like a lawn mower than a motorcycle – goes to show how much I knew about bikes). He was cresting a hill, swerved to avoid two cyclists and was thrown off (bloody cyclists!). He wasn't wearing a crash helmet; almost no one did in those days, apart from racers. Indeed, the first British helmet designed specifically for use with motorcycles was the Cromwell in 1926, prompted by the burgeoning popularity of speedway racing in Australia. Lawrence was in a coma for six days before he died, but had no significant injuries other than to his head. One of the doctors who treated him, Hugh Cairns, became aware of the huge numbers of despatch riders who were dying of head injuries and his research led to the introduction of helmets for military personnel in 1941. They were not required for UK civilians until 1973 and remain optional in many US states today. I'd always assumed it was obvious that bikers *should* wear helmets. It was interesting to discover that two things I associate so closely together (motorcycles and helmets) had such separate histories. Giving up my job as a history teacher seemed to be re-invigorating my interest in history.

Lawrence owned a succession of no fewer than seven Brough Superiors, and had an eighth on order, which was still being built when he died. All SS100s were guaranteed by George Brough to exceed 100 mph, (hence the name) and Lawrence once famously raced an RAF biplane on one. The SS100 on which he had his fatal crash is currently on display at the Imperial War Museum in London. Go up the stairs and turn left.

Helmets are compulsory in Canada, as they are in about half of the United States. Only three US states (Illinois, Iowa and New Hampshire) are completely compulsion-free. The official motto of New Hampshire is 'Live free or die', a sentiment which is no doubt shared by the bikers who spurn helmets and increase their chances of dying in an accident as a result. Laws requiring only certain categories of motorcyclists to wear a helmet are in place in twenty seven states. Generally, if you are under 17 you must wear one but over 17 you're free to take your chances with an unadorned bonce. Alaska is one of the above twenty-seven, as are Idaho, Montana and Utah through which I was also planning to ride. Florida laws require all riders under 21 to wear helmets; those over 21 may ride without helmets only if they can show proof that they are covered by a medical insurance policy. If you can pay for your head to be stitched back together, you can go ahead and risk smashing it.

I am all for freedom but to me it just seems silly not to wear a motorcycle helmet. Apart from reasons of self-preservation, if you don't wear suitable protection in the UK and have an accident you are going to be using the National Health Service and costing the state money to repair you. I suppose as America doesn't have an NHS and all medical work is covered by private insurance, it's different. As the State doesn't look after you it doesn't get as involved in telling you what to do. It almost made sense to me.

*

Petrol stations are few and far between in northern British Columbia and once through the forest fire I pulled in at the first opportunity. I didn't want to run out of gas with a couple of dozen bikers behind me – too embarrassing. Three other bikes also pulled in and one of them was the Irish Africa Twin. This time I said hello. Patrick was on the Alaska-Argentina route and was riding this section with Stuart (USA – BMW F800) and Paul (USA – Kawasaki KLR 650). Two easy bikes to recognise as they have their names and engine sizes clearly printed on the side! They'd met up a few days previously and were now riding south together. After paying and filling up we pulled over to the car park to have a chat.

"Have you heard of the road to Telegraph Creek?" I asked.

"No, we were just heading straight south on the Cassiar," replied Paul.

"Well, I briefly met this British guy in Anchorage who told me that when I got here I should take the gravel road leading off to the right and go down to Telegraph Creek. It's about seventy miles each way, a fantastic ride and well worth the detour, apparently. I was thinking of going that way now. Wanna come along?" What I didn't say was that I'd quite like the company as I wasn't all that keen on heading down a gravel side road in northern British Columbia all on my own.

"Yeah, why not?" said Patrick. And with that kind of logic and forethought such trips are made as the four of us headed west on a mini adventure.

The gravel road was in good condition and the only reason we weren't bombing along at seventy was because the views were so wonderful. The route meanders down through a large gorge, twisting back on itself through a series of turns and occasionally crossing some natural bridges as the road juts out onto the spur of the valley edges. We stopped off two or three times to drink in the scenery and take some pictures. We took about two hours to reach the bottom where, almost unbelievably, there was a little village with a tea shop. Parking up the bikes (it was so cool to see my bike parked up next to three other big, dirty overland bikes) we headed for the tea room and lunch. Which was great – I was hungry.

I usually started the day with a coffee and muesli bar (or three); occasionally I would find an all-American breakfast somewhere but being vegetarian I was somewhat restricted in my choice, even at breakfast. I could get plenty of eggs cooked in a myriad of ways but knew it wouldn't be good for me if I ate that every day. Muesli as I knew it (a healthy breakfast cereal made with wheat and oats and fruit) didn't exist in this part of the world. I could get Granola but that's just sugar masquerading as healthy food. I did love the American custom of endless free coffee refills though. Perhaps McDonald's did a good breakfast, but I was still sticking to my principles, and I hadn't seen any 'Golden Arches' anyway.

In the evening I would usually camp cook which, for me, meant pasta or rice. I'm not a very imaginative chef and it's all about ease, cost and cramming in as much as I can: content over taste every time; the opposite of *nouvelle cuisine – vieille cuisine*? Lunchtime, however, was all about saving time; I didn't want to sit around eating food when I could be riding. So lunch was petrol station food. That was easy enough in Alaska and Canada where all petrol stations sell food, be it a sandwich, pastry or my favourite, a 'bear's claw', which is a mincemeat-filled sticky bun. However, I'm sure this cavalier attitude to food was largely responsible for the events that led to me losing a pair of underpants near Valdez! So, it was a pleasant change to sit in a tea room, with three other bikers, eating a healthy homemade sandwich and shooting the breeze; and a great treat at the end of a wonderful road.

Back at the petrol station where we had all met up a few hours previously I was refilling my tank when yet another biker heading south rolled in. He pulled up right next to me on his GS Adventure and I prepared myself for yet another friendly American greeting.

"Hey mate, how's it going?"

"Hi there."

"Did you go down to Telegraph Creek then?"

"Er, yeah, we've just been down there. It was great, you should try it."

"Mate," he said as he removed his helmet, "It was me who told you about it!"

"Oh wow, sorry. I didn't recognise you with your helmet on." Nevil was British but has been living in Canada for eighteen years. The previous year he'd suffered a stroke and had vowed to make the most of his life while he still could. He'd always wanted to head north to Inuvik and Alaska and decided to just do it. There's nothing quite like a near-death experience to wake you up and make you appreciate life. Nevil had got himself a BMW 1200GS Adventure and had spent two weeks going as far north as possible. He was now heading back home to the Rockies and, as there was only one road heading south from here, we all saddled up and in a convoy of five bikes, headed south.

I was just loving this whole motorcycle convoy thing. I'd started that day alone in a camp ground at Watson Lake trying to get over a disappointing time at the Northern Lights Experience and a slightly bewildering time at the sign forest; several hours later I'd been on an exciting side trip down to Telegraph Creek and had hooked up with four other bikers for the ride south.

CHAPTER 4

URSUS ARCTOS HORRIBILIS

"It may be that we are puppets – puppets controlled by the strings of society. But at least we are puppets with perception, with awareness. And perhaps our awareness is the first step to our liberation."

(Stanley Milgram)

Continuing south we took another slight detour, this time heading for a place called Stewart. Situated on the coast of British Columbia, Stewart is a tiny fishing village surrounded by magnificent mountains, nestled at the end of a vast 70-mile sea inlet. It reminded me of Norway, which was strange as I'd never been to Norway. The road down to Stewart passed close to a glacier and we all stopped off for the obligatory photo. One of the great things about hooking up with other bikers was that now some of my photos actually had me in them, rather than just my bike on the side stand. We set up camp in the comfortingly named Rainy Creek campground and took a walk around town. Ten minutes later I was back at my tent. Stewart has little to distract the tourist, as the guidebooks would say.

We were actually going to cross a border and head back into Alaska. A 'spur' of Alaska's territory stretches a long way down the Pacific coast, separating the northern half of British Columbia from the sea. We were headed for its southernmost town, Hyder, which is right next to Stewart, British Columbia.

Hyder has a population of 97 and strangely, no road connections with the rest of the state: it can only be visited from Stewart. Hyder also uses Canadian money, time, holidays, schools and police. Which begged the question, what really made it American?

Its history is in mining: between the two World Wars, Hyder flourished as it was the closest point in the USA to Canadian copper, gold, silver, lead and zinc, presumably then shipped out to the 'Lower 48'. As the mining eased up in the 1960s the life-blood of Hyder sapped away. According to the ever-reliable Wikipedia:

Hyder became popular with long distance motorcycle riders in 1998 when author Ron Ayres set a record of riding to the contiguous 48 states in six days. Ayres went on to add to the 48 state record by continuing on to Hyder, Alaska to establish a new 49-state record of seven days, 0 hours and 20 minutes. Ayres named the new long distance ride the '48 Plus' and the 49-state ride has become very popular with members of the long distance motorcycle riding Iron Butt Association.

Hyder is also the location of the annual 'Hyder-Seek' gathering of long-distance motorcyclists who travel from all over North America each Memorial Day weekend.

I rode the two miles from Stewart to Hyder and then the five or so miles out of town. (I say 'town' but really it was a one-street hamlet with ramshackle wooden cabins which didn't look as if they could withstand the summer let alone the long, dark and freezing cold winters they must get here.) There was a post office and two bars (more on them later) and I continued out on a dirt track towards Fish Creek.

Between June and August every year huge numbers of salmon return to Fish Creek to spawn and the bears come out of the woods (where, I can only assume, they've been busy shitting) to catch them. Hyder has cashed in on this and turned it into a tourist attraction. We parked our bikes, paid a small fee and joined the dozens of other tourists on the walkway to gawp and stare at the bears; except there weren't any. The river was full of the largest salmon I'd ever seen. (Actually, I'm not sure I'd ever seen salmon before, but these were definitely big 'uns.) The riverbank was littered with half-eaten fish and the stink was almost overpowering for a delicate vegetarian like me. We jostled for position on the walkway. For the first time on this trip I encountered the species I'd most feared, full on, with no holds barred: the American tourist! Compared to your average European tourist they were like an American RV next to a VW campervan: large and loud. Displaying trainers, long shorts, golf shirt and baseball cap, this species has also evolved huge SLR cameras strapped around their necks, balanced upon their large stomachs. And that was just the females!

With the amount of noise these people were making I really didn't expect to see any bears at all but to my amazement the lure of the calorie-filled salmon clearly outweighed the noise of the calorie-filled Americans. Soon a black bear appeared out of the woods. She (I assumed it was a she, as most hunting in the animal kingdom appears to be done by females) plodded up and down the stream spoilt for choice. It was like watching a child in a sweet shop; keen to eat something but unsure what to go for with so much to choose from. She took a lazy swipe at a few fish before homing in on a particularly large salmon right below where I was standing. She sized it up and then pounced, much like a cat would. She came up out of the water with a salmon firmly in her grip, and what a huge grip it was. I must have been several metres away but even from that distance I could still make out each finger that made up the enormous paw of the bear. And it was clear from the way the fish was wriggling that each one of those huge fingers had skewered the fish with a couple of inches of claw. She was holding the salmon in one paw but there was no way it could squirm free. Then off she plodded out of the water and into the bushes where I assume a grateful cub or two were waiting. I got an excellent shot of it with my small camera. Paul and Patrick, next to me, were equally excited about the whole thing. Stuart was sitting down on one of the benches looking uninterested. In the three or four days we'd now been together I hadn't really connected with Stuart. He was friendly enough but always slightly distant and, it seemed, lonely. This was his first real trip outside the USA and he'd actually been looking forward to coming to Hyder more because it was 'home' rather than to see bears. I couldn't really relate to this so I left him there and headed further up the walkway as I'd heard a rumour that there was a grizzly about!

Black bear at Fish creek, Hyder

North American bears come in three types: polar, black and brown. Easy. Well, not quite. Polar bears reside in the polar region so I wasn't going to see any of them. In fact it's likely that in a few years none of us is going to see any of them but that's another story. So that leaves brown and black. Black bears are usually black (although they can also be brown and sometimes white) but not all brown (or grizzly) bears are brown; some are black. Blacks are smaller than browns (but you'd only really know that if you've seen both, ideally at the same time). They have shorter claws (how can you tell?) and lack a shoulder hump. That's the important bit. The only real way to distinguish between a black and a brown is the hump between the shoulders. So when a bear is charging at you and you've forgotten your pepper spray, look for that grizzly hump. It might save your life because if a black bear attacks you the advice is to fight back. They are notoriously cowardly animals, or to put it a better way, they don't want to get injured. So if you fight back they may give up. However, if a brown or grizzly attacks, play dead. The only hope you have is that they get bored and move on. So, it's important to know your browns from your blacks.

39

Posh brown bears prefer their Latin name which is *Ursus arctos*. Ursus means bear in Latin and Arctos means bear in Greek – obviously a compromise between scientists with different classical leanings. Grizzlies are a sub-species and their Latin name is *Ursus arctos horribilis*. Unfortunately the naturalist who named them knew they were known as 'Grizzlies' (for the grizzled or grey hairs in their fur) but thought it meant 'grisly' hence horrible. Even funnier than that, is this: occasionally polar bears cross breed with grizzlies, producing either pizzly or grolar bears, scientists can't decide. I'd go for pizzly.

I was learning all this from Nevil as we waited to see if there really was a grizzly upstream. Nevil had worked as a mountain guide in the Rockies while living in Canada and had a few scary stories about bears. He always carried flares and pepper spray and made sure his paying customers did the same.

"On one occasion," he said, "it all got a bit out of hand. We were just starting out on a hike through the woods and I'd told my group that there were certainly bears about and we needed to be careful. I reassured them that I had a flare gun, pepper spray and bear bells (to warn the bears that we were coming so they would move away). I had explained how the flare gun would work and had just explained that the pepper spray, which was made of Cayenne pepper, needed to be sprayed directly into the bear's face if it was going to have any effect. It is similar to, but stronger than, the pepper spray police use. Just as I was telling them this I heard a loud shriek from behind me. It was a child's voice and he sounded in a lot of pain. I turned around. There, right behind me, was a small boy, of about eight or nine, standing with his hands over his face screaming. His mother was next to him. She had been spraying pepper spray on her son, using it much as you would a mosquito repellent. The boy was in considerable pain and we had to go directly to a hospital."

Just as he finished this story there was a collective murmur from the group I was standing near. Camera lenses were lifted off stomachs and pointed upstream. There was something huge and brown walking down through the middle of the river as if it owned the place. It was indeed a grizzly. Usually blacks and browns avoid each other but as this river has such a high calorific content they didn't seem to mind and it was a real treat to see a black bear and a brown bear within minutes of one another. I really could appreciate the size difference, and I even noticed the huge hump on its back. I was quietly confident that in a given situation I would be able to recognise whether it was a black or brown attacking me. Now, which one do you play dead for again?

Patrick, Paul, Nevil and I watched the grizzly wandering around the river, often slightly obscured by trees and bushes so I never got quite as good a photo of it as I had of the black bear earlier. He (I assume it was a male, because it was less successful!) had a very similar fishing style to the black but didn't manage to catch anything. After about fifteen minutes of trying he gave up and disappeared back into the bushes. It was getting quite late by now (although not dark of course) so the three of us decided to head back to Canada. We couldn't find Stuart anywhere and when we got back to the bikes, his had gone.

Riding back through Hyder, I spotted Stuart's bike parked outside one of the two pubs. It was Monday night and the lonely man from America had stopped off "to watch the ball game." There was also apparently a tradition for Americans this far from home, to stop at the bars in Hyder and get 'Hyderized'. This 'rite of passage' involved drinking a shot of 75% alcohol. I guess we all miss home occasionally; after all there are Irish pubs all over the world, and fish and chip shops everywhere. Bears were a novelty to me, whereas for many Americans they are just a commonplace nuisance. I left Stuart to his ball game and headed back to Rainy Creek campground. That was the last time I saw him.

I slept soundly that night. I'd again cleared my tent of anything that smelt, and my pepper spray was still to hand, but somehow seeing a couple of bears had calmed my nerves. I don't know why, seeing how powerful and quick they were should have scared me witless, and knowing that they were out there in the mountains around the campsite was hardly a comforting thought. Maybe seeing them had rationalised their existence in my mind: a bear was no longer a mythical creature. Counter-intuitive perhaps, but that's how my mind works.

*

The people behind the Horizons Unlimited website organise several Adventure Motorcycle weekends and I was heading for the Canada West meeting in Nakusp, BC. I'd mentioned this to Paul, Patrick and Nevil and, as they had all agreed to come along too, the four of us arrived at Nakusp for a weekend of adventure biking heaven. There were over 150 people at the meeting, all with stories to tell, advice to give and bikes to look at. I introduced myself to Grant Johnson, the organiser and HU co-founder, and reminded him that I had agreed to do a presentation on 'My trip so far'. Being a teacher by profession I had no qualms about standing in front of a group of people and talking; the difference here was that they might actually listen to me! Grant told me I was down to present that evening at 9 pm. I had four hours to put something together.

The evening kicked off with a buffet-style meal in the local town hall followed by a couple of presentations. I sat at the back of the hall with my laptop hurriedly putting some photos together while the first two presenters did their thing. The guy who was up before me, Rene Cormier, had written a book and travelled everywhere and was a really good speaker. Damn, I had been hoping he'd be rubbish, so I might look good by comparison. It was closer to ten than nine by the time I got up to talk and most of the one hundred and fifty or so people present were well lubricated with Molson beer. I hoped that would make them more receptive, but it could go either way.

The previous speaker had done it all and his stories were incredible and fantastic. But in a way that made adventure bike travel sound unobtainable, dangerous, mysterious; a dream that wasn't achievable for most. Too often you read the books and watch the TV series and are captivated by the adventure but end up thinking, 'There is no way a mere mortal like me could do that.' I wondered how many people had been inspired by Ewan McGregor and Charley Boorman's trips to follow their dream and how many had been put off. It was a bit of a double-edged sword. You buy a book about adventure motorcycle travel because you want to try it yourself. Then you read about all the wonderful, dangerous, exciting and difficult things the author does along with their mechanical skills and in some cases, support vehicles, and decide that it isn't for you. I know I'd only been on the road for three weeks but my experience so far was that it was all fairly easy. Or at least it was as easy as you want to make it.

I hoped I was getting this across with my presentation. I explained what a fantastic time I was having, how wonderful British Columbia was (play to your audience!) and whenever I needed a laugh I just made fun of Americans and Harleys – that seemed to go down well. Paul, the Texan I was travelling with, had a wonderful sense of humour, and I repeated something I had said to him in Hyder in the wake of the BP Deepwater Horizon oil spill off the Texan shore. He'd just bought a litre of oil for his KLR and I asked him, as he was from Texas and I was from Britain, whether he needed help finding a beach to pour it on.

During my talk I also mentioned my fear of (I would say respect for) bears and how camping every night I'd keep my pepper spray within reach and had been careful to avoid leaving anything in my tent that might smell interesting to a hungry bear. This had my North American audience in fits of laughter which was a little disconcerting as I hadn't meant it as a joke. I had a few questions, commenting on my, alleged, hysteria about bears. I couldn't really understand it. Bears live in the woods; I'm camping in the woods. Bears are inquisitive; I don't want to die. It all seemed very logical to me. One of them asked, "But how do you deal with bears in Britain?"

It hadn't even crossed my mind that I would need to explain that we don't have bears in the UK. The thought of camping in the Cotswolds or the Lake District surrounded by hungry brown bears made me chuckle. We have no dangerous animals in the UK. Wolves disappeared over three hundred years ago, Lynx over two thousand. Bears became extinct before the Romans invaded. Bear baiting, popular in medieval England was done using bears bred especially for it or imported from the continent. Indeed, bear baiting – which involved tying the hind leg of a bear to a post and the animal being attacked (or 'worried' as it's called) by dogs – was hugely popular in Elizabethan England. (Oh, I feel a history lesson coming on…) In 1575 Queen Elizabeth visited her favourite, Robert

Dudley, at Kenilworth Castle, near where I live and records show that on one day, thirteen bears were baited for the Queen's sport. The *bear and ragged staff* forms the coast of arms, even today, of the county of Warwickshire. But these bears were not wild, although I am sure they were pretty livid at being bated.

"Oh, we don't have any bears," I said. "The only thing to disturb a happy camper in the UK today is a snoring neighbour. And EU law says we're not allowed to use pepper spray on them."

I finished my presentation to warm applause and headed off stage relieved, making a beeline for the bar. Before I could get there a guy in a biker jacket with a bandanna around his head approached me. I feared that he might be an American Harley rider and not at all impressed with my crowd-pleasing jibes.

"Hi Dom." It always unnerved me when people I didn't know used my name. "Hi."

"That was a great talk, man. Well done."

"Good. I'm glad you liked it."

"Have you tried couch-surfing?" What was this guy talking about? Was it some sort of weird Harley initiation ritual?

"Check it out on the net. You can stay at people's places for free. Anyway, I'm Tom and I live in Washington State, you're more than welcome to stay at my place when you head south."

And with that he thrust a piece a paper into my hand with an address and a number.

"That's very kind. Thank you so much." I headed off to the bar to get a drink, fully intending to return to Tom and get more details of the couch-surfing thing he had mentioned. But at the bar I got talking to Nevil and Pat and totally forgot about Tom. I don't know what I did with that scrap of paper, although, bizarrely, I was to see Tom again, months later and on another continent.

The HU weekend came to a close all too quickly. I'd had a great time meeting fellow adventure bikers and sharing ideas and tips. Patrick had hooked up with Brian, a Brit on a BMW 800 and they were heading off south together with Paul, my favourite Texan. As we exchanged emails and said our manly farewells, I wondered if I'd ever hear from them again. Nevil was going home to Canmore in the Rockies but I promised to see him in a week or so as I was heading in that direction too. I was going to Banff to meet my wife who had flown out for a three-week holiday. It was going to be wonderful to see Tracy and ride through the Rockies together but I was just a little bit worried because there wasn't much space for her on the bike. I'd had a brief chat at Nakusp with David and Jill, a British couple who were travelling around two-up on a BMW R80 G/S and they had agreed that space was tight.

I spent the whole day riding the two hundred and forty miles from Nakusp to Banff worrying about how I would fit Tracy on the back but also excited about seeing her again. I'd had a fantastic time on my own riding down from Alaska but I was also looking forward to spending the next three weeks riding through British Columbia with company.

*

Everything went to plan and I met Tracy at a hotel in Banff. We had two days doing the touristy thing and then went to visit Nevil in Canmore. He had offered to help make a couple of cosmetic modifications on the bike and he kept his word. I'd bought a bicycle bottle holder cage and Nevil screwed it into the left pannier, allowing us easy access to water and a little extra space in the tank bag. He had also constructed his own oil cooler guard for his GS Adventure and had some material left over. Very kindly he manufactured one for my bike. The oil cooler on a GS sits, exposed, at the front of the bike just below the main headlight and this guard would protect it from flying stones. I was bowled over by how kind Nevil had been. I'd only met him a few days previously and yet he had gone out of his way to help me. This was a phenomenon which was to repeat itself on my trip – the kindness of others – but it never ceased to amaze me.

Having a pillion really did change things. Initially there was a bit of rearranging to do; although typically, Tracy had been extremely frugal with her packing and all of her gear fitted into two small bags that sat nicely on top of the two panniers. The large grey bag I had on the rear of the bike was pushed back a little to make some room and, thanks to the tail rack I'd bought from Dan's son, we managed to squeeze it all on. It's not easy fitting camping gear and two people on a motorcycle, but we did. The first noticeable difference was how heavy the bike now felt. It was already a big heavy bike with just me on it but, as that was all I knew, it seemed normal. Now it was even bigger and heavier. This was no great problem on the well-maintained and civilised roads in Canada, but my mind jumped forward to when Tracy was going to meet me in Central America in a few months' time. I had images of crazy traffic, awful roads and 400 kg of fully-laden BMW 1200. Was I a good enough rider to cope with that? For now we just enjoyed the glorious sweeping roads and awe-inspiring vista of the Rockies as we rode up the Icefields Parkway from Banff to Jasper. For one hundred and forty miles, Highway 93 as it's also known, cuts a wonderful path through the middle of the Rockies. The mountains on each side of the road dwarf the vehicles, and although there was a bit of a chill coming off the snow-capped mountains and glacier fields we had good weather and stunning views.

Half way up we stopped at the Athabasca Glacier. In the interpretation centre we warmed up and learned all about ice. The literature informed us of the size and magnitude of this glacier. Like almost all glaciers in the world today the Athabasca is retreating and it was disturbing to read about the speed at which it was doing so. One hundred years ago, when the first visitors' centre was built, the glacier licked the edge of the road; now you needed to drive hundreds of metres from the road to a car park and then walk to get near its edge. It was retreating at a remarkable rate: two to three metres a year. As we walked closer to the glacier, marker posts with dates on recorded the years in which the glacier had passed this point. All very depressing. Of course, glaciers don't, in fact, 'retreat'. The ice isn't going uphill, it just thaws out in the summer and is not being replaced in sufficient quantities by the winter snow. This being North America, you could walk the twenty minutes or so from the car park to the foot of the glacier or you could pay $30 to sit in a huge Snow Coach Bus and be driven on a 'glacier tour'. We walked; most people didn't. I found the irony of this both disturbing and worrying. The glacier was retreating because of global warming, caused in part by unnecessary CO2 emissions, caused, in part, by unnecessary bus trips; (and, I would have to admit, long unnecessary motorcycle trips).

One of the many joys of motorcycle travel is being locked inside a helmet all day. All sorts of thoughts float through my head. I'd become aware that my thoughts had been changing noticeably in the month or so that I'd been on the road. Initially I was still stuck in work mode. I'd find myself thinking about school and teaching and education in general. It was as if my brain hadn't caught on to the fact that I'd given up my teaching job and didn't need to be thinking about education, at least for a while. The enormity of Alaska, Yukon and British Columbia had cleared my head little by little and by the time Tracy arrived my mind was drifting along tangents, taking my thoughts in weird and wonderful directions. Heading up the Icefields Parkway we passed a series of road works and I found myself thinking about a 1960s psychology experiment.

Stanley Milgram was a Psychology professor at Yale University who set up a series of experiments in 1961, in the wake of the trial of the Nazi, Adolf Eichmann. The object was to see whether a 'normal' or 'average' human being is willing to inflict pain on a stranger just because someone in authority tells him or her to do so. (The mantra for the defence from concentration camp guards and other 'minor' Nazis, immediately after WWII, had been "We were only following orders".)

The Milgram subjects were told to flick a switch to deliver an electric shock to someone they believed to be another volunteer student. They were told to turn up the dial and increase the severity of the shock every time the other student got a question wrong. Of course the whole thing was stage-managed, and the 'shocked' students were really actors, but the subjects didn't know this and genuinely believed they were inflicting pain on a stranger. The experiment has been repeated many times and on average, 65% of people tested will inflict severe pain on a stranger if told to do so by an authority figure. (How frightening is that?)

However if the authority figure isn't physically present and instructions are given by phone, subjects are less likely to comply. The message for would-be dictators, or indeed management, is clear. Humans are hardwired to respect authority but that authority really needs to be visible. Dictators have always known this; this is why autocratic leaders have always been so keen to have images of themselves displayed everywhere. George Orwell portrayed this idea brilliantly in *1984*. But why had a series of Canadian road works reminded me of this? Because the effect can also be positive. In Canada, when you come across road works there are people stationed along the way holding signs telling you to slow down. Not just the signs but real people holding the signs – and it works. Automatically I slowed down; whereas I am sure I wouldn't have done if I'd just seen a sign on its own. It's not as if those people can do anything about your speed, it's simply the fact that they are there. The psychology is the same on European motorways, where they use life-sized 'dummy robots' waving an arm at you to slow down for road works, because, from a distance, they look convincingly like a real workman. Even the speed limit warning sign, called Smiley SID (Speed Indication Display) uses this effect, rewarding drivers with a smiley face when they obey the speed limit.

Two-up and camping in The Rockies

Tracy and I had had a really pleasant first week in the Rockies, enjoying the clean air and clear mountain views of Banff and we hoped that three days' camping in Jasper would be just as good. Unfortunately, there was another forest fire in the mountains around Jasper and a blanket of smog hung over the town. It was really rather spooky; the sun was blotted out and there was a faint smell of burning in the air. Apparently Jasper is surrounded by stunningly beautiful mountain scenery, but we never saw it! At the tourist office I asked about the forest fire which had covered the place in smoke. "It's hard to say which one is responsible," I was told. "There are several fires near here. In fact at the moment there are two hundred and sixty-five fires burning in British Columbia."

Leaving Jasper in the rain, somewhat disappointed by the conditions, we headed back down the Icefields Parkway, but this time it was different. The wind had picked up and was blowing right off those ice fields and the temperature had dropped to about five degrees. I never really minded rain on a bike trip. Tracy and I both had good, waterproof, breathable riding gear but when rain becomes sleet and the temperature nose-dives, it's just miserable. I turned my heated grips on which helped me, but I knew Tracy was stuck shivering on the back. Riding north in the sun, with wonderful views, the 140-mile long Parkway had seemed too short; now, heading south in a mini blizzard it seemed to go on for ever. It had hardly rained since I'd left Anchorage but now we were having an awful time and what's more, it was Tracy's birthday. With my marriage under threat I agreed to find a hotel for the night and not force her to camp another night in freezing rain and an already wet tent.

We found an expensive lodge near Lake Louise. It took Tracy half an hour in the shower to warm up, but then she sat happily in the rooftop hot tub as it snowed around her. Marriage saved. Lake Louise itself is so perfectly beautiful it looks like a painted backdrop: a sea of calm sapphire water stretching back between diamond-capped mountains and emerald forests.

*

Leaving the Rockies the next morning, we headed west towards Vancouver and it was somewhere along this road that I gave my bike her name. The thought had been in the back of my mind for ages and although I was having trouble coming up with a name it was getting a little impersonal calling the BMW 'the bike' all the time. One morning, riding through the mountain scenery, it came to me: my bike was called Heidi. I have no idea why which is perhaps the best reason. Heidi just popped into my head and that was it.

The imposing mountain range gave way to a semi-arid desert region and the temperature shot up nicely. The land became quite flat and dry and having ridden for weeks through the huge forested regions of Yukon and British Columbia it felt really quite strange to be in a very different environment, but the mountains returned as we neared the coast and Route 99 swept us up and down and around on our way towards Whistler. During one particularly spectacular section of road Tracy got really excited and thumped me on the back a few times. I assumed it was because she was enjoying the ride. Only later did I find out that it was actually because she'd spotted a black bear running across an open field. It was the first bear she'd seen and she was hitting me to tell me to stop. How was I supposed to know? We hadn't actually agreed on how to communicate! We didn't have an intercom – neither of us thought they were necessary and anyway what would we have to talk about when we stopped if we'd been chatting away all day?

We were six months late for the Winter Olympics but still stopped off at Whistler to enjoy the mountains (if not the cost of camping in the Olympic village). The tourist office told us that we simply must do the Peak2Peak cable car ride across the world's longest unsupported span. So we did. And it certainly was impressive, taking eleven minutes to cover the two-mile gulf, as were the views from the top. We also got a great view of a mother bear and her cubs while riding the ski lift up the mountain, although it was slightly unnerving to be twenty metres *above* a bear.

Our next stop was Vancouver Island, where we had several friends. Our first visit was with Sebastian and Natasha. I'd worked with Seb in the UK and now he was teaching at a sixth form college near Victoria. I'd only been on the road for about five weeks at this point but it was lovely to stop at a friend's house, unpack everything, watch TV and have a break from the travelling. It may sound strange but anyone who travels for a long time says the same thing. It's hard work sometimes and occasionally you need a break from it. Seb and Natasha had to work during the day so we'd sleep, read and go for walks along the beach with their dog, Ridley. I even managed to find the time to give Heidi a proper clean. Now that I'd given her a name, I seemed more inclined to take better care of her. I wondered what Milgram would say about that? She needed an oil change and I rode into Victoria, the capital, to find a bike shop. I watched the oil change being done as I knew I really should be doing this sort of thing myself. Perhaps next time I'd pluck up the courage to have a go.

Moving on to Ucluelet on Vancouver Island, we passed through an ancient forest of Douglas fir, red cedar and sequoia. Called Cathedral Grove, this area is a major tourist attraction on the island. I'd been riding through forests and past trees for 6,000 miles in Alaska and Canada but nothing like this. The largest trees in Cathedral Grove are over 75 metres tall, nine metres in circumference and over eight hundred years old – by far the oldest thing I'd come across in North America so far. These trees were already several hundred years old by the time Europeans arrived here. It was thrilling and humbling to be standing next to such huge and ancient living organisms.

Most of the population of Vancouver Island lives on the east coast and there's a good reason for this. The west of the island, especially near Ucluelet and, just to the north, Tofino is famous for its rainforest. That means two things: lots and lots of trees and lots and lots of rain. Vancouver City, (which is on the mainland, east of Vancouver Island), has a reputation for being quite wet: it gets 150 centimetres of rain a year, compared to London's 65 cms, but Ucluelet gets 300 cms! That's three metres of rain a year. So it should have been no surprise that as we arrived in Ucluelet and found the pretty little campsite by the harbour, it started to rain. Just a drizzle to start with and we managed to get my aged and tired small tent erected before we, or it, got too wet. Then with all our belongings either stuffed into the tent or safely and dryly packed away on the bike we did what all campers do (when they don't have a car or an RV), we stood around in the rain wondering what to do next. It was only five o'clock, so far too early to go to bed but the weather was miserable. If we'd had a car we could at least have sat in it and perhaps gone for a drive and looked at the sea or something. We both still had our bike gear on as there was no point getting our other set of clothes wet but neither of us really wanted to get on the bike and ride anywhere. So we did the only thing we could do. We went for a long walk in the rain in our bike gear. We must have looked rather strange. We walked along the main road that runs through Ucluelet, past the shops and tourist centre and on towards the coast. We then turned around and walked back. It was now a quarter to six. Sometimes, just sometimes, I have to admit, it would be nice to have a car.

When we got back to the campsite it was still raining and we were not 'happy campers'. The tent was looking rather sorry for itself and inside, the floor of the tent was getting damp. We had good quality sleeping mats so I knew we wouldn't get wet but I wasn't really looking forward to the long night ahead. Reluctantly we climbed into our damp tent soon after six. Trying to keep the dry stuff dry and the wet stuff as far away from us as possible we settled down in our sleeping bags, to watch a film on the Netbook, do some reading and try to get to sleep before we could feel the rain. The floor of the tent was a bit damp but the sleeping mats would keep us dry, I assured Tracy.

Trusting my word (she's a slow learner), Tracy got to sleep quite easily; she has a wonderful knack for being able to sleep anywhere. I tossed and turned a bit, listening to the rain and wondering whether my old tent would stand up to three metres in one night. I also worried about the bike, sinking into the wet earth on its side-stand and keeling over in the night. Eventually I managed to sleep but the patter, patter of rain on the canvas seeped into my dreams, and into my bladder. The one thing I absolutely hate about getting on in years and camping, (especially in the cold and/or rain), is having to get up to pee in the middle of the night. I pulled on my soaking bike trousers and damp shirt, slipped on my wet bike boots and went outside. Standing outside in the dark and wet, in soaking clothes, I doubted that things could get any more miserable, but I was wrong, they most certainly could.

About an hour or two later, snugly tucked back up in my warm sleeping bag, Tracy woke me up. Now Tracy, as I have said, has a wonderful knack for sleeping and in the fifteen years we have been together I can think of only a handful of occasions when she has woken me up. So something must be wrong. On my trip to the toilet I hadn't really taken much notice of how wet the inside of the tent was but Tracy had woken me up because she'd had nightmares of graves swept open by deluge and found her hair, hanging over the edge of the sleeping mat, was floating. The floor of the tent was about half an inch deep in water. Everything, and I mean everything not on the mat, was wet. It was 5 am.

We did the only thing we could. We got up (it was light by now anyway) put on our wet bike gear and slowly packed away the tent. At least the bike hadn't keeled over in the night. Once packed and ready to go we rode to the nearest open café and had a hot breakfast and several cups of coffee. An hour later, feeling a little more human and a bit dryer, we began to see the funny side. Neither of us wanted to leave the west coast without seeing the coastline for which it was famous so we rode out to one of the beaches and walked round in the mist and rain on the beach in our bike gear. We also went on a nature trail around a bog. And although it was actually very interesting and full of informative facts about coastal bogs, I didn't take any notes in the rain and later I could only recall one single fact – Ucluelet gets three metres of rain a year.

CHAPTER 5

LOOKING FOR AMERICA

'Nice Guy Eddie: You don't tip?
Mr Pink: Nah, I don't believe in it.'

(*Reservoir Dogs*)

The sign said *Goats on a roof*. How could anyone pass a sign that said *Goats on a roof*? We turned off the main road and found ourselves at a grass-roofed café with, well, goats on the roof. Apparently it all started in the 1950s when a Norwegian, missing home, built a shack with a grass roof. Soon goats turned up on his roof, swiftly followed by tourists who wanted to see this. Over the years it's developed into a major tourist attraction and tourists need food and coffee and, now it seems, shops selling garden furniture, tie-dyed T-shirts and jewellery. The car park was full.

Just up the road was the World Parrot Refuge. Its car park was almost empty. Most of its parrots, macaws and cockatoos are victims of the illegal international trade in wild and exotic birds. Housed in what were essentially two huge cages, stretching for twenty or so metres, hundreds of birds were flying around, squawking and shitting. It was parrot mayhem. Even with our ears plugged (as advised by the ticket office) the noise was deafening. Tracy really didn't like the experience and it was one of the few times I've actually seen her unsettled. Parrots are very intelligent animals; they bond with their 'owners' and can live for seventy years. Clearly many of these birds had chequered histories and were slightly mental.

I was pestered by one little fella who kept pecking at my ankle. He couldn't fly and all he wanted was to be picked up and stroked. But as soon as I put him down he started pecking at my ankle again. While he was doing this, another had landed on my shoulder and was grabbing for my neck chain. I'm sure I heard him squawk "Pieces of eight". Tracy had a macaw on her shoulder nibbling away at her earring. The look on her face, somewhere between mild panic and despair, told me that my marriage was under threat once more. I was rather taken by the parrots and saddened that these intelligent, beautiful creatures were the victims of such a profitable worldwide illicit trade. The World Parrot Refuge was much more deserving of my time and money than a few scrawny goats on a roof. But Tracy's face told me it was time to leave.

World Parrot Refuge, Vancouver Island

I really wanted Tracy to enjoy her three weeks with me on the bike and since her birthday had been celebrated in the freezing rain of the Icefields Parkway I felt I owed her something special. My trusty Lonely Planet Guide came to the rescue: it described an exciting place to stay on the east coast of Vancouver island which I just knew she would love: we were going to spend the night fifteen feet up a tree in a wooden sphere.

Set in a couple of acres of woodland, near Qualicum Bay, Tom Chudleigh has built three wooden spheres, suspended by ropes in the trees. A spiral wooden staircase, suspended from the orb leads up to the room. It's a bit like a tree version of a hobbit hole – or perhaps it's where the Ewoks live. Either way, that night our wet tent stayed in its wet bag and our accommodation was in a wooden orb suspended above the ground. A unique experience.

Unique accommodation for the night on Vancouver Island

Travelling has a habit of making a population of seven billion seem like village neighbours and you can while away many an evening playing 'six degrees of separation' with new acquaintances. But somehow people from different parts of our lives had clustered in this part of the world and the next week became a slightly surreal series of encounters with our former lives. After Seb, my work friend, came Tony, my school friend, then Neal, Tracy's college friend, then Tracy's aunt and cousins, each separated by a scenic ferry ride. Obviously staying with people you know who are pleased to see you and happy to show you the neighbourhood is a great way to travel, especially on British Columbia's sunshine coast, since everyone seems to have a boat (and a dog). But that itch to keep on moving and see what was around the corner was getting to me and in any case, Tracy had to fly back to the UK.

It was a rather damp, gloomy morning when we waved goodbye to Tracy's cousin Steve and family, in Gibson's Bay and set off for Vancouver airport. The weather appeared to be reflecting my emotions. We'd had a wonderful three weeks on the road and I was certainly going to miss Tracy. She was flying out to Mexico three months later but I'd got used to having company and was feeling a little apprehensive about being on my own again. I was losing my companion and moving to a new country all in one day. That morning I'd woken up in a country I'd become familiar with next to my wife; by the evening I'd be in gun-toting America, alone. I rode away from the airport feeling scared, excited, emotional and alive. The same feeling I'd had when I left England to fly to Alaska. Why was I doing this? What on earth did I think I was doing? What the hell is going to happen next? I had a very real appreciation that I was totally on my own and fully responsible for what was going to happen to me over the next few weeks and months. It's not a feeling you get very often in your life but it was the very essence of why I was doing this trip in the first place.

But first, of course, I had to cross the border back into *The land of the free and the home of the brave*. I'd lost count of how many Canadians had told me of all the bad things about the USA. How they all carry guns and how I would get grilled at the border. I put all that down to the worldwide phenomenon, well known to travellers, of neighbourly suspicion. It happens across the globe with disturbing regularity. Everyone tells you bad things about their neighbours. Canada and the USA actually share the longest single border in the world. There's five thousand five hundred miles of it and I'd chosen to cross at its most westerly point, at the Peace Arch just south of Vancouver. I was actually quite laid back about the whole thing (I guess, in my mind I was thinking more about Tracy than some stupid border) but, as is often the case with these things, I got more and more nervous as I got closer. As I passed the arch itself I read the descriptions on both sides of the twenty metre high monument. On the Canadian side it read: 'Brethren dwelling together in unity' and on the US side: 'Children of a common mother'. An inscription above the iron gate read: 'May these gates never be closed'. All very touching, but I couldn't help feeling it was a little melodramatic. After all, this wasn't exactly Checkpoint Charlie.

I'd been in very slow traffic queuing to cross the border for nearly an hour and was getting thirsty and hot in my bike gear. It was the most frustrating kind of traffic: sitting on the bike constantly inching forward, not moving fast enough to benefit from an airflow but not actually stopping, so you couldn't get off the bike for a break. It's hard work and not conducive to a sensible and polite conversation with a US customs official.

"Good morning sir, can I see your documentation please?"

I handed over my passport, not sure whether I was supposed to get off my bike. Perhaps any sudden movement would have spooked her into tasering me, ending my American adventure before it had even begun.

"Where are you coming from?"

Now this one always confused me. Did she mean today, in which case the correct answer was: "My wife's cousin's house in Gibson's Bay?" or where did I start this trip, in which case I should say, "Anchorage" or where I was born, "Darwen, Lancashire." As she was holding my passport I wanted to cover all the options.

"Today I've come from Gibson's Bay, but I started out in Alaska on this trip. Originally I'm from the UK." That should cover it!

"And where are you going?"

Again – some sort of time frame would be useful.

"Well, today I'm heading for Seattle. Then I'm travelling around the US for a couple of months." At that point I managed to shut myself up. 'Too much information; you can give these people too much information,' I thought. And if I mentioned the word Mexico I just knew I was going to be arrested as a liar. No one, but no one who isn't a fugitive from justice, goes to Mexico.

"Is this your bike?"

'No I stole it,' I thought, but kept the sarcasm to myself.

"Yes," I said.

"Did you pack everything on that bike yourself? Are you carrying any weapons? What is the purpose of your visit?"

"Yes. No. Tourism." 'Wow,' I thought to myself, 'I can see how you manage to stop all the illegals and terrorists with this tricky questioning.'

This all reminded me of the palaver I had to go through getting my US Visa in the first place. I had to fill in an online form for the US Embassy in London. There were some taxing questions such as: 'Are you, or have you ever been a terrorist?' and 'Have you ever been involved in an act of genocide?' No, no I have never bombed a country or series of countries without exhausting all other legal, peaceful and democratic options. And I have never used excessive force to further my own domestic or foreign policy aims with scant regard for the citizens of other lands. Have you? I thought but didn't write.

I must have satisfied her that I was just another tourist and I was soon on my way heading south towards Seattle but, wanting to avoid as many large American cities as possible, I turned east at Everett and over the hills inland towards Spokane. Somewhere along the road I remembered that Tom from the HU meeting in Nakusp had mentioned that I could stay with him in Washington but I couldn't find the piece of paper with his address on it. It would have been nice to stay with a friend that night. In the end I checked into a motel and watched the local news on the TV. In two separate incidents, police in Washington State had tasered people, both of whom had died. So glad I'd been polite at the border, but perhaps those warnings from Canadians hadn't been hyperbole after all. Perhaps the USA really was full of gun-toting lunatics?

One thing I did learn in my non-descript chain motel was that Washington state had an unofficial state motto. I learned that most states have official ones but Washington's rather perplexing: 'Bye and Bye' hadn't been recognised by the state legislature. I decided to make it my mission to learn each state motto as I journeyed through the country and shout it out as I crossed the state border. It's the little things that keep you sane whilst travelling alone!

*

Everett to Spokane started with a wet ride up and over the highest navigable road in Washington, via a ski resort, not that I saw anything through the dense cloud and rain. Down the other side the sun came out. I love it when that happens. Then it all got a little weird. Having ridden through mile after mile of pine forest since Alaska, the environment suddenly changed and I was in Kansas. Or at least it looked like Kansas to me: hundreds of square miles of wheat fields and huge skies. I was surprised that the land was so flat and fertile here; it certainly wasn't what I'd been expecting. Geologists talk of a 'mega-flood' that happened near what is now Spokane 15,000 years ago. A massive sea of glacial water broke through a huge ice dam sending 500 cubic miles of water west across Washington State. In a matter of hours it not only washed away everything in its path, but reshaped the land, creating 'the scablands', terrain consisting of bare rock, deeply channelled by glacial flood water. Three hundred miles after leaving Everett, I arrived in Spokane. The main reason I'd come here was to pick up a new front tyre that I'd ordered from the BMW dealership in town, but first I had to find a campground. I'd googled Spokane while in Everett and located a State Park west of town that had a campground. I found it quite easily but it seemed all the pitches were pre-booked. I rode around wondering what to do. Just as I was about to leave, a camper waved at me and I pulled over. Andy and Janice were cruising around in a van and offered to share their pitch with me. Campsites in America mirrored their cousins in Canada: huge pitches with room to park your RV, a fire pit and wooden table; more than enough space to share. Andy and Janice were from Portland, Oregon and had just spent a month touring Canada. They were on their way home and he gave me their address in Portland should I want to "stop off and wash some stuff." This was extremely kind of them. I wondered how I would react back in the UK if I was camping and a solo biker was cruising around the campsite looking for a pitch. I was quickly learning that Americans are more likely to offer you a beer than threaten you with a gun.

Next morning was sunny and warm and I rode off to the BMW dealer certain that today was going to be a good day. Oh dear, how often does a trip to the mechanics turn out well? First the good news: they did have the front tyre that I had ordered. I'd noticed some worrying cracks all around the right-hand side and knowing as much about tyres as I do about mechanics I wasn't sure how serious this was, but decided to err on the side of caution. By the time I got to Spokane it was clear that I might as well get a new rear tyre as well, especially as I was heading towards some winding roads in Glacier and Yellowstone National Parks. My Avon Distanzia tyres had taken me over seven thousand miles from Alaska to Spokane but they hadn't been new when I'd started so it made sense to change both tyres in one go. The bike shop had a set of Continental Attacks which cost me around two hundred pounds.

They took the bike away and I had a wander around the showroom. Twenty minutes later the mechanic came out to tell me there was a problem. The spokes were loose (all the way around on both wheels). This had, partly, caused the 'cupping' on the front tyre and was potentially a big problem. He could solve it but, of course, it would take time and money. I was annoyed with myself over this. Spoke monitoring and adjustment had been covered on my bike maintenance course and over the previous seven weeks I'd occasionally tested the spokes by banging them with a spanner. They'd all sounded fine to me. This loosening wasn't good, either for the bike, or for my pride. If I couldn't even do a simple thing like check the spokes properly what chance did I have of making it to Panama, let alone Africa?

Still, at least it was noticed by a mechanic in a shop rather than having a wheel collapse on me in Glacier National Park in the pouring rain, or half way down Baja California in the heat. All I had to do was sit and wait. I also asked them to sort out the computer anomaly on my bike. I had a light on the dashboard telling me the front light wasn't working (when it was) and the gears were out of sync with the computer so it still said I was in neutral when I was actually in first gear, as well as that perpetual flashing red sign warning me that the anti-lock system on the brakes wasn't functioning. None of these issues were a real problem but I thought I might as well get them sorted while I was at a dealership with the official BMW plug-in computer system to do it. It's only money…

So I found the coffee machine and a comfy chair and settled down for what might be a long wait. It gave me the opportunity to catch up on my blog a bit and I managed to write down a few thoughts I'd been having while riding along over the previous couple of days…

Whenever I buy food or a drink I'm told to "Have a nice day". Are they just being polite or are they after something? We may speak the same language but I think we find it quite hard to read each other. Being English, I'm slightly suspicious of people who are overly friendly; I just can't tell when it's sincere, whereas I can read British sarcasm from half a mile away. I really like the friendliness of people here though, there's an air of optimism about and let's face it, if you're going to sell coffee you might as well be happy about it.

Or are they after something? I'm aware that tipping is big here but I agree with Mr Pink in Reservoir Dogs: tipping only encourages employers to pay lower wages. Are people just saying, "Have a nice day" because they want me to tip them? After all, it's not like I was thinking about having a shitty day when I bought the coffee but have had my mind changed by the waiter, and now that I'm certainly going to try my best to "Have a nice day" should I leave a dollar for planting the thought in my mind?

It's so difficult, especially when you only have superficial contact with people. From the one sentence conversation to buy coffee (you can see that I drink a lot of coffee) to the ten minute chat at a gas station with a Harley riding skydiver who used to live in Milton Keynes. (This happened yesterday). I'm sure most people are genuine enough. What does interest me, though, is why are Americans/Canadians like this and we Brits aren't? Now that is a question…

Talking of coffee, as I was, I'm intrigued by the little drive-thru coffee shops that I've noticed and can only assume permeate the country. Some are smaller than the trucks that pull up to them, most are shaped a little like gypsy caravans and all serve every conceivable kind of coffee. It's not the fact that they exist that I'm concerned about, it seems like a really good idea. It's more the fact that we don't have them in the UK. We have imported so many US food 'restaurants' and coffee shops but not this neat little idea – a drive-thru coffee hut. I must fly home immediately and sink all my money into setting one up.

Another difference I've noticed has nothing to do with coffee and all to do with politics. We're two months away from mid-term elections in the US. Many members of Congress are up for re-election as evidently, are many State representatives. TV is punctuated by what we would call party political broadcasts, and billboards litter the countryside. As a teacher of Politics, I am already aware of some of the similarities/differences between our form of democracy and America's. I believe it might even be against the law for billboards to advertise the party, it must be the person and every TV advert which is, say, promoting Bill Smith for Congress, must have a voice over by Bill Smith saying "I'm Bill Smith and I endorse this advert." Often these TV commercials go on for a minute or two and don't even mention the party Bill Smith is standing for. Politics here is much more personal.

But the thing that really surprises me is that in the USA judges and sheriffs stand for election. I hadn't realised this. In some ways this is refreshing and very democratic. We've just moved towards the idea of elected mayors in the UK, and even elected police commissioners. But voting for sheriffs and judges got me thinking. I passed one homestead, for example, that had a billboard telling me to re-elect John Smith as sheriff and Kevin Duke for judge. Now, what if Mr Smith and Mr Duke do get re-elected, won't they be fully aware in a small town who did and who did not support them? Could that have repercussions? Or am I just being super suspicious?

At least all of this gave me something to think about as I sat, waiting, in the bike shop. I'd arrived at 10 am and didn't leave until 4 pm. They changed both tyres and their computer had sorted out my glitches. One remaining issue was that a spoke broke and the dealership didn't have a spare! (That couldn't be funnier. The BMW dealership in SPOKane, broke my spoke and couldn't replace it) Of course I wasn't carrying any spare spokes. I had to phone the BMW dealer in Missoula, Montana and they ordered some for me. I ordered three just to be safe! It seemed that I was destined to travel around the US picking up a different part for my bike from each state I visited. I left Spokane $500 poorer but with a safer bike.

It was about three hundred miles from Spokane to Glacier National Park. I passed, briefly, through northern Idaho screaming the state motto: 'Let it be perpetual' as I crossed the border and then on into Montana whose motto: 'Gold and silver' didn't sound quite so deep!

*

I expected Glacier National Park to be cold (the clue being in the name) and I was pushing my luck a little visiting so late in the season. The trees were certainly warning me that it was autumn, even though it was only early September. I had ten hours in my tent but I can't really say I slept, at least not well. It was one of the coldest nights I can remember. I was in three layers of clothes, plus I had my biking jacket liner on and I was still cold.

I rode the famous fifty-mile Going-to-the-Sun Road, which passes right through the middle of the National Park. It was a good stretch of twisty tarmac but a combination of six weeks of amazing riding, and the fact that it was Sunday and everyone was on the road made it a slightly less than awesome experience. It was a long slow procession to the top with cars, RVs and trucks forming an orderly queue as we snaked our way up the pass. The views were stunning and I could see that, given a run at it, the road would have been brilliant fun on a motorcycle – narrow and winding with a huge drop off to the right – but it just turned into a long slow convoy. I was thoroughly disappointed. Several people, including Paul the Texan, had told me that I shouldn't miss this road and I'd come here specially. I suppose I'd built it up too much. It's always the surprising discoveries that stick with you; the places you feel you have discovered all on your own. I should just have been grateful that the road was open. In winter it lies under several metres of snow and only opens from mid-June to mid-October.

At the top I stopped at Logan Pass (6,600 ft or 2000 m), bought a huge Montana sticker for the bike and then headed down the other side. Probably because of the lack of sleep and problems with the bike's spokes I'd got myself into a bad mood that day and there was no one around to snap me out of it. Such are the pitfalls of solo travel. When you're having a good day, everything is going right and the roads are awesome, it's great but I felt there was something missing – there was no one to share it. When times are bad, when you wake up having had a poor night's sleep, it's cold and the road you've been looking forward to riding is jam-packed with traffic and road works, it's easy to forget that you're on the trip of a lifetime. Your mind exaggerates the negatives and there is no one there to help you see reason. Many solo travellers always emphasise the positive, but the truth (as I see it) is that there are many occasions when it's boring, lonely, disappointing or just bloody hard work.

And if you are in this sort of grumpy mood, without anyone around to snap you out of it, it can linger for a while. Had Tracy been there, she'd have told me I was being an idiot. Mind you, travelling two-up on a motorcycle also comes with a health warning: a huge amount of compromise. You really are living in each other's pockets twenty four/seven and you need a special sort of strong relationship to survive that. I remember Tracy telling some friends that she was coming out to Canada for three weeks to sit on the bike and camp with me.

"Three weeks? With your husband? That close to each other? Oh my God I can't stand spending a whole weekend with mine."

David and Jill, the couple I'd briefly met in Nakusp, were travelling two up on a 1982 BMW R80 G/S called Nancy and said that they'd come across the same sort of trepidation from their friends. How could you survive spending all that time with your partner? I was following David and Jill's blog which was refreshingly honest about this whole thing. They were clearly having 'issues', as they say, but were very open about it; a good reminder that that this kind of long distance travel is just as much a personal one as a geographical one. Meeting fellow travellers and then following their blogs was one of the wonders of the new travelling age. When I first started travelling in the late 1980s we still had to queue up to collect real letters from real *poste restante* offices. Now I could get an instant message on a phone in my pocket. I might be travelling alone but blogs made me feel part of a travelling community.

I was having these thoughts as I exited Glacier National Park and headed towards Browning, which is home to the Plains Indians National Museum and I felt it deserved a stop. There was just one other vehicle in the car park, in contrast to the huge Indian-owned-and-run Casino next door, where there were at least a hundred cars parked. The museum had the usual stuff you'd expect with a depressing graphic wall map showing how the Plains Indians, who had lived in this huge swathe of North America since the days of yore, were almost wiped out (they didn't use that phrase) in barely a century. In 1800 they were living, more or less happily alongside small numbers of white Americans, but the gold rush of the 1840s, among other things, led to land seizure and by 1900 the survivors had all been 'settled' on reservations.

In one room there was a grainy DVD of several Indian chiefs talking, using sign language. I didn't really understand why they were using sign language until I stepped outside. In front of the museum a monument explained it to me. In September 1930 the U.S. Government organised a conference of all the (remaining) Plains Indians at Browning – The Indian Sign Language Conference. At that meeting the Indians were filmed using a sign language they had developed as a way of communicating since they all spoke different languages. The monument was constructed by getting the twenty participants (sixteen Plains Indians, four US Government officials) to stand in a semi-circle in cement, their footprints marking the occasion for posterity.

I walked round the circle looking at the imprints. Clearly marked and preserved in concrete I could see the naked foot imprints of 'Deer Nose – Crow'; 'Tom White Horse – Arapahoe'; 'Strange Owl – Cheyenne'; 'Foolish Woman – Mandan'. And then I got to the US Government contingent including General Scott and Governor Dixon: their prints were of their shoes. Of course they were. You wouldn't expect upstanding representatives of the mighty US of A to lower themselves to going barefoot, like the natives! I could just imagine them having a conversation along the lines of:

"What should we do, Governor?"

"General Scott, we will keep our shoes on; it's what makes them savages, and us dignified."

I actually laughed out loud. It was one of those occasions when you really, really wished you had someone to share this with – and not just via the internet. Later I read that just one month prior to my visit, the Cheyenne had hosted another Plains Indians Sign Language Conference. It was the first one since 1930. The museum suggested that in 1885 over 100,000 Native Americans used 'hand talk'. Hardly anyone uses this form of signing anymore, and organisers were hoping that up to thirty people might attend.

At least General Scott had set up a conference in the first place. I still found it funny that he'd kept his boots on but perhaps I'd been a little hasty in my condemnation of him. It appears he did work hard, in his retirement, at documenting and studying Indian sign language. He actually learnt to sign and apparently was known as 'Mole-I-Gu-Op' which means, not surprisingly, 'one who signs with his hands'. I take my hat off to him – or perhaps my boots.

I was still smirking when I rolled into Augusta, Montana. And the smile was only going to get bigger. This was the America I had been looking for. A one-horse town, Augusta consists of one main road and three hundred souls. I pulled up at the town's motel and enquired about camping out the back. Fifteen dollars later I was pitching my tent on grass rather than gravel and for the first time I didn't have to pack all my food and toothpaste away. I was in open country here and a long way from trees. There wouldn't be any bears shitting in the woods anywhere near me tonight. It was a weird sensation to be camping 'properly' again. As the sun set over the distant hills I took a stroll along the main road to see what Augusta had to offer. I wasn't disappointed. I saw a guy in a rocking chair on his porch, under a star-spangled banner, smoking a cigar. Classic small town America. I went into a shop to buy some food and in addition to the usual commodities you'd expect, they sold bullets behind the counter. Rows and rows of bullets.

Next door was the town's bar, The Buckhorn. I had to go in. The interior was exactly as I had hoped: neon Budweiser signs, big TV, long bar with stools and trophies of dead animals all over the walls and ceiling. For someone brought up in the UK this was a surreal experience. It was all so familiar but in an unfamiliar way. I'd only ever seen this on TV before. I ordered a Bud and watched the ball game – I'd been looking forward to finding this America and I was having a great time. All was going well until I looked up and nearly choked on my beer. Behind the bar there was a big handwritten sign: 'Win a gun – and help the needy kids at Christmas. Ask our friendly staff how.' I know I should have asked. I know I should have. I just couldn't – not with a straight face anyway.

I moseyed on back to my tent (I felt I just had to 'mosey'). What a day it had been. It had started, freezing cold in Glacier National Park and ended camping under the enormous Montana night sky, on grass and away from bears. I'd ridden the Going-to-the-Sun Road, learned about Plains Indians and especially about their sign language, and I'd found real small town America. Talk about ups and downs. This was what it was all about. I'd witnessed more in one day than I'd normally pack into a whole holiday. As I drifted off to sleep, surrounded by food, with no idea where my pepper spray was, I was simply the happiest, most contented biker on the planet.

CHAPTER 6

FINDING AMERICA

"We are two countries separated by a common language."

(Attributed George Bernard Shaw)

The following day was just as fantastic as the last. The sun shone – it was the hottest day I'd experienced so far – and I rode for a glorious hundred miles through wonderful BIG Montana. I stopped at lunchtime for a cold drink at a place called Lincoln, just another small Montana town famous for nothing. Well that's not strictly true. Lincoln had been home to the notorious 'Unabomber'. Ted Kaczynski, to give him his proper name, was the subject of one of the FBI's most expensive investigations. A brilliant mathematician and neo-luddite, Kaczynski waged a bombing campaign in the US that lasted from the late 70s to the mid-90s. He was angry with the way society was developing, especially the destruction of the environment and loss of personal freedoms. But his bombings were erratic and confused, to say the least. He sent letter bombs to university professors, computer salesmen and even left one on a plane in 1978, which, if it had exploded, would have brought the flight down. The FBI got involved and used the code name UNABOM (University and Airline Bomber), hence the nickname. All in all he sent sixteen bombs which killed three people and injured twenty-three.

As is often the case with these things, it wasn't the FBI who caught him; his family actually handed him over. In 1995 Kaczynski sent a 35,000-word manifesto to the *New York Times* and the *Washington Post* demanding that it be published in return for him giving up his bombing campaign. Essentially the manifesto called for a world revolution against modern society. What a dilemma! The FBI urged the papers to publish – in the hope that someone would recognise the author. On September 19th 1995 they did so, Kaczynski's brother read it and his suspicions that the madman might be his brother were confirmed. Although he hadn't seen him for over ten years he still had some letters Ted had written to the press in the early 1970s. Kaczynski was arrested in his cabin outside Lincoln, Montana in April 1996. After pleading guilty he was spared the death penalty and sentenced to life imprisonment.

On through Lincoln, Heidi was purring at the fantastic Montana scenery. It's not called 'Big Sky Country' for nothing. Occasionally the grand vista was punctuated by a sign informing me that I was approaching a 'Point of Historic Interest'. This usually referred to something that happened in the nineteenth century involving the explorers Lewis and Clark.

America famously declared independence from Britain in 1776 and by the end of the century the young country had steadily expanded westward from the original thirteen colonies on the Atlantic coast towards the Mississippi. Then in 1803 a strapped-for-cash Napoleon sold America a vast tract of French territory to the west of the mighty river and following its course right down to New Orleans and the Gulf of Mexico. The 'Louisiana Purchase' included far more than present day Louisiana and actually included all or part of no fewer than fifteen states today. Covering 800,000 square miles (2 million square kilometres) the agreement doubled the size of the United States without a shot being fired. Now President Thomas Jefferson wanted to bridge the gap between the west and east coasts. The south western part of what we now call the United States (California, Nevada, New Mexico, Utah, Arizona and Texas) was all Spanish territory. So in 1804 Jefferson ordered an expedition to explore the Louisiana purchase territory and beyond, across the Rocky Mountains, to find a passage to the Pacific Coast north of Spanish-owned California.

Jefferson appointed US Army Captain Meriwether Lewis to lead the expedition and Lewis selected William Clark as his partner, along with about thirty others. They left St. Louis, Missouri, in May 1804 and met dozens (some say nearly fifty) Native American tribes on their travels. They wintered with the Mandan tribe in present day North Dakota where the temperature dropped to forty below and Lewis had to amputate several toes (not his own).

The following spring, with Mandan guides, they continued west upstream along the Missouri river, finally making it to the Rocky Mountain Range. (Although as they were, I think, the first white men to see them, I doubt they were called the Rockies at the time.) Near starving, they made it over the mountains in September 1805, having taken nearly two weeks to cover the 160 miles from Missoula, Montana to what is now Weippe, Idaho. Today it's a four-hour drive. The world of Lewis and Clark was so different from the one I was riding through. Not only were they travelling through unmapped territory, they were far out of reach of their own comforts and cultural norms.

While Lewis and Clark are as familiar to Americans as Drake and Raleigh are to us Brits, this was all new to me. I knew a little about recent American history but next to nothing about this period. And I found it fascinating. I suppose I'd always just taken it for granted that the USA was the size and shape it was. It was intriguing to think that the whole central belt could have stayed French and the western third Spanish.

Lewis and Clark's expedition finally reached the Pacific on December 7th 1805; the first white men to cross North America overland. However, in their three months on the Oregon coast they only had twelve days when it didn't rain! They made it back to St. Louis in September 1806. An epic twenty-eight month journey. They brought back not only knowledge of a route through the Rockies to the coast but a vast amount of detailed information about flora and fauna. It must also have been a huge psychological boost for the citizens of such a young country to know that it could straddle the continent.

Several times a day, I would see a sign indicating a 'Point of Historical Interest' and every time it was something to do with Lewis and Clark. I was impressed with what I had found out about the Corps of Discovery, (as the Lewis and Clark expedition was known), but it also seemed that nothing else had happened in this part of the world. However, soon after leaving Lincoln, I came across a 'Point of Historical Interest' that was different. This one declared that I was near the spot where the coldest temperature ever measured on 'Continental America' was recorded. I knew that the coldest point in the USA was near the Arctic Circle in Alaska, I had been near it on the Dalton Highway, but this was referring to the 'contiguous US' or 'the Lower 48'. Roger's Pass had got to -56C (-70F) in January 1954. I was there in September and it was warm at perhaps 25C (77F). It's quite amazing what five months can do. It was yet another reminder of how tame and gentle our UK weather patterns really are. In comparison, November 2010 was extremely cold in the UK. In England it got down to a highly unusual – 13C (+8F).

With about fifty miles to go to Missoula, and in no particular rush, I followed a sign leading off the main road and up a gravel track to a 'Ghost Town'. I wasn't expecting much but was pleasantly surprised. Garnet was a 'gold rush' town established in the 1880s and reached its peak in 1898. With over a thousand residents, Garnet had four stores, four hotels, three stables, a hall, a school, a doctor's surgery and thirteen saloons (many of which doubled as brothels). One thousand people and thirteen bars – doesn't take much imagination to know what went on most of the time in Garnet. But it didn't last for long. Garnet's population dropped to a few hundred by 1914 and although it struggled on until World War Two it eventually became the ghost town that survives today.

Ramshackle wooden buildings were peppered through a pine forest on the edge of a mountainside. Just the kind of place I'd expect the Unabomber to live. Exploring the derelict buildings and outhouses, I was reminded of how primitive people's lives had been just a century ago. Although it was a warm day when I was there, the 'Point of Historical Interest' sign had reminded me that winters in this part of the world are long and hard and cruel. The people who called Garnet home had lived tough, unforgiving lives with no modern comforts and little outside help. Their accommodation would have provided them with little protection against the fierce winter snowstorms. After just one hour there I could fully understand why there were so many bars in the place!

Stumbling across Garnet was an unexpected pleasure, in contrast to the over-hyped Going-to-the-Sun Road. It's often the way that places I'm particularly looking forward to are a little disappointing while gems like Augusta and Garnet pop up unexpectedly. It's an unavoidable quandary for the traveller since you have to plan your travels around the must-see places (which tend to be crowded and overpriced) while hoping that you'll bump into some hidden gems en route. Travelling under your own steam makes this all the more likely and was one of the reasons I was so glad to be riding solo on my own motorcycle.

The dusty gravel track took me back to the main road that twisted and dipped its way through the mountains and on towards the capital of Montana, Missoula. I was trying to avoid large cities in America but had to go to this one to pick up the spokes I'd previously ordered from the BMW dealer there. It seemed a little silly to go all that way just for a few spokes so I'd dipped into my bike manual to see if anything else might need changing, tightening, replacing or cleaning. You'll recall that motorcycle maintenance isn't my strong suit but that I had been on a one-day maintenance course in the UK the previous Easter. Run by World of BMW in the Brecon Beacons, Wales, the day was devoted to helping complete novices like me find their way around a motorcycle before heading off on a trip. I'd found it extremely useful to get down and dirty with someone else's bike, without having to worry about doing anything wrong. I'd spent the morning taking the wheels off, plugging the tyres (GS bikes, I'd learned, run tubeless tyres, despite having spokes) and learning how to pump water out of the engine. (Not that I could imagine ever taking my bike across a river.) In the afternoon we looked at what we should do to maintain the bike on the road. Ironically one of the easy jobs was to check the spoke tension. It was something I'd done a few times since leaving Alaska, which made me suspicious when the mechanic in Spokane told me they were all loose.

Another advantage of the BMW 1200GS is its shaft final drive, instead of the more common chain and sprockets which need frequent oiling. However, the shaft is supposed to have its oil changed every 12,000 miles. By the time I got to Missoula I'd done 8,000 miles but as I had no idea when the last final drive oil change had been done I booked Heidi in for one. After all, it couldn't cost that much, could it? I'd also started feeling a slight wobble on the front wheel. I wasn't sure if it was connected to the one missing spoke (unlikely), my imagination (possible) or something else (worryingly); so I asked Missoula to take a look.

I never like taking a motorcycle or car to any mechanic. It's a bit like going to the dentist. I go in confident that nothing is the matter and come out much later in all sorts of pain. With trepidation I arrived at the BMW dealership and handed over the bike. I went upstairs to their customer waiting area and, well, waited.

"Mr Giles, there seems to be a bit of a problem. Would you like to come and have a look?"

Not what you want to hear after waiting two hours. I followed the mechanic down to the garage area where Heidi was up on a bike-lift with the back wheel off and bits of the drive system lying on the floor. What they showed me made my heart sink. The drive shaft, the long metal rod that transmits the engine's power from the gearbox to the back wheel was, even to my ignorant eyes… knackered. It was rusted and corroded and clearly not in a good state.

"How, what, why, eeerrr?" I stuttered.

"It looks like either, the oil on this bike has never been changed, or water has somehow got into the system, or probably both. It's not good."

"Stupid question – Is it, well, fucked?"

"Yes."

"Fuck."

"Yes."

"I suppose I have only two questions then," I said. "First, can you fix it? And second, how much?"

"Yes, of course we can fix it. We don't carry the parts here but I can order them from Nevada and they will arrive overnight. We should be able to replace the whole drive system tomorrow. That's the good part. Unfortunately these parts aren't cheap. It will cost somewhere in the region of $3000."

I was lost for words. Almost.

"Fuck."

What could I do? It was true that the bike would actually still work but eventually (possibly in the middle of the Guatemalan rain forest) it would pack up and there wouldn't be anyone who could fix it. So, in a way, I was lucky. At least it had been found out at a BMW dealership and they could fix it. All I had to do was sit around and wait. And pay.

I found a cheap motel in town and soon became familiar with the three-mile walk from the motel to the bike shop. In much of America everyone drives everywhere, so I was the only person walking down the sidewalks across town. That first day it was a long, hot, depressing walk from the mechanics to the motel. I couldn't stop thinking about how expensive this was going to be and asking myself whether there was another option. Once again, I was feeling lonely and badly missed having someone to bounce ideas off. That night, for the first time on the whole trip, I phoned Tracy back in the UK. I'd kept in touch with texting and email but had a policy not to phone. I always liked to hear her voice but felt even more lonely and depressed once the conversation was over. Texting and email was easier. In the eleven weeks, between leaving Tracy at Vancouver and meeting her in Mexico City, I called her twice. This was the first time and as always Tracy was forthright, sensible and practical with her advice.

"It's only money. If you have to do it you have to do it. It's not like you're dead or anything. Stop being a grumpy git and enjoy your trip. And don't phone again while I'm watching Eastenders."

Maybe you can see now why I don't phone her very often! But it was sage advice. It was indeed 'only money' and at the end of the day (or at the end of three days as it turned out) I would have a safe, reliable bike. I remember going to a talk given by Peter Forward. Peter has ridden a Harley Davidson around the world and became the first person ever to ride the same vehicle to every single country in the world, all one hundred and ninety-three of them, as was. I remember Peter saying that whatever happens, wherever it happens there are always only two things you need: time and money. A combination of these will get you out of anything. He was right.

By the time I left Missoula, I had a lot less money. But at least the whole of the final drive aft of the gearbox had been replaced. They'd also changed the worn out rear disc, brake pads and spark plugs. I was certainly poorer for my trip to Missoula but Heidi was in the best condition she'd been in for years. And I had some spare spokes!

*

I headed south from Missoula on some wonderful mountain roads in the general direction of Yellowstone National Park. A fantastic day's riding was only interrupted by two interesting tourist stops. First was the Big Hole Battlefield site, where the Nez Perce were slaughtered by US Government troops. (The name is pronounced 'Nezz Purse'.) It appears that during the seven decades since the Lewis and Clark expedition, relations between the US Government and Native Americans had soured somewhat. The 1870s and 1880s saw the US Government chasing Native Americans all over this part of the world trying to 'civilise' them. The Nez Perce didn't want to be civilised and instead, somewhat understandably, they wanted to go to Canada. Government troops chased them for five months. At Big Hole, in August 1877 they managed to kill upwards of one hundred. The rest they pursued for a few more weeks towards the Canadian border until the Nez Perce chief surrendered. In 1805 the Nez Perce had helped Lewis and Clarke survive and triumph, seventy years later they were being rounded up.

Further down the road I stumbled upon Nevada City. Like a scene from a Western film, Nevada City was a collection of around fifty buildings all from the mid to late nineteenth century. Each building was original but all had been uprooted, moved and lovingly restored (is there any other way to restore?) at this site. I paid my $8 and wandered around. Not only had they rebuilt the buildings but each and every one of them was crammed full of furniture, products and trinkets from the era. Like Garnet, this was yet another example of America treasuring its history. Americans may not have a lot of history to cling on to but they certainly relish what they have.

Growing up in the UK, surrounded by lots of old stuff, it's all too easy to be blasé about the rich architectural history we have on our small island. In the USA I saw no buildings more than two hundred years old. I knew the Inuit, First Nations Peoples and Native Americans, had lived on this land for thousands of years but they didn't build anything permanent. So to stumble across a nineteenth-century ghost town in Garnet and then Nevada City, was wonderful. Yes they may have only been one hundred or so years old, but here that meant something. I overheard an American tourist say to the woman who ran the gift shop in Nevada City:

"It's so cool here. This stuff is so old. You're real lucky to have such amazing history out here in Montana."

I chuckled to myself, but perhaps I shouldn't have. Again, travelling was making me confront my inner prejudices and appreciate what I had back at home. I was also acquiring a much deeper understanding of Americans by travelling through their country.

Moving on, the road twisted up the mountainside and spat me out on top of the Madison Valley. Fifty miles later I was pulling into a campground in the foothills of Yellowstone. The only other tent in the campground belonged to a couple on a tandem bicycle. They were flying the Union Jack so I went over to say hello. Huw and Carolyn were cycling from Vancouver to Florida for charity, raising money for Shelter Box (Disaster relief). They were covering fifty miles a day, stopping off to give talks at schools and being helped along the way by the Rotary Club. It was nice to chat with someone 'from home' and as it was now getting dark at 7.30, it was also nice to break the evening up a little.

I always feel a little sorry for cyclists, especially when it's raining, but apparently everyone had been taking pity on them and they'd been inundated with offers of beds for the night, food and help. The following morning, as I went over to say goodbye, they pointed out that someone had left a few quarters on their table with a note saying that as it had rained in the night they might like to use the money to dry their clothes in the laundry. Needless to say there was no such note on my table!

I packed away my tent and set off for Yellowstone National Park, shouting 'Equal Rights' as I crossed into Wyoming. Established in 1872, Yellowstone was the world's first National Park. Famous for its wild animals (bears, wolves, elk and buffalo), geysers and stunning scenery, Yellowstone is one of America's top natural tourist attractions. Cue people, RVs, gift shops and queues. On average, two million people visit the park every year with a peak of almost a million in the month of July alone. I was there in mid-September and it was still extremely busy: nose-to-tail traffic along the main route towards Old Faithful, probably the world's most famous geyser. Erupting every ninety minutes or so, Old Faithful spurts up to 8,000 gallons of boiling water fifty metres into the air. Thousands of people see it erupt every day nowadays, but the first non-Native American to see it was only a hundred and forty years ago. I'd wanted to see Old Faithful for myself (I'd seen the original 'Geyser' in Iceland and wanted to compare) but at a fork in the road I couldn't face all the traffic and people and I took my chance to escape and headed east into a much quieter section of the park.

More by luck than judgement, I found myself heading north east out of Yellowstone and up the infamous Beartooth Pass. As I'd been a little disappointed by the Going-to-the-Sun Road, I was keeping my expectations low for this one. I'd been told it was a great biking road by some Harley riders so I knew it must be paved. The road passed through a stunning wide U-shaped valley with a large angry river carving its way through the bottom with meadows gently sloping up towards huge jagged mountains on both sides. I could see what looked like enormous cattle grazing on the valley floor. Wait, hang on a minute. They're not cattle. Bloody hell, those are bison! What's the difference between a buffalo and a bison? Well, lots of things actually, but not here, because the creatures called 'buffalo' in North America aren't really buffalo at all, they are actually bison. True buffalo are only found in Asia and Africa, although the word has been mis-applied to the North American creatures since the seventeenth century. *Bufalo* (with one F) is a Portuguese word, although its origins go back to ancient Greek, via Latin. There's a theory that the mis-naming of bison as buffalo came from French fur trappers' habit of referring to them as *boeufs*, (which can mean any kind of bovine animal such as oxen or bullocks as well as 'beef').

Whatever you call them, there used to be millions of these animals in North America, but they were hunted almost to extinction by the white settlers. Thankfully, there are now a couple of hundred thousand of them living on reserves.

There is something uniquely exciting about seeing a species of animal for the very first time. I knew what bison looked like, of course, but I'd never actually seen any. Not even in a zoo. And there, right before me were dozens of them. Roaming around on the prehistoric plains, munching away and just, well, being bison. It was 2010 but it could have been 1810 or 2010 BC. Awesome. I got that feeling you often get when travelling, of seeing something for the very first time, and being very much aware of that fact. I guess it's a feeling common to people who travel a lot and it's one of those sensations that keeps us going back for more.

The road climbed up the mountain, exited the park and continued up and up. Even though it was only September it was getting cold and the air was getting thinner. Would Heidi be able to cope with the thinning air? Although the internet is full of wonderful advice and help it is also populated by scare-mongers and stay-at-home grumpy bastards who will tell you anything you try to do is impossible and dangerous. One such thread I remember reading on a motorcycle website (not I may add the wonderfully helpful and supportive Horizons Unlimited site) warned against riding a BMW 1200GS at altitude as the fuel injectors wouldn't be able to cope with the lack of oxygen. The bike would splutter and die and you would be stranded and no doubt, murdered. As I didn't even know what a fuel injector was I took that advice with a pinch of salt and continued up. (I've since learned that one of the principal advantages of fuel injectors over old-fashioned carburettors is that they automatically adjust for altitude.)

Anyway, Heidi seemed to be coping extremely well with the lack of oxygen, even thriving on it and we continued up and climbed out of the forest through a series of zigzags and switchbacks to reach the peak at 10,947 feet (3,337 metres). I parked at the top and just gawped at the views: three hundred and sixty degrees of majestic mountains. I'd chosen an excellent day for it and could see for miles and miles. A few days later, online, I caught up with Pat who said he'd been there two weeks before me and had had to fight through snow to get to the top. He saw nothing at the summit and had a miserable time. So I was lucky. The pass is only open until early October because of snow. Standing at the summit in about four layers of clothing with a thermal balaclava on under my helmet I could well believe it.

By night it was bitterly cold (hovering around zero degrees Celsius) and as I was sure I'd read that Yellowstone was the number one place where bears attack campers, one night was going to be enough. In fact just riding a bike around Yellowstone can be dangerous. The park is so full of animals that it isn't uncommon for a biker to collide with one and be seriously hurt. Just the previous day a Canadian on a Harley had hit a deer. He'd broken his leg in several places. (He won't be going back to those places! Boom boom.)

As I rode through the park I still had one small bike issue lingering in the back of my mind. Although the new final drive was working perfectly, I had to change the oil after its first six hundred miles. In my rush to leave Missoula and get back on the road I hadn't really appreciated where I would be at that point. As I left Yellowstone I notched up my six hundredth mile, and I was a long way from a BMW dealer. I had thought about this a few days earlier and had pulled into a coffee shop to hook up to their free wi-fi. With time running out on my Netbook battery I had just managed to find a bike shop in Idaho Falls and had called them up. They said they could change the oil but there was some discussion about the type of oil they had in stock. Whatever oil I put in would stay there for 12,000 miles so I didn't want to settle for an inferior brand, but likewise I didn't want to have to ride on another four hundred miles to Boise, Idaho and the next dealership. I got back on the internet just before my battery died and found a Harley rental company along my route that also rented BMWs; perhaps they would have some oil.

So that's why I pulled over in Jackson, Wyoming, just south of Yellowstone. I found the shop and although they didn't have a mechanic on hand as it was Saturday, they did have some BMW oil, which they happily sold to me. I love it when a plan comes together. Two hours later the bike was in the capable hands of a mechanic in Idaho Falls getting the oil changed – and only one hundred miles over the stipulated six. For the first time since Gibson's Bay on the Sunshine coast, where I'd noticed the cracks in the front tyre, everything was fixed and working properly. Heidi was ready to go.

Perhaps for that reason, or because the landscape had changed, the ride to Sun Valley was liberating. Although I loved every minute of every piece of scenery I passed through I have a thing for deserts and was pleasantly surprised to be riding into one as I headed west from Idaho Falls. Caused by volcanic eruptions and lava flows, Route 20 took me past a huge atomic research centre, through Arco (famous as being the first town on the planet to be powered by atomic energy, in 1956), and on to the Craters of the Moon National Monument. Now, I've seen lava before and wasn't expecting to be overly impressed but it would have been rude to have just passed on by, so I pulled in and took the seven-mile circuit around the park. I learnt that several times during the past few thousand years, a parallel line of fissures had erupted through volcanic buttes and cones to spread a flow of lava across the area. The last eruption was only two thousand years ago, very recent in geological terms. This whole geological phenomenon has shifted from west to east over the millennium and the centre of the activity which was once under this area around the Craters of the Moon National Park, was now the cause of all the hot springs and geysers in Yellowstone.

Yellowstone, which is in effect a super volcano, is actually overdue for a massive eruption. The whole park, forty miles wide and thirty miles long, is one huge magma lake. Should it erupt, it will probably unleash a force some two and a half thousand times that of the famous Mount St. Helens eruption of 1980 in nearby Washington state. The dust cloud would cause a nuclear winter and we could, quite possibly, face extinction. Apparently scientists have measured a 75 cm increase in the ground level in Yellowstone since 1923. They also think the volcano erupts with reliable regularity every 600,000 years or so and the last one was 640,000 years ago. As the *Daily Mail Online* put it, in January 2011: 'Is the world's largest super-volcano set to erupt for the first time in 600,000 years, wiping out two-thirds of the US?'

The highlight of Craters of the Moon was the four or five 'caves'. Two thousand years ago, sheets of lava ran downhill, flowed into channels and cooled, forming tubes as the surface hardened. To quote the guidebook: "The formation of tubes is a complex process dependent on eruption rate, topography, and the chemical and physical properties of the lava." So don't expect any further explanation from me. I was delighted to be allowed to explore these caves and, armed with a torch, spent a good hour clambering around inside them. By the time I left, it was already getting dark but I didn't have to worry about where I was going to camp that night because I was heading for a friend's house and a warm comfy bed.

*

After my visit to the 'Crazy Dog Kennels' in Alaska where the owners and I had discovered a mutual acquaintance called Trent, I had made a concerted effort to track him down and eventually I found him online.

Trent had cycled across America in the late 1980s and it was his stories which had first instilled in me a desire to go to Montana and the western half of the US. When we had shared a house together in Argentina he had encouraged me to venture south to Patagonia on my Honda Transalp. And when he had finally replied to one of my e-mails he insisted that I stop off and visit him in Idaho. He was now living near Ketchum with his wife, Candida, and their daughter, Kali and it only took me a couple of hours to get there from the Craters of the Moon.

I hadn't seen him in ten years and it was wonderful to meet up again but Trent's the kind of person who makes you feel inadequate. I thought I was doing something adventurous with this trip. Not so. Since I'd last seen him he had learnt to run sled-dogs (as I had mentioned to John and Zoya at the Crazy Dog kennels in Alaska) and had completed the thousand-mile Ididerod challenge in Alaska, which explained the sixteen dogs and kennels out back in the yard. I arrived in mid-September and Trent had just got his new pack for the year, ready to train for the following year's race in March. Sled dogs overheat if they exercise above about five degrees so he was only able to take them out late at night and as it hadn't started to snow yet (fortunately for me) he took them out with an ATV (quad). I wasn't going to miss the opportunity to try this! With the engine running and Trent using the gears to hold the dogs back, he and I sat on the ATV with eight mad, enthusiastic, crazy dogs pulling us along the gravel roads in the Sun Valley mountains.

These were largely two and three-year-old dogs, full of enthusiasm and strength but short on obedience and understanding of basic road rules. Screeching around one tight corner, going faster than I'd even dare on my bike we were confronted by a huge moose just standing in the middle of the road. The moose looked at us as if it were the most natural thing in the world to see eight crazy canines, two humans and a noisy machine.

The dogs, who I assume hadn't seen a moose before, instinctively saw it as something to bark at and chase after and it took all of Trent's strength to keep them under control. We must have come within about five metres of the moose before it woke up to the situation and ran off into the bushes. Some of the dogs wanted to chase it down a ditch and into a field. The ATV tipped up onto two wheels and I don't know how I didn't fall off. Trent shouted something at the dogs and enough of them listened to him to right the quad; it bounced back onto all four wheels and we slowed to a stop. (He later admitted that he'd almost lost it.) After two months on the road this was the most exhilarated and frightened I'd been and I wasn't even on my bike (or in my bike gear). That would have been an embarrassing way to die.

"What happened to Dom?"

"Oh, he went off on a middle-age crisis thing around the world on his bike, and died. Lost control on an ATV powered by dogs and hit a moose. Twat."

At least, that's how I expect my wife would have delivered the eulogy at my funeral.

In addition to mastering sled-dogs Trent had also built his own house on land he'd bought in Alaska, and had taken part in the one thousand mile Yukon kayak race. And that's not all. The summer before I met up with him in Idaho he'd flown to Mongolia, built a kayak, transported it over the border to Russia and spent ten days kayaking on Lake Baikal, just for fun. Don't you just hate people like that? Before arriving at Trent's place I was feeling rather pleased with myself for giving up my job and starting my big trip. Not anymore. And what makes it even worse is that Trent is just about the nicest person you'll ever meet.

He did, however, help me in clearing up a query I had. In Canada and in the United States I'd noticed road signs telling me that a certain company or group had 'Adopted the Highway'. I asked him what this meant.

"I'm not sure if it's national but certainly some States let groups of people or companies put up these signs in return for keeping the highway clear of litter. They either arrange to collect the garbage themselves or they pay someone else to do it in return for the advertisement they get from the signs. It's kind of cool. Everyone wins."

It surely seemed like a good idea. The roads were certainly free from litter, which, when I thought about it, was a bit of a shock. As America is the home of fast food I'd expected more litter. And this way taxes are kept low as the state doesn't have to pay for clearing up. Why don't we do this in Britain? But the more I thought about it the more I realised how this exposed the differences between the British and the American psyche. In America individualism and low taxes take priority and the 'Adopt a Highway' scheme epitomises this. Britain has a more socialist outlook. The state is there to take control and care for its citizens and, through taxes, we pay for the privilege. I wasn't trying to make a value judgement as to which system was better; it was just that this scheme, in its own small way, highlighted for me a difference between our two countries.

I'd been brought up to believe that we had a lot in common with our

American 'cousins' and that there was a 'special relationship' between Great Britain and the USA. I think I'd always accepted this; after all, we speak the same language and share a lot of cultural references but the more time I spent in America the more I was beginning to think that this wasn't perhaps as clear-cut as it had seemed. I'd felt close to Canadians, sharing a very similar sense of humour (which is important) but America felt slightly different. More like second cousins, perhaps. I began to question if it was the language that held us together rather than the shared values. I wonder if the British have a lot more in common with the peoples of Scandinavia and Germany than we may think and less with America than we are told. George Bernard Shaw or perhaps Oscar Wilde, but certainly someone cleverer than me said, "We [the British and Americans] are two countries separated by a common language."

I'd been struck by another example of this in the way I was often asked how much I earned. It appeared to me that Americans were much more forward in asking about this than we would be in the UK. And I was particularly struck by the way it was phrased:

"How much do you make?"

This may just be semantics but it seemed revealing that I was asked what I 'made'. Not what I *earned*, but what I *made*. As if I could make more if I put in a little more effort. To a British ear, it sounded odd. I suppose it's fair enough; we're all probably interested in how much money other people have and how much they get paid. Perhaps Americans are just more honest and upfront about it. I'm not sure how much other Europeans discuss their earnings but the British tend not to. And when others do we see it as crass and brash and rather undignified. After all asking someone what they 'make' is tantamount to asking someone what they are 'worth' and that's just not on!

Our shared language makes us assume we are more similar than we are and we don't always allow for our many cultural differences. We're well aware of the cultural distinctions between us and, say, the Chinese, and make allowances for our quirks and differences; perhaps we should do the same with the Americans. I would be less shocked by what I thought was a slightly rude question and we would understand one another better.

It was hard to pull myself away from Trent's place but if I didn't move on soon it was only going to become harder and anyway, I still had a lot to do and see. I had four more weeks in the US and, I estimated, about four thousand miles. I left Trent's heading west for the Oregon coast conscious of the fact that I had no more friends or cousins to stop with. I rode out of Sun Valley feeling excited, brave, adventurous and a little worried. How was I going to cope with my own company for another two months before Tracy arrived in Mexico?

Crossing from Idaho to Oregon over Snake River at Nyssa I screamed "She flies with her own wings" grateful no one could hear me on the empty bridge.

Continuing on Route 26, I stopped for a break in a small, dusty 'nothing' kind of place called Unity; the kind of place where the locals can sniff out fresh DNA. I could easily have ridden through but wanted to stop just to get a sense of what these places are like. I pulled up at the only diner in town next to a couple of 4x4 trucks. The sign outside read: 'We welcome hunters'. No mention of vegetarians…

When I walked in every face in the place was looking at me. I went up to the bar and ordered a coffee. I was planning to eat something but there was absolutely nothing available that a vegetarian could eat. Just as my coffee arrived I felt a presence as someone sat uncomfortably close to me. I looked around and it was another biker. He'd obviously arrived just after me. Perhaps he was feeling as nervous as I was? Either way the presence of a fellow biker made me feel safe.

"Hi, you just arrived?" I asked.

"Yes. I've just pulled along next to your bike. At least I assume it's your bike?"

"Well, at least it's still there," I quipped. "I'm Dom by the way."

"JW."

We chatted for a few minutes about motorcycles (I could only manage a few minutes). JW had a KTM and ran a motorcycle lodge a few miles up the road. He'd also been travelling a lot abroad and I hardly had to say a thing as he told me about his trips, his lodge and a charity he was working with saving cats somewhere in the world. He was one of those overpowering Americans who likes the sound of his own voice, but is super-friendly with it. Although he knew I was British (he'd spent a year in Leighton Buzzard) and I was riding an Alaskan-registered motorcycle he didn't ask me anything about my trip, but kept me entertained with tales about his KTM. And then he said:

"Look Dom, it's been great chatting but I need to run. I'm J.W. Everitt, guitarist with Crosby, Stills and Nash. Here's my card. Ride safe."

And with that he was off, out through the swing doors and away. I was left stunned. What had just happened? It felt as if a whirlwind had passed through the sleepy diner. Had I just met a musician, biker and traveller or a total bullshitter? Later that day I logged on and checked his name on Google images. He certainly was J.W. Everitt: professional musician and biker. And he really had played with Crosby, Stills and Nash.

CHAPTER 7

UP AND DOWN LIKE A YOYO

"If you are lonely when you're alone, you are in bad company."

(Jean-Paul Satre)

I reached Cannon Beach on the Oregon coast and camping became fun again. It got dark at 7.30 pm, but I was camping on grass, near a beach, in beautiful weather. There were no bears around, in fact the campground was infested with cute little white rabbits hopping all over the place. All I had to worry about was being nibbled to death by bunnies.

I'd been looking forward to riding down the Oregon coast for some time and it didn't disappoint. It was the best two hundred miles of coastline I had ever ridden. Windswept sandy beaches, rocky outcrops, giant offshore stacks and quaint little seaside villages, all seen from a twisty, undulating and well-maintained road. Along the way I passed 'the world's smallest harbour' and 'the world's smallest river'. It was even sunny and warm. In short, motorcycle heaven.

The only slight disappointment was 'The world's largest sea cave', where I'd hoped to view sea lions. To reach it I had to descend in a lift, which was novel, but the cave itself wasn't particularly large or impressive, there were no sea lions to be seen from the viewing platform and nowhere else to walk to. But even the world's most boring cave didn't upset me because I'd enjoyed the ride so much. Oregon was quickly becoming my favourite US state – despite their really stupid petrol pump laws.

Oregon has a daft regulation which bans motorists from taking the nozzle out of the petrol pump but once it's out they are allowed to pump their own 'gas'. So the attendant will extract the pump and hand it to you, take your credit card and swipe it in the pump right next to you. When I first stopped for petrol in Oregon I lifted the pump and the attendant came over and told me that we would both be fined $500 if caught doing this. Why? Nobody seems to know. 'Health and safety' I presume.

I liked this part of the world so much that on the following day I stopped at 1 pm. I took a turn off from Route 101 toward the sea. Two miles down the road I came across the most magnificent beach: mile after mile of sandy, wild coastline and not a soul in site. Best of all, there was a campsite and absolutely no-one else around – and this just happened to be a Saturday, often the hardest day of the week to find a quiet spot to camp in the US. I couldn't believe my luck. I left $12 in the honesty box (honestly), pitched my tent and walked out to the beach. It was just wonderful to be totally on my own on this fantastic beach all afternoon. I thought there was bound to be someone else at the campground when I got back, but no, total solitude. Where was everyone? It was the weekend and it was warm and dry.

I spent the rest of the day just doing nothing. I caught up on my blog and listened to my radio. The only stations I could get seemed to be the local religious network and I was glued to it for a couple of hours. I'm not a religious man at all but I am fascinated by religious zealots and extremists. It was certainly novel to hear a serious phone-in discussion on whether or not animals have souls or could go to heaven.

Just before sunset I walked back out to the beach. I was still alone and as the sun set over the Pacific the wind picked up and was blowing straight into my face, making my eyes water. I stood on the bleached white sand, the wind blowing me backwards a little and the waves crashing on the shore in front of me. It wasn't the most wonderful sunset I'd ever seen but I was just overcome by the whole episode and started to sob. First just a few tears down my cheeks which I could fob off as watery eyes due to the wind but then deep down in my belly I felt something stirring and it wasn't long before it rose to the surface as pure, unadulterated blubbering. What started as a few tears erupted into a flood as I simply lost control. I sank to my knees in the soft, white sand and wept. The crash of the waves and noise of the wind masked my wails as I really let rip. I had no idea where it all came from but it poured out of me uncontrollably.

I wiped away the tears, checked I was still on my own and tried to get to grips with myself. What on earth was going on? Why was I standing on a beautiful beach at sunset, crying? It had only been five days since I'd left Trent and two weeks since Tracy had flown home. Surely I could cope with my own company and solitude a little better than this? In the planning stages I had wondered what it would be like to be on my own for so long. This was, in my mind's eye, what the America section of my trip was all about. I had left Tracy in Canada and would meet her again in Mexico. In the US I was on my own and I was interested in finding out how I would cope with that. In everyday life, most of us are surrounded by friends, relations or work colleagues. It is not very often that we spend more than a few hours totally alone and if we do we know we can reconnect with people quite easily. Now I was spending day after day, week after week, by myself. The experience was having a strange effect on me. I didn't need to pretend to be myself anymore. There was no history between me and the people I met and I found that bizarre but liberating. Ironically it seemed that travelling on my own and knowing that no one knew me gave me the freedom to be me. It had, in fact, been a little strange to roll up at Trent's place and be Dom, who Trent actually knew, rather than some strange British biker who was passing through. I became much more conscience of who I was, how I was supposed to act. I became Dom with added excess baggage. And it occurred to me that this must be how we live out our everyday lives. We carry around our own personal histories and relationships and make subtle changes to our personas to accommodate each and every social situation we encounter. Dom the history teacher was certainly different to Dom the biker and never the twain shall meet. No wonder modern life is stressful!

I remembered watching a programme on UK television where an explorer tried to spend three months on his own in Yukon. The plan was to live and survive totally isolated in the wild outback. He took a camcorder and recorded his experiences. In short, he nearly went mad. He had trouble getting food and (being British) was constantly worried about bears, but his main problem was the lack of company. I remember one scene where he broke down in front of the camera, blubbering, because he just wanted company; someone to speak to and someone to touch. He missed touching another human. He just about lasted three months, totally alone. I was losing the plot after a couple of days, and I wasn't even that isolated. I walked back to my tent confused and worried. Was I cracking up? Had the whole 'being alone' thing got to me? Was I going crazy? If so, how was I supposed to know?

I tried to calm myself down. Food always helps, so I boiled some pasta and took a look at my map. I thought if I concentrated on what I was going to do the next day I might get my emotions under control and regain my composure. It seemed to work and by the time I ate I was able to think rationally about what had happened. Well, I say that, but it's hard to unpick why you have had a minor emotional breakdown when you've got no one to talk to. I put it down to loneliness. Being at that campsite and beach all on my own had obviously just brought home to me how alone I was. I missed Tracy most when I was doing something she would have enjoyed, and I knew she would have loved being on that beach. I contemplated phoning her but knew I would just miss her even more when I put the phone down.

I also missed my parents, both of whom had died in the previous five years. In a way their deaths had spurred me on to do the trip – the, 'if not now, when?' syndrome. But more importantly their deaths had made me reassess my own life. I was no longer a son, my role had somehow changed. Perhaps children don't really become adults until their parents die. I'd heard this somewhere and thought there was a ring of truth about it. The expanse of sea and desolate beach brought home my isolation. I think that's why we love open spaces, mountain-tops and huge vistas: they remind us that there is so much more out there but that can also make us feel small, alone and insignificant. Just as it had in Alaska and Yukon, nature was telling me that I was nothing. I usually didn't mind that, in fact I often took solace in it, but that day on the beach it overwhelmed me.

*

The next morning I rode into California. Having first promised the 'border patrol' that I didn't have any fruit or veg. with me, I rode away shouting 'Eureka', the state motto, and continued on to the famous redwood trees. I'd never seen redwoods but I knew they were going to be huge and impressive because my guidebook told me so; it did not lie.

Redwood trees can be found all along the north California coast on the glorious Route 101; not only at Redwood National Park but also further south at Humboldt Redwoods State Park. Leaving Route 101, I entered Humboldt and rode along 'The Avenue of the Giants', which wound its way through redwood territory. The temptation is to ignore the road and focus on the magnificent trees. With groves and nature trails to stop off and explore, it took me three hours to cover the thirty miles through the park. The majesty of these trees is legendary but it's the utter silence beneath them that is so impressive; unforgettable, unbeatable. Perhaps it was because I was riding a motorcycle, open to the elements, and able to see them properly, I really think you get a much better feel for the trees on a bike.

I found a campsite in the park but it was set up for RVs rather than tents, which meant that there were no tables supplied because RVs supply their own furniture. They let me pitch my tent on the grass but I had to cook on my haunches and eat standing up (a usual enough occurrence in Europe but I'd got used to being supplied with a table and bench in North America). I went for a short walk before dark along the road, cricking my neck to gawp up at the trees. I was reminded of the words of John Steinbeck, from *Travels with Charley* (well to be honest I'd just read them in the Lonely Planet Guide). They were spot on: *"The redwoods once seen, leave a mark or create a vision that stays with you always… from them comes silence and awe. The vainest, most slap-happy and most irreverent of men, in the presence of redwoods, goes under a spell of wonder and respect."* Well said, and I thought *The Grapes of Wrath* was boring! I retired to my tent and read more amazing and astonishing facts about these big trees:

- Redwoods are so immense that they live in three climatic zones, from base to canopy.
- A large redwood can release up to 500 gallons of water into the air per day.
- It can take a fallen redwood 400 years to decay into the forest floor.
- The oldest recorded redwood was 2200 years old.
- Redwoods can grow more than 360 feet (110 m) tall.

This was all mind-blowing stuff. These things were more than huge and impressive trees, they were therapeutic. Steinbeck was certainly on to something. The anxiety and loneliness I had felt on the Oregon coast evaporated amongst the redwoods and I felt alive, calm and, most importantly, relaxed. On the beach I'd felt really low and had started to question what I was doing; now it all felt right. Almost.

For a while I'd been concerned about the performance of the bike. She had been working perfectly when I left Missoula but that had lasted for all of ten days. By the time I hit the Oregon coast I was feeling a worrying wobble. The front brake had started shuddering which had been somewhat unnerving, especially as I'd been riding eight hundred miles of the most fantastic winding and undulating coast roads down the Oregon and Californian seaboard. Good brakes would have been useful! I'd asked a few people online, emailed Nevil who had been extremely helpful as always and I'd done a little research. It seemed likely that the front brake discs were warped (how that had happened I had no idea). I decided to carry on with my route and get the problem sorted out in San Francisco. So, upon leaving Humboldt Redwoods State Park I rang a BMW dealership in San Francisco. They were fully booked and couldn't see me for at least a week. As I'm not a city person I didn't fancy spending a week in San Francisco, so I decided to head thirty miles inland to go to another bike shop I'd found online in Santa Rosa. (This was beginning to feel like a tour of America's BMW dealers!)

I'd spoken to them on the phone and they'd told me to just turn up, so I did. On a wonderfully hot Californian morning I found the shop just outside Santa Rosa. I wandered into the showroom and asked for help. A mechanic came out and had a quick look at the bike.

"Yep, your front disc is warped."

"So, I guess I need to get a new one then."

"That's right."

Silence.

"Well, do you have any?"

"No." That was helpful, I thought.

"Can you get any, or do you know where I can get one from?" I asked. I was trying to be polite and friendly but the heat and stress was getting to me and I was worried that I was going to be riding a bike with a warped front disc. Those feelings I had had back in Missoula and Oregon about whether I should carry on if Heidi was just going to break down every few hundred miles, came flooding back.

"No, we can't get one. Not for a while. You could try the dealers in 'Frisco."

"I've tried them; they're fully booked for a week. Do you know of anywhere else in California?"

"No, not really."

And with that he walked off. I was left standing in the hot sun next to my warped-disc bike. What now? I was rummaging around in my tank bag looking for my water bottle when a policeman came over to me. I'd seen him arrive on his BMW. This was a *bona fide* California Highway Patrolman, a real-life CHiP!

"Having trouble, sir?"

"Yeah, my front disc is warped." (Listen to me, as if I know what I'm talking about!) "I need a new one but they don't have any here."

"Have you tried 'Frisco?"

"Yes."

"What about Reno or Sacramento or even Chico? They all have BMW dealerships. Give them a call."

So, I went into the showroom and logged on to their free wi-fi, and had a coffee and a pee just to get my own back for their lack of customer service. I started making some calls. I rang Sacramento and Reno, even though I had no idea where these places were, but both were fully booked for at least a week. I was running out of options and wasn't sure how serious a warped disc was. Should I just carry on with my trip and sort it out next time I was close to a BMW dealership? Or should I drop all plans, book into San Francisco and wait a week? What would Ted Simon have done in 1973, I thought? (Of course, I didn't realise that his old Triumph couldn't have warped a disc because it had drum brakes!) Or all those other people who travelled around the world in the past without mobile phones, the internet, or the HU website? Whatever they would have done it wouldn't have involved breaking down in tears and throwing their toys out of the pram. I needed to get a grip, put things in context and work out what to do.

My last chance was Chico, wherever that was.

"Hi, I've got a BMW R1200GS and I need a new front disc. Can you help with that?"

"Sure, man. We can do that for you, no problem."

"Today?"

"Yeah, come along as soon as you want."

Problem solved! Now I just needed to find out where Chico was.

Looking at my map I located it approximately two hundred miles north east from Santa Rosa, roughly in the direction I wanted to be heading anyway. It should have been a pleasant three-hour ride but there was a heatwave with record temperatures for a September day all over California. I rode in over 100F degree (30+C) heat, the hottest I had ever ridden in. The previous week I'd been camping in near-freezing temperatures in Idaho. Hot and bothered, I made it to Chico and following my sketched map I found the BMW dealership.

Ozzie runs the BMW bike shop in Chico, California. I knew this as the place was called 'Ozzie's' and I'd spoken to someone called Ozzie on the phone. When I finally arrived, hot, sweaty and somewhat flustered I was met by, you guessed it – Heather. Ozzie was out! She took my details and directed me to a cheap motel, about a mile up the road. I left the bike at Ozzie's, walked to the motel, booked myself in for one night and flopped on my bed totally exhausted. I hoped they would be able to change the disc in the morning so I could be on the road by lunchtime. It was Tuesday; I could be in Nevada by Wednesday, riding Route 50 – 'America's loneliest road'. On a bike that didn't wobble every time I braked. Oh, how naïve of me…

I returned to the shop the following lunchtime, ever hopeful. The good news was that they'd changed the warped discs. But there was also some bad news. Heidi was up on a trestle in the workshop and two mechanics were looking at the front end. Heather introduced me:

"This is Mike; he's been working on your bike, Dom."

Are all mechanics in America called Mike?

"Hi. I'm afraid you have problem." Mike was looking, not at the disc but further up, at the handlebars.

"Listen to this." He turned the 'bars from side to side.

"What am I listening for?" I asked. In all honesty I couldn't hear anything.

"Listen."

Mike turned the bars again and I heard a faint squeak.

"Oh," was all I could muster.

"We changed the discs, that was no problem. But this is more serious: there's a crack in your triple-clamp".

A what in my where? (I thought). "The triple-clamp?" I nodded, knowingly.

"Yeah, the triple-clamp. Did you know that your front wheel has a kink in it as well? I think it's all from the same event. Have you had a front end crash on your bike? It looks like it. That would explain the kink in the wheel and, to be honest, I've only ever seen a crack in the triple-clamp when someone's had a spill."

By now Mike had pointed to the top triple-clamp enough times for me to realise what he was talking about. It's the bit of the bike that the handlebars are bolted to, which holds the fork tubes together and connects them to the frame. (I now know that there are actually two of these things, an upper and a lower one, and that they are also known as fork yokes.)

I asked the familiar question, "Can you fix it? How much? How long will it take?"

"Of course we can, Dom. We can fix anything! It will take a day or two to get the parts. I'll have to go and check the price."

Having ridden down all those twisty roads I suppose I should just have been grateful that I'd made it alive. But actually I was really annoyed that things kept going wrong with my bike. It was getting expensive and I started to think that 'thedomwayround' might only make it to Panama. I might not have the funds (or a functioning bike) with which to make it to Africa.

This had all been a bit of a shock to the system, so to speak. I'd been on the road for nine weeks and was having a really great time. So often I'd been asked by people what I was up to and I had got used to saying "I'm riding down to Panama and then shipping to South Africa and heading back to Europe." But now, being told that yet again there was something wrong with my *'Unstoppable'* BMW I was really starting to doubt it. Canada had been much more expensive than I'd expected and although much in the USA was cheap, fixing the bike certainly wasn't! But I needed a fully functioning bike if I was going to tackle Africa. It was one thing to have these problems in the US; on one level all I had to do was find a dealership and sit it out in a cheap motel while they fixed the problem. But it's a whole different kettle of fish to be told your triple clamp is broken in Africa. (That's if I could find anyone who could actually tell me that the triple clamp was broken in the first place.) It was sobering to think what I would have to do if either of the major problems I'd had so far happened in the middle of Guatemala or Malawi, instead of Montana and California.

So, I was trapped in Chico while the problem was fixed. Chico, California – not a great place to be stuck, even for forty-eight hours. One of the main attractions is The National Yo-Yo Museum. The literature in my motel room revealed: *"The National Yo-Yo Museum is the country's largest collection of yo-yo artefacts, which also includes a four-foot-tall yo-yo that is dropped with a crane every few years. Classes are available as well for those new to yo-yo and those who just want to get better."* When I was planning my big motorcycle trip I never once thought it might incorporate a visit to a yo-yo museum. I thought about going, then I changed my mind. Then I thought I should go… I just couldn't make my mind up as it yo-yo-ed back and forth.

I decided to stay in my motel and watch TV. I would have liked to watch a serious in-depth news channel, one that actually analysed what was going on, but the news was so shallow and 'bitty'. America was getting geared up for mid-term elections in November but there was very little in the way of debate. It was just opposing sides shouting at each other. As for news about the rest of the world – it just didn't exist. Central America meant Kansas City and Mexico is only ever mentioned if there is a gunfight or a mudslide. No wonder I kept getting told to be very careful when I went 'down there'. Two or three times I'd been asked if I was carrying a gun for protection in Mexico. I usually answered that I didn't have a gun, followed by an awkward silence. Once I said, "No. I don't have a gun, but I do still have my pepper spray!" The stare I got was memorable.

I left my room to search for a newspaper. It's funny how what may seem like a simple task can be a frustratingly difficult once in a foreign land. In the UK newspapers are on sale everywhere, and shops are everywhere, but not so in

Smalltown, USA. Chico had a population of 80,000 and my motel was within walking distance of the centre of town so I went out thinking it wouldn't be long before I passed a convenience store or shop that sold newspapers. I walked and walked and walked. Nothing. No small shops and no other walkers! I passed a McDonald's and a Denny's and a pizza place but not one single shop or store that sold either food or newspapers.

I must have walked for an hour before turning round and heading back. Even though it was late afternoon it was over 30°C and I was hot and parched. I passed a McDonald's and although desperate for a drink I stuck to my principles and walked on. My stupid stubborn pride would have to quench my thirst. I got back to the motel and just outside the foyer there was a row of small vending machines. At last, I could get a refreshing drink. I approached them visualising a long cool bottle of water. I just had to laugh at what I saw. These machines didn't contain drinks, they had newspapers in them! Of course they did. How many films had I seen where someone puts money in a vending box and gets a newspaper? God, I was so stupid. It just brought home to me how you can travel in a country and yet really not understand what it's like to live there. I knew a lot about the roads and how to buy petrol and where to find campsites. But there was so much I had no idea about whatsoever.

I popped my dollar in, bought *USA Today,* returned to my room and fell on to the bed ready to read some serious news. On page seven there was an article about Obama commenting on his Christian beliefs. President Obama had been in office for nearly two years at this point. According to a survey, 18% of Americans still thought Obama was a Muslim, only 34% thought he was a Christian. The article concluded:

Obama is the son of a Muslim father from Kenya. His mother was from Kansas. As a boy, he lived for several years in predominantly Muslim Indonesia. Some think his full name, Barack Hussein Obama, sounds Muslim.

The only place I could find any foreign news was on the back page in the weather section! I did, however, discover that Chico, California had been the hottest place in the USA the previous day, clocking in at 104°F (40°C). No wonder I was hot and flustered when I arrived in town!

USA Today vies with the *Wall Street Journal* for being America's best selling newspaper. It sells just under two million copies a day. I was staggered by these facts. With a population of 300 million I'd expect those numbers to be higher. *The Sun* sells two and a half million copies daily in the UK with a population one fifth the size. The British obviously read more newspapers than their American cousins. Or at least more national newspapers. America was so big, as I was learning, that in many ways it wasn't a nation at all, but a series of interlocking States. As I was finding out from TV, radio and print, regional news was much more important in America. I was in California, population 37 million with the eighth largest economy in the world. Why read a national paper when you can read the *LA Times* with a daily circulation of over half a million? I had nothing better to do so I did a little internet research.

Not surprisingly newspapers are more popular in wealthier countries. Scandinavia and Japan have the most daily newspapers per capita – five of the world's largest daily circulations are in Japan. *Yomiuri Shimbun*, a Japanese National Daily holds the record for the world's largest circulation, some 14 million copies! Even with a population of 127 million, that's still a lot of newspaper sales.

It was more interesting than a bloody yo-yo museum.

I woke up the next day in a much better mood. Maybe sleeping in a bed had given me the restful night I needed or perhaps it was just the dawning of a fresh day which had shone new light on my situation. I needed to keep everything in perspective, which is easier said than done when travelling alone. After all, what had really gone wrong? I hadn't crashed or got ill or injured. I was just spending money making my bike safer and better. If this was the worst that was going to happen to me on this trip then really I should be laughing. After all, what is a big trip about if it isn't about having an adventure? Okay, this might not be the same as crossing the Mongolian desert or being abducted by South American guerrillas but I didn't want those sorts of adventures. I was having an awesome time riding through some wonderful places in western USA and had just stopped off for a couple of days to sort out a few problems with the bike. In the grand scheme of things, when I look back on this trip in my old age I won't even remember this part, so I should stop worrying. I imagined that this would have been exactly what Tracy would have said if she had been with me – after she had finished telling me off for buying a motorcycle I hadn't checked out first and cursing the fact that she was married to a mechanical numpty. She would have put things in perspective for me, and that's why I didn't phone her!

Munching on my granola (the only vegetarian item on Denny's extensive breakfast menu that didn't come with half a dozen eggs) I promised myself that when Heidi was fixed and on the road I was just going to enjoy myself for however long it lasted. I wouldn't make any long-term plans about Africa just yet. After all, I was about to head off on a two thousand mile loop of Nevada, Utah and Arizona before heading back to the Californian coast and then south to Mexico. In the next three weeks I planned to go to: Nevada desert, Zion, Arches, Canyonlands and Mesa Verde National Parks, the Grand Canyon, Las Vegas, Death Valley, Yosemite National Park, Californian coast and Big Sur. If I couldn't look forward to that, and ride off into the desert with a huge grin on my stupid face, then I might as well kill myself.

I had also decided to write to Motoquest venting my frustration and concern at the motorcycle they had sold me. I didn't expect it to do any good but it made me feel better. I emailed Phil telling him that I'd had to spend over $5000 getting problems fixed that I really shouldn't have. The final drive was not maintained in Alaska and the cracked triple clamp was indicative of a crashed bike. My email was polite, but honest. I clicked 'send' and felt a whole lot better, and that was the end of that.

Ozzie's BMW had fitted a new triple clamp, front discs, front brake pads and changed the oil. They were extremely friendly and helpful people and I actually had a good time with them. Mike let me into the garage to watch him do the oil change – I was still suffering from the illusion that I would do it myself one day. He even showed me how to adjust the valve clearances, something which I just knew, in the pit of my stomach, I was never going to do. Ozzie's was now my favourite of all the North American BMW dealers I'd visited. Surely now Heidi was in tip top condition? Pretty much everything that could be changed on her had been and I really felt my luck must change.

Leaving Chico I headed back towards the Pacific coast. I'd been told, both by the guys at Ozzie's and a friend in the UK, not to miss Route 36. From Red Bluff, some forty miles north of Chico, Route 36 snakes its way down to the coast. And I mean 'snakes'. At the beginning of the turn-off there are two wonderful, smile-inducing signs. One tells you not to use this road if you have a trailer or are in an RV. The other warns that this road twists for one hundred and forty miles!

And it did. For three hours I fully tested out my new front discs and triple clamp as I banked and cornered on the smooth asphalt. It was the pure adrenalin rush of a roller coaster ride. The route had very few flat or straight sections and both Heidi and I were given a good workout as we headed down towards the sea. The eastern section started quite tamely, with open land, farms and hills if you had any time to look up from the twisting road. Initially it climbed up into the hills of the coastal range, then about half way along the route, it threw me out over the top. If anything, the route downhill had even more curves and thrilling one hundred and eighty degree switchbacks. The flora changed on this side of the mountain, the trees were bigger and taller and just toward the end of the road, redwoods started to appear. Just one or two to begin with, so unexpected that as I whizzed past I wasn't sure I'd seen them right. Was that a redwood tree I'd just passed? Of course, if I'd looked closely at my map I would have realised that I wasn't all that far from Humboldt Redwoods State Park again, but I had been so focused on the ride I'd almost forgotten where I was. I was back in the saddle, back on the road and right smack bang back in the middle of my adventure.

CHAPTER 8

CAN LIGHTNING STRIKE TWICE?

Burt Munro: *"If you don't follow your dreams Thomas, you might as well be a vegetable."*
Tom: *"What type of vegetable?"*

(*The World's Fastest Indian*)

Route 50 – 'The loneliest road in America' – sounded like a plan. I had entered Nevada having roared 'All for our country' as I left California just north of Reno. I was aiming for the Great Salt Lake Desert which was four hundred miles and six hours along I-80 according to Google Maps, but who wants to take an interstate when you can take 'the loneliest road'? I was heading west on US-50 and then north on US-93, four hundred and forty miles through the desert. And I was going to take two days over this, not six hours, and thoroughly enjoy every lonely minute in the desert.

As it had been so hot in northern California, I expected the heat to continue in Nevada. But the clouds closed in on me as I passed through Reno and as I climbed up and over the mountains, it started to rain. This wasn't part of the plan. After I passed through a small town called Fallon I wasn't by any means the only vehicle on 'the loneliest road' but the vastness of the desert around me certainly made me feel alone. The road was in excellent condition and the black asphalt carved an impressive line through the beige desert. As I steamed along I had plenty of time to look either side of me. The desert in this part of the world is rocky rather than sandy with a few low-lying bushes; no trees at all and nothing grows more than about three feet high. I could see for ten or twenty miles to my left and right and from glancing at my map I knew there were no roads or settlements for hundreds of miles. That's why it's called the loneliest road. North of me, perhaps a hundred miles away, was Interstate 80 then beyond that nothing for at least another hundred miles until I'd get to Trent's house in Sun Valley. (It was strange to think that two weeks and two thousand miles after leaving Trent's place I was now only two hundred miles from him.) Las Vegas was over two hundred miles to the south. I was riding through a state that is bigger than the UK in area, but less than one twentieth the size in population.

My brain was taking all this in when I saw a bright flash. I looked up at the sky which had filled with threatening clouds. There was no traffic behind me but up ahead I could see two vehicles coming towards me. They had their headlights and windscreen wipers on. Not a good sign. We crossed and I was alone again. The first few drops of rain started to hit my visor, proper desert raindrops: large, heavy drops of surprisingly cold water. I could feel them through my jacket as they started to turn to hail. Hail in the desert, this wasn't good at all. And then another flash: lightning. I was riding into a thunderstorm.

Now, I think a little background information is needed here. A few years before this, while on holiday in Malta, I had been struck by lightning. Tracy, who was with me at the time, told me that a bolt of lightning had landed two metres in front of us and I was hit by a splinter from it. I didn't see anything; I just felt a shock of electricity hit me on the head, run down the right side of my body and then exit via my big toe (honest). I jumped up in the air and landed in a puddle swearing and shouting, somewhat predictably: "Shit, I've been hit by lightning." Tracy was laughing. I've not made that up – she stood there laughing. Clearly I hadn't copped the full force but it still hurt. I consider myself slightly lucky to be alive as I could easily have been the main target of the electricity bolt. As it was, I caught what is called a 'side splash' but it still had enough power to give me a very nasty headache for two days. Since then I've had a morbid and, I feel, not irrational, fear of thunderstorms. I won't go out in them on foot, let alone on a big metal motorcycle.

So when I heard the thunder clap, I panicked. I saw another bolt of lightning and didn't know what to do. As far as I could tell the storm was heading towards me, coming from the south east. If I turned around the storm would be chasing me the fifty or so miles back to Fallon. If I carried on it was fifty miles to Austin, the next town. There seemed to be no other traffic on the road and absolutely nowhere to hide. What made it even worse was that I was the tallest thing, sitting on the only piece of metal for miles around: an obvious target for a lightning strike. And although it may sound crazy, I really felt the lightning was hunting me down.

Although it was raining I increased my speed to over 80 mph. I was watching out for the lightning and then counting how many seconds it was before I heard the thunder. I seemed to remember from my scouting days that each second meant one mile. Or was that one kilometre? I wasn't sure. Later Wikipedia informed me that three seconds equalled one kilometre, or one mile for every four and a half seconds – had I known this at the time I think I might have fallen off the bike. I was only counting five or six seconds; the storm was less than two miles away.

I don't mind admitting that for thirty minutes as I passed through the worst of the storm I was seriously afraid that I might not make it. I was riding along convinced that a bolt of lightning was going to hit me. I could visualise what was going to happen and how painful it was going to be. Memories of Malta came flooding back but this time there were no houses to run back to and absolutely nowhere to hide. Sitting on Heidi I was exposed and vulnerable. My heart was racing and I could feel my arms shake as I gripped the handlebars for dear life. I decided that the best thing to do was to race through as fast as I could, so I did.

Another flash, this time followed barely two seconds later by the crack of thunder. The sky had gone black: I was certainly right in the middle of it now. I heard a voice inside my helmet. What was going on? I could hear myself talking but I wasn't consciously aware of what I was saying.

"Tracy, Tracy, Tracy".

Crouched over the tank (as if that would help!) eyes wide open with my vision transfixed on the asphalt in front of me. It was still raining hard, occasionally hailing and I could only see about thirty metres in front of me. With my tinted visor it looked even darker than it was and at the speed I was going I just hoped I wasn't going to come across anything in the road that would cause me to swerve or brake.

"Tracy, Tracy, Tracy."

With my knees gripping the tank, my hands glued to the bars and my eyes fixed on the road ahead I had almost soldered myself to the bike. Not a good riding technique I was sure. But I didn't care about any of that anymore. I just wanted to be out of there. Even a bolt of lightning hitting the ground nearby would have been enough to unseat me. I thought back to Malta and the sheer power behind the splinter that had hit me. It had forced me up into the air and backwards a few feet. Anything like that hitting me on a motorcycle and I'd be history. Was this how it was all going to end?

"Tracy, Tracy, Tracy."

This time I saw a flash but it was certainly weaker than the last and definitely off to my right rather than in front of me. I reckoned I had a couple more minutes and then I'd be through. Perhaps one or two more flashes to survive. This was how I was calculating it now. One or two more flashes and I might live.

"Tracy, Tracy, Tracy."

I was muttering in rhythm to the bike, as if by saying her name I would move even faster away from the storm. These were the thought processes going on inside my helmet. Irrational, confused, and in the cold light of day, pathetic, but this was my world. I registered 95 mph in the hail and rain as I tried to escape the storm.

And then, almost as quickly as it had started, it was over. Within a few seconds the rain stopped, the clouds looked friendlier and I slowed to 75. As if to signal the end of the danger two cars appeared in the distance. We passed and somehow that was the end of it. I relaxed a little on the bike and lifted my visor, making everything even brighter, and slowed to a stop. I got off Heidi and turned to look at the desert storm disappearing into the distance in the direction of Fallon. I was cold and wet and shaking. But I knew the shaking had nothing to do with feeling cold, it was all nervous energy and I was getting over the shock. I was surprised how scared I'd been. Out in the desert on Heidi I had felt so vulnerable and alone. I hadn't really known what to do. I suppose I should have walked away from the bike and crouched down in a field, that's what they say you should do isn't it? Or was I being totally overdramatic about the whole thing? I didn't know but I certainly wasn't going to forget 'America's loneliest road' in a hurry.

I got back in the saddle and headed east, under brighter skies, away from the storm. As I rode along, I started to wonder about the realities of motorcycle travel and lightning storms. Are bikers often hit by lightning? I could feel another Google moment coming on, but would it really be wise to search "motorcycle accident + lightning"? I did it anyway: bad idea.

In the US, I learned, lightning strikes the ground 30 million times a year. 30 million! The National Weather Service estimates that 100,000 thunderstorms occur annually in the US and on average, forty to fifty people are killed by lightning each year. Lightning kills more people each year than hurricanes, volcanoes, tornadoes and earthquakes combined. I also read about a motorcyclist in Florida who'd been hit by lightning, crashed and died. It was really sobering to read this just a day or two after my experience. Perhaps I wasn't being irrational. Yes, it was extremely unlikely that I was going to be hit by lightning, but I could have said that in Malta. It does happen and if it happens while you are on a motorcycle it's likely to be fatal.

Eventually I made it to West Wendover, Nevada. I'd not come here because it has the world's tallest mechanical cowboy, although it does. Nor because it was where the crew of the 'Enola Gay' B-29 Superfortress were based before they dropped the atomic bomb on Hiroshima. Although it was. I'd come here because of the salt flats, just across the state line in Utah. I'd made it just in time for Bonneville Speed Week.

*

Shortly before leaving the UK I'd watched the 2005 film *The World's Fastest Indian* which is based on the amazing true story of an extraordinary man, Burt Munro. Between 1962 and 1967, New Zealander Munro travelled to Utah several times and set three land speed records on a motorcycle which had started life as a 600cc Indian Scout road bike, bought new in 1920 when he was 21. Burt spent nearly half a century steadily tuning and extensively modifying the bike in his own workshop in Invercargill. He set a New Zealand record of 120 mph in 1940, but in 1967, on his last and fastest blast at Bonneville he averaged 183.58 mph, with a best one-way run of 190.07 mph. By that time Burt Munro was 67 years old and the oldest parts of his home-built streamliner were 47. This certainly put what I was doing into perspective.

My impression of Burt Munro on the Bonneville Salt Flats

I was excited about seeing these speed freaks and spending a day out on the salt mingling with them. Obviously I felt totally out of my depth surrounded by lots of real men who knew which end of a spanner to use and how to take an engine apart. I was fortunate enough to have got there the day before the speed trials so all the vehicles were out on the salt parked up so I could have a close look at them. Again, this was not something I had imagined I would be doing on this trip but that was the joy of travelling – stumbling across new experiences. And one thing I'd never done before was ride a motorcycle on salt. It was a very strange sensation. It looked like snow and initially I was very tentative expecting it to be slippery. But it felt solid enough and quite smooth to ride on. I soon got the hang of it and clocked 85 mph before chickening out – the lack of perspective and blinding white salt was unnerving and besides, I wasn't being hunted by Thor, god of thunder and lightning so I had little impetus to go faster.

Just two weeks previously, Rocky Robinson had set a new land speed record of 376 mph (602 kph) sitting inside the 2,600cc Top 1 Oil Ack Attack streamliner: a recumbent, fully enclosed motorcycle powered by a pair of turbocharged Suzuki Hayabusa engines. He might have gone faster than me but he didn't have a couple of un-aerodynamic panniers to cope with!

From Bonneville I headed across the Great Salt Lake Desert. This awesome desolate landscape required an equally awesome desolate motto. Utah disappointed me as I quietly muttered 'Industry' in my helmet. Come on Utah you can do better than that! At Salt Lake City I turned south. I'd seen the light and in the middle of Mormon territory I was heading for Zion. Zion National Park. Now we're talking history. Zion has been evolving for at least two hundred and fifty million years and has created some of the tallest sandstone mountains in the world. The park is characterized by a maze of narrow, deep sandstone canyons, high plateaux and striking rock towers. I picked up some literature and was blown away by what I read: *Over 200 million years ago, the area where Zion is today was a great desert basin. Over vast spans of time, mountains eroded and material was transported by slow-moving streams and rivers depositing sand in a vast basin. Conditions and the environment changed as time passed and sea water covered dunes of sand. Calcium carbonate cemented loose grains of sand making hard sandstone. The seabed turned to limestone and mud and clay changed to mudstone and shale, forming the sweeping diagonal cross-bedding that Zion National Park is famous for… The rock formations that exist today in Zion are still changing. Slowly, over vast amounts of time, great monoliths will return to sand dunes from where they were born in ancient days. Forces of nature make their way through layers of sedimentary rock every day of our future, just as they have in our past. The largest monolith in the world, 'The Great White Throne', will slowly crumble to sand.* Looks as if I got here just in time…

It wasn't only the geological history which impressed me, I was also very much taken with the way the park dealt with visitors. Since the year 2000 they have forbidden cars from driving in the canyon and now you have to take a shuttle bus up the gorge. It stops at all the trail heads and gives you the information you need to have an informed experience. Even the twenty-minute DVD in the visitors' centre was impressive. I especially liked the fact that every time the narrator mentioned that something happened millions of years ago the Mormon women in front of me tutted and shook their heads. Only when the Mormons were mentioned (for 'discovering' the area in the 1860s) did they nod and look pleased. The Mormons gave the place its modern name – Zion, and the peaks and canyons all have names like 'Court of the Patriarchs', 'Mount Moroni', 'Angels' landing' and 'Altar of sacrifice'.

I checked into the campground for two nights and spent the following day hiking the trails. It was great to ditch the bike, get some exercise and then have an excuse to eat a lot. I took the courtesy bus and walked several trails including the infamous Angels' Landing: a four or five hour steep trek with long drop-offs and wonderful views. I passed two sunbathing tarantulas, which made me wonder whether I'd zipped up my tent properly that morning.

And there was even something to do in the evening. I had been working my way through my only book and had already watched all the films on my Netbook, but at Zion there was a Ranger Talk every evening. *'Noise pollution and Zion National Park'*, was the title for the evening and the ranger spent an hour explaining how they had set up microphones all over the park to monitor noise. She played some of the noises of the animals they had recorded and explained why it was so important to keep noise pollution to a minimum. In fact she proudly announced that Zion was the first National Park in the US to create a noise pollution policy! Surprisingly, although there must have been five hundred people camping in Zion that night and hundreds of others in the lodges nearby, only about ten of us could be bothered to turn off the TV, get out of our lodges and RVs, and learn something about the place we'd driven to. On my second night the talk was on *Mountain Lions and Cougars*. Again only a handful of us were there to hear it. Admittedly it was cold, (Zion is over a thousand metres above sea level and I was sleeping in all my clothes by now) but I'd expected more people to show up.

Every night, at the beginning of the talk, the ranger ran a little quiz and had a sticker as a prize. With only a handful of us there I had every chance of winning. I was going to get that sticker! On my second night the question was: "What is the most dangerous animal in Zion? The cougar, the mule deer, bats or squirrels?" Of course I knew the answer, I'd been listening on the bus tour and, like a good student, I'd read the literature. So I knew it was the squirrel. Hundreds of tourists get bitten by these cute little critters every year. But the way the ranger had said 'squirrel' was confusing for a Brit. In her American accent she had said "sqwerl", with only one syllable instead of two. Nevertheless, while my brain was dealing with the linguistic confusion, my arm clearly wanted the sticker and was in the air. No-one else put their hand up. The ranger came over to me with the microphone. What was I going to say? Squirrel or Sqwerl? I muttered "Squirewerl"– but I got the sticker!

As it was now mid-October the nights were drawing in but one of the pluses of early sunsets was wonderful night skies. At Zion I saw the clearest night sky I'd ever seen in the northern hemisphere. I stood outside my tent looking up just able to make out the silhouette of the ancient rocks towering above me pointing the way up to the stars. With the rocks telling a story that goes back at least two hundred and fifty million years and the stars going back a lot further, I had to admit that America does have some history after all. I'd had a minor epiphany at Zion.

So, I was learning a lot about a country I'd thought I already knew. I spent most of the following week riding through a geological history lesson. From Zion I headed north-east to Bryce Canyon. Geologically the whole region is called the Grand Staircase – starting at the bottom with the Grand Canyon, Zion is the middle and Bryce the top – so Bryce is 'only' about ten million years old. Bryce is famous for its hoodoos – spires of multicoloured rock formed by frost and rain weathering. They can range in height from a few metres to over fifty and the minerals in the rock give them a variety of colours at different levels. Many form strange shapes which have inevitably been given names such as 'The Rabbit', 'ET', and 'Wiseman'. From Bryce, I rode east and based myself in the town of

Moab as I explored the nearby National Parks.

At Canyonlands I peered down two thousand feet to the Colorado River and at Arches National Park I saw, well, arches. Millions of years ago, Arches National Park (indeed I believe most of southern Utah), was the world's largest desert with sand dunes probably over a mile high. Over time all of that compressed under its own weight and created sandstone which eventually eroded away to form the canyons and cliffs, outcrops and desert landscape that cover this part of Utah. The wind and water, over an enormous amount of time, sculptured the sandstone to create the most wonderful arches in the middle of the Utah desert. I wondered what the Mormons and other creationists thought of this place.

*

Having spent a week in some fantastic National Parks looking at lots of very old stones, it was time to move on and find some human history. I left Moab, crossed into Colorado ('Nothing without the deity') and headed to Mesa Verde National Park. Native Americans – or Ancestral Puebloans as they are called – have been living in this part of the world for at least fifteen hundred years. Initially living on the flat mountain top, these people farmed the land and, seemingly, prospered.

The Ancestral Puebloans farmed on the plateaux but lived below them, building their cliff dwellings in the recesses and alcoves along the canyon walls. The settlements that we can now see were only lived in for around one hundred years (in the thirteenth century) before the population mysteriously disappeared. But what they have left behind is quite unique and wonderful. There are over six hundred settlements, although only a handful are accessible, via steep steps and ladders. In fact the first five minutes of the ranger's tour was spent explaining how hard it was going to be – they usually have to medically evacuate at least one person a week.

The buildings are circular or keyhole-shaped and made of sandstone and mortar. Called Kivas, they were originally roofed, presumably with grasses of some sort, and they think these rooms served as a sort of meeting room. Apparently the hole in the middle of the roof was both the entrance and the chimney. Beyond that it's all conjecture. The Ancestral Puebloans left no written record and just seemed to disappear from the area in the early fourteenth century, giving the whole place a spooky feel. I really loved the idea that there's probably more we don't know about these people than we do. Why did they move from settlements on the plateau to build below in the alcoves? What function did their Kivas really perform? Why did they disappear so abruptly? And why did no one occupy the cliff dwellings after they left?

By the time Europeans were exploring this part of North America, the Ute people were living in this area although they didn't live in the dwellings because they believed them to be sacred. It wasn't until the 1870s and 1880s that knowledge of these dwellings became known to the outside world. President Theodore Roosevelt created the Mesa Verde National Park in 1906. Those are the known facts but I was much more intrigued by the unanswered questions. Seeing new things, understanding them a little but being left with more questions than answers was my idea of fun and I found Mesa Verde fascinating for this reason.

I was having a fantastic time riding Heidi through this part of the United States and from Mesa Verde I headed west towards the mother of them all, the Grand Canyon. Crossing into Arizona I yelled 'God enriches' as I wondered why I was keeping up with this pointless, and occasionally embarrassing, self-imposed ritual.

The road was smooth, the sun was shining and as I sped along the desert towards the world's largest canyon, I tried to grapple with the mind-blowing statistics. The canyon is over a mile deep, ten miles wide and two hundred and seventy seven miles long. Yes, it is indeed grand. For perhaps seventeen million years, the Colorado river has cut down through layer upon layer of ancient rocks exposing nearly two billion years of history. Like much of America it's so big it's almost impossible to comprehend as you stare into it. But the colours at sunset are just magical. As the light fades and the sun dips below the Arizona desert the multicoloured layers of rock across the canyon turn a variety of deep red and orange: layer upon layer of colour, mapping out thousands upon thousands of years of deposition and erosion. They say that nothing can prepare you for your first glimpse of the Grand Canyon. They may be right.

The following day I explored the edge of the canyon and walked down into it for a few hours to get away from the hordes of tourists. I'd spent the last ten days in National Parks, and although some had been quite busy nothing had prepared me for the Grand Canyon. I thought I'd met American tourists in Hyder – I had no idea. Grand Canyon was packed full of bus-loads of people, everywhere, all of the time; unless you took one of the trails down into the canyon.

By 8 pm I had cooked and eaten my dinner and just about had the energy to stand in the cold autumn air and stare at the amazing stars. I was content. The last few weeks had been wonderful and I knew I was doing what I had been born to do. To travel, seeking out new life and new civilisations, or something like that. I was seeing some wonderful things and learning a lot about the world, myself, and even a little about motorcycles. Three months into my trip, I knew I had changed. All the worries of 'normal' life had disappeared on the road; as if by simply riding along I'd shed my worries, concerns and the baggage that comes with everyday life. One of the great things about motorcycle riding is the peace and solitude you get inside that helmet. Your mind is free to roam and on long days on the road it gets up to all sorts of things. By the time I got to the Grand Canyon I wasn't just in a new physical place. I was in a whole new emotional and psychological space as well. I had never felt so at peace with the world and my place in it. Everything seemed right; I was where I wanted to be.

The rocks, dating back millions of years, were reminding me how insignificant humans are on earth. The stars, shining so brightly, were showing me how insignificant humans are in space. My journey was showing me how completely insignificant and yet wonderful my own existence was: existential angst but in a good way. The realisation of the meaninglessness of my existence was freeing me to appreciate every living minute.

Shit, it was time to get a grip on reality. Luckily my next stop was Las Vegas.

CHAPTER 9

LEAVING LAS VEGAS

"We won't talk about the obesity, the greed, the extravagance, the waste, the hard-worn looking people or our depression about seeing it all."

(David and Jill)

The ride from the Grand Canyon to Las Vegas could have been a simple two hundred and fifty mile jaunt through the desert but I extended the ride with a trip down memory lane and a date with a bridge. It so happened that a one hundred and thirty mile stretch of the original Route 66 lay west of the Grand Canyon and I couldn't resist the chance to 'get my kicks' on a bit of the legendary road; which is also officially known as Will Rogers Highway.

I stopped at a few 1950s memorabilia gas stations and tourist traps, got a sticker for the bike but I found the whole Route 66 thing rather underwhelming. Errol (whom I'd met in Anchorage) had ridden the whole of the old road from Chicago to Los Angeles. I couldn't help but wonder why? There was nothing wrong with the section I rode (the longest continual stretch now remaining, apparently) but neither did it have anything outstanding to recommend it. After all, Route 66 was just the main highway for those migrating west during the 1930s in search of work; it wasn't meant to be scenic or challenging. Presumably it's all just down to the 1946 song written by Bobby Troup and made famous by Nat King Cole, Chuck Berry, The Rolling Stones, Billy Bragg (sort of) and all the others…

Heading north west from Route 40 towards the Hualapai Indian reservation in Arizona, there was one section of Route 66 which began to look strangely familiar… as if I'd been here before. This had happened a few times in America and each time I'd managed to trace the familiarity back to a film. America does that to you. I focused on the road and the desert trying to work out which film I was riding though. And then it hit me as I passed a series of Burma Shave adverts. Popular between the 1930s and 1960s the adverts were usually spread over several road signs, each one providing a couple of words from a poem. I passed a sequence of signs which read:

> *If daisies / Are your / Favorite flower / Keep pushin' up those / Miles per hour / Burma-Shave.*

I remembered having seen them in *The World's Fastest Indian*; I was back on the trail of Burt Munro.

Vaguely disappointed by Route 66, I headed south to fulfil a twenty-five-year-old dream. When I was a boy, my history teacher at school told us about a millionaire American who had bought London Bridge and transported it in small pieces to the Arizona desert where it was re-assembled. Crazy enough on its own but the poor (or rather extremely rich) American had thought he was getting Tower Bridge. I had always remembered the tale of London Bridge being in the Arizona desert, so when I saw a road sign that pointed one way to the Hoover Dam and the other way to London Bridge I just had to make the two hundred mile detour to see this relic from Olde England.

This particular London Bridge was built in 1831 to replace the original thirteenth-century medieval one with houses on it, as immortalised in the children's song for 'falling down'. But the 'new' bridge lasted little more than a century before the weight and volume of modern traffic began to overwhelm it. In 1968 Robert McCulloch bought the bridge for $2.5 million as a propaganda stunt to help develop Lake Havasu City in Arizona. It was dismantled, shipped over and rebuilt at a total cost of over $5 million. The purchase also included the cast iron bridge lampposts, moulded from French cannons captured at the Battle of Waterloo in 1815.

Having been on the road for nearly three months and clocked up 14,000 miles it was very strange to come across something so 'British' in the middle of the Arizona desert. London Bridge spanned the lake connecting an island to the main part of the Lake Havasu City. It actually made me feel a little homesick. I rode across the bridge, turned around and rode back. Then I rode over it again and then back again. I parked in the very expensive adjacent car park and walked across the bridge and back again. (Not something I would recommend in full bike gear and thirty degrees heat.) It was rather surreal walking across British stone and touching French cannons disguised as lampposts. I had to remind myself that this was not a movie set.

Feeling hot and sweaty and slightly confused at seeing Union Jack flags all over the place I went into the visitors' centre to find a suitable sticker.

"Hi there," I said in my best British accent.

"Hello. Can we help you?"

"Well, I've just come all the way from the UK – to claim our bridge back!" I just couldn't stop the words coming out. What a ridiculous thing to say.

"Oh, well. We get that a lot," came the reply.

"I'm sorry. Look, I do have a question. I remember being told that the guy who bought this bridge thought he was getting Tower Bridge, which opens in the middle. Is that true?"

"No. No, it isn't," came the rather curt reply. "Robert McCulloch knew full well which bridge he was buying. That is just a myth that has grown up around the story. Indeed McCulloch let the story develop as it simply increased interest in Lake Havasu City which was, after all, the whole point of the project. It was also, I might add, a face-saving story told by the British."

And that was that. I'd embarrassed myself and been told I was wrong. Perhaps I should have gone to the Hoover Dam? There was nothing more to do so I went back to Heidi, added my 'Lake Havasu London Bridge' sticker to my increasingly impressive-looking sticker collection on my panniers and headed north for Vegas.

*

Las Vegas. Hum, what can I say? I arrived in the scorching heat of a Friday afternoon rush hour. I'd ridden four hundred miles, all the way from the Grand Canyon, along Route 66 and down to Lake Havasu City. It had been one hell of a day, one that needed a calm, peaceful and cool ending so I could process all I had seen. Instead, I was stuck in traffic on 'The Strip' in by far the largest conurbation I'd seen since starting out in Anchorage three months previously. Las Vegas has a population of about half a million and I think most of them were either walking or riding down The Strip when I arrived. (The official name for this four-mile stretch of road is Las Vegas Boulevard South and it's not even within Las Vegas city limits, but it's the heart of tourist Vegas, and is far better known simply as The Strip.)

I had a motel booked and was using my hand-drawn map to get me there. This was one time I really could have used a GPS. Heidi didn't seem to like Vegas either and was soon overheating, stuck as we were in nose-to-tail traffic. For the first time the digital oil temperature gauge was climbing dangerously up the scale.

There can be nothing quite as uncomfortable and annoying as riding a big heavy motorcycle in 30C degree heat through slow-moving traffic in desperate need of a pee. As always, I was wearing full bike gear and I was slowly cooking. In a high-speed crash I would be very grateful to be wearing my black Alt-berg bike boots, black BMW trousers and armoured Hein Gericke jacket, but right now this ensemble seemed cumbersome and ridiculously hot. As I stopped at yet another set of traffic lights a Harley pulled up next to me. The rider was in a T-shirt and shorts and really did look, well, cool. I lifted my flip-front helmet and greeted him, sweat dripping down my face. He looked at me through his Ray-Bans.

"Dude, you're not from round here are you?"

By the time I'd found my motel and checked in I was exhausted, dehydrated and had gone just a little crazy. I had the longest, coldest shower, drank a litre of water and then lay on my bed to rest. It was a big effort just to log on to the internet to see if I had any friends in town.

David and Jill, whom I'd met in Nakusp, were in the same part of the US on their BMW bike 'Nancy' and I'd been following their blog closely ever since I got into Utah. They'd always been a few days ahead of me but I was slowly catching them up and knew they'd been heading to Las Vegas. I really felt I could do with some company and was secretly hoping they were still in town. I logged onto their blog. Just that morning David had posted:

"As the saying goes 'what happens in Vegas, stays in Vegas' so we won't talk about the obesity, the greed, the extravagance, the waste, the hard-worn looking people or our depression about seeing it all, but will just leave you with the hope of many who come here."

They'd left that very morning. This news hit me hard. I don't know if it was heat exhaustion, the long day's ride or the effect of being alone in a big city but reading that David and Jill had just left Vegas left me feeling lonely and deflated. I lay on my bed in my motel room in Las Vegas and started to sob. "Oh no, not again!" I thought. This was getting silly. I needed to pull myself together and go out and see what Las Vegas had to offer on a Friday night.

It was all quite hard to cope with. After three months in the wilderness, *any* big city was going to be an assault on the senses. But Vegas took the biscuit. The first casino I came to was MGM and I went in to see what all the fuss was about. It was unreal. Row upon row of slot machines, poker tables, gambling machines and TV screens showing every sport you could think of. And hundreds of people. The saddest part was that nobody looked happy. People were concentrating and focused but clearly not happy; losing money they couldn't afford in a sterile, business-like environment. It was actually hard to watch but then, in one corner, I saw the most horrible thing I had seen so far on my trip: a glass cage with lions in it. Inside a casino in the middle of a desert there were four large adult lions in a glass cage. I really couldn't believe what I was seeing. I walked over, mouth wide open.

"Shit. Shit. Shit," was all I could say. I'd spent the last twelve weeks living outside and travelling through some of the world's most wonderful scenery. I'd got used to the great outdoors, watched the cycle of the moon as it waxed and waned, felt the heat of the days and the frost in the nights. I'd stood spellbound by North America's nature. Yet here in Las Vegas I was looking at MGM's iconic symbol, the lion, four of them, in a glass cage inside a casino. I actually felt a little sick.

*

The following morning I felt a lot better; it's amazing what a good night's sleep can do. I ventured out to see what Vegas had to offer by day and came back six hours later physically scarred and $500 poorer.

I began by walking up and down The Strip and it was a shock to the system to see so many people, so many shops, so many fast food joints, so much *stuff*. I went back into MGM to see the lions again (just to check that I hadn't actually imagined it the night before) but thankfully the glass cage was empty. The casino area was already filling up with punters at 10 am. I passed one slot machine and was convinced that the middle-aged woman sitting there, feeding in coins from her bucket, was the very same woman I'd seen in the very same seat fifteen hours previously. Surely not, surely she hasn't been there all night? Has she?

"the greed, the extravagance, the waste, the hard-worn looking people"

The words from David's blog resonated with me as I walked out of MGM and down The Strip. Las Vegas did seem to be a thoroughly depressing place. People looked unhappy, haggard; almost as if they were trying too hard to have a good time. At the entrance to a huge shopping mall I saw a queue snaking its way back at least a hundred metres. What were all these people queuing for? It must be something important. Perhaps a famous actor or pop star was signing autographs? The doors to the mall were swinging open as people came and went so they weren't queuing to get in. I approached the front of the line. People were queuing to have a free go at a one-armed bandit. In exchange for your email address (so companies could later bombard you with literature) you got one free swing on the one million dollar prize machine. Perhaps if I'd flown in from the UK on a week's holiday geared up for everything Las Vegas had to offer I would have thought differently. After all, millions of people back home gamble away a few pounds every week on the lottery. Good friends of mine had flown out to Vegas to get married a few years ago and although I can't think of a worse place to get 'hitched', they thoroughly enjoyed themselves. Horses for courses. Las Vegas was never going to be my favourite place under any circumstances, but coming at it as I did, from being on the road, it was a strange brew.

A few minutes later I came across the Harley-Davidson Café. I just had to go in. I would imagine the Las Vegas Harley-Davidson café needs little introduction. It looks, feels and smells exactly as you would imagine. Situated on a major crossroads on The Strip, the two-storey building screams 'Harley!' at you with the front end of a twenty metre high Hog smashing its way through the second floor window, apparently in the process of jumping on to the main road. There were some tables and chairs set out on the pavement and most were already full with patrons tucking into their brunches: huge people with huge plates full of huge portions of food. I wanted to see what the décor was like inside and strolled through the Harley-decorated doors. Surprisingly, considering how packed the outdoor area was, there was hardly anyone within. I sat myself down in front of a massive American flag in the far corner so I could watch everyone and everything.

"Hi. My name's Eva and I'm going to be your server today," said Eva, as she handed me the menu. She was dressed more like a biker chick than a waitress:

tight black jeans held up with a large studded Harley belt and a tight black Harley T-shirt. As you might expect, the menu had a motorcycle theme. Breakfast was called *Kickstarts;* side orders, *Sidecars;* and dessert, *Vroooom! For more!* I loved this; I didn't like Vegas but this I could buy into. Eva returned with an all-American smile on her face.

"Are you ready, Hon?"

I was. I ordered my breakfast and a coffee (under the *Standard lubrication* section) and settled back to survey the scene.

Largely decked out in polished wood, most of the seats were black leather-backed and set around polished wooded tables. In the corners and around the edge, especially under the flag, were a few stylish leather booths: classic American diner set-up. The walls were covered in Harley-Davidson memorabilia: shirts, pictures of bikes, framed records, all signed. Higher up, Hogs hung from the ceiling and in front of the flag a conveyor belt of Harleys moved around in a circuit. And that flag. It must have been fifteen metres high and twenty metres across but the most amazing thing about it was that it was made of heavy-duty motorcycle chains. "Here we are, Hon." Eva had returned with my huge plate of eggs and beans and toast. "I see you're looking at the flag?"

"Yes, it's huge."

"World's heaviest flag." She said it in such a way that I just knew I needed to be impressed by this piece of information.

"Wow," I said.

I ate my food but to be honest I was more interested in drinking in the scene. I was eating brunch in the Harley-Davidson Café, Las Vegas. And I'd got here by riding a BMW motorcycle all the way from Alaska. This just made me chuckle. Somehow I felt as if I had taken on Las Vegas and won. It could keep its casinos, all-you-can-eat buffets and sordid, semi-legal prostitution. (Nevada is the only state in the US where prostitution is legal, but it's officially outlawed in the whole of Clark County, in which Las Vegas is situated, along with three quarters of Nevada's population. The nearest legal brothel to Las Vegas is about an hour's drive away, but the city is still teeming with 'escorts' whose services are widely advertised.) I'd come to the home of the hog on a boxer and what's more I even knew what I was talking about. I felt like a spy who'd infiltrated the headquarters of the enemy.

There was almost a spring in my step as I walked back down The Strip. Vegas is what it is, and it can be whatever you want it to be. I might not enjoy it but I could at least learn something from the experience. Without really thinking about where to go next or what to do I turned into one of the huge malls, just before the million-dollar slot machine queue. Most of the shops were designer label places selling ridiculously expensive stuff I wasn't interested in. But then I stumbled across a sight that made me stop: a tattoo shop. Ah, I thought. Could I?

Should I? After all I was going get one before I left England and just never got around to it. Why don't I do it now? What better place to get one done than Las Vegas? So I went in to *Club Tattoo* and had a look at their designs. Three hours later I came out with a dragon tattoo on my leg. Las Vegas had certainly scarred me.

*

The following morning I hit the road for Death Valley. Cruising at 70 mph across the desert I could feel the stress and anxiety of Las Vegas slowly evaporate as the morning sun warmed my back. I was back on the road; back in the wilderness; back on track. Stopping at a nondescript town to fill up with petrol and water before hitting Death Valley I was amazed to spot an overland motorcycle parked outside a motel. Then I recognised the bike. Even I could now spot an Africa Twin when I saw one and there weren't many of those in this part of the world with an Irish flag on the front.

It had to be Patrick. The very same Pat I'd hooked up with way back in the Yukon and with whom I'd travelled for four or five days. We'd kept in touch but I hadn't actually caught up with him, until now. The motel formed a horseshoe shape around the car park and I had no idea which of the fifteen rooms he was in. But this wasn't going to deter me.

"Pat." I shouted. "It's Dom. PAT. PAAAAAT!"

A door creaked open and a smiling Irish face peered out. The first familiar 'mug' I'd seen since leaving Trent's a month earlier. It was great to see someone I knew and we had a good long chat comparing notes on the places we'd been to and the whole experience of being on a long bike trip. We rode together that day, down into the Valley and along to Death Valley Lodge at Furnace Creek, famous for being the world's lowest golf course, selling extremely expensive food and even more expensive stickers for my panniers. Pat and I sat out in the baking sun by our bikes and chatted. It was great fun to catch up with him and what he had been up to. Since leaving Canada he'd parted from Paul the Texan and zigzagged his way slowly down Montana, Idaho and Colorado. We'd been to many of the same places, sometimes only a few days apart and it was really interesting to get someone else's perspective of the same things. Often we'd agree but occasionally we'd have very different experiences of the same place. Beartooth Pass certainly sounded very different in the snow!

Planning ahead, it was clear that Pat and I had slightly different agendas. He was heading for southern California whereas I was heading for Yosemite. We made tentative plans to perhaps meet up in Mexico and said our goodbyes at Furnace Creek, so I rode into 'the valley of the shadow of death' all on my own-some.

Death Valley sounds dangerous and I'm sure it can be. But on a motorcycle full of petrol with two litres of water on board, it was just another day's ride. And it wasn't even that hot. It even rained for five minutes (first time in ten years apparently). Riding below sea level was weird but not in the same way as riding at altitude. It's not as if you really notice anything about being fifty metres below sea level. The barren, rocky desert was certainly uninviting, with little in the way of vegetation managing to survive in such an environment. Furnace Creek holds the record as the hottest place in the Western hemisphere, the mercury rising to 56.7 C in 1913, just one degree below the world record set nine years later in Libya. In October, the month I was there, the daytime temperatures at Furnace Creek usually hovered around 30C (86 Fahrenheit).

I rode through Death Valley and on towards Yosemite National Park without really stopping. Part of me was being pushed as far away as possible from Las Vegas and part of me was being pulled towards Yosemite, where I was hoping to catch up with David and Jill. Also, with a day-old tattoo on my leg, Death Valley was probably the worst place I could be. New tattoos need to be kept moist and every few hours I needed to apply a moisturising skin cream, with clean hands. Not an easy operation on a bike trip.

I stopped for the night in Bishop, California, a small town on Route 395. Since coming out of Death Valley I'd been riding parallel to the mighty Sierra Nevada mountain range. Running four hundred miles north to south and about seventy east to west, the Sierra Nevada are certainly impressive. Home to three National Parks: Yosemite, Sequoia and King Canyon, the mountains are also the highest in the contiguous United States. The tops of the mountain range were dusted in snow and a cold wind was blowing down into the valley. I found a cheap motel in Bishop, unpacked and moisturized.

Next morning, to get into Yosemite, I had to climb up the nine thousand feet pass north of Bishop. This was the famous Tioga pass road, only open between the end of May and late October due to heavy snowfalls. I was there in mid-October and although the road was open there was snow at the top. The previous day I had been at 30 degrees centigrade and fifty metres below sea level, now I was at zero degrees and three thousand metres above sea level. And it was snowing. No two days are ever the same in this 'job'!

Yosemite was very pretty, very well organised and very busy. All the RV-type campgrounds were booked up months ahead – even for a Monday in October, but the walk-in campground wasn't full and was only $5. It was busy though, with some sort of rock climbing convention in progress. Yosemite has several one thousand metre sheer granite cliffs and it draws climbers from all over the world. I heard more French than English being spoken and there were lots of skinny young people carrying ropes.

Yosemite is also famous for its black bears (here we go again). The statistics I saw said that in 1998 one thousand cars were broken into by bears in Yosemite. When I was checking into the campground I was told to leave absolutely nothing in my tent – I was to put it all in the bear lockers. I did as I was told, and went to bed that night with my trusty old pepper spray.

Next morning I got up, grabbed a muesli bar from my bear locker and boiled some water for my breakfast. It had been a cold night and I took a walk around the campground with my coffee to help the blood circulate. My fingers and toes were numb even though I'd slept in about three layers of clothes inside my sleeping bag.

While stamping around the campground I spotted David and Jill's bike, Nancy. I'd finally caught up with them! David and Jill, who hail from England's south coast, had been on the road in North America for six months already. Shipping their bike to Halifax on the Canadian east coast, they'd ridden across Canada and the United States to California, then up to British Columbia in Canada and back down again. I'd been following their trip on their blog and as we had been on a similar route since Montana it was really interesting to read their experiences and perceptions of the places I'd also been to. It is quite amazing how people can visit the same place, almost at the same time but have a totally different experience. Partly it's down to luck as to whom you meet and what you do, partly it's down to personal preferences as to where you stay and what you visit but it's also down to how you see the world. I suppose everyone can only ever see the world through their own eyes but it brought home to me how different this trip was because I was mostly on my own. If Tracy had been with me in the US it would have been a very different experience. Not better, not worse, just different.

David and Jill had been very honest on their blog. Travelling two up with camping equipment is tough. Space is limited both during the day and at night and they had got on each other's nerves at times. I guess this is an area of travelling that isn't often talked about and it was refreshing that they were so candid. Travelling is hard and there are bad days as well as good ones. People often only remember and write about the good ones but I think the immediacy of email and blogging now allows travellers to be much more honest and forthright about *all* their travelling experiences. Of course it also helps let off steam; as an alternative to moaning at each other they could use the blog to express their frustration and anger.

The day I met them they were at least talking to each other! Even though we'd only met once before, several weeks previously, it was like meeting old friends and we spent the day together riding around Yosemite and walking through some wonderful woods. We stopped at Mariposa Gorge to see the world's largest (by volume) living organism *ever* on this planet – the Sequoia tree. (Redwoods are also Sequoia, *Sequoia sempervirens* – coast redwoods but these Sequoias are Giant

Sequoia — *Sequoiadendron giganteum*.) Not quite as tall as the Redwoods, the Sequoia are immensely thick. Up to twelve metres in basal diameter, and they can live for well over two perhaps even up to three thousand years. It was quite something to be standing next to such old and huge trees. Yet again, America's National Parks had come up trumps. And yet again I was learning that America does have history.

David and Jill were heading for San Francisco and I was going to Los Angeles so we said our goodbyes, hoping to meet up again in Mexico or beyond. It had been really quite odd to have been on my own for so long and then to bump into fellow-bikers that I knew. My usual conversations were to do with asking for things or explaining what I was doing. So, even though they were brief encounters, catching up with Patrick and then David and Jill was just the tonic I needed and as I left Yosemite I felt confident that I could cope with solo travel once more. Indeed, I was going to relish the time I had left on my own as I knew it was running out.

CHAPTER 10

A CHANGING STATE OF MIND

"What the United States does best is to understand itself.
What it does worst is understand others."

(Carlos Fuentes)

Unfortunately the southern Californian coast was shrouded in fog when I hit Route 1 towards Big Sur on the much-talked-about section of coast road south of San Francisco. I'm sure it was lovely but I couldn't see much of it. I was heading for Los Angeles and stopped off for the night, camping near Point Buchon just a few hours' drive north of the metropolis. This was possibly going to be my last night sleeping outside for a very long time since I didn't expect to do much camping once I hit Mexico. As I settled into my sleeping bag, wearing a T-shirt, fleece, jacket and woolly hat, I was sad that this aspect of the trip was coming to an end. In Alaska and Canada, camping had supplied me with some of the best memories of the trip but once in the 'Lower 48', with the temperature dropping and the days drawing in, it was becoming more of a chore. Time to spend my evenings in nice warm Mexican bars, eating good food and supping on a beer.

But first I had to navigate Los Angeles. As usual, I'd drawn myself a map. I had an address for a BMW dealer and had arranged to get a new rear tyre and an oil change. The Continental Attack fitted in Spokane had lasted 8,000 miles and there was still some tread left, but not knowing what to expect in Mexico, I decided to change now in the hope that the new tyre would get me all the way to Panama. I'd calculated that I should cover six to eight thousand miles in Central America. I still didn't trust myself to change my own oil.

I found the bike shop quite easily (who needs a GPS?) and I left Heidi with a BMW mechanic, surprisingly not called Mike. As usual, American customer care was excellent and I picked my bike up later the same day, this time with no nasty surprises. Heidi had a lovely new Continental Attack rear tyre and fresh oil. Perhaps my luck was changing – or perhaps I'd simply replaced all the most fault-prone parts. I knew this would be the last BMW shop I would see in a long time so I asked if there was anything else I should be aware of before heading for the border. I should have known what was coming next.

"Have you got a gun?"

"No. No I haven't," I replied.

"I wouldn't go down there without one. Those crazy bitches will shoot you just for fun."

It was hard to know what to say apart from, "That's what they said about you lot in Canada." But I refrained. "What about gas? I've heard that the octane level is quite low. Is that an issue?" I asked, changing the subject.

"Yeah, you'll want to take some. Mexican gas is shit. Your engine will have trouble with the shit they sell you. You really need to take some octane booster."

I'd already heard that Mexican petrol can be low on octane and that high performance engines suffer if fed on low octane fuel. As I had no idea what 'octane' was, it just worried me that I was going to trash my engine. I'd searched online, of course, and now my head was full of technical stuff that just made me even more confused. In Britain, regular petrol is rated at 95 RON. RON stands for Research Octane Number. 95 stands for, well 95. Super Unleaded is 97 RON. In the US the rating is in AKI (Anti-Knock Index); 91 AKI equals 95 RON. I'd heard all sorts of scare stories about Mexico's petrol and was hoping the guys at the BMW dealership in LA which was, after all, just a few hours' ride away from Mexico, would be able to fill me in on the details. It seemed not. I'm not sure any of them had ever been south of the border. They were friendly and helpful, like most people I'd met in the previous seven weeks, but similarly, they also had a morbid fear of Central America, and Mexico in particular!

One of the universal truths about travel is that as soon as you get near to the border of any country people will start to scare you with stories of what will happen to you once you cross. They will talk of the land and peoples on the other side as if they were aliens. All through the US, when I'd mentioned to people that I was going to Mexico I was told not to.

"They're crazy down there. They all have guns and will shoot you and steal your bike."

What is it about our human psyche that makes us so wary and resentful of our near neighbours? Ask an Englishman why he dislikes the French and he might not be able to tell you why but he'll sure know that he does. And it's often people who have never been to the neighbouring country who are the most opinionated.

This was all compounded by American TV news. Whenever the news mentioned Mexico it was to show a bloodbath, drug seizure or film of illegal immigrants crossing fences and rivers to get into the US. No wonder then that Americans who'd never been south of the border had a pathological fear of doing so. I'd started my trip with absolutely no qualms about going to

Mexico and Central America but after weeks of hearing and seeing only negative reports, it was hard not to feel a little reticent about crossing the border at Tijuana and heading south.

The media have an enormously powerful influence on us (after all where else do we get our opinions on foreign lands from?) and the closer you get to a new country the more patriotic, scaremongering and xenophobic the media become. A conversation travellers often have is about how each and every country is full of nice, friendly, helpful people and not the stealing, lying cheats we were told about in the previous place. One of the things I found most frustrating during the planning stage of my trip was the number of times I had to explain to people who rarely strayed from package holidays that I didn't expect to get mugged or killed. In a way I blame package holidays. They are sold almost on the assumption that it's going to be dangerous where you are going and before you step outside of your nice clean European style hotel you must make sure you ask the rep. if it's safe. Don't drink the water and don't talk to the locals. They are only going to try to steal from you.

And, of course, package holidays are based in tourist resorts, where there may be a certain resentment of the tourists from the locals. We've imposed what we want, taken their beaches and created an environment and culture that they cannot afford, may not understand and probably don't want. I'd once made the mistake of taking a package holiday to Egypt (it was a cheap way to go diving in the Red Sea) and on the flight out we were advised to buy our cigarettes from the tour operators, as they couldn't guarantee the quality of the 'foreign cigarettes' available in Hurghada. Once there, I was surrounded by European and North American food outlets and badly behaved, drunken Europeans inappropriately dressed for a Muslim country. It dawned on me that this was most people's view of travelling abroad and it depressed me. Mind you, the diving was good.

As I continued down the coast road towards San Diego and the border I mulled over what I had seen and done in the previous seven weeks since I'd left Canada. I'd been to fourteen National Parks; slept in thirty-six different places; visited six BMW dealerships; ridden eight thousand, five hundred miles. I'd also seen some wonderful landscapes and incredible wildlife; ridden some fantastic roads; met up with friends old and new, and I'd even phoned my wife once.

If truth be known, when I was planning my trip I had got very excited about Alaska, Central America and Southern Africa but had always sort of skipped over the US. I'd looked at it as just somewhere between Canada and Mexico. Now, as I was leaving, I had a whole new appreciation for the place and the people. Nearly everyone I'd met had been friendly and helpful and the quality of service was usually exceptional. We in the UK could certainly learn something about customer care from the yanks. Lots of people had come up to speak to me about the trip and were good fun to talk to. Some of the roads were the very best I'd ever ridden, and even the boring ones were well-maintained and relatively free of traffic. What traffic there was obeyed the road rules and gave me space. The National Parks surpassed all expectation. I loved the 'hugeness' of it all. Yes it had been easy: the language was, well, similar; food, water and lodging were abundant and whenever I'd had a bike problem, it had been quite easy to find someone who could solve it.

There were a few negatives though. The abundant food was of limited variety. It's far too easy to eat poorly in the US. Portions are ridiculously large – especially drinks – and I soon got fed up with vegetarian burgers and pizza. And although America is cheaper than Canada, camping was expensive. With campsites charging per site, I was paying $15–25 even though it was just me and a bike. And many of the campsites don't tailor for tents so the pitches aren't flat; are gravel rather than grass and there's nowhere to wash your dishes as it is assumed you will have brought the kitchen sink with you. And don't even get me started on the bears!

And despite the friendliness, much of the USA still scared and worried me; like the fact that people kept asking me if I was carrying a gun. What did they think the world was like? Fundamental Christianity also worried me. Perhaps I'd just listened to too many religious radio stations along the way but socially conservative America seemed alive and well. In a recent survey people were asked if the following statement was true: *"Human beings, as we know them, developed from earlier species of animals."* In Britain about 80% agreed, in the USA it was 40%. Fox News also worried me. Those people are so angry! And so suspicious of foreigners. Realising that Sarah Palin wasn't unusual worried me. One leading politician (in Utah I think) expressed concerns that Barack Obama was a Marxist.

But that was about it. On the whole America had been 'awesome', and a pleasant surprise. I'd never travelled to the USA before and that was partly because I'd assumed it was going to be similar to the UK, that travelling in the United States would not be as exciting and different as travelling in, say, India or Chile. But I had been wrong. Our shared language masks our differences, and the 'special relationship' and continual references to being 'cousins' obscures the fact that we are, actually, quite different. I found America fascinating, intriguing and exciting. It had eased me into my adventure. So as I rode down Interstate 5 towards whatever Central America would throw at me, I was as prepared as I was ever going to be. And I didn't have a gun.

*

The numbers, however, are certainly scary. At least 40,000 people have been killed in Mexico since President Felipe Calderon dispatched the army to fight the drug cartels in December 2006. That's about eight thousand a year, or twenty-two per day. Eight hundred people are killed every year in Tijuana alone, more than in the whole of the UK. Tijuana and Mexico were certainly, statistically speaking, dangerous.

Statistics aside, I wasn't going to get paranoid about riding through Tijuana. The vast majority of crime in Mexico is tied up in smuggling – drugs, guns and people. If you're not involved in it you're unlikely to get caught up in it, hard as that is to explain to people who watch Fox News. I had no doubt that the average Tijuanan would be as friendly, helpful and nice as the average American. More so perhaps, as my experience had shown me that people who live in poor areas seldom visited by tourists tend to be open, welcoming and hospitable.

I rode the mile or so from my Motel 6 to the border somewhat apprehensively. I passed under a big sign that said MEXICO, and was stopped by a couple of military border guards who asked me, in Spanish, what I was doing and where I was going. I spoke a little Spanish but my answer was obviously not good enough because they wanted to take a look at my luggage. I had a large grey bag slung over the pillion seat and I had to untie it and open it up at the side of the road. After a quick rummage around they said I could move on and they walked off to inspect a truck, leaving me at the side of the road to repack my bike. And that was that.

I got back on Heidi and started to ride off. But where to? The four lane road I was on headed off around a corner but seemed to be an open road and not part of the border itself. Nobody had looked at my passport yet and I had a feeling that I should at least get someone to stamp something. I had heard that the whole of the Baja peninsula is a sort of 'Zona Franca' and Americans can cross the border with ease; a little like Europeans can within the EU. But I wasn't American and needed to leave the US and enter Mexico officially. Perhaps, I thought, I do that when I get the ferry from Baja to Mexico proper. I just didn't know and there didn't seem to be anyone to ask. This was all rather bizarre. That morning I'd woken up worried about being pushed and pulled from pillar to post at the border by officials keen on taking their cut from me. In fact I'd been left alone and could ride off at will, but the road down the narrow Baja peninsula was a thousand miles long. I didn't want to get to the bottom only to be told I would have come back up again.

While sitting on Heidi thinking this through I spotted a sign at the side of the road. It said 'Transit Vehicle visa' and pointed off to the right. I took a

111

chance and followed it. Within seconds I was right slap bang in the middle of a new country. The American side of the border had been ordered, with neat streets and sidewalks; the usual American food joints, shops and buildings, sensible drivers and law-abiding pedestrians. Within two miles all this had changed. I was now riding along potholed dirty roads with people, animals and vehicles weaving their way around the holes, past each other and in every conceivable direction. At the traffic lights hawkers were selling everything from water to newspapers to beach balls. My nose was also aware that I had moved country: the sweet smell of peanuts being barbecued and roadside fried food filled the air. My ears were also aware that things had changed: car horns blazed away in an apparent belief that simply by pressing on your horn you can magically make the traffic in front clear the packed road. I had to keep one eye out for the sign I was following and the other firmly fixed on everything else that was going on.

Within five minutes I had arrived at the Transit Vehicle visa office but I got off my bike a little shaken and dazed. Tijuana was such a contrast to what I had spent the past three months riding through. And the change was so quick. I don't think I have ever crossed a border which marked such a stark and obvious difference between two cultures.

Having made sure everything was locked down on the bike ("Man, those Mexicans are all thieves") I went into the building hoping I'd come to the right place. It was exactly 8 am on a Sunday morning, a perfect time to cross a border quickly and quietly. I found a man sat behind a desk in a small office. He was a classic Mexican border official – cigarette hanging from the corner of his mouth and two-day-old stubble on his face. This was going to be the man who would let me into Mexico. I handed over my passport and documents and explained to him, in my limited Spanish, that I wanted to enter Mexico with a motorcycle (which should have been obvious as I was wearing full bike gear and carrying a helmet). He gave me a couple of pieces of paper to fill in and pointed around the corner. I took the paperwork and walked in the direction he suggested. Around the corner was a small office with two counters and behind the glass screen sat two officials each seemingly ready and willing to help me. There was no queue and within ten minutes I'd paid my fee, got my passport stamped and was legally in Mexico. They assured me that all was in order and I could go on my way.

"Make sure you don't lose the paperwork," I heard from behind me. I turned around to see a biker standing in the queue.

"Hi, my name's Jim," said Jim with a huge smile on his face.

"Hi, I'm Dom. I guess you're heading south then?"

"Yep, down to La Paz then on the ferry to Mazatlan. How about you?"

"The same. Look, why don't I wait for you to get your stuff stamped. I'll see you outside."

"OK. You can keep an eye on the bikes. I parked up next to you."

Jim was from Canada and had ridden his Kawasaki KLR 650 down from Vancouver. He was going to spend the winter in Mexico and, happy to have company, I was more than pleased when he suggested we ride together down Baja. I hadn't ridden with anyone since Canada and it would be great fun to share the ride south. So we headed off together down the world's third longest peninsular.

As always, I'd done my homework before entering Mexico and I knew more about Baja California than just the murder statistics. People first settled on the peninsular perhaps 10,000 years ago but Europeans didn't arrive here until 1539. The Spanish colony of California was divided into Alta (Upper) and Baja (Lower) in 1804, separating the Franciscan from the Dominican Missionaries. In 1848, Alta California was annexed by the United States; Baja California didn't officially become part of Mexico until 1952. Although most people probably associate Baja with desert, the flora and fauna is surprisingly diverse. A mountain range runs down the middle and the valleys offer good agricultural climates. This climate is Mediterranean and olive groves and vineyards thrive here. As we rode south, we passed fields of the blue agave plant, from which tequila is made.

Signs of civilisation thinned out as we got further south. We were now passing huge cacti several metres tall: one large stem sticking out of the ground splitting into three or four giant 'fingers' that reached up to the sky pointing to the sun in recognition of the heat. These were Cardon, the redwoods of the cacti world, the world's largest. A Cardon cactus can grow twenty metres high and live for three hundred years. The thickness of the stem and longevity of the plant would explain how and why so many had been 'graffiti-ed' at the roadside with names and dates engraved into them.

Jim and I rode two hundred miles down the peninsula that first day, stopping off at the small dusty town of El Rosario as night fell. There were two small motels in the town and Jim inspected one while I went to the other. There was little difference in price but Mama Espinoza's had a restaurant so we booked in, parked the bikes up by our rooms and went to get some food. I was looking forward to my first real Mexican meal. We walked into the restaurant and couldn't quite believe what we saw. It was in many ways a regular little bar/restaurant with small wooden tables covered by red chequered plastic tablecloths but the walls were filled with memorabilia and photographs, many showing motorcycles. Turned out Mama Espinoza's was the first checkpoint for the first ever Baja 1000 desert race back in 1967.

The walls were testament to the motorcycles, cars, trucks and quads that had competed in this famous annual off-road desert race ever since. It seemed a fitting way to spend my first night in Mexico – and the food wasn't bad either.

"Has this place been here long?" I asked the old lady at the counter.

"Oh, yes," she replied. "My mother supplied food, lodging and fuel to any passers-by. About ten cars a year made it down here in the 1930s."

"Amazing. I guess the road wasn't paved then?"

"No and it wasn't paved heading south until 1973. Up until then it was only dirt road for the next eight hundred miles south. Mum used to say – 'bad roads bring good people; good roads bring all kinds of people'."

I liked that. I liked the food and I liked that fact that I could even buy a Mama Espinoza sticker for the bike. All in all I'd had a great day.

On our second day in Baja we rode south east along Route 1 towards the Sea of Cortes. We'd been warned that there were no gas stations between El Rosario and Santa Rosalia on the coast and we should take extra fuel with us. Having learnt from my Alaskan episode I knew I could manage at least two hundred and probably two hundred and fifty miles on a full tank but Santa Rosalia was over three hundred miles away. Besides, I hadn't filled up with the notorious low octane Mexican fuel yet, so I had no confidence at all as to what my fuel range might be. I bought a plastic gallon bottle of water from a shop, redistributed the water into smaller bottles and filled the empty container with fuel at the gas station. Jim did the same and with our 'auxiliary fuel tanks' strapped to the back of the bikes we headed off into the baking early morning sun. Not really wanting to ride for longer than necessary in the heat with a gallon of petrol in a flimsy plastic container wedged behind us, we stopped about a hundred miles down the road – ironically in a burnt out, derelict petrol station – and emptied our plastic bottles of petrol into the bikes' tanks.

That day we rode long and hard. It was hot under the Mexican sun and there was no shade. My black bike trousers made my legs warm and even with all the 'aeration' zips on my jacket open I was still cooking. It was bearable but I was beginning to speculate on how hot Central America was going to be if it was like this here. Generally we rode for a little over an hour before stopping for a break, some water and in Jim's case, a cigarette. Riding with someone can be difficult, you have different agendas, speeds, interests, but I was enjoying my second day with Jim. He was a laid-back casual guy with a good sense of humour. A helicopter pilot by trade, he was now semi-retired and, not for the first time, wintering in Mexico. This is not uncommon amongst retired Canadians (who can afford it) and they are collectively known as snowbirds. I'd come across a similar affectionate term for retired Australians who buy a camper van and drive around Australia – grey nomads. Travel seems an enlightened way to spend one's retirement.

Just before sunset, after covering three hundred and fifty miles that day, we took a bend in the road that swept us up and around a hill and, for the first time, afforded us views of the sea of Cortes. The road curved around and down towards the lovely deep blue water and as we descended, the humidity rose sharply. By the time we motored into Santa Rosalia it was dark, the temperature had cooled to about 25C but the humidity was up to 90%. Riding around a small Mexican port in the dark looking for a hotel, dripping with sweat and trying my best, after a long day's ride, not to hit the children, chickens and drunks who were crossing the cobbled street in front of me – I was the happiest I could be. This was different, this was an adventure. Santa Rosalia looked, felt and smelt foreign to me. I was slightly out of my 'comfort zone' and having to think on my feet; there were no neon lights leading me to cheap, clean motels, Jim and I would have to work it out for ourselves. We stopped in the main square, consulted my Lonely Planet Guide and looked around. I spotted a cheap-looking hotel near the square but there was nowhere even remotely safe to park the bikes. Jim headed around the corner while I stayed with the bikes and came back five minutes later with a grin on his face.

"I've found somewhere with parking and I've even managed to dicker them down."

"You've done what?"

"I've dickered them down. They wanted $25 but we got rooms for $20."

We parked the bikes in the courtyard and dumped our overnight bags in the rooms before heading out for a drink. It had been such a long, hot day that I only managed one beer before crawling back to my room and falling on to my bed. I was asleep within seconds.

Next morning, after a breakfast of eggs and beans, we continued south, skirting the Gulf of California, which separates the Baja peninsula from the rest of Mexico. The deep blue sea, stark white desert and blue sky filled my vision as we rode throughout the morning in the hot sun. After about a hundred miles we stopped in the small fishing port of Loreto. I was surprised at how wealthy the place looked. There were several hotels and cafés and I even spotted a couple of North American number plates on the vehicles parked up in the square. I didn't realise it at the time but Loreto is a major Baja tourist resort for North Americans. There are daily flights from the US and many snowbirds winter here enjoying the fine weather and fishing. We parked in front of the mission of Our Lady of Loreto, next to the Jesuit Missions Museum. I wasn't surprised to discover that Loreto had been founded three hundred years earlier by Jesuit missionaries. It was my first taste, on this trip, of somewhere historic and I took to it immediately.

"Jim, do you fancy staying here today? I know it's only eleven but it's hot and I'm in no rush to get to La Paz."

"Sure, why not?"

Leaving Jim to watch the bikes and have a smoke I headed around the block to see if I could find a hotel. I found a few but they were all set up for snowbirds, asking over a hundred dollars per night. Walking back towards the plaza somewhat dejected I veered up a side street and stopped at a small hotel with a beautiful covered entrance which would have been excellent to store the bikes. I rang the bell and when no one answered (it was siesta time) I walked around the back to find two BMW GSs in the small dusty car park!

Ralph and Carol were from Alberta, Canada and were heading down to Argentina. They, like us, had stopped in Loreto because it looked nice and they were suffering from the heat. Carol especially seemed really hot and bothered by the weather and was finding motorcycle travel a little more exhausting than she had imagined. Ralph had been riding bikes for years but his partner was new to the game and had only passed her test a few months before they set off on the trip. After returning for Jim and checking in, I left them to chat about all things Canadian and wandered down to the shoreline. Even in the mid-afternoon sun the Gulf of California looked impossibly blue and inviting. I stood there staring out at the water reminding myself where I was and how I had got there. I gave myself a few minutes to take it all in and then headed back towards the town centre. I bought a bottle of water in a small shop and drank it under the shade of a tree in the main plaza. I seemed to have the place to myself, as anyone with half a brain was inside sleeping off the heat of day. And this was late October; I wondered what it was like in the height of summer.

Back at the hotel, the three Canadians had gone for a siesta and I sat in the courtyard catching up on my paperwork. I usually updated my blog every week but wrote something every day or so, as it happened. I found this much more enjoyable than I thought I would, as it gave me the discipline of thinking through what I'd seen and done and how I was feeling. I didn't put everything on the blog but it certainly helped me rationalise my thoughts and process the data.

In the evening I went out for dinner with my three Canadian friends and we had a really pleasant evening talking about travelling and bikes. Jim and Ralph obviously knew more about motorcycles than I did (if truth be told, Carol probably did as well but she was quite quiet). Ralph and Carol were going to spend another day or two in Loreto, but Jim and I decided we would move on. We were all heading to La Paz so were fairly sure we'd meet up again somewhere. We didn't. I often wonder what happened to Ralph and Carol.

*

On the fourth day Jim and I made it down to La Paz, the capital of Baja. We found an excellent little *pension* in town for only $15 a night and, most importantly, it had off-road parking for the bikes. I decided to stop in La Paz for a couple of days. As a tourist destination I didn't feel it had much to offer except lovely weather and some nice beaches but both Heidi and I needed a little rest and, Heidi at least, a good clean. So the next day was spent washing the bike and getting my clothes washed at a launderette.

Jim needed to get the ferry from La Paz to Mazatlan on mainland Mexico the next day, so the pair of us rode out to the port to book him in. Jim had been wonderful company and I was sad to see him go. He always had a smile for every occasion and although his Spanish was even worse than mine, he just smiled at people and repeated what he wanted to say with an appalling accent until they understood. He never got agitated, annoyed or angry. Life was a blast for Jim and he saw the good in everyone and everything. I'd only ridden with him for a week but it felt like we had been friends for years. He'd rented a villa on the mainland and was going to spend a few months there with his girlfriend who was flying down from Vancouver. He gave me his address and I promised to stop off and see him when I made it over. And I meant it.

After three quiet days in La Paz and now with clean clothes and a clean bike, it was time to move on and I headed down the coast to the bottom of Baja. It was a short day's ride, less than a hundred and fifty miles, but a significant one. About half way down the road I pulled over onto a dusty lay-by next to a derelict old building. The Mexican sun was beating down onto a rather odd-looking papier-mâché style, six foot diameter white globe with some Christmas tinsel wrapped around a barbed wire fence. A sign by the side of the road told me that I had reached the Tropic of Cancer. Dismounting from the bike I stood there for a few minutes in contemplation. I had ridden all the way from the Arctic Circle to the Tropic of Cancer. I still wasn't convinced that I was going to make it all the way to Panama, let alone through Southern Africa but at least I'd made it this far. It had taken ninety-nine days and I had covered 16,500 miles. Of course there was no one to share this amazing personal triumph with. I was proud of myself and really wanted someone to be there so I could tell them what I'd done. I just had to talk to myself: "Hey, Dom. You've just ridden a motorcycle all the way from the Arctic to the Tropics. That's some feat. Well done mate!" And with that I rode into the tropics and on to Cabo.

The town of Cabo San Lucas (Cape St Lucas) is, as the name implies, at the very bottom of the Baja peninsula and it was probably a lovely place thirty years ago. The sandy white beaches and wonderfully warm blue sea formed the backdrop to the desert, stretching back inland as far as the eye could see. The natural harbours created by rocky outcrops and sweeping bays would have supported small fishing fleets enabling the locals to eke out a living from the rich abundance of life in the ocean. But times change. With the completion of a fully tarred road from the American border, ("bringing all kinds of people") tourism had hit and now Cabo San Lucas sits at the bottom of Baja California as the jewel in the crown of the Baja tourist board. But if the cream always rises to the top then I guess shit must sink and Cabo, in my opinion, had collected all the crap Baja had to offer: tequila bars, fast food joints and lots and lots of *gringos*. Within ten minutes of walking down the main strip I'd been offered Cuban cigars, a good time and drugs. One dubious looking character passed me muttering: "Party accessories for sale." I'm still wondering what that actually entailed – invitation cards, some balloons and a kid's magician perhaps?

I did buy some drugs though. Even before I left the UK I'd been having a debate with myself as to whether I should or not. Opinion is very divided, especially amongst the travelling community. The Horizons Unlimited website often has long conversations on the matter and everyone is entitled to their own opinion. Some say it's a waste of time, others that you're a fool if you don't. By the time I got to Baja I'd weighed up the odds, looked at it from both sides and decided to get some. I was pleasantly surprised to find that they were also a lot cheaper in Mexico than they would have been in either the US or the UK.

So armed with my two month supply of anti-malaria medicine, I found a semi-Mexican eatery on the waterfront and had to convince the waiter that I just wanted a main course and didn't need a cigar, small boy or marijuana as a starter. I had a huge but bland burrito in front of three big TV screens. One was showing an American college football game, one the World Series baseball and the last a basketball match. I'd left America but it seemed that America had come with me. By 8 pm on a Saturday night in wild Cabo San Lucas, I headed back to my room for an early night. The Lonely Planet told me: "Come to Cabo and expect to toss your inhibitions to the wind – everyone else does." Hum, perhaps I was getting old.

The next day was the hundredth of my trip, a milestone worthy of celebration. Unfortunately, it was marked by a puncture instead. I'd spent the night in a small guesthouse in Cabo and had parked Heidi up in the courtyard. In the morning I packed my gear, loaded the bike and heaved her off the centre stand. As the back wheel hit the shiny tiled floor it made a strange squeaking noise: my first flat of the trip. I unloaded the bike and put it back on the centre stand. It wasn't hard to find what I was looking for: a huge screw was sticking out of my nearly new Continental Attack tyre. In a strange kind of way I was quite excited. I knew the theory of how to plug a tubeless tyre and I'd even done it once as practice. I got out my puncture repair kit and read the instructions. It all seemed quite straightforward. First I had to find and extract the 'foreign object'. That was easy enough; the head was about a centimetre in diameter and I pulled it out with a pair of pliers. Somewhere, somehow, the previous day I'd managed to ride over a three inch screw. I then had to screw a metal prod into the hole and wiggle it about so the hole got bigger. Very counter-intuitive but I did it anyway. The next task was to plug the hole. To do this I had a special tool, a little like a huge needle. Once I'd threaded a four-inch sticky worm on to it I had to screw the needle into the hole. Then when I pulled the needle out the gummy worm stick would remain in the hole, thereby plugging it.

Amazingly, it all seemed to work and once I'd cut off the excess sticky stuff I was ready to inflate the tyre. I plugged my little 12V electric pump into the bike's power socket and the motor started, pumping air into the tyre with ease. I wasn't even going to have to break sweat. Within half an hour of discovering the puncture I'd mended it. I was pleased with myself and felt as if I was almost turning into a bit of a biker. Again, no one to show off to, but never mind. Now all I had to do was test the repair. I rode the fifty miles from Cabo San Lucas to Todos Santos rather tentatively that morning. As luck would have it, I was going to stop for a couple of weeks at Todos so I had plenty of time to see if my plug would hold.

CHAPTER 11

ON A DARK DESERT HIGHWAY

"Nothing will ever be attempted if all possible objections must first be overcome."

(Samuel Johnson)

Before I'd started my trip I'd already signed up to do two stints as a volunteer on projects in Central America. The first one was on a turtle conservation centre in Todos Santos, just north of Cabo San Lucas. I was going to spend two weeks with a small family-run turtle rescue and research centre. I was met at the gate by a couple of barking dogs, two small children and a smiling woman. Francesca, originally from California, now lived in Baja with her Mexican husband Herman and between the two of them they ran *Tortugueros Las Playitas*.

I was shown to my room, a small wooden hut containing a double bed, cabinet and table; it even had a small TV. I unpacked my things and looked around at what was going to be home for the next fourteen days: a weird feeling after three months living like a nomad. Later, I sat down with Francesca to find out what I would be doing and she taught me all about turtles. There are seven distinct sea turtle species in the world today and even though they have been around for at least 150 million years all of them are now officially either 'threatened' or 'endangered'. Two of them, the Olive Ridley and Leatherback come ashore in Baja to nest. Unfortunately the sand is not warm enough for the eggs to incubate successfully so Francesca and her organisation patrol the beaches at night trying to find the nests. They then dig up the eggs and re-nest them in an incubator.

Olive Ridleys are the smallest of the world's sea turtles, often only two to three feet in length. Sexual maturity is reached after about fifteen years and females reproduce at least once, sometimes twice a year. They lay around one hundred eggs at a time, which take fifty to sixty days to hatch. Although there are thought to be 800,000 Olive Ridley turtles in the world their numbers have halved in the last fifty years and they are classed as endangered. A healthy Olive Ridley, if you can find one, can live for fifty years.

Leatherbacks are critically endangered. The largest of the turtles and the fourth largest species of reptile in the world, they need all the help they can get. The Leatherback is the only sea turtle without a shell. Its outer protection is a leathery, scaleless skin made of tough, oil-saturated tissue raised into seven prominent ridges, giving rise to its name. Little is known about their lifestyle but we do know that they can dive to around one thousand metres and live to be over a hundred. They are also just so damn huge – regularly up to eight feet in length! In fact the largest known sea turtle was a male Leatherback, found on the coast of Wales in 1988. It was 9.5 feet long (about 3 metres) and weighed almost 2,000 pounds (908 kg).

Numbers of Leatherbacks have halved in the last thirty years and there are now thought to be only between 30,000 and 60,000 adult females in the world. Leatherbacks eat jellyfish and it is believed that the dramatic drop in their numbers is largely due to the turtles mistaking plastic bags for jellyfish. Mature females will lay around a hundred eggs at a time and will nest several times in a season. It takes between fifty and seventy five days for the eggs to hatch.

The turtles that come to Todos Santos to lay their eggs probably used to go further south but the coastal development that has sprung up in the last thirty or forty years has driven them north. It can take twenty years for a Leatherback to return to its birthplace to start laying, so the ones turning up now are confronted with all the development (and lights) that have sprung up on the Mexican coast since 1990. The noise, light and general pollution forces them to move on and they move up the coast. Todos Santos has a near perfect environment for nesting turtles – long sandy beaches with a gentle slope and little human pollution. It's a shame the sand isn't quite warm enough. For turtle eggs to hatch they need the temperature to be around 28–30 degrees centigrade; any lower and they just won't incubate.

I was really hoping to see a Leatherback or two but Francesca explained that they don't actually get many coming ashore. Last season only *one* female nested, three times, and the year before, fourteen nests were found, probably from three or four females. And, of course, even if a Leatherback does lay a nest it only results in a hundred or so hatchlings. That might sound like a lot until you find out that statistically it is thought that only one in a thousand hatchlings makes it to adulthood.

"What exactly will I be doing then?" I asked Francesca. We'd been sitting out in the late afternoon sun for about an hour by now talking about the depressing plight of the turtles.

"Well your main job will be to go out at 4 am with Herman and patrol the beach on an ATV looking for the obvious signs of any nesting turtles. If you find any you dig up the eggs and take them to the nursery where Herman will bury them again. The turtles have only just started to come ashore. We have a few nests in the nursery but I'm afraid there won't be any turtles hatching for a while."

I went to bed early that night excited about what the following day would bring. My alarm sounded and I rose before dawn with enthusiasm, fully expecting to find at least one nest. I jumped on the back of the ATV and Herman and I rode off down to the beach. It was strange to be sitting on something other than my own motorcycle and even stranger to be riding over sand and to not feel terrified by the experience. We were looking for turtle tracks coming up from the beach, to lead us to each nest. Three hours later we got back home without seeing anything.

Day Two: still keen and eager, I found it easy to get up and put on my fleece and woolly hat as it was surprisingly cold in the early morning breeze. I remembered to pack my camera because I was confident that we would find some nests this time. I returned home three hours later, cold and turtle-less.

Day Three: still full of enthusiasm but three hours of searching resulted in nothing. These turtles really are endangered!

Day Four: I was beginning to understand what 'critically endangered' really meant. At least I'd seen some dolphins and at daybreak on day four we saw some spouting grey whales off shore. But I was here to single-handedly save the Leatherback turtle population and I couldn't do that if the little critters didn't come ashore and lay their eggs.

On the fifth morning we spotted something. Herman stopped the ATV and in front of us I could see small tracks leading out of the water and up the slope. They were very definitely turtle tracks but not a Leatherback's, since they were only about two feet wide. I'd hardly had time to get off the ATV and there was Herman, kneeling down on the sand with a wooden stick in his hand, slowly pulling small turtle eggs out of the ground. He seemed very excited, which was wonderful to see. He'd been doing this for years and yet he still seemed to be pleased to find another turtle nest.

He produced forty-seven eggs from the nest, which we put in a plastic bag (the irony was not lost on me) and transported to the 'hatchery' – a plastic greenhouse on the beach. There he buried the eggs again and stuck a lollipop label on top with the date on it.

When I got back 'home' Francesca translated for me that Herman thought we had found a black sea turtle nest, which was extremely rare – there were perhaps only 5–10,000 individuals in the whole world. They would have to wait ten weeks for them to hatch to find out for sure, by which time I would be long gone.

I'd been in Todos for almost a week now and had fallen into a wonderfully lazy rhythm. After the early morning turtle run I'd take a walk down to the beach and sit around reading. When it got too warm towards lunchtime I'd head back to the project and take a siesta. This would be followed by an afternoon walk around town or back to the beach. I'd go to bed early and wake up at four to start the day all over again. Riding a bike on a long distance trip is, essentially, a very selfish thing to do. It's all about doing what you want, whenever you want to do it, and I wanted my trip to be a little more than that. I also thought I might get bored just riding a bike day after day and by the time I got to Baja in some ways this was true. I needed a holiday from the holiday and stopping somewhere for two weeks afforded me the opportunity to rest, delve a little deeper into a community and make myself useful.

I must have ridden through dozens of places like Todos Santos: a fairly nondescript place, set out in a grid pattern. Todos has one paved main road that leads into town from the south, continues for about a dozen blocks, then makes a ninety degree turn to the right, just past the only set of traffic lights, sweeping up a small hill for another dozen blocks or so and then curves around to the left and off out into the scrub and desert again. Either side of the main street, sandy roads stretch out in a grid pattern for several blocks each way. Along these tracks, large houses hide behind concrete walls and fences, protecting the five thousand or so people who call Todos Santos home. And many people do call it 'home' as Todos has an interesting mix of locals and 'gringos'. Numerous Americans and Canadians live there, some seasonally, but many permanently.

Todos also has lots of artisan shops, several guesthouses and rental villas and perhaps the most famous Hotel in Central America. Opened in 1948 by a Chinese immigrant, Hotel California was, in 1950, the first place in town to have ice and sell cold beer, and that is probably where the story should end. But somehow, and nobody really knows why, how or when, Hotel California got associated with *the* Hotel California in the song by The Eagles. Although there is absolutely no evidence of any connection between the two, and indeed I think The Eagles themselves have said the song has nothing to do with Baja and is more a reflection of life in California at the time, this particular hotel has managed to hold on to the myth. It is very careful on its website not to lay claim to any direct connection, but it certainly doesn't hold back from cashing in on the supposed link. On their website they say:

Although the present owners of the hotel do not have any affiliation with the Eagles, nor do they promote any association, many visitors are mesmerised by the 'coincidences' between the lyrics of the hit song and the physicality of the hotel and its surroundings.

- *Hotel California is accessed by driving down a long desert highway*

- *The Mission Church of Pilar is located directly adjacent to the hotel and the mission bells ring daily*

- *Countless stories and first-hand witnesses relating to spirits and ghosts in the courtyard*

- *In the 1950s and 1960s many people grew their own marijuana and rolled it into 'colitas' which is Mexican slang for a joint.*

A hotel in or near a desert by a mission church with stories of ghosts and dope smoking – can't be many of them around, can there? Annoyingly, it just became impossible to walk around town without humming the bloody song to myself.

Back on the project, after the initial barren first week we were starting to see evidence of nesting turtles on a regular basis. But that was the easy bit. After finding the tracks we would have to locate the nests. Turtles are surprisingly good at disguising their nests and sometimes even dig more than one as a decoy. But Herman was an expert. We would follow the tracks across the shoreline until the turtle tracks merged with the deeper sand and then Herman would walk around a bit working out where the nest was. Once he had located it he would take his stick and carefully prod it into the sand. Turtles dig out nests with their hind flippers in a sort of bell shape – deep and wide at the bottom but with a small neck and entrance. They then lay their eggs, which can take several minutes. After that they cover the eggs with sand to fill the hole. A little stamping around, hopefully covering and disguising the entrance follows and then she heads off back to the sea. This is, incidentally, the only time female turtles ever come ashore. Male turtles never come ashore, ever.

Turtles have been around for millions of years – preceding the dinosaurs – and have found it quite easy to lay eggs in safety. Not anymore though. Even if a turtle can find a deserted beach with an accessible sandy shore (turtles can't cope with steep climbs so the beach has to be flat) there is no guarantee that the eggs will incubate. Dogs, cats and other land-based predators will joyfully dig up the eggs and eat them. On a few occasions we found a fresh nest but were just too late. Something had dug up the nest and we arrived to witness the horrible scene of a hundred turtle egg shells scattered along the shore, beyond help.

Humans are another threat. Turtle eggs used to be a local delicacy, in fact the reason Herman was such a good nest finder was because he and his family used to harvest turtle eggs and eat them. This still goes on although it is now illegal in Mexico and not such a problem, but ATVs and fishermen are. Every morning as we finished our patrol at sunrise, dozens of locals would hit the beach with their fishing rods. The problem is how they get there, riding ATVs and trucks and unwittingly crushing the turtle nests and destroying the eggs. Francesca and Herman were working closely with the local community trying to educate people about this.

On the sixth night, Herman gave me the stick when we found some tracks and asked me to try to find the nest. He'd made it look easy but it wasn't. Although it was a beautifully starry night the moon was low and I just had the light of my head torch to help me. The turtle had tramped over a large area. The nest could have been anywhere within a five metre diameter. I had to be careful where I stood and even more careful where I prodded my stick. The idea was to feel the stick slip into the void and to stop pushing before hitting the eggs. I pushed the stick into the sand and it went down a few inches but… nothing. I tried another spot – nothing again. Looking around I saw a patch of sand which clearly the turtle had been digging in and tried that. Kneeling down next to my 'hole', with the stick on a slight angle I teased it into the sand. It went down an inch, then another. If this was the nest the next inch would find the air pocket. I was trying my best to push the stick in but not wanting to push too hard. Herman must have been laughing to himself at how rubbish I was at this. I was getting a little embarrassed so I pushed a little too hard, and heard a horrible sound: a quiet popping noise. I looked up at Herman. I'd found the nest but I'd popped an egg in the process. I'd come here to save turtles but I'd just managed to kill one.

Using my hands I scooped out the sand to uncover a perfectly formed turtle nest. I had, indeed, smashed an egg but below that one I could see dozens and dozens of others. Each egg was about the size of a table tennis ball but as they were freshly laid, the shells were soft and warm rather than hard. Delicately scooping them out of the nest I counted them as I put them into a plastic bag Herman had supplied: ninety-seven eggs. I'd popped one but I'd saved ninety-seven.

These were Olive Ridley eggs and by the beginning of the second week we were finding one or two nests a night. Each time we would collect the eggs and place them in a plastic shopping bag and with me on the back of the ATV, desperately clutching on to a hundred little warm turtle eggs, we would shoot across the sand to the nursery and rebury them.

This was great and I was really pleased that so many Olive Ridleys were nesting, but what I really wanted to see was a Leatherback. A study in 1982 estimated that 115,000 adult female Leatherbacks existed worldwide and that around 65% of them were nesting in western Mexico. Now the world population is between 30,000 and 60,000 and less than 1% nest in Mexico. A group of sea turtle biologists recently concluded that, along with plastic bags, gill-net and longline fisheries were probably causing this decline. In short, the Leatherback will probably become extinct in my lifetime unless something drastic changes soon.

I was thoroughly enjoying my turtle patrols and got a real buzz finding turtle tracks and then nests and then digging up the eggs and 'saving' them but in the back of my mind I knew this was a drop in the ocean. And we weren't seeing any Leatherbacks at all. The first true sea turtle evolved over one hundred million years ago and human activity meant that quite possibly, in my lifetime, many of the last seven species would become extinct. How do we explain that to our children? There is a glimmer of hope on the other side of the continent however, in the Atlantic, where Leatherback numbers are increasing and the turtles seem to be thriving further and further north, right up into Nova Scotia, as globing warming heats up the icy waters.

For the whole two weeks I was working on the project I was the only volunteer. I was a little disappointed at this as I had hoped to meet up with other travellers and have people to talk to but it did mean I could go out on all the turtle patrols. I did make one friend however. Maria had rented one of the rooms from Francesca but wasn't interested in actually volunteering. In her mid-fifties, Maria was an American escaping the winter by driving around Baja in a clapped out old car with her two corgi dogs. She was delighted to meet a Brit (because the Queen loves corgis and I must surely know her) and offered me a bottle of beer and a spliff over breakfast the first day we met.

Maria, it transpired, had checked herself out of rehab in Palm Springs, bought the car and driven across the border into Mexico with a supply of (medicinal) dope, a boot full of her favourite beer and the dogs (Diana and Charles). She had no real plan but it seemed like a good idea to head down to the south of Baja, and as she felt the same as me about Cabo she opted for sleepy little Todos to set up base for a few weeks. Maria was one of those people who gave away little about herself while talking a lot; I could tell there was a really interesting story behind the façade and half-truths, but I never got anywhere near hearing it. She was far too clever for me. It was only on my last night, over a *mojito* or two in Hotel California, that I learned that Maria wasn't her real name.

"No, Dom, never use your real name if you don't have to. My travelling name is Maria. Everyone should have a travelling name. I've been thinking what yours should be, seeing as you're on this amazing trip."

"Oh, I don't know about that. I don't think I could look someone in the eye and lie about my name."

"It's not lying. You're just using a different persona. I never lie to people about important stuff; I'm always honest with them. I'm a different person when I travel and that person has a different name. Don't you feel the same? Surely you're not the same person riding a motorcycle around the Americas and volunteering at a turtle sanctuary as the man who teaches history back in Britain?"

I had to admit, Maria had a point; after all, this thought had already crossed my mind on the Oregon coast. The strong *mojitos* were helping but I certainly thought she was on to something.

"Ok then," I slurred. "What's my name?"

"I'm going for Nico. Your travelling name is Nico," Maria slurred back.

"Thanks," replied Nico. And with that Nico and Maria had another *mojito* and, as the familiar sound of a certain 1970s Eagles song wafted over the heavy night air, we toasted all travellers everywhere who were on a journey, be it geographical or personal.

"You know what, Maria? I'm going to try. I certainly feel that I'm changing as a person on this trip and I'm going to try to remember that as I head for Panama. Thank you, thank you, thank you."

"Nico, remember – we are all just prisoners here, of our own device..."

Last thing I remember, I was running for the door...

*

In no time at all my two weeks had come to end. It was interesting to just stop for a while and scratch below the surface of places I would normally just pass through and it was also good to feel useful again. 'Volunteering' is a bit of a misnomer as I was actually paying for the experience but I really couldn't think of a better way to spend $750. Francesca, Herman and their two children had been welcoming and fun to be with and I was in awe of how they had dedicated their lives to trying to save the local turtle population. Francesca had been a schoolteacher in California but had given it up to follow her heart and Herman worked tirelessly on the project. I was just passing through, but it is people like Francesca and Herman who are really trying to make a difference.

Although I was sad to be leaving the turtle conservation project I was keen to get back in the saddle and on the road. My rear tyre was still fully inflated which was as welcome as it was surprising and I rode the fifty miles back to La Paz without incident. I was booked on the overnight ferry to Mazatlan on mainland Mexico but as I was early I stopped off in La Paz at a little café on the corniche. As I sat there, content in the mid-morning sun, sipping a coffee and looking lovingly at Heidi, I wondered what would happen that day. Who would I meet? Who would I talk to? Where would I sleep? This was one of the exciting aspects of travelling: not quite knowing what each day would bring and how it would pan out. Deciding to stop at that particular café, how long I stayed for, where I boarded a boat, any of these small details could make a big difference to my experience. From meeting Nevil, or Jim, or J.W. Everitt to going to the Bonneville Speed week or that unnamed beach on the Oregon coast, all of it had happened by luck, chance meetings which need never have happened. I drank my coffee and headed for the ferry.

I had an uneventful night on-board (which is always the best kind of night to have on the seas) and the following morning I rode down the coast of Mexico for a day to catch up with Jim who had rented a villa on the hillside above Guayabitos. It was great to ride around the local area with him and his girlfriend, Cathy, and great not having to get up at 4 am, but I needed to be in Mexico City within a week as Tracy was flying out to join me. Jim and Cathy rode with me as far as Puerto Vallarta where we said goodbye. I was sad to leave them behind. As I rode away through the cobbled streets of the port I took one last look in my wing mirror; I might very well never see Jim again but I knew that I had made a friend for life.

I spent the night in Barra de Navidad (Christmas Bay), a small, quaint port with significant history. In 1564 the shipyards here built the galleons used by the conquistadors who sailed west and claimed the Philippines for King Philip II of Spain. I'd got into the routine of travelling without a tent now and with it getting dark at 6 pm and secure, clean accommodation relatively cheap and easy to find, I knew I'd made the right decision not camping in Central America. I'd left my tent and cooking gear with Francesca and had posted my sleeping mat and bag back to the UK. I needed to make space on the back for Tracy and travelling without camping gear certainly made a big difference. I went for a walk to see the harbour of Barra but was disappointed to find it somewhat unimpressive, notwithstanding its historical significance. Apart from a large monument at the end of the pier there would be no way of knowing how important Barra had been four centuries earlier.

It took me most of the following day to ride the two hundred and fifty miles down the coast but I only caught sight of the sea a handful of times, despite my guidebook telling me that the road 'hugged' the coast. On top of that, Mexico's famous *topes* (speed bumps) had, by now, raised their ugly heads. Coming out of nowhere these small, unpainted but steep little bumps played havoc with the shock absorbers (and my backside!) not to mention severely reducing my average speed. That's why it took me seven hours to cover two hundred and fifty miles. Every little village had *topes* to slow traffic down which was fine in itself, but they were seldom signposted, so were hard to spot and often very steep. One grinding of the bash plate on a *tope* was enough to warn me to keep an eager eye out for them and I tried my best to slow down whenever I came to a settlement.

Occasionally a *tope* would appear out of nowhere but usually they were in groups of three or four. This 'multiple hit' really made the bike shudder and shake as it jolted over the top of them. Heidi had been performing admirably since her last visit to a BMW dealer and I didn't want the *topes* to start loosening any nuts or bolts. I was also still a little concerned about my rear tyre. The plug looked good but I just had no confidence whatsoever in my own ability and had taken the decision to change the tyre once I got to Mexico City. I'd asked for advice on the internet and although some people had boasted about how they had ridden their rear tyre with two dozen plugs for thousands of miles others had suggested that really it's best to change the tyre as soon as possible. I would never have forgiven myself if I had left the tyre as it was only to have a blow-out or an accident with Tracy on the back.

Although I didn't glimpse the sea very often the weather was wonderfully warm and the scenery stunning. I'd left the desert of Baja and this part of Mexico was much more lush and vibrant. With the Pacific Ocean (somewhere) to my right and the huge Sierra Madre mountains to my left, I was riding down a wonderfully well-maintained tarmac road with little traffic. However that didn't mean the road was empty. I passed several sun-worshipping iguanas, and something else… coming up a rise I saw a large tarantula crossing the road. I doubled back to get a better look but it had gone. Riding on I couldn't shake this horrible thought that the spider had jumped on to the bike and was slowly crawling up my back.

It was a lovely ride on a hot day, despite all the *topes*. Thick vegetation encroached on the side of the road and I rode past mango, coconut, papaya and banana plantations. In fact I was enjoying it so much I forgot to keep an eye on my fuel gauge and came close to running out. There was one stretch of coast with no settlements for at least a hundred miles and I hit it with a half-empty tank. I'd been quite worried about running out of fuel in Alaska, but now it really didn't seem to worry me at all – what would be would be and with less than thirty miles of petrol left I saw a handwritten sign offering *gasolina* in the first village for well over an hour. What made it even more fun was that with no electricity or fuel pump the attendant filled my tank by sucking petrol through a hose connected to a gallon bottle of fuel that he was holding above his head.

From Playa Azul ('Blue Beach') I turned north and headed inland to Morelia. The Lonely Planet Guide says it's *'the coolest place you've never been'* whatever that means, but it was on my way to Mexico City and about an hour's ride from the famous Monarch Butterfly Reserve which I wanted to visit. I arrived in Morelia, parked by the cathedral and looked at my map to get the lie of the land.

Morelia was my first real experience of a mainland Mexican city and I was stunned by how old everything was. The sixteenth-century *Plaza del Armes* and eighteenth-century cathedral dominated the city centre. I hadn't appreciated how long I'd been away from 'old stuff'. North America has very many wonderful sights but it doesn't do this kind of history. It was great to be reunited with what we in Western Europe perhaps take too much for granted. Morelia was a typical Latin American city centre but I wandered around it for an hour, mesmerised.

However, there seemed to be a few too many Federal Police around for my liking, and there were even a few mobile metal detector boxes I had to pass through to get into the *Plaza del Armes* (the town square). I began to wonder if I should be worried. Unbeknownst to me I had arrived in Morelia on Mexico Revolution Day and there were going to be festivities in the plaza that night. So, having found a suitable hotel with secure parking near the centre of town I returned to the square in the evening to watch the music and dancing and general mayhem that is Mexican Revolution Day celebrations. It was only later I read that in 2008 grenades had been thrown in Morelia during the celebrations, killing eight people. Morelia was the home town for Mexico's President Felipe Calderon and security was high. Sometimes ignorance is bliss!

Unfortunately for me, Morelia will also be remembered as the place I lost my AirHawk seat. Or rather, the place where it was stolen. Before setting off from Anchorage I'd bought an inflatable AirHawk seat to ease the pain of bike riding and it had been a wonderful investment. It cost nearly $200 but it was the most comfortable thing I've ever sat on and every day I was glad I'd purchased it. But when I packed up my stuff in Morelia I couldn't find it anywhere. I searched for over an hour around the room and hotel but to no avail. I don't know how or when it was taken but it was.

I tried to cheer up as I headed for the butterfly reserve. Situated in the pine forests at an altitude of 3000 metres, millions and millions of monarch butterflies spend the winter months here. I was escorted up the mountain by my local guide, Pedro. Surprised perhaps to be taking a biker on a tour of a butterfly reserve, he tried to make me feel at home by talking about Premier League football. I didn't really learn much about the life cycle of the monarch butterfly but I did learn that Liverpool were the best team in the world and England would never win the World Cup if they insisted on playing Gerard and Lampard together!

After an hour of walking uphill, at altitude, in my bike gear, we started to see the first butterflies; initially just a few flying around overhead and then some on the ground and trees. Then suddenly there were thousands of them. These large orange and black butterflies have travelled over two and a half thousand miles from North America to winter on the oyamel trees; the longest migration of any insect. That was amazing enough but the next thing Pedro told me really blew my mind.

In North America when a monarch metamorphoses from a pupa to a butterfly it only lives for about three to four weeks. In that time its job is to mate. This means that in the American summer three to four generations of butterflies occur. It is only the last generation emerging at the end of the summer which will fly the two thousand five hundred miles south and winter in the Mexican hills. Nine months later those very same creatures will head north and the cycle will start again. This is extraordinary. First it means that one butterfly lives for nine months, migrating the five thousand miles south and then north again, while the other butterflies only live for a few weeks. But even more astonishingly, the butterflies seem to 'return' to the same locations in Mexico and, apparently, even to the same trees as their ancestors. As this isn't the same butterfly which left Mexico several months previously but something like its great grandchild; this information must somehow be passed down through three or four generations. Scientists still don't fully understand how.

I no longer needed to walk as I could just stand still and see thousands upon thousands of monarchs all around me. In fact I had to be very careful where I stood as the forest floor was also littered with the little critters. I'd thought twice about coming to see the monarchs – after all, I was supposed to be on a motorcycle trip and this was hardly a macho thing to be doing – but standing there seeing and hearing these incredible, colourful and large creatures was worth it. The vivid orange insects were quite mesmerising as they fluttered all around me. And that fluttering created an eerily loud noise, which added something unique and special to the whole experience. Once Pedro had told me of the life cycle of the monarch I stood there staring at these delicate little butterflies in awe of their accomplishment.

I left the Monarch Butterfly Biosphere reserve and headed towards Mexico City. The plan was to stop in a town just before I got to the city so I could ride in on the Monday morning rather than late on a Sunday night. It was only a few hours' ride and I wasn't expecting anything to happen. I certainly wasn't expecting rain, and hail, and lightning. I was on a *cuota* toll road and there was lots of other traffic around but the sound of thunder and the sight of the flashes still made me nervous and I was desperate to get off the road and into a motel, somewhere. But first I had to queue to get through a tollbooth. Some countries let motorcyclists ride around tollbooths and avoid paying, but not in Mexico. So I joined a queue of cars inching our way towards a booth as the heavens opened and torrential rains came straight down out of the sky like stair rods. Out of the blue, a BMW motorcycle pulled up next to me. It was a huge shock as I hadn't seen another bike for five days. Not only was it a fellow adventure motorcyclist but he was also British! I couldn't remember the last time I'd met a Brit on a bike.

"Hey, how's it going?" I shouted through my helmet. The rain was falling so hard I could hardly hear myself speak.

"Good. Gotta get to Mexico City quick. I'm meeting someone and I'm late," came the reply.

And with that he was off. Weaving in and out of the slow-moving traffic he disappeared as quickly as he'd arrived. I only knew he was British because of the accent and number plate but I didn't even catch his name. I was left somewhat shocked and bewildered. Had that really happened? Five days is quite a long time to be totally alone and then suddenly out of nowhere someone turns up and disappears within seconds. And all during a brief but violent thunderstorm!

I turned off the toll road and into the town of Tolima, hoping it would be easy to find the centre of the city and a cheap hotel. It wasn't. It was dark and without a GPS it took me half an hour just to find the city centre, another half hour to find a hotel. I was wet, tired, hungry and dazed by the events of the day. I made some notes for my blog:

Seat stolen, awesome butterflies, lightning, Brit on a bike.

Then I went to sleep. I was going to need to be on my toes in the morning. Everything was about to change.

CHAPTER 12

TWO-UP AND HEADING FOR THE HILLS

"Never go on trips with anyone you do not love."

(Ernest Hemingway)

I had not been looking forward to Monday. Not because Tracy was arriving, I hasten to add. I was, of course, very excited about that. But it meant I had to ride into Mexico City without a GPS. Before leaving Todos Santos I'd drawn myself a map of how to get into the city and where the BMW dealership was, but as I was relying on following this sketch I started early and prayed for the best. Surprisingly, I found it much easier than I had expected. The traffic wasn't that bad and it all seemed to behave itself. I'd heard rumours of crazy driving in Mexico City: people going the wrong way around roundabouts, six lanes of mayhem and no road signs. Not to mention car-jacking and road robbery as you sit in the endless traffic. It wasn't like that at all and I managed to find my way to Motohaus, the BMW dealership, without too much trouble. Yet again, the anticipation of an event had been more worrying than the reality.

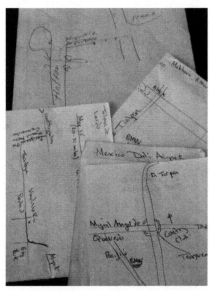

Who needs a GPS to find the centre of Mexico City?

The staff were very welcoming and extremely obliging. They proceeded to change the tyres (and oil) and they even washed the bike for me. Roberto, the manager, was very helpful and tremendously excited about my trip. He asked if he could 'sponsor me' by not charging me labour and also by putting a sticker on the bike. How could I refuse?! Two birds with one stone: I got to save a little money and I gained a free sticker. He also gave me two little bottles of visor spray – what a great guy! I left Motohaus with two brand new Avon Distanzia tyres, fresh oil and a clean visor. Nothing was going to stop us getting to Panama now.

Finding the hotel Tracy had booked proved a little more difficult but I finally got there after an unintended detour around the city centre and checked myself in. It was only early afternoon and Tracy wasn't landing until six so I had plenty of time to get the shuttle bus to the airport to meet her. I was obviously very excited that she was coming out for two months to travel with me through the rest of Central America, but it also meant that this was the end of my solo trip in the Americas. It had been nearly three months since Tracy had flown out of Vancouver and I'd crossed into the United States. I had been on an adventure through the US and Mexico but also on a different sort of journey as well. I'd found it fascinating to spend so much time alone. It was an incredibly liberating, refreshing and selfish way to live. For Maria this had manifested itself in a *'nom de voyage'* as she learned to cope with her changed persona as she travelled through Baja. I hadn't managed to live as 'Nico' as she had suggested; I was unable to force the words out of my mouth whenever I introduced myself. But I felt I didn't need to. I knew who I was and I was happy with that. I hadn't undertaken my trip to try to forget the past or deal with deep-seated personal problems (I think Maria was trying to come to terms with both). I knew I was changing but I was fairly sure it was subtle rather than palpable. I would soon find out – Tracy would tell me!

Early next morning we loaded Heidi up to head out of the capital. All of my gear needed to fit into the panniers and the large grey bag which had been slung across the pillion seat. Tracy hadn't brought much kit and it all fitted into the same two small daypacks as she'd brought to Canada, which we strapped on top of the panniers. I moved the grey bag to the small rack on the back of the bike, placed sideways; this made it tall but thin, so Tracy had quite a lot of room on her seat. I got on the bike, started her up and Tracy climbed on. Heidi felt incredibly heavy and slightly wobbly as we left the car park. I turned left out of the hotel and then left again, following my handwritten notes.

Then I felt a slap on my shoulder. What was going on? We still hadn't invested in an intercom and I had no idea what Tracy wanted. We'd only gone about fifty metres so it couldn't be a toilet stop already!

"The grey bag's coming off," Tracy announced. It had slipped right back and was half way down the back of the bike obscuring the number plate. This was no good. There was no way we were going to get to Panama like this. The only option was to tie the grey bag on, as I had done previously, flat and low. This made it much more secure but gave Tracy far less space. I edged forward at the front, nestling up against the tank to give her a little more room, but still she can't have been that comfortable. To her eternal credit she never complained, not once, all the way to Panama.

We rode the forty miles to Teotihuacan. Short in distance but long in time as I found navigating out of Mexico City much harder than getting in and it took us two hours to get there. Teotihuacan was once Mesoamerica's greatest city. Built between the 1st and 6th centuries AD, about 125,000 people lived there making it the largest city in all the Americas at that time. Teotihuacan is known for its two vast pyramids – dedicated to the sun and moon. The pyramid of the sun is the world's third largest – 222 metres long on each side and 72 metres tall. At the height of the Teotihuacan empire the pyramids were painted bright red and would have been a magnificent sight at sunset. It was wonderful to have Tracy with me; visiting somewhere like Teotihuacan is so much better if it can be a shared experience. We spent most of the day walking around the huge site, watching tourists come and go. Tracy was especially pleased to be out in the sun having just left a very cold UK.

From Teotihuacan we headed south; first to Puebla and then on to Oaxaca. Puebla was a bit of a challenge. With over a million inhabitants and very few street signs it wasn't easy finding my way into the centre (I was beginning to think that a GPS might have been a good idea). Once there, we had a pleasant evening in the lovely colonial centre of town. Next morning I found it equally hard getting out of the place but a friendly policeman gave me some directions and eventually we made it the two hundred miles south to Oaxaca.

We spent two nights in Oaxaca (pronounced 'Wahacka') so that we could take a day visiting the nearby ancient ruins of Monte Alban; the ancient capital of the Zapotec, an indigenous pre-Columbian civilisation. Building started around 500 BC and the place was occupied until the fifteenth century and it looked exactly as I expected a Mexican archaeological site to look. Pyramids, artificial mounds and terraces all carved out of rock sat atop a flattened mountain. We had both been looking forward to visiting the ancient sites of Mexico and so far had not been disappointed.

Oaxaca is one of Mexico's most beautiful and vibrant cities; a great place to soak up the atmosphere of Mexican culture and colonial elegance. In the evening we went back to the main plaza to experience some more of that famous Oaxaca culture and food. Although we didn't sample the ant larvae or deep fried grasshopper we did try the famous *mole negro* ('black sauce' – a smoky, savoury sauce with a hint of chocolate), and Oaxaca's favourite hot drink – *chocolate caliente* – ('hot chocolate' – a mix of cinnamon, almonds and sugar with cocoa beans). The plaza itself was full of life, with street theatre including fire jugglers, dancers and clowns and lots of stalls selling food, trinkets, clothes and jewellery. We visited the impressive cathedral, watched some dancing in the main plaza and then I got accosted by a drunk who wanted to tell me that Manchester United was the best football team in the world, ever. Over and over again. I told him that I knew a butterfly man who thought differently but he wasn't having any of it.

This was the Mexico I'd been looking forward to finding. Days spent riding down well-maintained, quiet roads through wonderful mountain scenery in warm but comfortable weather. In the evening we'd stop at picturesque colonial towns; plazas full of evening life and excellent Mexican food. Each night we'd find a hotel near the town centre with safe parking and just soak up the atmosphere. Heidi was running perfectly; I had full trust in my tyres for the first time since the puncture. Tracy and I had settled into a great little rhythm of daily packing and unpacking and we'd even managed to put a little more gear into the panniers, thereby slightly reducing the size of the grey bag. I'd got used to riding two up and Heidi no longer felt unusually heavy. Everything was just perfect and we were having the time of our lives.

Due to the wonders of the internet (and I'd been pleasantly surprised by the availability of wi-fi in Mexico) I had been able to keep up with Pat, the Irishman on the Africa Twin I'd first met in Canada. By the time we were riding south from Mexico City he was already in Costa Rica and back with Brian, whom he'd started out from Canada with. They were both speeding their way to Panama in order to get across to Colombia before Christmas. I wasn't going to see Pat again. But as one door closes another one opens and I'd also stumbled across a blog called 'Oneworld2explore'. It was written by Daryll and Angela, a Canadian couple, who had set off at about the same time as me. Currently in Panama, they were heading for Argentina and then planning to ship their Suzuki DR650s to South Africa. As we were on roughly the same schedule I'd been in touch and said we should talk once we both made it to Africa. Both Pat and Daryll talked a lot about rain. The rainy season in Central America should have come to an end by October but even in late November it seemed to be in full flow. Whenever we had a TV in our hotel room that worked I was keen to catch up on the news and see what the weather was like further south. This wasn't just a case of not wanting to get wet, Central America can suffer from flash floods and roads can get swept away. Daryll had just posted some photos of himself and Angela wading waste deep in water with their bikes through what was essentially a river but apparently should have been a road. I think this was the 'La Niña effect' and Central America was suffering from an exceptionally long and intense rainy season.

La Niña, (literally, 'the girl') and its counterpart El Niño ('the boy'), are both ocean atmospheric phenomena. In lay terms, La Niña happens when the Pacific Ocean is cooler than normal. This results in different conditions around the Pacific Rim and importantly for us, heavy rains and flooding in Central and Northern South America. There were strong La Niña episodes in 1995, 1999, 2007 and then in 2010. But none of this was obvious to us at the time, we were just riding south in glorious weather and I couldn't actually remember the last time it had rained on me.

It took us two days to travel the four hundred or so miles from Oaxaca to San Cristóbal de las Casas stopping in a nondescript but pleasant enough town half way. We were now firmly in the tropics and by eleven it must have been at least 25C. All was going well until I tried to navigate through a town called Tuxtla Gutiérrez. We'd climbed six hundred metres from sea level into the Chiapas mountains. Tuxtla was a fair sized place with a population of over half a million, and I had hoped to link up with the bypass road and not have to go into the city centre. I was carrying two maps of Mexico and one map had a ring road going north around Tuxtla, whilst the other showed it going south. I didn't find either of them and we ended up in the middle of the city in a huge traffic jam at 2 pm. It was now about thirty degrees and both Tracy and I were beginning to boil in our bike gear, stuck in a traffic jam in the middle of a city. The sweat started trickling down places you don't want sweat to trickle down and I began cursing my black bike gear. Heidi wasn't having much fun either and began overheating. I was trying to concentrate on finding my way out of the city and was desperately looking for road signs that would point us in the right direction, but the nearer I got to the middle of the city the fewer road signs there were. I admitted defeat, swallowed my male pride and pulled into a petrol station.

Following directions from the attendant it took us almost another hour to get though Tuxtla by which time we were both hot and bothered but at least we were back on the road to San Cristóbal de las Casas. We crossed the mountain range and mercifully, the sun and heat disappeared behind it. But then, it started to rain. By the time we got into San Cristóbal it was teeming down – huge, tropical droplets of rain. The cobbled streets had turned into streams and two or three times I had to ride up a street with so much rain flowing against me I wasn't certain how deep the water was and what lay beneath the surface; a little nerve-racking to say the least. This was the most challenging riding I'd done in a while: two up on a heavy bike, along wet cobbled streets in the rain, suffering from mild dehydration. And I could tell I had an unhappy pillion on the back – six hours on the bike, boiling hot at 2 pm, soaking wet by 3 pm.

I found the central plaza and parked up. The usual plan was that one of us would stay with the bike and gear while the other walked round looking for a decent place to stay. This typically meant somewhere clean with safe parking. The safe parking came first but accommodation in old town centres was short of space and places with car parks were few and far between. It took me over an hour and I must have tried four or five places before I found somewhere that would do. By the time I got back to Tracy, who had been standing next to the bike in soaking bike gear all this time, I feared the worst but she was happily singing to herself.

I parked the bike in the courtyard of our *pension* and proceeded to hang all our wet stuff up around the room. We went out in the evening drizzle to look around but it was still wet and miserable so we gave up and went back to our wet and miserable room. We didn't even bother finding any food that night, gave up on the day altogether and went to bed – wet and miserable. Some days just pan out like that.

The following morning, under cloudy but dry skies we ventured out into the city determined to give it our full attention and we liked what we saw. San Cristóbal is a very attractive colonial town with three interconnected plazas that are artistically illuminated at night. The surrounding cobbled streets that had caused me so many problems the night before now glistened in the morning light and looked lovely. The single-storey buildings that led off from the central plaza were brightly painted in colonial reds, pinks and blues, topped off with ceramic red-tiled roofs. We visited the eighteenth-century cathedral, market and a very interesting Mayan Medicine Museum where we watched a twelve-minute DVD on childbirth, Mayan style. This included passing a large axe and then a large live hen over the woman's stomach in order to ease labour. I wasn't quite sure what the hen was supposed to do but I've no doubt that passing an axe over a heavily pregnant woman has some sort of effect on her! Next, I wanted to go to the Coffee Museum; Tracy wanted to go to the Amber Museum. So we 'compromised' and went to the Amber Museum and I learnt that real amber doesn't float.

San Cristóbal is a major tourist attraction in this part of Mexico and we were certainly on the 'gringo trail' here. Shops and eateries pandered to the travelling clientele and although Mexican food anywhere can be great, in San Cristóbal we were spoilt for choice. We left the Amber Museum just as it started to rain again and dived into a small coffee shop nearby (so in a way I won!). With the heavens opening outside we gorged ourselves on excellent burritos and spicy hot chocolate – the joy of compromise.

The following day we were aiming to cover 150 miles to Palenque, site of one of Mexico's best Mayan ruins. It was supposed to be an easy little run. Unfortunately it was still raining. It had been raining all night and we were told that it was likely to be raining all day. We put on our dry gear and packed the bike up. This wasn't going to be a fun day.

By midday we were both totally soaked. My waterproof gear was pretty good but water still managed to find its way through, especially down into my boots. Tracy's jacket was holding up well but she hadn't bothered bringing the waterproof liner for her trousers (apparently I'd told her there wouldn't be room) and her boots were also filling up.

"I need a wee," I heard from behind me. We were riding along a narrow road through a very hilly section and there just wasn't anywhere to stop. The road was tarmacked but the edges were quite severe drop-offs and very muddy and I really didn't fancy pulling off on to steep slippery mud. There were also no flat sections and lots of bends so I really wasn't keen to just stop on the road in case a large truck came around the corner.

"Just hang on a minute," I shouted.

Twenty minutes later: "I really need a wee," she pleaded again.

I did keep looking for somewhere safe and easy to stop but nothing presented itself. A car came speeding up behind me, overtaking on a blind bend in the rain, reinforcing my belief that I really couldn't stop anywhere on this road as it would be too dangerous. I had to wait until we came across a lay-by or at least something flat. And anyway Tracy had gone quiet and wasn't demanding a toilet stop any more so perhaps it wasn't as urgent as she'd suggested.

It took about another twenty minutes to find a suitable place to stop and I pulled over. I needed a toilet break myself now. Pulling my helmet off I smiled at her.

"Here you are then. You go for a pee first."

"Don't need to," she said, looking a little pissed off.

"Oh, I thought you said you needed to stop?"

"Yes, that was forty minutes and a lot of bumps ago. I've gone now."

"What do you mean?"

"I've peed myself."

I wasn't sure what to say to that.

"Well, I needed to go and I was soaked through anyway so I thought, what difference does it make?" Sometimes it's just best to say nothing so I went for a wee and then got back on the bike. By now everything was soaked through, and although it was warm, this was quickly becoming the worst day of the trip so far. I could only hope that the weather would improve. We were only an hour or so away from Palenque so I hoped that within two hours we would be shacked up in a nice warm *pension* laughing at the day we'd had.

We continued along the road but it had obviously been raining for a long time in this area. We were now dodging fallen trees, riding through little streams as they crossed the road and slaloming around small muddy landslides. I thought back to those emails and blogs I'd read from Pat and Daryll. So this is what it was like. It was all very exciting for a while until we came across a very flooded river that had almost covered the road. It was then that I first thought we might not actually make it to Palenque. There was little traffic and as we continued, the fields on either side of us were flooded and it looked like the only dry piece of land around was the road we were on. There was no way of telling where the river (if there had even been a river) ended and where the fields began. What if the road got flooded? What if the rain continued and we were stranded?

As the afternoon progressed I began to wonder what we were getting ourselves into. Or, to be more accurate, what I was getting us into. Tracy hadn't spoken to me since the toilet stop and I dreaded to think what kind of frame of mind she was in. She'd been looking forward to a two-month trip in Central America having worked really hard all year and here she was, sat on the back of a bike, soaked through, having wet herself.

I rode around a corner and saw a traffic jam in front of me. We hadn't seen any traffic for quite some time so it was a bit of a shock to stumble across four or five cars, a few minibuses and a large coach. Luckily I wasn't going too fast so I straightened the bike up and squeezed gently on the front and rear brakes. I slowly passed the traffic wondering what the holdup was. Presumably a tree in the road or a landslide, which I hoped we would be able to navigate past. We can't have been more than twenty miles from Palenque.

As I passed the large coach I saw the problem. My heart sank. In front of us the whole road had disappeared. The two-lane tarmac road had simply been washed away. I was confronted with a ten metre long gap in the road. Obviously a build-up of water on the left-hand side of the road had become too large and heavy and had eaten away at the earth underneath. It had broken through and washed the road away. There was no getting around this.

There were several men standing around looking at the situation and I asked one of them when this had happened.

"Just an hour ago. It happened an hour ago."

"How are you going to get to Palenque?"

"We are taking everything off the buses, walking around the mud slide and getting on those other buses."

He pointed across the gap in the road. There were, indeed, several buses on the other side of the gap. And when I looked to the left I could see passengers clambering around the undergrowth at the side of the road, many carrying suitcases. But there was no way we were going to get a motorcycle around there. I walked back to Tracy.

"I'm sorry. I don't know what to do. There's no way we can get around this. We'll just have to go back and try to find somewhere to stay the night. Although I can't remember the last time we passed a village."

"We did pass a junction a while back," Tracy said. "It might take us to a town or something?"

Dejected and disappointed, we turned around. Neither of my maps showed an alternative route to Palenque and it looked as if we might even have to return all the way to San Cristóbal. If this was the case we wouldn't be able to get to Palenque at all and therefore we wouldn't be able to go on to Tikal in Guatemala. Our whole plan, since leaving the Pacific coast, was to head into Guatemala via Palenque on a reasonably new route. Most travellers stick to the Pan-Americana route down by the coast and we wanted to try a less well-known way into Guatemala and on to Tikal. This could change everything and alter our whole path through Central America. This was a total disaster. I was cursing and moaning into my helmet as I headed back the way we had come; something I never like doing.

All these thoughts were swimming (almost literally) around my head as I headed back down the road but then we came to the fork that Tracy remembered seeing. The route leading off to the right looked as if it might be heading in the right direction for a Palenque detour. Several taxis were parked up on the corner. I stopped the bike and asked a taxi driver if the road led around to Palenque. He told me, in Spanish, with some excellent sign language, that this road was fully open and, although full of potholes, we could take it to the main road which would eventually take us to our destination.

"That's great," I said. "Can we do it in three hours?" I was conscious of the fact that it was now mid-afternoon and we only had about three hours of daylight left.

"Yes, yes. No problem," came the confident reply.

If we wanted to visit Palenque, Tikal and northern Guatemala we would have to trust this taxi driver and take the road. If he was right, we would be at our destination by dusk and back on track. But if the road *didn't* lead to Palenque, or if it was blocked further along the route, we would be in big trouble. We didn't have a tent with us and had no idea if there would be anywhere we could stay for the night. My biggest worry was that the road would be impassable and we might get totally stranded. This was a big decision. Standing in the rain, soaking wet, hungry and tired we both tried to think through the options. Neither of us really knew what was best to do. Taking this new road was a leap into the unknown but eventually we agreed that this was what an adventure was all about. We might get into trouble but we would only regret not trying. With boots full of water (and in Tracy's case, not just water), soaked to the skin and having not eaten all day we did what we were told (the taxi driver was very insistent that we should go this way) and turned off the main highway on to this small road.

*

It all started quite well, in fact the road seemed in better condition than the main one but I just had this nagging feeling that it could all so easily go wrong. As the miles passed I got more and more nervous that we were getting deep into something that could go horribly 'pear-shaped'. Eventually I realised what was bugging me. I'd made a schoolboy error that could cost us dear. I'd said to the taxi driver: "Can we do it in three hours?" whereas I should have asked: "How long will it take?" Travellers' tales are full of examples where well-meaning locals have simply agreed with what the tourist has said in order to please them.

It was still raining, although lightly now and while the forest encroached on the road in places, there were no fast-flowing streams or mudslides and the way ahead seemed clear. What I was really hoping to see was a vehicle coming the other way. That would suggest that the road was open – at least to somewhere. Being the only vehicle on the road in either direction was worrying.

My mind was racing away now and I was beginning to appreciate how amazingly easy it is to mess things up. Two poor decisions in a row can turn a good day into a disaster. I never felt that our lives were in danger (well, perhaps mine was at the hands of Tracy) but we were tired, hungry and wet. Under those circumstances it's easy to make a series of poor decisions and end up in a real mess. I also remembered reading in the guidebook that tourists had been robbed on these roads, and as we were fairly close to the Guatemalan border, smugglers used these routes at night. The Lonely Planet had advised, 'For your own safety it's better to be off these roads by nightfall.' I was trying!

The detour went on for mile after mile and the road slowly began to deteriorate. For long stretches the tarmac was smooth and flat and then suddenly part of the road would be missing, or there would be a series of large potholes, or those damn *topes* would appear out of nowhere. Twice I went over *topes* that clattered against the bash plate.

Then we came to a particularly tricky section. There had been a tarmac road here in the past but now it was really just dirt with the odd island of tarmac. A huge flooded hole right across the road blocked my way. To enter it

I would have to ride down a steep muddy bank and into dirty water, without knowing what lay beneath. The alternative would be to ride along the edge, between the hole and the foliage at the side of the road. I opted for this route. A two foot wide stretch of tarmac ran along the edge of the hole.

Tracy got off the bike and walked ahead of me clearing away some of the bamboo and other flora from the path. Gingerly I rode along the edge. The first few feet were easy, after all, the tarmac was two feet wide. But as soon as I started contemplating what I was doing I began to panic. I was navigating a big heavy machine along a wet narrow path. I thought it would be best to go as slowly as possible with both of my feet down on the path walking myself along. But the tarmac wasn't quite wide enough and although my left foot was firmly down on tarmac my right was hovering dangerously over the edge, slipping on some mud which was sliding down into the hole. The drop to both my left and right was several feet and would cause major damage to the bike and, more importantly I realised, to me, if we toppled over. If I fell to my right I would fall more than ninety degrees into muddy water with the bike on top of me.

This was not helping me keep the bike steady. I needed to be positive. I tried my best to forget what could go wrong and concentrate on what I was doing. I had to take control of the situation and speed up a little. All I had to do was ride in a straight line. I told myself that this was easy. I focused on the front wheel, revved the engine a little, lifted my feet up and trusted myself. I made it across. It was only afterwards I realised that it would have made a wonderful photograph. But neither of us was in the mood for taking photos and there was no way I was going to ride back to get the picture! Tracy hopped back on and within a mile we came to the main highway where there was a wonderful sign pointing me in the direction of Palenque. Dusk was creeping up on us fast but we were going to make it.

Or were we? My aim was to make it to a place in Palenque called El Panchan; a series of cheap *cabanas* only a few kilometres from the Mayan ruins. In pouring rain and fading light we rode through Palenque and I found the muddy turn-off. Around the corner I had to stop and laugh. We were within sight of our destination but a stream had broken its banks and was washing across our road. It was probably only eight to ten metres wide but it was now dusk and I had no idea how deep it was and it was flowing very fast. I contemplated walking across to see if we could make it but then I noticed that, on the other side, the car park was flooded as well. The water was halfway up the wheels of the three or four vehicles parked there and I decided there was just no point trying to cross the stream. We certainly weren't going to leave the bike anywhere near here for the night.

We turned around and headed back towards Palenque, stopping at the first hotel we came to. It was only 6 pm but felt like midnight. Tracy had really suffered on the bike and was very pleased to finally get some food and a warm bed. We had to ignore the budget to stay in this hotel but neither of us cared. We were just pleased to have made it through and to have ended up in a warm, dry room with a bed. Tracy was understandably also quite pleased to finally get out of her bike trousers. She had a long bath and then soaked them in the tub overnight.

CHAPTER 13

A MAYAN ODYSSEY

"It just ain't possible to explain some things. It's interesting to wonder on them and do some speculation, but the main thing is you have to accept it — take it for what it is, and get on with your growing."

(Jim Dodge)

Next morning, after a civilised breakfast on the beautiful terrace of our posh hotel, we rode back down the road to El Panchan. The raging torrents had receded to a trickle and everything was drying out in the very welcome sunshine. The car park, which had been two feet under water the evening before, was now accessible and we checked in, unloaded the bike, scattered a few wet items around the room and headed off to see Palenque.

We spent a full day there exploring the Mayan ruins and being amazed and impressed by what we saw. At its height, between AD 500 and 700, Palenque was a vast city set in the foothills of the Chiapas. Built by the Mayans and occupied for hundreds of years much has been discovered but there is still a lot of mystery about the site, the occupants and their traditions. Even the name, Palenque, is new; its original name lost in time. The remains of the site now centre around several stepped pyramid buildings and courtyards set in a forest clearing. Howler monkeys, howled in the distance, taunting the tourists as they clambered around the site. It looked exactly as I had expected and hoped it would. Teotihuacan had been impressive, but it was situated in barren landscape surrounded by settlements on the edge of Mexico City, not in the middle of a sweaty jungle. Mayan settlements, I felt, needed to be in the undergrowth. Palenque certainly was.

The mystery of Palenque lies in the fact that soon after AD 900 it was abandoned and left untouched for centuries. Indeed the entire Mayan civilisation seems to have collapsed quite quickly. The Empire arose around 2000 BC and was the only American civilisation to produce a written language. It grew for two millennia, reaching its peak between AD 250 and 800 and then largely died out, although further south, the last independent Mayan states were not conquered by the Spanish until 1697, over 200 years after Columbus first landed in the Americas in 1492.

The mysterious decline of the Mayan empire is intriguing. The latest theory is that climate change had a lot to do with its collapse. Abundant rainfall in the 6th and 7th centuries may well have led to a rise in population which was unsustainable, especially as recent analysis of lake sediments shows severe drought during the next century. This is not to say that climate change is solely to blame for the collapse of the Mayan empire but it was probably a contributory factor. There seems to be growing evidence that the decline of many of the world's empires can be associated with climate change – even a suggestion that there may be a correlation between population size, climate change and wars. Empires grow but changes in climate mean they become unsustainable so they have to expand and invade other areas. Still, that's all history. Thank God we don't live in a world of expanding population, limited natural resources and rapid climate change!

Palenque was unknown to the Western world until 1746 and it wasn't seriously mapped and explored until the middle of the nineteenth century. Perhaps the most famous explorer of the site was Jean-Frédéric Maximilien de Waldeck or *le Comte de* Waldeck, as he liked to style himself, (when not giving himself the title of duke or baron). A little like Palenque itself, Waldeck's life is shrouded in mystery and many of the things he claims to have done cannot be verified. However, according to one biography, by the time Waldeck was fifty years old he had travelled the world; been mixed up in forty-two revolutions; fought in Napoleon Bonaparte's Italian campaign and in Egypt; sailed the Indian Ocean as a pirate and fought to help Chile achieve independence from Spain. He was a friend of Lord Byron, and Marie Antoinette, whom he supposedly visited in prison shortly before her execution.

In 1832, at the age of sixty-six, and already living in Mexico, he embarked on a jungle expedition into an area of hostile natives, incredibly difficult terrain, heat, mosquitoes and rain and set up camp in the ancient Mayan city of Palenque. He made a home on top of one of the pyramids and spent two years creating ninety extraordinary drawings of the ruins. The drawings included some notorious 'embellishments' which were not actually present in Palenque, the classic example being carvings of elephants, which of course have never existed in the Americas. Waldeck's travels had convinced him that the Mayan world had its roots in the ancient world and that everywhere there could be seen strong Hebrew and Egyptian influences. He returned to Paris in 1836 and much later, aged eighty-four, he married for the third time, to a seventeen-year-old who bore him a son. Allegedly, '*Le Comte de*' Waldeck died, aged one hundred and nine in 1875. Phew! Palenque and Waldeck left me speechless.

I'd never considered myself to be a trailblazer but we were certainly off the beaten track when we left Palenque to head for another Mayan ruin at

Tikal in Guatemala. Most tourists head south for the Pan Americana and cross into Guatemala at Tapachula. However, I'd done my homework and found a direct route from Palenque to Tikal that had only recently opened up as a viable crossing for overlanders. The road was paved and had been for years but bureaucracy had prevented its use. Previously, it had been impossible to get a vehicle permit on the Guatemalan side of the border. Travellers would have to enter the country without one and travel across it to the Belize border, leave Guatemala and then re-enter. But a few months before I got there all that had changed and entry visas were being issued for people and vehicles at the border. Happy days.

So it was with a heady mix of excitement and relief (it wasn't actually raining) that we left Palenque heading for the frontier. On twisty roads it took us just under two hours to ride the sixty-odd miles to Tenosique where we found the last PEMEX (Mexican petrol station). I filled up, not having noticed any difference in Heidi's performance since entering the country – so much for the need for octane boosters – and we rode the forty miles to the border (El Ceiba). This was going to be our first border crossing in Central America and I was quite apprehensive. I'd heard and read a lot about the hassle, the noise, the paperwork, the frustration, the time it took. I wasn't looking forward to the experience but surely, I thought, it couldn't be as bad as all that?

The Mexican side of the border had full services for checking out of the country in a lovely new, air-conditioned building. We seemed to be the only vehicle and the whole experience could hardly have been easier. First I had to cancel my temporary import card for the motorcycle and then get our passports stamped. Tracy stayed with the bike and I dealt with the paperwork. In all, it took us fifteen minutes to check out of Mexico. I'd spent six weeks in the country and had ridden 3,500 miles. I'd thoroughly enjoyed my time and had really grown fond of the land and its people. It's a crying shame that most North Americans think of drugs, guns and murder when they think of Mexico – it has so much to offer: wonderful food, amazing ruins, beautiful colonial cities, gorgeous beaches with turtles, whales and dolphins and warm friendly smiling people. *"Viva Mexico!"* I muttered into my helmet, as I headed for country number four.

*

As we rode through the gate separating Mexico from Guatemala a guy called me over to stamp our passports. This was quickly done and he then ushered us across the road to a parked-up lorry on stilts where I needed to go to get the bike stamped in. The two guys in the 'building' were fantastically helpful and there wasn't even a whiff of bribery in the air. They apologised as the electricity wasn't working in the lorry-cum-office and I had to jump into a tuk-tuk to go to a photocopy shop because I needed to have a copy of the Guatemalan stamp that had just been put in the passport. But once I'd done that he got me my temporary Guatemala bike import papers and a sticker to put on the bike. This cost 40 Queztals ($6). We then had the wheels ceremoniously sprayed with something that cost 20 Q ($3) and we were done. It all took less than an hour.

Just as we were about to leave, the cheery officials insisted on taking a photo of us on the bike and then waved us on our way. It turned out to be a relatively pleasant experience; partly, I think, because we arrived early in the day at a crossing that wasn't busy and wasn't used to seeing lots of independent travellers, but also because we approached the whole thing with an open mind. It really is amazing how far a 'Thank you' and a smile can go. I dare say that having a female pillion helps too.

The new country was not as drastically different as Mexico had been from the USA at Tijuana but I did notice some subtle differences as we rode towards Tikal. Guatemala was obviously poorer than Mexico. There were more pack animals (and just animals in general) on the road – lots of pigs, chickens, horses and turkeys. In the villages, girls carried heavy stuff down the road and little boys played in the dirt and mud with machetes. There were noticeably fewer private vehicles around, but more small motorcycles and lots of *collectivos* – minibus taxis. People seemed friendly and were much more inclined to wave at us than they had been in Mexico.

It only took a couple of hours to get to Flores, which was going to be our base for two nights. Flores is a town on an island in Lake Petén Itzá. Only a few square miles in size, and connected to the mainland by a 500-metre long causeway, the island was picturesque and full of tourists. It is the main place to stay when visiting nearby Tikal and although we didn't find it hard to find a hotel, parking was at a premium – so much so that I had to leave Heidi on the main street overnight. Flores itself was a wonderful surprise. A colonial town made up of cobbled streets, red-roofed buildings, a historic plaza and church. It was small enough to walk, so we spent the rest of the day exploring every nook and cranny and then found a small café where we supped our first Guatemalan beers.

Sipping a cold beer on a warm evening having just crossed our first border together, Tracy and I couldn't quite believe what we were doing. Guatemala! We were in Guatemala and we'd got there on a motorcycle. I'd forgotten about the rain in Mexico and the broken road and the soaking wet clothes in San Cristóbal. Guatemala was warm and dry and Flores was beautiful. I got out my guidebook and started reading about the history of the place.

In the sixteenth century the Spanish *conquistadors* worked tirelessly to subdue the Mayan peoples of the Yucatan. The Itza people left Chichen Itza in the Yucatan and set up their capital on this small island, which became Flores; they called it Tayasal. The Spanish seem to have left them alone until 1697 when they attacked and destroyed Tayasal, the last independent Mayan state. Those who weren't killed or captured, fled and hid in the jungle. And that was the end of the place. The conquistadors built the church out of the ruins of the Mayan temple and destroyed everything else. The island had once been covered in Mayan temples and pyramids, but the Spanish soldiers destroyed it all. This revelation took the edge off my enjoyment of my beer but I still managed a smile on the way home to our hotel, tapping Heidi on the tank as I passed, hoping that she would still be there in the morning.

Eager to spend most of the next day at Tikal, we got up early and headed off towards the National Park. The road took us eastward first before turning north, around the lake but not close enough to see it. Near El Remate I could see a large motorcycle coming towards us. Initially I thought it might be a local bike but as it got nearer it was obviously another adventure biker. I slowed down, stopping on the crest of a menacingly large *tope*. The other bike also slowed to a stop. It was an old Triumph of some sort and by his accent, the rider was British.

"Hi, how are you?" I asked.

"Great. Great. Are you guys going to Tikal?" he said.

"Yes, we're just heading that way now."

"Look. Why don't you have my ticket? It's valid for twenty-four hours so it will let one of you in, and I don't need it anymore."

"Thanks, Thanks a lot. That's really kind."

"Take care," and with that he was off. I never learnt his name or saw him again.

Tikal itself was spectacular. Set in dense tropical jungle, its iconic pyramids soar above the jungle canopy. This is the largest excavated ancient city on the American continent and a UNESCO world heritage site. Inhabited for a much longer period of time than Palenque, its ceremonial centre contains fabulous temples, palaces and public squares. Tikal was the capital of one of the most powerful kingdoms of the ancient Maya. At its height its population could have reached 90,000. We know much more about Tikal than Palenque and can even list the thirty-three leaders who ruled it for eight hundred years.

By the ninth century the crisis of the 'Classic Mayan collapse' as it is known reached Tikal and its population plummeted. Again, no one really knows why, but over population and agricultural failure were probably to blame although other theories include foreign invasion, revolt, collapse of trade routes, epidemic disease and even aliens in space ships.

When you visit somewhere like Tikal, with its huge buildings towering above the jungle, it's hard to imagine that these places could remain 'lost' for centuries but Tikal certainly was, at least to outsiders. Hernán Cortés passed within a few miles in 1525 but never mentioned it and although stories were rife of a lost city in the jungle, Tikal was not recorded by Europeans until 1848. The site wasn't properly excavated until the 1960s but by the late 1970s it had been seen by millions on cinema screens worldwide. Space ships really did come to Tikal in 1977 when it was used as the site of the rebel base in the original Star Wars film – *Episode IV: A New Hope*.

Next day we left Flores and headed south on Route 13. Another well-maintained tarmac road, this one ran parallel to the Belize border. Initially I had planned on visiting all of Central America's countries but after talking it through with Tracy we realised that if we did that we would really be on a whistle-stop tour, not affording ourselves time to stop and enjoy any of the places we were passing through. It was a difficult decision to make and not perhaps the one I would have made if I'd been alone. I always like to be on the move and get annoyed if I miss anything out. Missing out the whole country of Belize was hard to take but deep down I knew that Tracy was right. The best experiences and most memorable times are had when you have time to stop, reflect and get under the skin of a place – I'd learnt that at Todos Santos. So with one eye on the road and the other staring at the mountain range off to my left that formed the border with Belize, we headed off to see what would happen to us next. We seemed to have left the rains of Mexico behind us and it was a gloriously sunny day – surely nothing could go wrong.

At Rio Dulce we turned west onto Route 7E. Marked as a dirt road on my map, this road had recently been paved and was in perfect condition. There were two tourist attractions down this way, and it wasn't long before we found the first: Guatemala's only castle. *El Castillo de San Felipe de Lara* was built in the seventeenth century to ward off nasty pirates (who seized it anyway in 1686). It was more of a fort than a castle but it was still quite exciting to find in the middle of Guatemala. Tracy likened it to a toy Zorro castle and ran around the place doing Zorro style swishes with her arm – or perhaps Tikal had left a lasting impression on her and she was fighting the Empire with her light-sabre. At least she seemed to have forgiven me for the rain of Mexico, so I kept quiet.

Half an hour further down the road we came to *Finca El Paraiso*. The attraction here was a hot spring waterfall which dropped twelve metres into a cool pool, surrounded by jungle. A hot spring waterfall is not something you come across very often; it was a magical spot and great to get a hot thermal 'power shower'. We both swam out to the waterfall and stood under the powerful torrent as we let it pound our shoulders and necks. That night we stopped across the road in a farm next to the lake. The farmer had built a few cabins by the water and we were made to feel at home. We told them we were vegetarians and they cooked us up some lovely tortillas, with eggs, re-fried beans, cheese and sour cream. All washed down with Guatemalan beer. Some days just couldn't be more perfect and that was most certainly one of them.

*

Having taken four months to cross three countries, they were now coming up on me fast and it wasn't long before we were saying goodbye to Guatemala and hello to Honduras. I'd been reading several bikers' blogs and they all complained about the Central American border crossings: chaos, bribery, heat/rain and three to four hours to cross. I think they had all chosen the wrong crossing points. We crossed into Honduras at Copán and it took an hour. Absolutely no hassle or bribery and as no one else was crossing we had the place to ourselves. The Honduran border officials were friendly and helpful, even if I was interrupting the Champions League football match that was on the TV – and all in all it was another surprisingly positive experience.

My theory was that because we were crossing at small border posts with little traffic, and few gringos, we were a novelty not a nuisance. The Pan American highway border crossings are filled with busloads of tourists, trucks and other traffic: a honey pot for 'helpers', pickpockets and chancers. I'd read how people had rushed through Honduras in a matter of hours as it had a reputation for bribery, theft and corruption. Just the previous year Honduras had had a revolution where the military had removed the president. It was an unpredictable time to be in an unpredictable land but I refused to accept that a whole country could be corrupt and felt sure that with the right attitude and a little luck we would find Honduras to be as welcoming and friendly as anywhere else. Tracy didn't care. She was still playing at being Zorro or a Jedi Knight – I still hadn't worked out which.

Honduras made the international news for its 2009 revolution and tourism had died. We arrived the following year and were certainly made to feel very welcome. It was a little ironic that Honduras should be the one Central American country to be rocked by recent revolution as in the 1980s it was the bastion of stability. The USA bankrolled capitalism in Honduras as El Salvador, Guatemala and Nicaragua all experienced uprisings and coups. President Reagan bolstered Honduran democracy and aided anti-left groups from El Salvador and Nicaragua (the infamous 'Iran – Contra Affair') from bases in Honduras. Therefore Honduras had much more of an American feel to it than anywhere I'd been since leaving Los Angeles – there were Wendy's, McDonald's and even Dunkin Donuts. It was slightly weird to see those eateries again having left the land of fast food two months previously.

Our first stop in Honduras was Copán Ruinas. The third and final Mayan ruins we would visit. While Palenque and Tikal might fight it out for splendour and architectural supremacy, Copán has sculptures and hieroglyphics. It is also the least visited of the three and although there weren't many people at Palenque or Tikal we thought we would pretty much have Copán to ourselves. Divided into two sections, the main site was only a short walk from the pretty town of the same name which was our home for two days. The second section, called Las Sepulturas, was a little further away and we thought we might give that part a miss. We set off under the early morning sun to walk to the ruins. The ruins were a couple of kilometres along the only road out of town and as it was the country's number one tourist attraction we didn't have any doubts that we would find the place.

After about an hour we began to worry that we must have somehow missed it. There was no traffic on the road and we seemed to be walking past cultivated fields near a river, with no sign of a huge archaeological complex. But how could we have passed Copán? We gave it another ten minutes before turning around and heading back. Half an hour later we came to a small track leading off to our left, down towards the river. There was no sign at the gate but there was a small empty car park at the bottom. I didn't think this could possibly be the famous ruins of Copán but we had nothing to lose: we'd already been walking for over an hour and it was now past 9 am and starting to get warm.

When we got down to the car park we noticed a small hut off to the right. There was a very bored looking soldier smoking a cigarette and someone who looked like a gardener. I went over and was about to ask, somewhat embarrassingly, for directions to Copán when he said:

"Hello, welcome to Las Sepulturas. Can I see your ticket?"

"Ah," I thought. "We don't have a ticket. Can we get one here?"

"No, no. You need to get your ticket at the main ticket office. Did you not go there first?"

I was stumbling around thinking of something to say when Tracy came over and saved the day. "We didn't realise but we wanted to come to this part of the ruins first, before everyone else. Is there no way you can let us in and we can pay for our ticket later?"

He looked at us for a minute and then said, "Of course, come with me."

And with that we had our own private tour guide showing us around the Las Sepulturas section of the Copán ruins. It was fascinating. This part is called the 'Residential Area' although, as with all things Mayan, nobody is completely sure. But certainly there were the remains of lots of houses here. Our guide spent about half an hour showing us around and filling us in on what he knew. By the eighth century AD this residential area was home to perhaps two hundred and fifty people housed in forty buildings organised around a dozen courtyards. Connected to the Great Plaza, which was part of the main ruins, by a causeway, archaeologists believe that Las Sepulturas was home to the rich and powerful. After the tour we had the place to ourselves and spent a further hour just wandering around, enjoying the place and the sights and sounds of the jungle. We left the way we had come in (the causeway that linked the two sites was not open to tourists) and I gave our guide $5 for his help in letting us in without a ticket and showing us around. He was over the moon.

Twenty minutes later, back up the road towards the town, we came across the main site. An open gate to our left revealed a large car park, now with several *collectivo* minibuses in it and an office off to the left. It was hard to imagine that we had walked right past it earlier in the day. My only excuse is that we were in such a rush to get there early we had marched off with heads down, not realising the entrance was a lot closer to town that we'd imagined; and the fact that we'd walked by before it had opened. Feeble excuses I know. I can ride a motorcycle, without a GPS, all the way from Alaska to Honduras but I can't find the country's largest tourist attraction.

Occupied for more than two thousand years, Copán reached its zenith from the fifth to ninth centuries. It certainly wasn't as large as Tikal and Palenque but it had three important features which, in my opinion, made it just as impressive overall. First, the stelae: Mayan stelae are sculptured stone monuments standing several metres tall. Created to glorify and honour great leaders, each stela records the deeds of the leader in hieroglyphics with perhaps a relief of their face or their exploits. These monuments were popular throughout the Mayan classic period (AD 200–900) but Copán is perhaps the best place to see them. Secondly, Copán has 'The Hieroglyph Stairway'. Built in AD 710, this stairway, measures twenty-one metres in length and climbs ten metres high through sixty-two steps. It takes its name from the 2200 glyphs that together form the longest known Mayan hieroglyphic text. Tourists now can't climb it and it is permanently shrouded with a cloth canopy to protect it from the elements. But it is still impressive to see. I left Tracy to marvel at the staircase as I headed round the corner for what was, for me, the highlight of the day: Copán's third big feature: the Mayan 'football pitch'.

Immediately north of the Hieroglyph Stairway is a genuine Mayan ball-court. Although little (again!) is really known of how this game was played, ball-courts are found all the way from the southern United States to

Nicaragua. The courts are usually very similar, a rectangular playing surface, in this case about twenty metres wide and twenty metres long, flanked by sloping walls which encroached on the playing surface. Originally the walls would have been plastered and brightly painted. At either end these walls opened up a little to give the whole pitch an 'I' shape when viewed from directly above. There is a lot of variation in pitch sizes; the one at Chichen Itza in the Yucatan measures ninety-five metres long and thirty wide. The ball was made of rubber and the idea seems to have been to keep it in the air, although I'm not clear whether there was some kind of net or goal to score in. Some literature suggests there was a human sacrificial aspect to the game with competing captured armies forced to play for their lives. Losing captains could even be beheaded and then, of course, the suggestion is that their head was used as a ball. It would certainly focus your concentration on the game. I've written to Sepp Blatter at FIFA, suggesting a change to the rules of football, but haven't, as yet, received a reply.

The modern town of Copán Ruinas, with its red-tiled roofed buildings and steep cobbled streets is very picturesque and that, along with some excellent coffee shops and restaurants made it a travellers' Mecca. One café even had banoffee pie on the menu! Honduras is famous for its cigars and bananas (it is the original Banana Republic after all) and every little shop was stocked to the rafters with them. They also had some lovely Mayan masks for sale. We'd seen these all the way from Mexico City and Tracy was getting a little fed up with not being able to buy any – the joy of motorcycle travel: no souvenirs. We spent the evening, eating wonderful food, drinking good beer and talking about the weird and wonderful world of the Mayans.

We left Copán the following morning with one aim in mind for that day: beer. An American beer enthusiast had built a brewery and hotel in the middle of the jungle near Lake Yojoa. I wrote down the directions and hoped it wouldn't be too difficult to find. I'd emailed the brewery and had been told: "If you have trouble finding us just ask for the gringo with the beer."

We rode for several hours through the gently rolling hills of eastern Honduras. Again, the road was in excellent shape, well-sealed all the way and, outside of the villages, blissfully free of traffic. Heidi was purring like a kitten, which was just as well as I was acutely aware that in Honduras I was probably about as far away from mechanical help as I was ever going to be. Honduras had no BMW dealers and, it seemed, very few large motorcycles of any make. I was sure Guatemala and Nicaragua were the same. Every time I turned the ignition key I prayed she would start up and I wouldn't get the dreaded 'error message' from the on-board computer. I had no reason to think that I would; after all, Heidi hadn't actually broken down at all and I'd renewed most of the 'serviceable' parts and more in the US.

We turned south just before San Pedro Sula and I started to pay attention to the instructions I'd been given: *From San Pedro Sula head south on CA-5 towards Tegucigalpa. About 10 Km after the bridge over the Ulua river turn off at the exit called El Caracol.*

This seemed easy enough and indeed I did spot a sign for El Caracol, as I sped past it. Turning around I pulled over at the junction and asked a local who was waiting at a bus stop if this was the way to El Caracol and Peña Blanca. He looked at me, looked at the sign clearly pointing down the road to El Caracol and nodded. Tracy muttered something about me being an idiot but I just wanted to make sure I was going the right way.

The next instruction read: *Pass through Rio Lindo, Pulhapanzak and Peña Blanca in each of which you will find a D and D Brewery sign guiding you to the brewery.* So I headed down the road, not a major road now, but still paved. Lake Yojoa was somewhere off to our right and we passed through a couple of small villages. Neither of us saw any D and D Brewery signs or indeed any signs at all. I was starting to get that sinking feeling. Why, oh why, didn't I have a GPS?!

After perhaps twenty minutes we came to a sizable town. I rode through it hoping to see a sign for either the brewery or the name of the place. I came out the other side none the wiser. Turning around I went back into the town and stopped the bike. Tracy jumped off to ask someone where we were. She came back telling me that we were in Peña Blanca. We were back on track. The instruction continued: *Pass through Peña Blanca until you reach the intersection and turn right on the road to Las Vegas and Santa Barbara.*

Turning the bike around again I headed along the main road until we reached the outskirts of the town and came to a junction. Again no street signs, but the road was at least heading off to the right. A small boy was walking past. He must have been about twelve years old and had obviously never seen such a huge motorcycle before. He was staring at us with a mixture of amazement and panic on his face. I lifted my flip-front helmet: "Hola," I greeted him in Spanish. "Do you know where the D and D Brewery is?"

He stared at me. I tried again. "D and D Brewery?"

Again, nothing. So I played my trump card. I asked him: "Do you know where the gringo is, who has beer?"

Tracy told me to stop scaring the poor child and we drove off as he gawked after us. I have no idea what he said when he got home, but I doubt anyone will ever believe him.

Taking a chance, I took the minor road that led off to the right. It curved around a small hill and then dropped down towards the lake. It came to an end in a very small village where the road just literally ran into the lake and ended. There was no D and D brewery here and yet again I turned the bike around and headed back to Peña Blanca. I was getting really rather frustrated now; we couldn't be far away but the light was starting to fade and we needed to find it before dark or we would have no chance. I didn't fancy wandering around Peña Blanca at night asking for a gringo with beer!

Back in the town I spotted a hotel sign and pulled up in the car park. Surely they would know where the competition was? Tracy wasn't too keen to humiliate herself again by asking for directions so I went up to the hotel and knocked. An old lady came to the door.

"Hello," I began, "We are looking for D and D Brewery. Run by an American gringo. Do you know where it is?"

"Yes," came the reply.

A moment's silence and then I added, "Can you tell me?"

"Yes. Go a little further down the road and take the road to the left. It's down there."

I got back on the bike and hoped that these meagre instructions would suffice. I took the turn-off she had suggested and immediately found myself riding through the middle of a street market. This was obviously Peña Blanca's market day and everyone was out on the streets buying chickens, brooms, clothes and just about anything else you could think of. They weren't expecting a motorcycle to get in their way and it took a little swerving and weaving to manoeuvre ourselves through the crowds. Once through, the road opened up and we crept up a hill that took us away from Peña Blanca and into the surrounding hills.

The instructions I had written down said: *Drive 4 km until you see the D and D Brewery sign. We are down that road.* I kept an eye on my dashboard and as we took a corner the way ahead opened up. There was a football pitch on our right and a series of buildings on the left. By the entrance to the last building which looked like a shop and bottle store, I saw three men standing together talking. I slowed down, pulled over and lifted my helmet. But before I could even ask for help, one of them said: "D and D brewery? Over there on the right."

And indeed, there it was. A large sign beckoning us to the D and D brewery. We had made it!

So, six hours after leaving Copán we were finally booking into D and D Brewery. We were shown into one room which had a jacuzzi. We were asked if we wanted to see a cheaper room. I said yes and then looked at Tracy and realised that the right answer was no. We took the jacuzzi room. That night, in the middle of a Honduran rainforest we had apricot beer with hops bought from Stowmarket, England, and a long bubbly soak.

CHAPTER 14

SANDINISTAS AND SLOTHS

"A few months ago, I told the American people I did not trade arms for hostages. My heart and my best intentions still tell me that's true, but the facts and evidence tell me it is not."

(Ronald Reagan, admitting to the Iran-Contra affair, 1987)

Tegucigalpa might win a competition for the best-named Central American capital city but it certainly has nothing else to recommend it. We could find no reason to stop off in the city and thankfully found the quickest way in and out as we headed on towards the border with Honduras. Like Guatemala, Honduras had happy smiling people who were welcoming and friendly; and lots and lots of lush, vibrant and, more importantly, *dry* jungle. It hadn't rained on us since we'd left Mexico and we were grateful for it. The roads in Honduras were generally fine although occasionally there were some huge potholes that could end a trip if you rode into them.

Passing one of those large potholes I wondered what would happen if I had an accident in this part of the world and whether it would be a good idea to involve the local police. We'd had nothing but positive, friendly dealings with police so far. I'd been stopped a couple of times heading down the Baja peninsula by very young military conscripts. They'd just asked me where I was going and wanted to see some documentation. From my encounters in Argentina I knew it was best to show a photocopy of something rather than the original. If the official takes your original, be it a driving licence or passport and then holds on to it, you are at their mercy. I'd had a colour photocopy of my UK driving licence made up and so far that had proved effective, although I never felt threatened and they always handed it back. In Mexico we'd stumbled across a couple of road-blocks set up by the drugs police but had been quickly waved through. One was on the coast road before I met Tracy and then again entering and leaving Tenosique near the Guatemalan border. So I hadn't come across the notorious Central American police, especially the Honduran ones, famous for their gun-toting demands for bribes. Then I banked around a corner on the road out of Tegucigalpa and was flagged down by a couple of gun-toting Honduran policemen.

'Here we go,' I thought. I'd heard stories of how they fine you for not carrying a fire extinguisher and red triangle on your bike and how they take all your documents and put them in their back pocket until you 'pay up'. I pulled over, lifted my flip-front helmet and smiled.

"Hola, ¿cómo estás?" I tried my best to smile, hoping my limited Spanish would impress him.

"Hello, señor. Where are you coming from?" he replied in Spanish.

"I'm from the UK, but we are travelling around Honduras. It's very nice."

"You have a big motorcycle. How fast can you go?"

"Oh, I don't know. I think it can go over 100 kph but I don't do that."

"Can I see your documents?"

So the pleasantries were over and I presumed we were about to get shafted. I handed over my spare UK driving licence and waited.

"You are from the UK. A long way from home. Where are you going?"

"Today we are heading for Danli. And then the border and Nicaragua."

"You must be careful on the roads: very dangerous drivers. And when you cross into Nicaragua. They are crazy."

He then shook my hand and smiled at us. The other policeman who had been eagerly looking around the bike stood to attention and saluted.

"We hope you have enjoyed our country and come back one day."

And the truth was that we *had* enjoyed our short time in Honduras. These two policemen had summed up the place for us beautifully. Initially it might look and sound quite scary and it certainly has a bad reputation but scratch beneath the surface, explore the place a little and open yourself up to new possibilities, and a whole new world emerges. Yes, just like Mexico the statistics are frightening. In 2010, according to UN published figures, Honduras had the dubious honour of being the murder capital of the world. With a rate of 82 murders per 100,000, Honduras was number one, ahead of El Salvador (66), and Ivory Coast (57). The USA figure was only 5 per 100,000 and the UK was well down the list at only 1.2. The magic number for Mexico was 18.

But statistics can deceive. I wouldn't think twice about riding Heidi up the east coast of the USA and visiting the capital. And yet Washington DC has a murder rate of 22, making it statistically more dangerous than Mexico. And in 2005 Scotland had the second highest murder rate in Europe (beaten, I was very surprised to discover, by Finland). The numbers are largely unimportant. As in Mexico, the vast majority of murders in Honduras are to do with smuggling: drugs, guns and people, and if you are not involved in any of those then there really shouldn't be too much to worry about.

If you rush through Honduras you may well only see the worst of it. It is no surprise that policemen, paid only a pittance, try to up their salary by stopping fast-moving *gringos* who have no interest in stopping and visiting their country. It is also probably a bit of a self-fulfilling prophesy as well. I'd read about people who were so anxious that they had got up before sunrise in El Salvador to cross into Honduras, sped across it as quickly as possible and exited into Nicaragua, all in one day. Perhaps, when stopped by Honduran police, their anxiety might display itself in anger and frustration. They then post their unpleasant experiences online and the whole thing snowballs. My tip is to take the inland route. I can't speak for the Pan American Highway but the route we took through the country was wonderful and the people friendly. And that is still the only time I've ever been saluted by a policeman!

By now we'd got into a daily routine with our riding and had it down to a fine art. Usually we'd be up and on the road by 9 am. Tracy doesn't eat breakfast so I usually would have to try to find a cup of coffee somewhere. Coffee in Mexico and Honduras was quite good; not so good in Guatemala. A typical 'local' breakfast would involve eggs, usually scrambled with tomatoes, chillies and onion. In Mexico this was called *Huevos Mexicana*, the colours of the Mexican flag – green, red and white. We generally tried to cover two hundred miles or thereabouts in a day. This could take between four and six hours depending on the road surface and traffic. We'd tend not to stop for lunch but would dip into petrol stations to rest and snack (there are no lay-bys in this part of the world). The plan would be to arrive at our destination between two and five in the afternoon. We'd have a look around if there was anything to see and then have a rest in our room – write the blog, read a book, plan the next day, wash socks, use the internet if we had it. Sometimes I would even look at the bike and check that the wheels were still there or something technical like that.

Early evening we would go out to eat and sample the local beer, then head back to our room. I'd downloaded some TV series and audio books onto my Netbook and we both had paperback books on the go. Yet another benefit of travelling was the fact that I was reading a lot more.

It was around this time that I got an email from Phil at Motoquest. I had written to him while I was still in the United States about all the problems and expense I'd had with Heidi so soon after buying her. I didn't really expect him to reply but he did and what's more he agreed that what had happened with Heidi wasn't right and even suggested that he compensate me. He agreed to post me a cheque for $2000 and wished me well on my travels. I really hadn't expected this and wrote to thank him for being so honest. He could have totally ignored my email and, although I still did feel a little aggrieved over all the problems I'd had, Phil had restored my faith in humanity with his gesture.

On our last night in Honduras we found the only hotel in town, parked up in the secure car park out the back and settled into our room. About thirty minutes later I heard some English being spoken in the corridor and opened our door to find two bikers standing in the hallway.

Chrissy and Alan were from New Zealand and had been on the road for six months. They'd flown to America and bought two Kawasakis. Alan was on a KLR 650 and Chrissy on a smaller KLR 250. It was great to meet up with other bikers again and spend time comparing notes on where we'd been and what we'd done. We went out for a pizza together and planned to cross the border into Nicaragua the following day.

Before starting my trip I really didn't know much about Guatemala or Honduras but I had heard of Nicaragua. Growing up in the 1980s it would have been hard not to. And I associated Nicaragua more than any other country in this part of the world with revolution, class struggle and protest. I remember it as a *cause célèbre* of 1980s UK protests. I was a student in those days and Nicaragua was one of those places left wing British students banged on about. I even remember buying expensive Sandinista-friendly Nicaragua coffee. Later, being a history teacher, I'd updated my understanding of the place and as we crossed from Honduras my knowledge came flooding back to me as we rode towards Esteli.

The USA has always seen Central and South America as coming within its 'sphere of influence' (known as the 'Monroe Doctrine' after the nineteenth century US President). Nicaragua has been no exception to this and throughout the twentieth century, America had a hand in guiding (and selecting) Nicaraguan governments. In the 1920s and 30s in particular the USA dominated Nicaraguan politics, installing and ousting governments as it saw fit. In 1933 the US marines headed home from Nicaragua having handed power over to the US-trained conservative *Guardia Nacional* led by Anastasio Somoza Garcia. The following year Somoza (as he was known) engineered the assassination of his Liberal opponent, Augusto C Sandino. This resulted in Somoza becoming President and de facto dictator by 1937.

Thus began two decades of oppression. Somoza became an internationally recognised and notorious dictator amassing huge personal wealth, while the people of Nicaragua remained poor. Somoza supported the USA and the CIA used Nicaragua as a launch pad for missions into Guatemala and the failed Bay of Pigs invasion of Cuba in 1961. In return, successive US Governments supported Somoza. He was assassinated in 1956 but succeeded by his eldest son (Luis Somoza Debayle) who was himself succeeded by his younger brother (Anastasio Somoza Debayle).

Opposition to the Somoza dynasty grew in Nicaragua in the 1960s and various groups merged to form the *Frente Sandinista de Liberación Nacional* (FSLN) led by Santos Lopez, an old fighting partner of Sandino in the 1920s and 30s, who'd become a general at the age of only 15! Poverty, inequality and the corruption and embezzlement of the Somoza family fuelled support for the FSLN. Then a massive earthquake struck Managua, the capital in 1972. Between 5,000 and 10,000 people died and 300,000 were made homeless. Interestingly Mick Jagger's wife, Bianca, returned to her homeland to look for her parents, increasing public awareness of the tragedy.

International aid poured in – and Anastasio Somoza stole it. This was the last straw for Nicaragua and even the small but influential middle class turned against the corrupt regime. By 1974 opposition was widespread. The assassination of one of the leaders of the opposition, Chamorro, in 1978, led to a general strike and the FSLN occupied the National Palace. By early 1979 the Sandinistas were ready for their final offensive and Somoza knew it. On July 17th 1979, as the Sandinistas entered Managua, Somoza resigned and fled the country. He was assassinated the following year in Paraguay. 1979 was a busy year for America as it was also in this year that General Pinochet, backed by the CIA, overthrew and killed democratically elected Salvador Allende in Chile, but that's another story.

In 1980 Daniel Ortega Saavedra became effective leader of Nicaragua and the Sandinista set about righting the wrongs of the Somoza years. I will not pretend the Sandinista were perfect. They ruled by decree and committed human rights abuses themselves but they did at least spend some of the country's money on health care and education.

The Carter administration tried to salvage its influence in Nicaragua by offering aid to the Sandinistas in 1979. However, by 1980 America was becoming concerned with the increasing number of Cuban and Soviet advisers in Nicaragua and allegations that the Sandinistas were beginning to provide arms to leftist rebels in El Salvador. And the dove-ish Carter had been replaced by the hawk-ish Ronald Reagan. President Reagan funded the anti-Sandinistas (known as *Contras* – based in Honduras). The CIA planned to mine Nicaraguan harbours, as revealed in 1984 and declared illegal by the International Court of Justice. America initiated a Cuban-style embargo of Nicaragua in 1985. This created hardship for the embattled people of Nicaragua, cemented the popularity of the Sandinistas at home and called attention to their cause around the world. While Reagan was keen to push further, the US Congress thought he was going too far and rejected further military aid for the Contras in 1985. Story over? No. Oliver North (allegedly without Reagan's permission) orchestrated an ambitious plan whereby the CIA illegally sold weapons to Iran (so they could keep fighting Iraq to whom America was also selling weapons) and diverted the proceeds to the Contras: the infamous Iran-Contra affair. This history still makes my blood boil.

So it was with a totally open mind and unbiased heart that I crossed the border and rode into the Sandinista town of Esteli. Four of us on three bikes made crossing the border a breeze and we rode into a new country with confidence and excitement. These Central American countries were small compared to North America and there was actually very little that changed from border to border but a new country was always exciting, and we rode down to Esteli and our first stop.

*

Little did we know that Esteli was holding some sort of fiesta that night and finding somewhere to stay wasn't easy. The first two places we tried were totally full and the third only had one room. We tossed a coin and Chrissy and Alan took the room and we moved on. A few blocks away I found a place with a room. It was dark and dreary, the mattress was lumpy and filthy but we took it – both sleeping in our sleeping sheets. Going to the toilet in the middle of the night I spotted several creatures running for the cracks in the floor and the only reason we couldn't hear the wildlife crawling around was because they were not as loud as our neighbours, who were having their own private 'fiesta' in the room next door! The room's shortcomings were tolerable because it was so great to be able to walk around the fiesta-fuelled streets and soak in the atmosphere of small town Nicaragua in party mode.

We said goodbye to Chrissy and Alan the following morning as they were heading for Leon and we were going to Granada. We had only been together a day but had got on well. They were a great couple and we wished them well on the rest of their journey down to Argentina. I later read on their blog that Alan had had a nasty accident in Ecuador. He was overtaking a cycling peloton when one of the cyclists veered over the road and hit him. Alan broke his shoulder and fractured his elbow. He took a few weeks to recover and needed to get the bike fixed as well, but they managed to carry on, and eventually made it all the way down to Argentina.

Finding somewhere to stay in Granada was even harder than little Esteli. Leaving Tracy to guard the bike as usual (I wasn't quite sure what she would be able to do if a group of machete-wielding thieves came along) I headed off around town to look for somewhere suitable. I found some cheap places with no parking and some expensive hotels, but nothing in between. I went back to Tracy who was sat chatting to a local pottery seller. Perhaps she thought the pots could be ammunition to throw at the machete-wielding thieves if they arrived.

After our experience at Esteli we opted to upgrade and stay in an expensive place that was connected to a small chocolate museum and made some really wonderful hot chocolate. The price of our room included an 'all-you-can-eat' breakfast, use of the swimming pool and a free massage. So, we used the pool in the afternoon, got up early for a big breakfast and then had a massage before checking out – and agreed that every now and again, luxury is good. The masseurs had spent ages working on our backs – riding the bike had taken its toll and I felt so much better for having had a masseur beat me up a little.

So with aspirations for continued relaxation, we headed on to the stunningly beautiful *Laguna de Apoyo*. The lake is a 48-square kilometre stretch of shining blue water nestled within the old jungle-covered crater walls of the Apoyo volcano. Riding into the crater we caught tantalising glimpses through the trees of inviting cool water. The volcano is not completely dormant and at some spots on the shore you can see steaming bubbles coming through and stick your fingers into hot sulphurous mud. The Lonely Planet guide mentioned the 'Monkey Hut' as a cool place to stay and I'd phoned them the previous day to check they had space. We arrived at midday to find they were full. So much for planning ahead. There was, however, a new place next door. We walked over and met Tim. Nicaraguan-born, American raised, Tim said we could stay although they weren't really open and no one else was staying; he offered up the spacious lakeside flat at a very reasonable rate. We were going to stay just one night, but ended up staying there for three. Tim was super-friendly and helpful and made us feel right at home. We had a private balcony overlooking the lake, with a hammock and a canopy of pink jasmine. It was idyllic and perhaps the best place we stayed in the whole of Central America.

While we were there we went on a night tour up another nearby and very active volcano, where we visited a lava tunnel and saw hundreds of bats as they emerged from their cave at dusk. This part of Nicaragua made us feel like we were on holiday, but it was getting close to Christmas and we had to be in Costa Rica for that, so with a heavy heart we said goodbye to Tim and headed for the Nicaraguan/Costa Rican border. By now I felt I had the hang of Central American crossings but Tim warned me that this one could be frustrating and as we were on the Pan Americana now I did expect it to be busy and chaotic. I had no idea!

This particular border was undoubtedly the most frustrating and certainly the worst experience we had moving between countries. There were no signs telling us where to go, just lots of queues of equally baffled-looking tourists. After the ease with which we'd crossed into the country it seemed ridiculous. I asked around and eventually was directed to a line of people outside a nondescript building. The queue went into the building but I didn't know how far or indeed what was in there. It moved very slowly in the morning sun. Obviously I was in full motorcycle gear and was getting hot and flustered before we'd even started. Eventually we made it into the building where, if anything, it was hotter. But at least I could now see my destination. There was an official sat behind a desk surrounded by piles of paper. He was checking people's passports and stamping them. It appeared that he was simultaneously stamping people both into and out of Nicaragua.

After about forty-five minutes I got to the front. Even though every person in front of me seemed to take two or three minutes to get through their paperwork it took me only thirty seconds. Isn't that always the way? With passports stamped, we just had to deal with the bike paperwork.

Crossing Central American borders with a motorcycle can be a bit of a lottery because each country has its own rules and ways of doing things. Generally you need to get a piece of paper confirming temporary importation of the bike and sometimes you have to buy insurance. This was not intrinsically difficult; the hard part was discovering the precise requirements, and then where exactly to go in order to meet them. Sometimes it appears as if no one has ever done this before and they are trying to make it as difficult as possible. Of course this isn't the case and a little perseverance and a friendly smile usually does the trick.

Nicaragua, however, was trying my patience. There were no signs whatsoever on any of the buildings and I had no idea what to do next or where to do it. Again I asked, but the problem of asking for help at a border is that the 'helper' will latch on to you, show you what to do and where to do it but then expect payment for it. I'd managed to avoid needing any help at any other border but at this border I think the helpers' union and the Customs and Excise people had teamed up and created such a confusing system that it did actually pay to get some assistance. I asked someone to show me what to do next and with his 'help' we got the bike inspected, checked and the paperwork done. It took about half an hour but on my own I would have had absolutely no idea and we could have been there all day. Altogether, it took almost two hours to get out of Nicaragua and we had to pay $2 each for the privilege.

The Costa Rican side was better organised and at least it was free to get in. Costa Rica was, however, the first country that insisted on Tracy actually standing in a queue and handing her own passport over. I also had to get motor insurance at the border: $25 for three months. It's never really very clear how official these insurance papers are but I assumed a fine for not having it would cost more. In Nicaragua I'd paid $15 for something similar. So finally, we were through.

Nicaragua, while geographically and culturally similar to Honduras or even Guatemala, had also been a land of contrasts. Crossing into the country had been totally hassle-free but leaving was a nightmare. Our first night's accommodation had been the worst on the trip whereas Tim's lodge on the lake was pure bliss. Again I was reminded that our opinions of places (and people) are guided by our experiences of them and those experiences can occur at random. Chrissy had said that she thought the driving in Central America was awful, whereas I didn't think it was that bad. Everyone's view of the world is tainted by their own experience and so much of that is just down to luck.

*

So the next link in the chain was Costa Rica – 'rich coast' in Spanish – hard to argue with that. Costa Rica was always going to be different. It has a very well-developed tourist industry and is a popular destination for North Americans and Europeans, especially around Christmas. It was going to be richer, more developed, cleaner, busier and more expensive. This is what I wrote on my blog after being there for a couple of days:

Costa Rica is wonderful. Full of colour, animals, birds and North Americans. It is also noticeably more expensive than any other of the Central American countries we've been to. And much more Americanised. American food chains, supermarket, prices in US$ and most people speak to us in English. All a bit of a shock after two months in Central America. There is no doubt that Costa Rica is a beautiful country but I can't help thinking that crossing the border from Nicaragua I crossed out of Central America and into some sort of Disney-fied, US version of it. Costa Rica has taken the good bits out of Central America, cleaned them up and presented them to the tourist with 4 and 5 star facilities and prices to match. Great if you've come here straight from London or Los Angeles; a little disappointing and even disturbing if you've spent two months getting here overland.

No visit to Costa Rica would be complete without a stay in a rainforest so we headed south from the border and then east into the hills, to Monteverde. The road was interesting, especially as I had assumed that Costa Rica would have some of the best roads in Central America. I was wrong. Once we left the Pan Americana we were soon on a steep gravel road heading up into the mountains. It only took about an hour to climb up to Monteverde ('green mountain') but the steepness of the road and the potholes and wash-boarding made it one of the worst roads we'd been on. Tracy certainly wasn't a happy bunny and by the time we got to the top she was less than impressed with Costa Rica's infrastructure, taking into account its general pricing and profile.

Once settled into the friendly little 'Pension Eddy', with extra blankets as it was quite cold at altitude, we soon forgot about the bumpy ride up and explored our surroundings. Situated at 1,400 metres (4,600 feet) Monteverde is technically a cloud forest and supports more than a hundred species of

165

mammal, four hundred species of bird and countless insects and plants. The cool mountain air was fresh and invigorating and having spent a few days on the Pan Americana sucking in fumes I filled my lungs with life-enhancing oxygen. Leaving the bike at the hostel we went for a day's walk through the cloud forest hoping, in vain, to spot a few frogs. I'd always associated Costa Rica with fluorescent tree frogs and wanted to see a real live one for myself. With little success on our own, we opted for a guided night walk and saw some coatis (raccoon-like things), orlinga (lemur-like creatures), two orange-kneed tarantulas and, finally, some frogs.

Our next stop in Costa Rica was San José, and yet another BMW shop. There was nothing wrong with Heidi this time but I needed to change the final drive oil as I'd now done 12,000 miles since Idaho Falls. I met Alvero, whom I'd been emailing, and he got the mechanics to have a look at the bike while he quizzed me about my trip. I reeled off the places I'd been to and how long I'd been on the road and Alvaro was amazed and impressed. He had been to the United States, but never to any other Central American country and was interested to hear what I thought of his neighbours. This surprised me a little but he hadn't been the first person like this. Many middle-class, educated Central Americans had travelled to the US but very few had visited the country next door. I suppose America is the 'Promised Land' – why would you spend your valuable time and money going to somewhere very similar to where you live? But it seemed a shame, since it helped reinforce the misconceptions and fears people had about their neighbours. Again and again I talked to people who were excited about the trip I was on, hoped I really enjoyed their country, but were extremely worried about me moving on to the next country which was full of crazy murderers, thieves and corrupt police. Talking to people like Alvaro, however, also reminded me to cherish every minute of my trip. It wasn't going to last forever – we were now only one country away from Panama.

The guys at BMW San José were efficient, friendly and helpful and checked that everything was as it should be. Alvaro did suggest that the battery was getting a little 'tired' and I made a mental note to possibly change it when I got to South Africa. He gave me a Motorrad Costa Rica BMW sticker to add to my Missoula, Chico and Mexico ones and then we were on our way again. Heading north east of San José we were off to the Caribbean coast to stop for two weeks, over Christmas, on a volunteer programme.

*

Situated thirty kilometres south of the port of Limon on Costa Rica's Caribbean coast, Avarios Sloth Sanctuary is unique. It was set up by Judy

Avey-Arroyo in 1992 when some locals brought an injured sloth to her hotel. Avarios has now expanded and looks after over a hundred injured and orphaned sloths. When planning my trip I knew I wanted to stop and volunteer in Costa Rica and when I stumbled across this place it just seemed ideal. We arrived at the sloth sanctuary three days before Christmas and were met by Judy and the other volunteers. There were eight of us in total: two American veterinary students, two from the UK and an older French couple. The first thing we needed to do was to learn more about sloths, so over a cold beer our new friends told us what we needed to know.

There are two types of sloth: the two-fingered (Choloepus) are omnivorous, and eat mainly leaves and fruits, whereas the three-fingered ones (Bradypus) are herbivores, subsisting solely on a variety of leaves. The sanctuary housed about ninety two-fingered and ten three-fingered sloths. All sloths live in trees and only ever come to the ground to defecate (which happens about once a week) and occasionally to move tree. When people think of sloths they assume they sleep most of the time. This may be true in captivity but recent research suggests that in the wild they may sleep for as little as ten hours a day. The other assumption about sloths is that they don't move very quickly and this is certainly true. They have a very slow metabolic rate and don't need to get anywhere in a hurry. Sloths do have natural enemies – harpy eagles, jaguars and snakes – but as sloths don't really taste very nice they don't have a huge problem. They are very light for their size and can retreat to the smallest branches if pursued. Should they be attacked they often survive thanks to their tough hides, tenacious grips, and extraordinary ability to heal from grievous wounds. Sloths have been known to survive a ninety-foot fall to the forest floor, and withstand respiratory arrest for forty minutes.

However, as man has encroached on their pristine forest environments things have got tougher for sloths. They are an easy target for children who, not knowing any better, catch them, try to make pets of them or even try to sell them on the road to passing tourists. Sloths climb telegraph poles thinking they are trees and get horribly maimed when they are electrocuted, and many sloths are now attacked by domestic animals, especially dogs. Every couple of weeks a new animal is brought into the sanctuary and as sloths can live for thirty years the work of the sanctuary goes on and on.

So, having settled into our new home and having learnt a little about the creatures we were there to help, Tracy and I quickly fell into the routine of sloth volunteers.

Unfortunately, although sloths sleep a lot they do wake up at dawn, so our days started at 5.30 am. We began by going into the sloth enclosures and waking them up. Each sloth had their own personal towel, a sort of foliage substitute, and most of them wrapped themselves up in it at night. Our first job was to remove that, shake it out and check it wasn't infested with ants or other animals. We then had to record whether there was any poo in the cages. Any urine or faeces was recorded, along with whether they had eaten all of their dinner overnight. Some sloths are in individual cages but many share, in which case you obviously didn't know who'd been poo-ing but it seemed that one would set the others off and if there was one pile of poo there was probably another one somewhere as well. I was also amazed to discover that sloths have unusual necks. Almost all mammals have seven cervical vertebrae. Only manatee and sloths don't. Choloepus sloths have five and a special adaptation on the skull that allows them to rock their heads backward at a 45° angle as they hang from a branch to look for food or danger. Bradypus have nine vertebrae, which allow them to rotate their heads up to 300 degrees. Quite amazing.

After searching for sloth poo we prepared their breakfast. The Choloepus ate leaves for breakfast which we had to check for tiny snails (which could kill them). This was probably the most unpleasant job of all as the morning mozzies were hungry but we couldn't use repellent while preparing sloth food. After checking and washing the leaves we fed them breakfast, placing a handful of leaves in the cage and encouraging then to get up and eat by hand-feeding them a leaf of two. After a few days we began to learn that each sloth had its own personality and each took to breakfast, as we do, in a different way. Every sloth had been given a name (although, or course, they didn't answer to it) and over breakfast, while a hundred sloths were munching on crisp, crunchy leaves the odd volunteer voice would be heard saying:

"Chewbacca! Come on, you really should eat the stems."

"Oh, Jonny, what have you done?"

"Hershey, don't do that to Mocha, she's your sister. Leave her alone and eat your leaves."

"Winston! No Winston, that's not yours!"

"Latoya! Come on, time to wake up."

It was almost like being back in a classroom again!

It took about two hours to prepare and feed the sloths and then we would head back to the volunteer house for our own breakfast. At 9 am we would return to the enclosures to 'walk the babies'. The young sloths need to get out of their cages and see and smell the jungle so we would each take one (they happily cling to you) and go for a walk. There was something quite magical about taking a year-old baby sloth out into a forest. The baby would cling to my T-shirt with its rather large claws. The Choloepus liked to look over my shoulder and up longingly toward the trees. The Bradypus had incredibly flexible necks and would constantly have their heads turned around, looking at the way ahead and up, hopefully at the canopy above.

By 11 am it was time to prepare lunch. We peeled and cut up hundreds of carrots and other vegetables into long, finger-sized chunks. This took about an hour, by which time our own lunch (rice, beans, plantain,) had been prepared for us in the volunteer house. At 2 pm we would return to the sloths to feed them lunch. Each Choloepus sloth would get a plate full of carrots, potato and a little dog food while the Bradypus could only stomach leaves. By 3 pm we were done for the day. Afternoons would be spent canoeing up the mango creek looking for birds, racoons and even some wild sloths. Or we could walk up the road to the local beach. If it was raining, which it did a lot of in the first week, we just sat under the thatched roof of the creekside shelter using the sanctuary's wi-fi. Occasionally a cruise ship would be docked at Puerto Limon and coach-loads of tourists would arrive at the sanctuary to be shown around by the local staff. It destroyed the peace and quiet of our afternoon but brought in much-needed revenue. On Christmas day we had over two hundred visitors.

On our first day off from the sanctuary we decided to take the bike out (I hadn't even sat on her for six days) and head down the coast exploring. For once it wasn't raining and we'd chosen a good day as over 300 cruise ship tourists were about to descend on the place. We donned our gear and got on the bike. And then the dreaded event happened. I'd been fearful that this would happen one day and got that horrible feeling you get when you press the ignition key and – nothing. Well not exactly nothing. It made a 'click click click' noise. I thought back to the mechanic in San José who'd told me the battery was getting tired. I hadn't touched the bike for a week and it didn't take a genius to guess what had happened.

I posted a few questions about BMW batteries on the horizon website and then we caught a bus to the nearest town to have a look around. It was raining so coastal Costa Rica wasn't at its best but we were still in warm, lush jungle rather than in the midst of a European winter.

Back at the sanctuary that evening I went online to find that I had already received several useful comments. Most people seemed to think that it was probably just a dead battery although it could be something more serious. The first thing to do, however, would be to test the battery. Luckily this had happened in Costa Rica and only four hours by bus from San José – I dreaded to think how I would have dealt with this if it had happened in Honduras or Guatemala. I slept on it, thinking that I would have to take the battery out and take it to San José so I could get a new one. However in the morning I remembered that one of the staff, who went by the wonderful name of Milady, had commented on my bike when we'd arrived. She had a small motorcycle herself and I went to find her to ask if, by any chance, she knew a mechanic. She did. She gave him a call and he said he would come over the following day, New Year's Eve.

The mechanic turned up on New Year's Eve, took a look at my battery, declared it dead and told me he could get a new one the following day. He did; it worked and only cost me $50. I have no idea how he managed it or where he produced it from but the New Year had got off to a great start.

To celebrate, Milady took us out for a ride; we two on the 1200 and she on her 125. We were heading for her brother's house and her niece's first birthday party. She said it wasn't far which I took to mean less than half an hour. It took well over an hour to get there. We rode along dirt tracks, through a massive banana plantation, over a very rickety bridge and finally made it to her brother's farm in the middle of the plantation. Her whole family was there, which included five sisters and two brothers and each sister had a handful of their own children. There must have been over fifty people partying in the cowshed in the middle of a banana plantation and we were the centre of attention. Milady was proudly showing off her foreign friends and Heidi certainly got a lot of attention. It was wonderful to have been invited to such a joyous Costa Rican party, it was just a shame that, as I was riding I couldn't partake of the festive alcohol. That didn't stop Tracy however, or indeed Milady, and we left in the small hours, riding through the dead of night, past row upon row of huge silent banana trees. Milady swerving across the road on her bike and Tracy falling asleep behind me, occasionally banging her helmet against mine. I felt like I was in some weird Gabriel Garcia Marquez novel.

Although I had been very keen to do some conservation work, and the two weeks at the turtle project in Baja were wonderful I had always been a little dubious about helping out at a sanctuary. However, some animals cannot be returned to the wild so what can you do? And I felt the sentiments of the Sloth Sanctuary were spot on. They were there to '*Rescue, Research and Educate*'. Rescue sloths in Costa Rica who have been run over, electrocuted on the pylons and captured by people. Educate the local population but also the wider world and research these little-known creatures. There is so much we still don't know about sloths; indeed I think it was only four or five years ago that their anatomy was first mapped.

Obviously all one hundred or so sloths are well looked after but they are still caged. It's depressing to see so many animals in small cages and it's hard not to think they would be better off (or at least the ones who survived would be) in the wild. But it's easy to anthropomorphise and if any wild animal is 'suited' to living in a cage it's got to be a sloth. In the wild they mainly live in a small area. They don't move around much, are fairly solitary and like hanging upside down. So a wire cage with poles for climbing on is fine.

Volunteering had been good fun and very educational. I'd learnt a lot about sloths, challenged some of my preconceived ideas on conservation and had a rest from riding my bike. I'd also got a much better understanding of what Costa Rica had to offer and ended up refreshed and renewed for the last leg of my North American journey. And Heidi had a brand new battery. However, all good things come to an end and it soon became time for us to move on once more.

Our second to last day at the sanctuary, however, started badly: two of the baby sloths had died. It is notoriously difficult to rear orphaned sloths and although Judy had kept a twenty-four hour watch on them, rearing them in special incubators, they had died in the night. We carried on with our chores and jobs but there was an air of sadness hanging over the place.

Later that day I was cleaning out some of the cages when I came across a very agitated sloth. Mocha shared a cage with her brother Hershey and she was whimpering to herself and moving quite swiftly around the cage when I unlocked the door. I noticed a few spots of blood on the ground of the enclosure and looked up at Mocha who was swinging from a bar at eye level. Initially she looked all right but then I noticed something odd. Her left hind leg looked much thicker than it should and was wet and matted. On closer inspection I realised why. Clinging to her leg was a tiny newborn baby sloth! It can only have been six inches long, was covered in fur and holding on for dear life. I couldn't believe it. Mocha had given birth and nobody had even known she was pregnant! I was just about to close the cage and go and get Judy when something alerted me to her other leg. And there it was: another baby clinging to her other hind leg. A double Mocha!

I rushed to get Judy. The excitement and bewilderment on her face was palpable. She quickly prized the twins from Mocha and took them to the infirmary. It seems that captive sloths are notoriously poor mothers and the best we could do would be to take the young from Mocha and hand rear them. Judy took over, she'd done this a few times before, and later that day Tracy and I visited the newborns who were housed in a specially built small infirmary annexed to Judy's bedroom.

The twins were wrapped up in blankets sleeping in a small incubator. Judy brought them out to meet us. Measuring about six inches long they were tiny, frail and vulnerable. It was hard to see how they would survive.

"We do have a sort of tradition here that if a volunteer finds a sloth they can name it. And this is special, Dom. These are the first ever sloth twins found in either captivity or the wild. I have never heard of it before and although we thought that sloths could have twins it has never been documented. You are the first person in the world to find twin sloths."

I was speechless. This was a responsibility, to name the world's first sloth twins. Tracy and I would have to go away and think about it.

Mum was Mocha and Dad was her brother Hershey, so some sort of chocolate-based name seemed appropriate. But when not masquerading as a biker chick, Tracy worked for the Royal Shakespeare Company so I asked her if there were any famous Shakespearian twins. Immediately she said that as the sloths had been born on January 3rd which was nearly 'Twelfth Night', they should be called *Sebastian* and *Viola*. We went to tell Judy the good news and to have one sneaky last look at the baby sloths.

Months later we heard that *Animal Planet* had been down to Costa Rica to make a programme about the sanctuary and the twins had featured on it. We found a clip on YouTube. Judy had heard Viola as Violet, but it was still great to see that they'd become famous and had brought attention, and hopefully funding to the sanctuary.

Christmas with Sloths

CHAPTER 15

PANAMA HERE WE COME!

*"Wandering around our America has changed me more than I thought.
I am not me anymore. At least I'm not the same me I was."*

(Ernesto 'Che' Guevara)

It was a short ride down the Caribbean coast on Route 36 from the sloth sanctuary to the Panamanian border. At Sixaola, formalities for leaving Costa Rica were completed within minutes but to get into Panama we had to cross the river by bridge. This was the only place to cross, short of riding hundreds of miles back to San José and then down the Pacific coast on the Pan Americana. I would have assumed that the bridge would be maintained in a reasonably good condition if I hadn't already read about a biker crossing it in the rain who had slipped and put his foot through a gap in the wooden boards. Chrissy had also emailed me to tell me that the bridge was 'scary and bloody horrible'. So I approached with some trepidation.

About two hundred metres long, the bridge was built in 1908 and looked even older. It was surprising to learn that the Panamanian government had actually invested $500,000 in repairing it since the millennium. I didn't see any evidence of this. Built of cast iron that was now rusting, with plants and even small trees growing out of the supports, the bridge was in a state of total disrepair. It had a train track running down the middle and on either side of that about a three-foot-wide walkway for vehicle wheels and pedestrians. The whole thing cannot have been more than nine feet wide and the fences at the edges were more for show than support.

People were walking down the middle of the train tracks on both sides, in both directions. When a large truck crossed over, the pedestrians would have to shuffle to the sides of the bridge leaning outwards and clinging to the shaky railing which, in all honesty, didn't look strong enough to support the strain. I rode up onto the right-hand side walkway and started to ride very slowly along the loose planks of wood. Through the gaps in between you could clearly see the drop of about sixty feet into the muddy waters of the Rio Sixaola. It was less scary than the road to Palenque in Mexico, since I was at least doing it on a warm sunny day and without any trucks behind blaring their horns, urging me to go faster. It was an interesting experience, but as an

173

international border crossing it was a disgrace. I'd read that there were plans for a new bridge but at $13 million, they were still just plans. A big gap in funding still had to be bridged before a new structure would be built...

The Panamanian side of the border was chaotic. There were no signs telling us where to go and when I joined the back of the queue to get our passports stamped it didn't move an inch for thirty minutes. I finally got them stamped and then went to the window labelled *Aduana* to start the process for importing the bike. They told me I first had to go and get insurance and when I asked where that was they just pointed vaguely down the road. We got on the bike and rode off. After a few hundred metres the road opened up and we were clearly heading out of town. I stopped at a police hut to ask and they sent me back to the aduana office, claiming it was somewhere nearby. We rode back and found a side road and optimistically headed down it. I stopped the bike near a small row of shops, a man came over and without me even asking, told me that the insurance office was upstairs in the building I had stopped next to. I went up the stairs and found myself in a huge hardware shop.

Just as I was about to turn around to leave, presuming I'd got the instructions wrong, the lady behind the counter gestured to me that I should walk through the shop and out on to the balcony! I did as I was told and there indeed was a tiny office tucked into the corner of the balcony with the word *Seguro* (Insurance) hand-written on the door. Unbelievable. Here was the office where everyone who brings a vehicle into Panama must come to buy insurance. It consisted of a woman with a computer and a printer. Why she couldn't be in the aduana office, or next to it, I had no idea.

I could have just ridden off, past the unmanned police checkpoint and into Panama without stopping and buying insurance and I probably would have got away with it. The only answer I could come up with was that nobody who worked in this system had ever or would ever have to use it so they were unconcerned about its obvious defects.

I bought the 'compulsory' $15 insurance and returned to the aduana office. I then waited for over an hour as they laboured to fill in the correct forms in order to process my details. This involved, amongst other things, a long debate about where I was from. Even though they had my passport in front of them they kept asking me. And then we had the whole 'where is the bike registered?' problem. Initially they thought Alaska was in Russia and it took some convincing to get them to put USA on the form. All of this was conducted with the three customs officers sitting in an air conditioned office whilst I, in black bike gear, was standing out in the sun talking through a small hole on the window which was positioned four feet off the ground. I was starting to lose my cool, both physically and metaphorically. Payback time for all those previous, smooth border crossings I guess.

After spending ten minutes answering their questions it all went quiet inside. They didn't seem to be doing anything so I knocked on the window and asked what was happening.

"No internet, senor," came the reply.

One of them got some food out and they all sat around eating and talking. I stood by the window getting hotter and hotter and madder and madder. Tracy was with the bike sitting in the shade and talking to some children so she wasn't too bothered but I was really getting wound up by these guys. Suspiciously, the internet had gone down at midday and I was convinced they had just stopped for a half hour break at lunchtime.

Once their lunch break was over they wanted to know how I was intending to leave the country and expected me to produce paperwork to prove it. I explained that the bike was being transported by ship to South Africa whereas I was flying. For a while I was worried that they wouldn't let me in as they insisted that I show proof of this, which I just didn't have. Eventually they relented and handed me the one-page typed form that had taken nearly two hours to produce. I meticulously checked the details. Everything was right except that they had written that I would be flying the bike out of Panama, not shipping it. I pointed out the error and they said it wasn't important and I shouldn't worry. After all this time spent filling out the official form, I shouldn't worry that one of the details wasn't right! Fantastic!

Fuming, I moved to the next window – I wasn't done yet. Another official checked the paperwork, stamped it and then charged me $3 per person to put a stamp in our passports. I had no idea why; I assumed it was really just a bribe by any other name but I didn't want to get stopped down the road and fined for not having the official stamp. I walked back to Tracy a broken man. It had taken over three frustrating, hot and pointless hours. I had been ignored, pushed around and charged for things I had no control over and I had no idea what had been going on for most of that time. I looked back at our crossings into Guatemala and Honduras with fondness. Leaving Nicaragua had been frustrating, long and annoying but I think the Panama experience took the biscuit. The only reason I had a huge smile on my face as we rode off was because I knew we'd just completed the last Central American border crossing. Surely freighting the bike couldn't be as much trouble?

*

Whilst in Mexico, I had received an email from someone who had visited my blog. Norman introduced himself as a Brit who used to live in the same town as me in the UK. He now lived near the town of David, in Panama and had kindly invited us to stay. How could we refuse? We turned up at dusk on a

Sunday to find the local motorcycle gang all there, drinking and singing. Norman introduced us to everyone (and his six monkeys) and plied us with alcohol. It was great, if a little weird, to be sitting in the middle of Central America with a complete stranger talking about our home town in the middle of England. He was used to it though. He was a regular contributor to the Horizons Unlimited forum and had given an open invitation to all bikers passing through Panama. I had read several other biker's blogs and knew that lots of people had enjoyed his hospitality. Norman told me that Pat, who I'd last seen in Death Valley, had stayed with him a few weeks previously and he'd heard that he'd just made it down to Chile.

We had a great evening but having just spent nearly three weeks getting up at 5 am and going to bed at 9 pm it was a bit of a shock to the system. I buckled first and crawled to bed at 11 pm while Tracy fared better and managed to stay up until the party ended around midnight.

We only had one night at Norman's as time was tight for freighting Heidi to South Africa. So we said thanks and goodbye and hit the Pan Americana for the final stretch down to Panama City.

With 99% of my Alaska–Panama route complete I finally got stopped by my first traffic cop. I'd heard that Panama was notorious for having cops with speed guns but having not seen one since the USA I guess I'd forgotten what to look out for. As we crested a hill I spotted a 60 kph sign and then saw a policeman standing in the road waving us over. The cop asked for my passport and licence and then started entering some details into his phone. He told me I'd been doing 103 kph and showed me the speed gun. I may well have been doing 103 but luckily Norman had warned me that sometimes the police try to trick you by having the speed gun pre-set on a specific number. I asked to see the date and time stamp to prove that it had recorded me speeding. He seemed a little annoyed by this and I walked back over to Tracy and the bike to give him some space to come up with a face-saving way of backing down. It worked. He continued typing away and then came over and said: "No ticket this time. You can go."

He gave me back my passport and licence and we were off. For the last two hundred miles into Panama City I kept the speed down and must have passed two or three more traffic police with speed guns.

Panama City had been in the back of my mind ever since I'd started out in Fairbanks, Alaska, where I'd stood at the signpost that said 'Panama 5000 miles'. I had actually covered 21,000 miles in 170 days to get there. As we rode over the impressive 'Bridge of the Americas' which took us over the Panama Canal and down into the city itself, I felt a lump in my throat. I knew I should think of something profound and deep to shout into my helmet:

"YEAHHHHHHHHHHHHHHHHHHHH."

I'd been in regular email contact with LMT-Corp shipping and the day after we arrived in Panama City they sent someone to our hostel to take us to the packing company. I followed on my bike and rode my last eight miles in Central America through the busy streets of the city. I knew I should have very little fuel in my tank when shipping the bike and arrived at the packing company with the dashboard computer telling me I had only enough petrol for three more miles.

I took the windscreen and mirrors off to lower the height of the bike and disconnected the battery (even though the guy told me that wasn't necessary). I had my bike gear and a few other things stashed in my big grey bag which I left with the bike, to be tied down next to it in the crate. We then went to the office to start the paperwork. I thought this might take a while but within half an hour I was on my way. I would have to return after the weekend to sign a few things (and pay) but for now I had done everything required. It all seemed too easy really.

I returned to the packing company the next day to see the bike all crated up. They'd done a good job and I was happy it was as secure as it needed to be. I just hoped it would turn up in Cape Town.

Heidi was all packed up and ready to go and I felt at a loss. The bike had been central to my life for the previous six months and it had just become second nature to be on her, with her or worrying about her. My life revolved around travelling and now there was a void. It seemed a little strange, but with a few days free to ourselves Tracy and I managed to put that to one side as we flew off to tiny *Isla Contadora* (part of the Pearl Islands, in the Gulf of Panama, on the Pacific side of the isthmus). The weather was wonderful and when we weren't diving we were sunbathing on beautiful deserted white sand beaches. While diving, Tracy spotted a pair of Harlequin Shrimps. These impressive little critters live off starfish, gruesomely eating a couple of legs and then letting them go. Our dive instructor had been there ten years and never seen one. Not as impressive as being the first to see twin sloths, but not a bad find.

Back in Panama City I phoned the freight company and they told me that Heidi was about to be put on a boat heading for Europe. Once there, she would be re-routed on another vessel heading for Cape Town. The whole journey should take about six weeks. There was nothing more I could do. Heidi had gone and Tracy and I had a few days to wait in Panama until our flights back to the UK.

Panama City wasn't really our idea of a fun time. With its high-rise buildings, shopping malls and opulent wealth in the harbours it felt more like a city in the United States than a city in Central America. Panama was certainly keen to lure the American dollar (so much so that it was actually the official currency) and there was an aggressive campaign to attract retirees to the country. Literature alluded to the safe, clean environment, the fact that English was widely spoken and, somewhat unbelievably, we were told that Panama City was the only place in Central America where it was safe to drink the water.

Fortunately, Panama City is surrounded by tropical forests. The country boasts more than nine hundred recorded bird species and over ten thousand plant species; more than one hundred of the local animals are found nowhere else on the planet. Panama rivals Costa Rica in this respect but so far the lucrative ecotourism trade has largely passed it by. This makes it a great place to visit for the independent traveller and we took every opportunity to get out of the city and into the jungle, which wasn't hard. A short taxi ride from our hotel took us to the *Parque Natural Metropolitano*, allegedly the only rainforest in the world set within the city limits of a metropolis. It was a haven of peace and tranquillity, which we relished. Walking around the hilly park we managed to spot some of the nine hundred species of birds, titi monkeys and even a couple of sloths in the trees.

The main tourist attraction, however, has to be the canal. Completed in 1914 the 50-mile length of waterway connects the Pacific with the Atlantic. Ferdinand de Lessops, the French builder of the Suez Canal, opened in 1869, began the construction of the Panama canal in 1880. Commissioned by the Colombians who then owned Panama, de Lessops thought it would be a straightforward exercise. It wasn't. Although it was only half the length of the Suez waterway it was much harder to construct a canal in the tropical environment of Panama. Furthermore, de Lessops' canal was going to be built at sea-level, without locks, which proved incredibly difficult. The French effort was finally abandoned after ten years, $287,000,000 and the loss of no fewer than twenty-two thousand lives.

That figure staggered me when I first read it at the Miraflores Visitors' Center, overlooking the huge Miraflores locks. Not the money – the lives. Twenty-two thousand people had perished, in little more than ten years. Most died from disease, mainly malaria and yellow fever, both of which are carried by mosquitoes. The yellow fever virus is introduced into the bloodstream via the saliva of the mosquito as it bites. If another mosquito then bites the infected human it can pick up the virus and pass it on, resulting in an epidemic. As a traveller I only knew about yellow fever as one of those vaccinations you need to get for certain countries. And in the UK it costs around $75. I'd grumbled at this, but upon reflection, reading about so many people dying from the disease, $75 seemed like a small price to have paid.

By the turn of the century American doctors had linked the cause of yellow fever to the mosquito and in 1904 Dr William Crawford Gorgas, who had cleared up conditions in Havana, Cuba, moved to Panama. His efforts to improve the sanitation conditions reduced the larvae breeding grounds and the death rate from all diseases amongst canal workers fell below that of any American city. They dug ditches to drain standing water, sprayed puddles with a film of oil and even emptied out the fonts in the local churches. The colonel in charge of the US Army in Panama apparently complained to Gorgas that each mosquito must be costing $10. To which Gorgas replied: "I know, Colonel, but what if one of those ten-dollar mosquitoes were to bite you?"

The French hadn't been the first to think of building a canal. King Charles V of Spain (who was also the Holy Roman Emperor and nephew to Catherine of Aragon, first wife of Henry VIII) ordered a survey way back in 1524, only thirty-two years after Columbus first sailed across the Atlantic. Plans were drawn up, but seemingly Charles was distracted by events in Europe and nothing came of it.

A much smaller European nation got involved with Panama in the late seventeenth century. As a way of getting hold of the lucrative spice trade of the East Indies, William Paterson, a Scottish trader and banker (who was, ironically, a founder of the Bank of England), started the Darien Scheme in 1698. In essence, he was trying to set up a trading post in Panama with the aim of garnering vast amounts of money for Scotland, which was still politically independent from England at the time. Paterson raised the £400,000 needed to set forth on Scotland's first major colonial enterprise. This was a risky venture, but the hope was to reap huge profits and increase Scotland's standing in the world. Five ships and 1,200 settlers set off in July 1698 carrying the hopes and wealth of the nation with them. It took them over three months to reach Panama with seventy people dying on the way. Apparently only the captain and Paterson knew what the destination was when they left Scotland. The other passengers were only told once they had set sail!

Arriving in the tropics, the Scots found it almost impossible to survive. They just weren't equipped or prepared for the heat, humidity, terrain or the belligerent Spanish. They had brought goods with them to trade with the indigenous population but found it hard to sell products made out of wool.

Without actually planning to construct a canal, the Scots had nevertheless hoped to set up a free port as a base to link the Atlantic to the Pacific across the narrow strip of land between the two, and thereby trade much more easily with the Far East. But within two years the Darien expedition was over, despite a second expedition being launched without knowing that the first had already abandoned the colony.

Paterson's wife, son and 2,000 of the 2,500 settlers who had finally arrived in Panama had died. The venture nearly bankrupted the country and, many argue, made the Scots aware that they could never be a major player in European affairs alone, and that if they wanted to share in the prosperity of the *Sassenachs,* closer ties with England would be necessary. So the doomed Darien Scheme provided impetus to the 1707 Act of Union which united the parliaments of England and Scotland, a century after the unification of their crowns. (King James VI of Scotland had become James I of England and united the two countries' sovereigns on the death of Queen Elizabeth I in 1603.) Indeed, amongst the terms of union there was compensation for many of the losses suffered by Scottish investors in the Darien Disaster (as it became known).

But I digress: back to the canal. At the turn of the twentieth century the canal project got tangled up with Panamanian independence. Until that point Panama had been controlled by Colombia but, sensing an opportunity, the USA agreed to back Panama's call for independence. In 1903 Panama freed itself from Colombia and in return for its support America won concessions. Philippe Bunau-Varilla, who had been one of de Lessops' chief engineers thirty years earlier, was appointed Panamanian ambassador to the USA and it wasn't long before he and the US Secretary of State, John Hay, signed the Hay-Bunau-Varilla Treaty. The USA was granted 'sovereign rights in perpetuity over the Canal Zone'. In exchange, America guaranteed Panama independence from Colombia.

In 1904 the USA moved in and built the canal. The world's greatest engineering marvel was completed within a decade. The first ship sailed through on August 15th 1914, just two weeks after the outbreak of World War One. I was fascinated by this complex, detailed and amazing history. I'd had no idea about any of it, even though I'd known of the canal's existence for most of my adult life. I like to think that I'm an intelligent, inquisitive and curious individual and yet there is so much about the world that I don't know anything about. As I stood outside watching a huge ship enter the Miraflores lock I thought back over the preceding six months and the trail of events which had led me to Panama.

It was almost impossible to quantify. I had seen and learnt so much. I had met some wonderful people and found out quite a lot about myself. I still didn't know as much about motorcycle maintenance as I should, but I had most certainly been on an amazing journey. The Panama Canal marked the end of one huge section but I was still only about half way through my adventure. As the container ship exited the lock and headed east towards the Caribbean I imagined Heidi on board and allowed myself a wry smile as I knew I had Africa waiting and whatever was to come it was going to be fun, exciting, challenging and life-affirming.

Dom in Ushuaia in 1995

"One day I'll make it to Alaska."

Fifteen Years Later

"All roads lead south from here. I wonder what they'll be like?"

The road to Monument
Valley, Utah

Avenue of the Giants,
Humboldt Redwoods State Park

Trying to get to Palenque, Mexico

Sixaola-Guabito International Bridg,
between Costa Rica and Panama

Apparently my drive shaft
shouldn't look like that

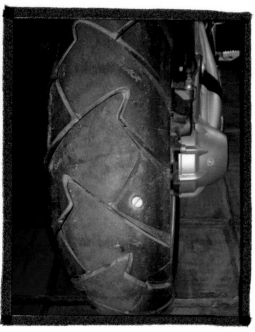

Flat tyre, Baja California

David and Jill on Nancy

Possibly *The* Hotel California, Baja California

World's heaviest flag, Las Vegas

Daryll on his Suzuki DR 650   Daryll and Angela

Angela enjoying the Namibian gravel   Tom on his Suzuki V-Strom
on her Suzuki DR 650

Pat and Chris with battery problems in Namibia

What happens when you wave at the locals

What must they think of us?

Children are never far away
In Southern Africa

The humbling Isandlwana battlefield site

Great Zimbabwe

Pat and Chris walking on the enormous sand dunes at Sossusvlei, Namibia

Wonderful Namibian sunset

The very photogenic Deadvlei,
Namibia

Spotting leopards on safari in
the Serengeti

PART TWO

Southern and Eastern Africa

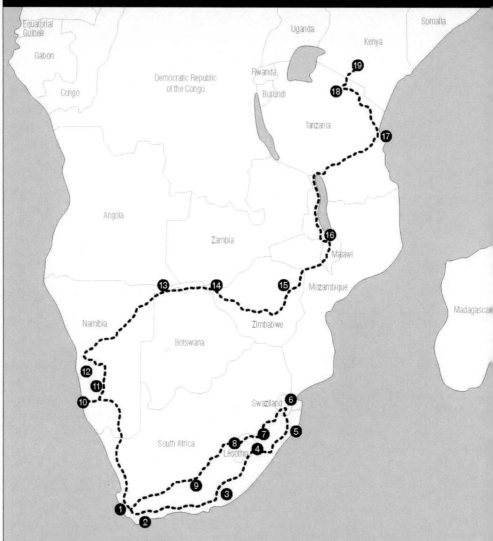

SOUTHERN AFRICA

1. Cape Town, South Africa
2. Cape Agulhas, South Africa
3. Hogsback, South Africa
4. Sani Pass, South Africa
5. St. Lucia, South Africa
6. Mbuluzi Game Reserve, Swaziland
7. Ladysmith, South Africa
8. Maseru, Lesotho
9. Graaff-Reinet, South Africa
10. Luderitz, Namibia
11. Duwisib Castle, Namibia
12. Sossusvlei, Namibia
13. Popa Falls, Caprivi Strip, Namibia
14. Victoria Falls, Zimbabwe
15. Harare, Zimbabwe
16. Monkey Bay, Malawi
17. Dar es Salaam, Tanzania
18. Arusha, Tanzania
19. Nairobi, Kenya

CHAPTER 16

THE SANI PASS, SOUTH AFRICA

"Many of life's failures are people who did not realize how close they were to success when they gave up."

(Thomas A. Edison)

I committed the cardinal sin: I wasn't looking far enough ahead. Instead of looking up the rough mountain pass I was staring down at the front wheel and the metre or so of gravel just ahead of it. The bike reared up and the handlebars wobbled as I tried to hang on. As the engine bash plate scraped on the rock I needed to 'give it some gas' to get the rest of the bike over the uphill obstacle but I was afraid of overdoing it and then careering off the edge of the cliff and I wimped out. The rear wheel made it half way up the rock before Heidi juddered to a halt. Fortunately I refrained from pulling the clutch in. Somehow I knew instinctively that this would only help the bike to roll backwards while the front brake would, in all probability, be useless as all the weight was at the back – Heidi would just slide back downhill in the gravel with the front wheel locked and me a helpless passenger. Although it felt counterintuitive, I let go of the clutch and let her stall. She rolled back a few inches but then stopped as the engine compression locked the back wheel.

I'd been standing up on the pegs at the start of the assent, but by now my arse was firmly planted in the seat which allowed my feet to find firm ground on which to anchor myself as we came to an ignominious stop. My heart was racing and my arms were shaking. I was staring ahead at the next hairpin bend in the climb, amazed that I was still upright and hadn't fallen off. I looked to my left. I was about three metres from the edge of the road and I could see the drop-off which would have taken us hundreds and hundreds of metres down the side of the rocky mountain, with absolutely nothing to break our fall.

But what to do now? I had to be very careful; one small slip could be disastrous. I tried to have a look at the accursed boulder that had caused the problem in the first place. But as I leaned over and down to inspect it the bike began to wobble and I realised this wasn't a good idea. I looked up the mountain to check that there wasn't a huge overland truck coming down. Fortunately there wasn't. I'm not sure what I would have done if there had been, but at least I had time to get myself out of the predicament I was in. I didn't want to roll back. Knowing that I would have much more control of the bike going forwards uphill under my own steam rather than freewheeling backwards, there was only one thing for it. I put Heidi into neutral and hit the start button. Kicking her down into first I started talking out loud to myself: "Look, just give it a bit of juice, look ahead and remember – speed is your friend."

I wasn't sure if speed really was my friend (wasn't that for sand?) but it seemed like the right thing to say. I had about five metres of gravel road in front of me before the next hairpin bend curved up to the right. I had to get this right – just enough power to pull the back wheel up and over the boulder but not so much that I'd go crashing into the side of the mountain. Simple really.

"Come, on you idiot. You've got this far without dropping the bike. Don't drop it now. You can do this."

I knew I probably should have stood back up on the pegs at the earliest opportunity but that was asking too much. The plan was to rev it in first gear keeping both feet just off the ground to work as stabilisers should I need them. I was also fully prepared to 'jump ship' should Heidi decide to head for the cliff edge. I let the clutch out until it started to bite, took a deep breath, looked up and went for it.

Except I didn't. Heidi rocked up on the boulder and then stopped again. I stalled, rolled back and ended up exactly where I had started. This was getting ridiculous. Repeating my pre-flight check, I had a serious word with myself and ventured to give it more beans. With the engine screaming I rode up the boulder with the rear of the bike rising alarmingly underneath me. I tried to ignore that and focus on the five metres ahead. The rear of the bike came down with a crunch but thankfully without skidding sideways. As soon as I was clear of the boulder I eased off the gas and the steepness of the slope meant that I slowed down quite quickly. A better rider would have then swept around the corner in one go and off up the mountain but I came to a stop with the bike pointing straight at the cliff face rather than up the track in the direction I should be going. But I was upright, unscathed and alive. With both feet firmly planted on the ground, I looked around to see just how large the bolder had been. The track was strewn with small rocks and piles of gravel. I expected to see the mother of all boulders but I couldn't see anything anywhere; it was as if there had been nothing there at all! I took a deep breath. What the hell was I doing trying to ride through Africa? I'd only been on the road a matter of days and I'd almost killed myself. How the hell did I get myself into this situation?

CHAPTER 17

GETTING A SOUTH AFRICAN EDUCATION

"Cowards die many times before their deaths
The valiant never taste of death but once."

(*Julius Caesar*, Shakespeare)

Having spent a month back in the UK, the start of the Africa section of the trip felt like a whole new beginning. I flew down to Cape Town with mixed emotions. I wasn't going to see Tracy for three or four months (she wasn't coming out to join me on this part of the trip) and the doubts and worries that I had felt when leaving her for Alaska reared their ugly heads again. It's a difficult emotion to describe: a mixture of excitement and trepidation. Again I had the feeling of extreme nervousness. Why was I doing this? What had I let myself in for? Of course this time I didn't really have a choice as Heidi was arriving in Cape Town so I had to go and get her. I thought I would have more confidence having just ridden 20,000 miles from Alaska to Panama but Southern Africa was going to be different. This wasn't going to be as easy as North America. And if I had any problems with Heidi, BMW dealers would be few and far between.

As the plane took off from Birmingham I watched England disappear in the mist and clouds of a cold February morning. I was off again; off on an unknown adventure. Off to do what I wanted, where I wanted, whenever I wanted to, and all from the seat of a motorcycle. I couldn't help smiling to myself and I felt a warm glow of contentment sweep across me. I was anxious and nervous but I was also excited just thinking about all the things that could happen over the next few months. I was back on the road.

However, I still didn't have a definite arrival time for the bike. The ship Heidi was supposed to be on had sailed from Rotterdam but until it arrived I wasn't totally convinced that she was on board. I knew she had been put on a vessel in Panama but couldn't be sure whether she had been moved from that boat, when it docked in Rotterdam, on to the right one heading for Cape Town.

Even if she were on the right ship it was going to be difficult to get the timing right so I had arranged to do some voluntary work in Cape Town while waiting. I had spent a long time researching different volunteer programmes online to make sure I got the most out of the experience and finally settled on three weeks teaching English in a primary school in a township just south of Cape Town with an organisation called *African Impact*. It was a locally run, non-denominational outfit geared up to help the local townships. They ran various projects across southern Africa and had volunteers working in local animal rescue centres, township medical centres and in schools. The volunteers lived together in a purpose-built compound near the projects and I was looking forward to meeting up with other travellers.

Quite a few African projects have a religious bent and, as a non-believer, I wanted to avoid them. For example, one project had looked good but I'd decided it wasn't for me when I received the following email:

Dom,

It is wonderful that God has called you to work in South Africa. I hope you find the attached of some use.

In His Grip,

Peter

No doubt Peter was a lovely guy and I was grateful to him for having expressed his faith to me so that I knew what I would have been getting into. I explained this in my reply, which he accepted, in good faith, so to speak.

Warren, from *African Impact*, met me at the airport and we drove the hour or so south to Masiphumelele, near Fish Hoek, where I was going to be based. On the way he explained what I would be doing and what the school was like.

The school in Masiphumelele had 1400 children, aged between about seven and fourteen, and I was going to help teach English to Grade 7.

"Grade 7. Is that 11–12 year olds?" I asked Warren.

"No. They're supposed to be 13–14, but some of them might even be older than that, we're not sure."

Each class had about thirty-six to forty students, housed in prefabricated rooms with intermittent electricity. Beyond that Warren didn't know much else. Most volunteers work with very young children in the pre-school and kindergarten classes. I'd asked especially to teach older ones which was, I was learning, quite unusual.

We arrived at the accommodation and I met the other volunteers. There were a dozen of us in total. Most of them were American University students studying medicine and were in South Africa for a couple of months getting experience 'in the field'. The only other guy was Neil, a financial consultant from London in his early thirties, who was spending his two-week annual holiday leave volunteering in Masiphumelele. Everyone was friendly enough but with so many of them twenty years younger than me it made me feel as if I was back in my teaching job leading a sixth form school trip.

However, I was sure that I was going to get a lot out of the experience and I was really looking forward to getting stuck into working in a township primary school, even if it was only going to be for a few weeks. I didn't expect to make any real difference to the lives of these students, (after all, I hadn't single-handedly saved the world's turtle or sloth populations) but I was certainly going to learn something and, I hoped, understand the land I was travelling through a little better. I also hoped I might meet people who'd been travelling in Southern Africa who could give me some advice on where to go and what to do.

On my first day I arrived at the school bright and early, eager to get stuck into some teaching. I'd actually surprised myself at how much I'd missed teaching in the six months I'd had off. Masiphumelele Primary School is situated on the edge of the sprawling Masiphumelele township. Originally, and rather uninspiringly, called Site 5, residents renamed their township Masiphumelele, which means 'we shall succeed' in Xhosa, one of South Africa's eleven official languages. Built in the early 1990s, it had been designed for only 750 families, with no provision for community based businesses. The township has grown rapidly and although official figures suggest around 16,000 residents, unofficial estimates reach as high as 30,000. Some residents lived in brick buildings but the vast majority are housed in wooden shacks. However, the township was perhaps in better condition than I had expected. I had imagined mud huts, dusty roads and long queues at water pumps but Masiphumelele was more developed and more prosperous than that. Overhead cables confirmed there was a communal source of electricity, TVs blared out music from the small shops dotted along the tarmac road and large solid buildings (the local clinic, library and community centre) near to the school gave the place a sense of permanence and hope.

The school itself had certainly seen better days but the majority of its buildings were constructed of bricks and mortar set around a covered central courtyard. The gated entrance led to the largest building on site, a single-storey construction measuring perhaps fifty metres across. I sat in the reception area waiting to be met by the Grade 7 teacher whom I was going to be assisting. Looking around, it was clear that the building was in need of some repair. Cracks in the glass on the front doors and windows and paint peeling off the walls and ceiling gave the place a well-used feel. Students were filing through the entrance area as I waited; some were looking at me perhaps wondering what this strange white man was doing here but most were just getting on with the early morning rituals of school life familiar to all students across the globe. In a uniform of black trousers or skirt, bright yellow shirt and black jumper, they looked like busy little bumblebees as they scurried and shoved their way down the narrow corridors and into their classes.

Then one of the secretaries appeared and asked me to follow her. We walked through the building and out into a large, covered courtyard. Walled on all four sides by long, narrow, single-storey buildings, each housing three or four classrooms, the whole place had the feel of a prison. Each long building didn't quite meet at the ends, so at the four corners I could see out beyond to the playing area. On the left I could see a couple of basketball courts and already some classes were out there running around between cones. Judging by the level of noise, they were thoroughly enjoying themselves. The right-hand corner led to a set of six prefabricated classrooms. That was where I was heading.

It was clear that the English teacher I was assigned to help had no idea I was coming. Mr Nyoni seemed rather surprised when I turned up but he was very accommodating and much more laid back about the whole thing than I would have been if he'd just turned up out of the blue into my classroom in the UK. He was just starting the first lesson of the day and once he'd got the class busy copying off the board, we sat down at his desk.

"I did not know you were coming. Welcome to my class and the school. You have come to help, yes?" He spoke clear, slow English, a little staccato, like many South Africans, but with a wonderfully deep, resonant tone.

I explained that I would be there for three weeks, and that back at home in the UK I was a secondary school history teacher. I apologised for him not being told that I was coming and felt rather uncomfortable about imposing myself on him and his classes without prior warning, self-conscious of any hint of colonialism, as in, 'Here comes the white man to show you how to do it'.

"This is not a problem. You are most welcome. Let me explain what we are doing. I teach English to all of Grade 7. That's five classes. Lessons are either thirty minutes or one hour, but as we don't have a bell and I don't have a watch we just move when we are ready." He had a huge smile on his face as he said this. I was going to like Mr Nyoni.

I'd expected to just be helping him that day, perhaps going around and working with a few individuals, or perhaps taking a couple out of class to listen to them read. Mr Nyoni had other ideas. He told me what they had been doing the previous week and then suggested I take the class for the rest of the lesson. "You can teach them about active and passive voice," he suggested. And that was it. I was up! I stood up and faced my audience. The classroom had a teacher's desk and chalkboard at one end and several waist-high cupboards along one side with piles of books stacked on top of them. The students were sitting on small wooden chairs around desks which were clustered together so that four or six sat facing each other; they were not in single rows and columns as I had expected. They had an exercise book each and one text book between two. Thirty-six inquisitive faces stared up at me as I walked over to the board, a single piece of chalk in my quivering hand. Had I really missed teaching after all? Active and passive voice: what the bloody hell was that?

After stumbling through for a few minutes, and using the relevant pages of the text book to explain active and passive I asked if there were any questions. Silence.

"So, is this sentence active or passive?" I pointed at the example I'd written on the board:

The teacher wrote on the chalkboard.

I was nothing if not original in my choice of examples! Silence from the class. Oh, dear. Had they not understood a word? Perhaps they couldn't actually speak any English and they hadn't even understood what I had said. After all, I'd just turned up with my funny English accent and started talking to them. At home I would have asked someone to answer but here I didn't want to pick on anyone on my first day and I waited in the hope someone would be brave enough to speak out. No one was. I'd been teaching in the UK for twenty years but within ten minutes of being in Mr Nyoni's class I felt like a trainee teacher again. Totally out of my depth, totally unsure of what to do, and totally aware that I was standing in front of a class of thirty-six children who were all waiting for me to do something.

I had to do something so I asked the table nearest me for a volunteer.

"Can someone from this table tell me?" I asked in my friendliest voice, pointing at what I had written.

The teacher wrote on the chalkboard.

"What is a chalkboard?" came a quiet reply.

"Oh. A chalkboard – er, a blackboard. Do you call it a blackboard?"

Suddenly the class came alive with mutterings and gasps of understanding. They had not understood my sentence. I was so used to political correctness in the UK where one didn't refer to blackboards as such. In trying my best not to be offensive, I had, instead, been incomprehensible. Of course it was a blackboard. It was a board and it was black. Crazy bloody Englishman!

I spent three edifying weeks at Masiphumelele primary school. I have no idea whether my students really ever understood active and passive voice or anything else I tried to teach them. They were wonderfully well behaved, inquisitive, friendly, polite and desperate to learn. With limited resources, poor infrastructure and a home life that I could only guess at, the young people in front of me every day were grateful for the education they were receiving. They also seemed delighted to meet me. It took a few days for them to get over the shyness but once they had they found out that I was just a normal person they opened up a little. The whole essence of travelling, for me, was summed up in those students. They were finding out about me and my culture just as much as I was about them and theirs. In those fifteen days I learnt a whole lifetime of information about life in modern day South Africa, much more than I would ever pick up just travelling through the place. I'd always believed this – gap years should be obligatory.

It was no surprise to me that the less people have, the more they appreciate the little they *do* have. At the school the rooms were messy, students were in uniform but very untidy, and resources were limited. They all had exercise books and pens but textbooks were usually one between two and quite old and we certainly didn't have anything like interactive whiteboards/projectors or computers. Electricity wasn't even guaranteed. I was teaching with chalk for the first time in ten years. But (and this is a big but) the students were keen to learn and worked hard. Back in the UK the Secretary of State for Education had recently suggested that schools would improve (by which he meant exam results would improve) if students were forced to wear blazers and ties with their top buttons done up. In my view this was, on its own, unimportant and largely misses the point.

What students need is a desire to learn and motivated, well-supported teachers. By and large in the developing world poor parents know that education is the key to the door of progress. It's a way out of poverty and many poor parents will sacrifice everything so their children can get a good start in life. Many students appreciate this too and I witnessed this first hand at Masiphumelele. The school had no library, (apparently only about seven per cent of schools in South Africa do), but just down the road the community library was packed every afternoon with primary and secondary students doing homework, research on the few computers they had or just playing chess. They knew it was in their own interests to learn and they had a thirst for education and a desire to find out about the world that I found refreshing and uplifting.

Of course many parents and children in the UK are also aware of this but many are not. We have developed a 'too cool for school' culture in the UK where education, school and learning are too often not valued as highly as celebrity status. Apparently, in a recent opinion poll in the UK, when asked what they wanted to be when they grew up, 54% of teenagers said they wanted to be famous. Not that they wanted to be doctors, or lawyers, or fire-fighters or train drivers or scientists; just 'famous'. I interpret that finding to mean that 54% want to get rich quickly and easily. When asked who they see as a role model the top three answers were Kate Moss, Wayne Rooney and Lady Gaga. As a British teacher this just depressed me.

Recent changes to the UK education system have only made matters worse. Teachers have to teach to the test and are judged on tangible results in an intangible industry. Successive governments have now devalued education and seem to be trying to replace learning with testing, enquiry with evaluation and ingenuity with accountability. English children are now the most examined in the industrialised world. The average child will be formally tested about seventy times in their school career. In the words of the US educational psychologist, Joseph Renzulli, we have created a new version of the three Rs: 'ram, remember, regurgitate'.

Working in the township reminded me why I'd needed a break from teaching. You can't appreciate what you've got if you've always had it. I was aware of this already, partly because I'd spent ten years of my life teaching abroad but Masiphumelele opened my eyes to it again and I was so pleased I had decided to volunteer. That's not to say that life was easy for me at the school. I found some aspects of working in a township hard, as cultural beliefs clashed and I witnessed a few things I would rather have not.

First, I never got used to the welcome I received every lesson. As I entered the room all the students would stand up and say (in a drawling, slow-singing way that groups adopt when speaking together) "Good morning teacher how are you?" To which I had to reply "Very well, thank you. How are you?" And they would then say "We are well thank you teacher." Then I would tell them to sit down. I always felt uncomfortable doing this and I'm sure there was an undercurrent of sarcasm in their collective voices but there was no way I could stop them doing it.

Secondly, every so often someone would come to class, say something in Xhosa (pronounced Koh -sa) and the whole class would just get up and walk out. It was their time to go to the kitchen and get some fruit, regardless of where we were in the lesson. I suppose on one level the school is there to provide a safe haven for young people during the day and it's just as important that they get an apple to eat as it is to conjugate a few verbs, but it took some getting used to. I was used to my lesson being the all-important thing, and here I was being reminded that there are some other basic things that are just as important.

Thirdly and more seriously, I never felt comfortable with the punishments that were handed out. Corporal punishment was outlawed, but the threat of it seemed to linger in the air. Mr Nyoni was a kind and gentle man, with me anyway, but if one of his students got a question wrong, or was not paying attention, he would threaten to clip them around the ear or pretend to throw a board rubber at them. On one occasion he threw some chalk at a boy. I never saw him actually hit anyone but I had to wonder what he might have done if I wasn't there. I saw a letter pinned on the staffroom notice board reminding staff that corporal punishment was not acceptable but it seemed to me that this wasn't necessarily adhered to.

Back at the volunteer house I was getting along with my new friends but to be honest I didn't have much spare time. The mornings were tied up at the primary school and in the afternoons I was helping out at one of the other projects. This could be at a home for AIDS orphans helping them with their homework, spending the afternoon painting one of the container huts at the pre-school, or at the library helping out with homework club for High School students.

Impact Africa worked in three different areas, each showing a very different side to life in a Cape Town township. Ocean View was a well-established, reasonably wealthy community, more like a council estate in the UK, by which I mean it had roads, structured housing and mains water and electricity. But the relative wealth of Ocean View brought its own problems, mainly drug-related. Several of the American medical students worked at the clinic there and while I was helping teenagers conjugate verbs and checking their spelling, they were dealing with gang-related injuries such as stabbings and dog bites and, as always, lots of HIV/AIDS. The best guess was that about 40% of the people in the township had HIV/AIDS.

Masiphumelele was a poorer township, at least in the sense that it looked and felt slightly less well established. There were some permanent structures but many people seemed to be living in converted containers or ramshackle dwellings made from whatever they could get their hands on, with sporadic electricity and water supplies. There was a clinic, an animal rescue centre, an orphanage for children affected and infected by HIV/AIDS, a pre-school and a primary school.

Red Hill was the third township. This was really little more than a collection of shacks on the hillside. *Impact Africa* worked in a pre-school and a nursery there. The history of this township was quite interesting. It was on private land owned by a white man who, during the apartheid era, had allowed blacks to set up temporary homes. The idea was that while travelling around that part of the Cape they could use Red Hill as a bolthole should they be chased by the police whilst breaking curfew. Now the government leased the land off the landowner and 2,000 people called it home. It had water but only limited electricity; the houses were made out of bits of wood and corrugated iron and it was certainly the poorest of the three.

My first weekend in Cape Town saw me doing the touristy things – up Table Mountain and over to Robben Island. Both were good; Robben Island, home to many prisoners of conscience during the apartheid era, including

Nelson Mandela, was particularly interesting. I found it quite moving to be taken around by a former leader of the PAC (Pan African Congress – an offshoot of the African National Congress) who relayed his stories with enthusiasm and dedication. He continually thanked people and countries who had supported the anti-apartheid movement and it made me feel proud to have boycotted Barclays Bank and South African oranges when I was a student in the UK in the 1980s.

I was particularly struck by the constant reference to 'Truth and Reconciliation' as we toured Robben Island. This was how South Africa had managed to deal with its past without descending into a bloodbath. It's worth recalling that a lot of people were predicting that when the apartheid era ended, in the early 1990s, South Africa would collapse into civil war and tear itself apart. But that didn't happen, partly due to the policy of 'Truth and Reconciliation' which allowed people to admit their crimes and give testimony in return for amnesty from prosecution. This was all based on the ideas and beliefs of the 'big three Ms' as our guide called them – Mandela, Martin Luther King and Mahatma Gandhi.

I also learnt that Robben Island had become something of a university for the prisoners. I was amazed to discover that despite strict censorship measures prisoners could continue their education and study for a degree. Books were allowed for this purpose but prisoners also managed to smuggle in other literature, including a *Complete Works of Shakespeare*, disguised as a religious text. This was passed around, with much reverence, amongst the inmates, with many signing off next to their favourite passage. Nelson Mandela's signature can be found next to a short speech by Julius Caesar. He signed this in 1977, by which time he had already been incarcerated on Robben Island for over twelve years:

Cowards die many times before their deaths
The valiant never taste of death but once.
Of all the wonders that I yet have heard,
It seems to me most strange that men should fear;
Seeing that death, a necessary end,
Will come when it will come.

Julius Caesar, Act II, Scene 2

You might expect that visiting a former prison would be a depressing or upsetting experience, but I left Robben Island actually feeling good about humanity; an unusual sensation for a history teacher.

By the time I entered my second week at the primary school I was learning quite a lot about education in modern day South Africa. Grade 7, who were 13–14 year olds, had three hours of English per week (They also had lessons in Xhosa, Science, Maths, and Geography.) Grade 7 was the top class in the Primary school. If they passed the year they moved on to the High School in Ocean View. Most of them would do this but there were one or two in my current classes who were clearly older than thirteen. It seemed that if they didn't pass the year they stayed where they were, although I couldn't really get a firm answer from anyone on whether this was official policy or just *de facto* practice.

Children playing at Red Hill Primary School, South Africa

The students themselves (or 'learners' as they are called in South Africa) were very polite and generally well behaved but they were initially quite shy and distant. However, they were very keen to please and this meant that if I asked the class if they had understood something I would get forty voices chorusing "Yes Teacher". I was accustomed to a more friendly relationship, with dialogue and lessons conducted in a caring environment in which students feel their views matter, opinions are heard and failure is seen as an opportunity to learn. Here it felt that there was a more rigid barrier between the staff and the learners at the school. Teachers taught and learners learnt.

One morning I went into school with Jen, a UK gap year student and volunteer who had joined me in the primary school to teach maths. Jen had spent most of her gap year in Australia and South East Asia doing the usual tourist things but was now spending a month volunteering with *African Impact*. She had no idea what she was going to do when she got back to the UK but had been thinking of teaching. Normally Mr Nyoni and the other Grade 7 teachers would be in their classrooms first thing but this morning was different – they were in a meeting. Jen and I went to the Grade 7 block; just us and 180 learners. As it was a Tuesday they were supposed to have a year assembly. At 8.15, unprompted, all of the learners trotted out of their classrooms and lined up on the dusty yard between two of the prefab huts. They then spent ten minutes singing, first in Xhosa (it's a mesmerising language which utilises lots of clicking noises using the tongue – in fact to pronounce Xhosa correctly you push your tongue to the roof of your mouth, then flick it backwards and down creating a click noise, then say Koh-sa). Then they sang the Lord's Prayer in English. Jen and I were the only teachers there. They had done this all without supervision and neatly and sensibly filed back into their classrooms to wait for the teachers. We both stood there utterly amazed. I had never witnessed anything like it. I'd taught in countries in which assemblies involved singing the national anthem and a lot of flag waving but never without staff there to oversee it. And this unsupervised performance was all done with pride, enthusiasm and dedication. It was breath-taking to witness.

Back in the classroom we settled down to our English lesson. Mr Nyoni had still not returned from his meeting so I took it upon myself to teach the class. We started with some work on adverbs using examples in the text book but it was dull stuff and none of us had our hearts in it. I don't know whether it was because I'd been in the school for over a week by now or it was the absence of Mr Nyoni, but one of the learners mischievously put up his hand and asked in broken English if I could read them a story.

"Of course I can," I answered, probably even more relieved than them to escape adverbs. "Would you like to pick one from the book?"

"Can you read the poem, page 134 please?" came the eager reply.

I turned to the relevant page and my heart nearly stopped. I could read the poem but I wasn't so confident that I would be able to interpret it. Oh well, nothing ventured…

> *'Twas brillig, and the slithy toves*
> *Did gyre and gimble in the wabe:*
> *All mimsy were the borogoves,*
> *And the mome raths outgrabe.'*

I read the whole thing to a stunned, silent class. As I finished the hands went up. Oh dear.

"What is 'frumious Bandersnatch' mean?"

"What is 'Tumtum tree'?"

"How you 'gyre and gimble'?"

I had no idea what to say. How do you interpret Lewis Carroll's 'Jabberwocky' with a class who have rudimentary English? I was out of my depth and about to fall back on the pedagogical maxim, "What do you think it means?" when the door opened. I'd never been more pleased to see Mr Nyoni.

"Right children, it's time for some more English grammar. Get your books open to page 57 please, we're going to look at prepositions."

*

Later that week it finally happened. On the Thursday of the second week I got back to the volunteer house and checked my email. And there it was: a message informing me that my bike had actually arrived. I could pick it up in the morning! I phoned the guy who'd sent the email and he very kindly offered to come the following day and give me a lift to the depot.

I asked Warren if it would be OK if I skipped school the next day and like an overexcited child on Christmas Eve I went to bed early that night but just couldn't get to sleep. Was Heidi really in Cape Town? Would I be able to get her out of customs in one day? How much would it cost? Would she still work? What would I do if she didn't? I'd almost forgotten that I was here to ride a motorcycle to Kenya. I'd got so wrapped up in teaching at Masiphumelele. But now the big trip was back on.

In the morning I was picked up, as promised, and by 11 am I was at the depot watching a fork lift truck gently depositing a familiar looking crate at my feet. It was such a relief to actually see Heidi again. She had been crated pretty well and with help from the forklift truck driver and his handy crowbar we got the crate dismantled. Once I'd got the bike out of the crate I put the mirrors and screen back on and re-connected the battery. This was the battery I'd bought new two months and just a few hundred miles previously in Costa Rica at the sloth sanctuary. I didn't expect it to work.

I turned the ignition key and all seemed good. The lights worked and the computer kicked into action. However when I hit the ignition switch Heidi turned over but didn't fire up. I tried again, pumping the throttle a few times first. Nothing. Perhaps I didn't have enough fuel in the tank. The forklift truck guy called a labourer over and I sent him off to the petrol station to get me five litres. He returned an hour later and I put the fuel in. Nothing had changed; the bike wouldn't start and now the battery was getting flat. Heidi was just making a 'thud thud' noise and we weren't going anywhere. I feared the worst. She had been crated up and transported over the ocean for nearly two months, anything could have gone wrong. And, of course, I didn't have a bloody clue.

CHAPTER 18

HOW HIGH CAN YOU GET?

"It is not the mountain we conquer but ourselves."

(Sir Edmund Hillary)

Fortunately I had the phone number for the Cape Town BMW dealer in my pocket. I gave them a ring and they arranged to have me and the bike picked up and taken to their shop. An hour later a guy with a van and a trailer turned up. The driver handed me his calling card with a friendly grin: *Steve 'The bike collector' Roadside assistance for bikers. Anywhere/Anyhow/Anytime/Anysize.*

He reversed his trailer into position and in a flash Heidi was up on the back, tied down and we were on our way. This was not the way I had envisaged the start to my African trip.

"Come far?" asked Steve.

"Well, I started in Alaska," I said, expecting some sort of respect.

With a thick South African accent he replied, "Well, you're not going anywhere fast now are you, man."

I wasn't sure if he was being sarcastic, ironic or just honest.

"No. Not today anyway. I was really hoping to drive out of the harbour and finally get on the road. How far is it to the BMW dealer?"

"It should only take us half an hour. And the guys there will take good care of you. You'll be on the road soon."

And sure enough, thirty minutes later we were pulling into the BMW Atlantic underground garage.

"So, how much do I owe you?" I asked Steve as Heidi was lowered back down to the ground. I was dreading the answer.

"That'll be US$35. And here's my card in case you need me again."

I was pleasantly surprised by the price, took his card and paid him, hoping I would never need him again.

The BMW guys in Cape Town thought the battery was flat. Of course the battery was flat: I'd been running it down as I turned the engine over repeatedly, trying to start the bloody bike! I was sure there was something else wrong, but since I knew nothing about mechanics, I listened to their advice. Time was tight: it was a quarter to five on a Friday afternoon and as it was a bank holiday weekend, the shop wouldn't be open again until Tuesday. I had really hoped I could take the bike for a spin over the weekend before my last week of volunteer teaching. My plan was to be off the following Saturday morning, heading up the east coast of South Africa. I was then aiming to come back down to Cape Town and get some new tyres before heading for Namibia. I mentioned all this to Shane, the mechanic. (I was very disappointed that he wasn't called Mike.)

"Look mate, why don't we put a new battery in your bike and charge up your flat one. Then you can head off up the coast and when you come back in a couple of weeks we'll swop them back."

This was great news. That fitted with my plans perfectly. By 5 pm Shane had swopped the batteries over and Heidi had been revived. I put my jacket, gloves and helmet on and was just about to sit on the bike when she cut out! Shane came over and said it was probably because the bike was on the side stand and the fuel intake was on the right side, so it had run dry. I thought about all the times I'd started Heidi on the side stand and she had never cut out before. I didn't have the confidence to say that I wasn't sure that this was the only problem and anyway, I was so eager to get out of there and on the road, I just nodded and put her on the centre stand. She started up first time. Of course Shane was right and I was just being an idiot. Again.

Somewhat tentatively but with a huge amount of excitement I got on the bike and headed up the ramp, out of the car park and into the African sun. In many ways I just couldn't believe it. After the long wait since Panama and the hassle I'd been through that day I was, at long last, actually riding Heidi in Africa. I headed for the coast road that I knew would lead me south towards Masiphumelele. It was just fantastic to be on the bike in a totally different continent. Although it took some getting used to, I was now riding on the left-hand side of the road. I'd never ridden Heidi on the left before. Being British it should have felt natural but on Heidi it felt all wrong.

After stopping to fill up with fuel, I'd chosen to ride back to my volunteer house along the beautiful Chapman's Peak road which runs along the rugged windswept South Atlantic coast. It reminded me of the Northern Californian or Oregon coast and for a moment I'd actually forgotten I was in Africa. I had a huge grin on my face as I sped around the curving coast road heading south – in Africa! I was riding in Africa! For nine miles; then she cut out again.

I was heading up an incline and the engine just died. It fired again for a moment, but then she died and I cruised, in deathly silence, to an ignominious stop at the side of the road. I had absolutely no idea what was wrong.

I'd just filled up so I knew there was plenty of fuel. And that's about as far as my diagnostics went. I tried to start her up and although the battery sounded fine she wouldn't fire. It sounded, to my uneducated ears, like the same problem I'd had at the customs depot but it was getting near to dusk and I had no idea what to do. One minute I'd been on top of the world, feeling great and full of life; the following minute I was as low as I could go without crying. Solo travel can have this effect; the peaks and troughs can be huge. I needed to think and come up with a plan.

And then I remembered Steve. But where the bloody hell had I put his card? I checked the pockets of my jacket. I looked in my wallet, which would have been the sensible place to put it. But it wasn't there. What about in my 'muggers' wallet? (I carried an extra wallet with a small amount of money in it, in case I got mugged.) Steve's card wasn't in it. Think! Think, you idiot. Where did I put it? I rummaged around in my tank bag in case I'd just thrown it in there but I couldn't see it. It wasn't in the side pockets of my trousers either. Where else could it be? I was starting to curse now (because that always helps). Almost subconsciously I delved my right hand into my back pocket, one of the two back pockets in my riding trousers which I never use. And I felt something small, rectangular and card-like.

"Steve. It's Dom again. Yeah, the guy from Alaska. I've broken down again. I'm on the M6 coast road, nine miles south of Cape Town, heading for Hout Bay. Any chance you can come and pick me up?"

"Sorry mate. I'm on another job and the traffic is crazy. It's Friday night, man. It'll take me at least two hours to get to you. Sorry. Try ringing Johnny at Atlantic Motorrad, he may be able to help if he's still there. If he can't help, ring me back."

Not only was it getting dark but the battery on my phone was looking dangerously low as I rang the bike shop. It rang and rang and I was just about to hang up and phone Steve back when I heard Shane's voice. I explained the situation to him.

"Sounds like your fuel controller. Hang on, I'll be out with you soon."

I just love blokes who know about motorcycles. Shane turned up at 5.45 pm with a spare second-hand fuel pump controller. He changed it over (it look seconds) and the bike fired back into life again.

"Fantastic. Thanks Shane. How much do I owe you?"

"Oh, don't worry. It's nothing, just enjoy your trip. I'm going home."

And with that Shane put on his helmet, jumped on his bike and was off to enjoy his weekend. Thirty minutes previously I'd been stuck at the side of the road unable to move the bike, unsure what to do next with a long weekend ahead of me. Now I was on the road again and the adventure was back on. I headed off on the sweeping coast road south towards home, thankful that Heidi was working again. It was a glorious feeling to be on the road in Africa at last but I was perturbed by the fact that I'd broken down twice already and that if I hadn't been so close to a BMW bike dealer I'd have been in real trouble. And yet I was planning on riding north to Namibia, then north east towards Kenya. Had I bitten off more than I could chew? Was this really a sensible thing to be doing given my minimal mechanical expertise? What on earth would I do if the same thing happened in the middle of Zimbabwe? I just had to believe and hope that Heidi would be fine and I'd make it. After all, this was supposed to be an adventure.

*

I still had a week of volunteering ahead of me but the day after I picked the bike up I went on a 320-mile round trip to Cape Agulhas – the southernmost point in Africa. I suppose this was my African equivalent of the Arctic Circle in Alaska. It was another obvious starting point but there the similarities end. At the Arctic Circle (once I'd actually found it!) there was someone there to take my photo, give me some information, have a chat, congratulate me on making it that far and wish me a good day. At the southernmost point of the continent of Africa there was nothing. Well, there was a sign but it was at the end of a narrow walkway, past a car park. The walkway had obviously been put there to stop people from driving their cars right out to the end. Perhaps if I'd ridden all the way down from the UK I might have felt the need to cover the last fifty metres to the green plaque built into a small stone cairn which informed me that I was at Cape Agulhas – the southernmost point in Africa and the official dividing line between the Atlantic and Indian oceans. But I hadn't, so I didn't.

The wind was blowing fiercely into my face and the waves were crashing against the rocks. It was a spectacular place but I felt it would feel slightly disappointing if it marked the culmination of a ride down the whole length of Africa. I could now see why the Cape of Good Hope, with its stunning scenery, photo friendly signs and proximity to Cape Town had become a more iconic place to start/end a trip.

I jumped back on to Heidi, nervously turning the ignition key in the hope rather than expectation that she would start, but all was fine, so I pointed the wheel north, kicked her down into first gear and as I rolled out of the car park and up the road screamed: "Let's go to Nairobi, Heidi!"

We headed back to Cape Town and another week of teaching.

I must admit to feeling a bit emotional when I finally did leave Cape Town the following weekend. I was obviously very excited and thrilled to be on the road but as I rode along I realised that it had been four whole months since I'd been on my own. Four months since I'd ridden without Tracy on the back and to be honest, I felt a bit lonely.

I enjoyed the easy ride along N2 towards Mossel Bay. I got there in the early afternoon, found the caravan park by the sea and pitched my tent. As I put up my new tent for the first time, I realised that it had been five months since I'd camped; the last time was just north of Los Angeles and it felt good to be back under canvas.

The following day, I rode 'The Garden Route'. Admittedly I didn't stop at any of the surfing beaches or take any side trips so I may have missed some of the best parts but I have to say it was just a little disappointing. It is a lovely part of the country, very green and rural with lots of sandy beaches and (I'm told) some great surfing. After Kruger National Park and Cape Town, The Garden Route is the thing to do when in South Africa, but perhaps I was expecting too much.

At the end of a long day (400 miles) I stopped in Hogsback, north of East London. A very young J.R.R. Tolkien used to visit here when he lived in Bloemfontein and the Lonely Planet waxed lyrical about a veritable 'Hobbiton'. I camped at a place called 'Away with the fairies' and some people there certainly seemed to be. While I was setting up camp a guy came to say hello.

"Nice bike. Hi, I'm Glen. Have you come far on it?"

"Well, I've come up from Cape Town but I'm from the UK and I started this trip in America six months ago."

"Ah, hang on. You're Dom, aren't you? You're thedomwayround. I've been following your blog."

I was somewhat taken aback by this. I knew that people I didn't know had been reading my blog but it was weird to actually meet someone who'd been following me. We spent a couple of hours in 'The Wizard's Sleeve' bar drinking the local cider and talking. Glen gave me lots of tips on where to go in South Africa, suggesting I ride The Sani Pass. I'd not heard of this place but he insisted it was a famously snakelike pass that wound its way uphill into the land-locked country of Lesotho. He talked me into it and in the morning I headed off for The Sani Pass to see what all the fuss was about.

A hundred miles out of Hogsback, I rode into an almighty thunderstorm. Initially I didn't feel as scared as I'd been in the US, as there were other people around, and buildings, but I seemed to be riding straight into it. As I crested one hill, the wind picked up and the rain was almost horizontal. And then FLASH! About fifty metres in front of me, right over the road, a God-Almighty bolt of electricity slammed into the ground. Within a millisecond, CRASH! I heard and felt the thunder. It was so intense I honestly felt my sternum shake. I stopped the bike as quickly and safely as I could without falling over. I turned the engine off, kicked the sidestand down and jumped off. Shaking from head to foot I scurried away from the bike, about twenty metres or so, and just sat down in the wet grass at the side of the road. I waited, and waited. I knew it was the right thing to do but I felt really foolish sitting on the grass at the side of the road in my bike gear in a torrential thunderstorm; yet I knew this was the safest thing to do. I could only guess at what the cars passing me were thinking. The next bolt flashed over to my right and the noise came a few seconds later. The thunder lasted for six seconds – I counted. I just sat there getting soaked – my waterproofs remained nice and dry since they were still packed in my panniers.

A few minutes later there was another bolt of lightning, even further away, and I began to feel a little better but I wasn't going to move, not yet. And then the wind and rain picked up again and I saw another flash. I couldn't tell, through the clouds, where it was coming from but after about five seconds I heard the thunder. This time, worryingly, it came from behind me. This was a new storm. What should I do? I decided I'd had enough of lying in the grass, getting rained on and being sensible. I'd try my luck on the road again. I got back on the bike and rode off. I wasn't sure it was the right thing to do but I didn't want to wait for the second storm to come over the hill towards me.

It was twenty minutes before I came to a town, where I pulled up at the first petrol station. I parked the bike, jumped off and stood next to her, soaked to the skin. I was shaking, my senses were on edge and I must have looked a state. I stood there in a mild state of shock for about ten minutes before I calmed down enough to think what to do next. I really wasn't coping with lightning very well. I had hoped I'd seen the last of it in America and I could only hope that this was a one-off.

I had about another hundred miles to go to make it to the Sani Lodge Backpackers Hostel which was my destination for the night. At Kokstad I turned north on the R617. It had stopped raining but I kept looking up at the clouds and listening out for thunder. Ahead of me were the huge grey and foreboding mountains which formed the border with the Kingdom of Lesotho. The road was tarmacked; in excellent condition and with little traffic, but I felt a little vulnerable to the elements as I headed towards the mountains. I had convinced myself that the weather must be lovely down on the coast and I started to question what I was doing heading towards mountains, poor weather and the possibility of more thunderstorms. This bloody Sani Pass had better be worth it.

Two hours later I was checking into the backpackers' lodge and pitching my tent in a wet but beautifully green garden area next to the main lodge. The place was set up for backpackers, independent travellers and more organised tours and there was a wealth of information in the main room about the local area and the Sani Pass itself. The lodge was situated at about 1900 metres above sea level and the top of the pass was 1000 metres higher than that;

making it the highest pass in the country. The summit was only about fifteen miles away so I was going to do a lot of climbing – on gravel roads. Going up would probably be fine but coming down might be a little scary and I would also have to cross the border, twice: within five miles of leaving the lodge I would exit South Africa and at the top of the pass there was a border crossing into Lesotho. I would have to pass into Lesotho to reach the Sani Top Chalet – with Africa's highest pub and I hoped, a little shop selling stickers – then I would turn around and head back down. The gravel road continued on into Lesotho and although it did not have a good reputation it was supposed to be passable. But I wasn't done with South Africa yet and I wanted to head back to the coast. I consoled myself with the knowledge that this wouldn't be my only trip to Lesotho as I had plans to head into the country from the northern side on my way back to Cape Town later in the trip.

I sat in the lodge, recharging my Netbook and phone, and writing my blog for about an hour (after all, I'd met one of my readers and felt I had a duty to update him on my progress!). Then I went outside to find the toilet. I looked up and saw something I don't think I'd ever seen before: lightning but no thunder or rain – a silent electrical storm. It was quite cloudy too, so the whole sky lit up with flashes of bright white light, then total darkness, but no sound whatsoever. It was really quite eerie. On my way back to the lodge I wondered if I should say something. For me this was a unique experience but I could only assume it happened a lot here. If I said something I might look a bit foolish but equally if I didn't say anything my fellow travellers might be missing out on a rare event. If only I had been travelling with someone, we could have talked about it in loud voices to see if anyone overheard and said anything.

I found the guy who was running the lodge and asked him about the lightning outside.

"Yeah, we get that a lot here at this time of year – often with rain or hail. You're camping aren't you? Ha, good luck with that, man!"

I wished I'd kept my mouth shut. I took that as a suggestion that I should go to bed before the rain started and headed off to the campground. There were only three tents set up and one campervan. It had only cost me $8 to camp, but a dorm bed would have been $12. I had a feeling I might regret trying to save $4.

At nearly 2000 metres (over 6,000 feet) I knew it was going to be a cold night so I put my thermals on, plus my fleece and woolly hat and crawled into my sleeping bag. It started raining as soon as I'd zipped myself up and I lay in my tent for about ten minutes wondering if it would pass. It didn't. The rain got harder and then the whole tent lit up as if someone had parked their 4x4 right outside and flashed their full beam at me.

I couldn't stand it. There was no way I was going to get to sleep in a tent in a lightning storm. The fact that the lightning wasn't followed by any thunder at all just made it worse, almost as if the light was taunting me. I got up, grabbed my sleeping bag and headed back to the lounge. Everyone else had gone to bed by now and I was just about to settle down on a sofa for the night when I heard a huge crash on the tin roof; then another, and another. Monkeys? Branches? What was going on? I opened the door and looked out. I just couldn't believe it: it was hailing. But these were no ordinary hailstones, these were the size of golf balls and falling heavily now. Standing there in the doorway looking out all I could do was hope that it wouldn't last long. The noise had become deafening on the tin roof and I could see some of the chalet doors opening as other guests took a look outside. There was no point trying to speak to anyone as you couldn't be heard, so we were in this rather odd situation of all standing in doorways taking photos of the golf ball-sized hailstones in the middle of the night. Just as I began to feel a little smug about getting out of my tent in time I thought of Heidi. She was out in the hail, unprotected. Surely this ice must be doing some damage to her bodywork? There really wasn't much I could do about it but I feared for what I might find in the morning; not to mention whether my tent would make it through the night.

The hail eased up after about ten minutes but it continued to rain and the lightning show didn't abate so I got in my sleeping bag and settled down on the sofa. I had a restless night, worried about the Sani Pass, worried about lightning and worried that my poor bike was outside in the hailstorm.

I woke to a beautiful sunny morning as so often happens after a storm. I rushed down to the campsite fearing the worst, but the tent looked absolutely fine, everything inside was dry and Heidi was unscathed. The other campers were emerging from their night-time ordeal and I asked how they had coped. One had ducked into a dorm for the night but the Australian couple had stayed in their tent. What's a bit of hail and lightning when you're used to camping with crocodiles and black widow spiders?

After fortifying myself with muesli and local organic milk from Jersey cows I gave the bike a once-over (for me, that meant checking the tyres weren't flat, checking the oil and petrol and packing my puncture repair kit in the pannier). Then I headed off to the Sani Pass. Every day on this trip I had felt excited about what I was doing and always reminded myself that I was doing something special – special for me at least – but on this particular day I was excited and nervous. I genuinely had no idea what I was getting myself into and whether I would be able to get myself out of it. I'd told myself in the night that I wouldn't attempt the pass if it was wet and would most certainly turn around and head back if the weather looked bad. There was no way I wanted to get stuck on the side of a mountain at 2000 metres in a hailstorm like the one I'd witnessed the night before. But at nine in the morning the weather looked really good and I just had to go and give it a try.

The eight miles to the South African border post were relatively straightforward. The road was compacted mud and earth and even though it had rained the night before it was comparatively dry and easy to ride. I didn't see any other traffic and when I got to the border post the customs officials told me I was the first person going up that day. I asked if there had been any other motorcycles recently and, reassuringly he said that they got quite a few. He smiled at me and with a glint in his eye added: "And most of them come back down safely too!"

I exited South Africa and prepared myself for the five miles ahead. That's all it was, five miles, but in those five miles I would climb 1000 metres to reach an altitude of 2850 metres above sea level.

The compacted earth road changed to gravel and rocks as I reached the foot of the climb. I looked up at the foreboding mountain ahead. I could clearly see the route I was going to take as the road cut its way up the side of the mountain, twisting and turning with the contours of the land as it stretched out ahead on the way to Lesotho. Originally, of course, the Sani Pass had been a trade route. No doubt for hundreds of years, Basotho traders had carried wool and mohair down the mountain and exchanged it for food and clothing. Then in 1948, Godfrey Edmunds, an ex-RAF pilot, decided to drive up. It took him several hours and he enlisted the help of a gang of Basotho men, their mules and lots of rope. As far as I could tell, from the reading I had done, he did it just for the hell of it. The kind of 'Well, it's there so let's give it a go' attitude that I greatly admire.

The night before I'd picked up a small leaflet in the backpackers' lodge which had a map of the route I was taking up the pass. I don't know why I was carrying it, I didn't need directions as there was only one road but the literature scared the shit out of me. Seemingly all the bends had names and it was very unnerving to know that I had just passed 'Haemorrhoid Hill' and was about to attempt 'Suicide Bend'.

I made it past 'Suicide Bend' without any mishaps. I was standing up on the footrests, with Heidi mainly in second gear. The road was quite steep so there was no need to use the brakes and all I really needed to do was keep away from the edge and out of the deep gravel which formed at the edges and middle of the road. I still hadn't encountered any traffic coming down and as the mountainside was devoid of any vegetation it was easy to see further up the route. The bends were, indeed, quite sharp but in order to get trucks and 4x4s up the route they had obviously extended the corners a little so they could manage to sweep around in one go. As I approached what was reassuringly called 'Ice corner' at 2750 metres I was almost enjoying it! But then I had the contretemps with the boulder described in detail in Chapter 16.

Having finally cleared the troublesome rock, I stopped at the apex of a sharp bend, put Heidi into neutral, turned off the engine and took a deep breath. I lifted my flip-front to help cool my face and looked up the road at what lay ahead. I couldn't quite see the top but I knew I must be close. Looking down at my map, I saw that I was on 'Reverse Corner' and only had seventy-five metres of vertical height left to climb. Just then I heard an engine from above and saw a motorcycle coming down towards me. It was a BMW 1200GS. The rider was wearing blue jeans, a black jacket and a backpack. He didn't have any luggage or even any panniers so I assumed he'd just gone up for the day and the border guard who'd said I was the first that day had lied to me.

"Hi, how's it going?" he asked.

"Oh, great thanks." I didn't mention my struggle with the boulder. "No problem going uphill. But I'm a little more worried about coming down. How are you finding it?"

"Just take care, mate. Slap it into first gear, get up on your pegs and look ahead." Almost as an afterthought, with a smile on his face, he added "Oh, and don't forget to turn the ABS off of course." He laughed as if that last little nugget was so obvious it almost didn't need saying. I had no idea what he was talking about.

"Er... Sorry to ask this, but how do I do that?" My fear overriding my shame.

Even I couldn't really believe this but I had no idea I could turn my Anti-Blocking System off. I was eight months, and 22,000 miles into my trip and I was asking a complete stranger, on the side of a mountain, how to turn my ABS off. What on earth must this South African have thought? Here he was on the Sani Pass and he meets a British biker on an Alaskan GS who is planning to ride all the way to Kenya and yet he doesn't even know that he can turn his ABS off, never mind how to do it.

Evidently it's quite easy to turn the ABS off on a GS. It involves the tricky operation of pressing the button that says ABS. Why would you want to turn the anti-lock braking system off? Because on a really loose surface it can stop your wheels locking up, but it can also stop the brakes working altogether, so you need to be able to feel for the limit of grip in a way that the ABS won't allow.

He seemed in a bit of a hurry and after showing me how to turn the ABS off he said goodbye and headed off down the mountain. This little encounter had given me time to calm down and reassess the road ahead. I knew I only had two or three bends to go and I now had the confidence to push on and make it to the top. This guy, whose name I never learnt, would never know what sort of impact he had on me. At that point I was seriously contemplating turning Heidi around and riding back downhill (with the ABS on). I wasn't convinced that I could make it to the top after that last little stumble, but meeting this other biker had reassured me. I pushed on for the summit, taking the last three corners in style and as I reached the top I saw the welcoming sign of the Lesotho border post. This was possibly the most pleased I've ever been to see a border post. It was also the most dilapidated one I'd ever seen. There was a wooden gate ahead of me and to the left a small wooden hut. Behind that was a red and white caravan. I parked up and headed over to the wooden hut.

"Welcome to Lesotho. How long will you be staying sir?"

"Oh, about an hour." I'd never said that on entering a country before!

"And you have a bike?"

"Yes."

"Can I see your road tax for the motorcycle?"

"Eh? No. This is not a South African motorcycle. It's American, so I don't have road tax for it."

"But you must have. All vehicles coming into Lesotho must have valid South African road tax."

"But, this is not a South African motorcycle."

This went on for a few minutes. It was a friendly misunderstanding and after repeating several times that Heidi was not South African (I showed him the Alaskan licence plate and even the map on the side to show him where I'd been) he seemed to lose interest in pursuing the whole road tax thing. He stamped my passport, charged me about $5 and welcomed me to his country.

The only thing to do at the top of the Sani Pass is to ride a couple of hundred metres to the Sani Top Chalet. Looking just like an old-fashioned wooden ski chalet, this was home to Africa's highest pub.

The local beer has the strapline: 'How high can you get!' and I sat on the veranda and almost found out. The stress of the morning and the low oxygen levels at altitude made for a heady mix. I hadn't even finished a bottle of beer and my head was spinning as I looked out at the amazing view. It was simply stunning. It was now late morning and the warm African sun was high in the sky which was a wonderful deep blue. Below me, stretching out for miles, were the Drakensberg mountains. Rocky by nature but with a greenish tinge, they rolled off into the distance and I couldn't see a single building or any manmade structure at all, apart from the gravel road that twisted and snaked its way down the mountainside right in front of me. From my spot on the veranda I could see the hairpin switchbacks that I had just ridden up. I tried to imagine what I would have thought if I'd been sitting here after coming up in a car and then seen a motorcycle attempt the road. Would I have been impressed, shocked or amazed or would I have said: "Oh yeah, that looks easy. I reckon I could do that." I'm fairly sure I would have looked on in wonder, never imagining that I would be capable of such a feat. I sat there, surveying the vista as if I had conquered it and it was all mine, a sense of invulnerability swelled up inside me and I felt quite proud of what I had done.

Then the alcohol wore off and I remembered that I had to ride back down. I went back into the chalet to see if I could get a sticker for my panniers. There was no one around and I couldn't see any for sale in the bar. Damn! All that effort and no sticker to show for it. I got back to Heidi, left Africa's highest pub, and nervously headed out to the border post to descend. I wasn't looking forward to it. I knew I had to stand up on my pegs (and I'd turned my ABS off) but standing up going downhill makes everything look a long way down. Still, I knew the theory. Slam it into first, use the engine braking through the transmission to control the speed, rather than the brakes themselves, look ahead and plan ahead.

I left Lesotho and headed for the first downhill bend with Heidi in first gear, letting the engine do the work. I was standing on the pegs, gripping the tank between my knees and, if I needed to, I was using the rear brake. I was consciously trying to keep my focus on what was ahead and not what was right in front of me, and trying to remember never to look at where I didn't want to go or else I would end up there. And it worked. I only had one scary section where I slid a little sideways as I locked the rear wheel, but I was down in no time. So, all in all, I'd covered thirty miles, entered and left a country and gone up, then down, a thousand metres, all in about five hours; quite some day. A few days later I stumbled across this gem about the pass on Wikipedia –

> *This pass lies between the border controls of both countries and is approximately 9 km in length and requires above average driving experience. It has occasional remains of vehicles that did not succeed in navigating its steep gradients and poor traction surfaces, and has a catalogue of frightening stories of failed attempts at ascending the path over the Northern Lesotho mountains.*

I chuckled to myself.

Coming down the Sani Pass with ABS off!

CHAPTER 19

MOTORCYCLE SAFARI

"We live in a wonderful world that is full of beauty, charm and adventure. There is no end to the adventures we can have if only we seek them out with our eyes open."

(Jawaharlal Nehru)

Leaving Sani I stopped at a petrol station and while there saw a BMW R1200GS with a UK number plate go by. I managed to catch up with him and we stopped for coffee and a chat. Mike had been on the road for a few months and was at the end of a UK–South Africa trip that saw him get through Egypt just before the overthrow of President Mubarak during the so-called 'Arab Spring'. He was in his sixties and had to walk with a stick, yet he was riding a huge bike through Africa. His achievement put my little accomplishments back into perspective just as I was beginning to feel a bit too pleased with myself.

We talked about South Africa and I commented on how strangely similar it seemed to home. It wasn't just the language and the driving on the left, it was also the scenery. I had described Alaska as being 'like Scotland on steroids'; well the South Africa that I'd been riding through was a bit like 'rural England on steroids': rolling hills (with Jersey cows on them) towns and village churches (some of them deliberately resembling English Norman churches); golf courses, crown green bowling and cricket pitches. Obviously there are one or two more banana trees, rooibos tea plantations and wineries than in middle England but I couldn't help feeling it was similar. The fact that I could buy Marmite everywhere also helped with the illusion. Over one hundred years ago my great grandmother emigrated to this part of South Africa, perhaps it wasn't as far from home for her as it looked on a map.

Mike smiled at me. "Just wait until you get to the Great Karoo."

Although he'd seen and done a lot, Mike was an unassuming guy and I milked him for all the information I could before we parted. He was heading south towards Cape Town for a few days before returning to Durban to arrange to ship his bike back to the UK. I told him I was thinking of going to Sodwana Bay to scuba dive. He said I should check out the Aliwal Shoal just south of Durban. So, not for the first time, I changed my plans and headed for the coast.

I took the beautiful winding R612 down to the sea and headed north a little way until I got to Umkomass and checked in to the Aliwal Dive Centre. I'd done quite a lot of diving in the past but I'd never heard of the Aliwal Shoal. Apparently it's quite famous! The local literature told me that this was one of the top ten diving sites in the world. Four miles out to sea, the shoal was created from dune rock about 30,000 years ago. (Yes my Zion National Park Mormon friends – that does say thirty thousand years ago.) Six and a half thousand years ago the sea level had risen, creating the reef. So, I was effectively going to be diving on an old sand dune. I was getting quite excited at the thought of diving now and needed to celebrate. I went into town to find a small bar and have a quiet beer.

Sure enough, I found an appropriate dive and went in. Dimly lit, it was a small place with a long bar at one end and a pool table dominating the whole room. The three televisions were all showing a rugby match and the cheering audience were mostly shirtless, smoking and drunk. A guy who was hardly sober enough to hold his cigarette was staggering around the pool table swinging his cue over his head. The only females in the place were behind the bar. I'm not sure if they were working or just there for their own safety. I didn't have the guts to just turn around and walk out so I ordered a beer in an accent which I tried to make not too obviously British, although I wasn't sure why.

I must have stood out like a sore thumb and I felt quite self-conscious as people seemed to be staring at me. I leant against the bar watching the rugby and feeling slightly uncomfortable, as if I'd gate-crashed a party. Had I been there with someone else then I'm sure the atmosphere would have felt much less sinister; it was simply because I was alone that I felt out of place. I knew I was being stupid but, subconsciously, I was drinking my beer quickly and already planning my escape. All I had to do was keep my head down, melt into the background, finish my beer and disappear.

"Hello."

Damn.

"Hi, how are you?" I replied.

"I'm Henry. You're not from here are you?"

Oh, no here we go, I thought. "No, no, I'm from the UK."

"Wow, so what are you doing here?

Just leaving, I thought. "Oh, I'm just travelling around. I'm going diving tomorrow so thought I'd come and have a beer."

Henry then insisted on buying me a beer and asking me more about my travels. He was a really friendly guy and absolutely amazed at what I was doing. He was built like a rugby player and must have been six foot two and 110 kilos. He spent most of his time out on the high seas fishing and wasn't the sort of person you would want to mess with, and yet the thought of travelling through Africa, let alone riding solo on a motorcycle, scared the crap out of him. He was very concerned about me travelling on my own and insisted on giving me his phone number should I need any help whatsoever. He was a genuinely nice guy and I felt ashamed that I'd gone into that bar with all my preconceived ideas about white South African men clouding my judgement.

Once again I'd had one of those magical days that, upon reflection, seemed almost unreal. I'd briefly met Mike, an inspiration to all overland bikers everywhere, and Henry, who had met a stranger in a pub and had given him his phone number. I had no doubt whatsoever that Henry meant what he said and if I were to phone him up in a few days' time he would have dropped everything to come to my assistance. I berated myself for being so worried and suspicious and returned to my room content that actually, people are quite nice and want to help. And I'm sure it wasn't just the beer that made me feel that way.

I had a great day's diving. My dive buddy seemed to be more interested in looking for sharks' teeth in the sand but I saw lots of exciting fish and even a couple of Hawksbill turtles. My mind flashed back to Baja and I wondered if the black turtles had hatched... It had certainly been more than fifty days since I'd been there.

The following day I headed up the coast. Mike had also suggested I stop off at St Lucia. So I did. The small town of St Lucia is completely surrounded by a Natural World Heritage Site and is the most ecologically diverse tourist destination in Southern Africa. My guidebook told me I might see elephants, leopards, rhinos, buffalos, turtles nesting, crocs in the water and hippos walking down the street. The area was famous for having the highest number of black rhino in one place on earth, 525 species of birds, 35 species of frog, 36 species of snake, 800 hippos and 2000 crocs. Rather bizarrely, the tourist brochure I'd picked up at the dive lodge had a timeline of St Lucia. This is what had happened in 1928: *Huberta, St Lucia's most famous hippo, left her pod and began an epic journey of 1600 km across South Africa. In 1931, after crossing 122 rivers, she was killed by hunters in the Keiskamma River.* I had so many questions...

Keeping an eye out for Huberta's relatives crossing the road I cruised into St Lucia on Heidi hoping to find a campsite. Unfortunately I couldn't see any signs and as it was getting dark I decided to check out a couple of the motels. It proved to be a decision that was to have a huge impact on my trip through Africa. I hadn't stayed in a motel yet in South Africa, but I was feeling a little lazy and wanted to see what sort of value for money I would get. I rode up the main street and as I came to the first motel on the left I could see the front wheel of what was clearly a large motorcycle sticking out from behind a car in the car park. I pulled in to take a look.

Parked up next to one of the rooms was a yellow Suzuki V-Strom 650 with a South African number plate, loaded up on the back and with black metal panniers on the side. This was clearly the bike of a serious overlander, and a trusting one, as it was now seven in the evening, dark and he'd left several items just tied on with a bungee. However, there was no one around to talk to. Hoping that we would meet up later, I parked next to the V-Strom and went to the reception. I had no idea what a nice room in a motel would cost in this part of the world but was confident it wouldn't be the $50 I'd had to pay in the USA. I was right. I got a nice clean room, double bed, fan and really hot water all for $30. Camping would have probably cost me about $10 so I wouldn't break my budget by using motels every now and then.

After a quick wash and sort out I went for a stroll around town. St Lucia was certainly geared up for tourists, with a main street full of souvenir shops, restaurants and tour guide offices. I found a reasonably cheap pizzeria and ate while watching rugby on the large TV. This seemed to be the thing to do in South Africa and something I would just have to get used to. Food, beer and rugby – guess I couldn't complain. Eating out in the evening, when I wasn't camping, was often a lonely experience. Somehow a person sitting on their own in a restaurant, or even worse, sitting with a book, looks sad. There's no rationale to this. They may well be very happy and a good book beats bad company any day, but eating is a communal thing and it was often the one time of the day when I felt lonely. I wasn't really lonely, I just thought I looked lonely – which paradoxically made me feel lonely.

When I got back to my room (there were no hippos about) I found a note on my bike. It read: *'Alaska, we are in room 14. Leaving early in a.m. Want to do breakfast? Tom – Washington, Pat and Chris, Quebec.'* How could I refuse? I don't think I've ever *done* breakfast before.

What a surprise I got in the morning. 'Tom – Washington', was the same Tom I'd met briefly in Canada at the motorcycle rally, the one who had offered me a bed for the night when I crossed over from Vancouver. He'd just bought the V-Strom in Johannesburg. Pat and Christianne were riding two-up on Pat's Canadian-registered Honda Africa Twin 750 which had been parked around the corner. The three had known each other for a few years and were planning to ride all the way up to Europe. We had a very long breakfast and swapped stories and pieces of advice for over three hours. Eventually they left, heading south, but we exchanged phone numbers and I was sure we'd meet up again. We were all planning to head up to Namibia from Cape Town and they'd also been in touch with Daryll and Angela, the Canadian couple whose blog I'd been following in Central America. It looked as if my days of eating alone might be coming to an end.

However, I'd come to St Lucia to see some hippos so as Tom, Pat and Chris rode off on their bikes, I went off to find the local wildlife. I rode up to the estuary and saw some hippos but didn't see any crocodiles, rhinos or elephants. They were to be found further north in the 'Eastern Shores' park but this was closed to motorcycles; I suspected that this would not be the last time that seeking wildlife would be impeded by my choice of transport.

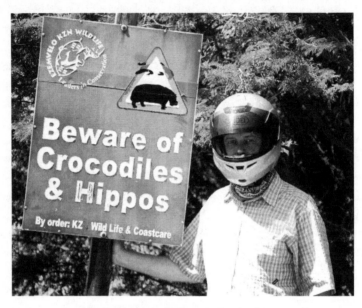

No bears to worry about in South Africa

From St Lucia I headed north to my third African country, Swaziland. Like Lesotho, Swaziland was a country I'd heard of, and could find on a map, but knew very little about. I knew it was land-locked and had gained independence from Britain in 1968. It was also one of the last remaining absolute monarchies in the world. King Mswati III, with a personal fortune of around $200m, rules over one of the poorest countries on the planet. Famous (or rather infamous) for his lavish lifestyle, this is an African king who has at least thirteen wives and holds an annual dance where he can choose a new bride from the tens of thousands of bare-breasted virgins. Meanwhile, Swaziland has a horrific HIV/AIDS problem. The HIV infection rate is currently the highest in the world at about 26% of all adults, and over 50% of adults in their twenties. This has severely limited possible economic and social progress, and is at a point where it endangers the existence of its society as a whole. HIV has reduced life expectancy to below fifty and Swaziland could well become the first country in the world to collapse because of an epidemic.

I went online to improve my Swazi-knowledge. I came across this: *Swaziland also has one of the highest numbers of people struck by lightning per capita in the whole world and it is common to know (or know of) somebody who has been struck by lightning.*

Great! Just what I *didn't* want to read.

With memories of some of the Central American crossings I'd had to endure, I approached the South African/Swaziland border at Lavumisa with some trepidation. However, it took less than thirty minutes to leave South Africa and enter Swaziland. No photocopies of anything were needed and South Africa even refused to cancel my *carnet de passage*. Most African countries (but none in the Americas) require vehicles to have a carnet. This is a sort of passport for the motorcycle and I had been told that I would have to get it stamped at every border. Fundamentally it worked as a guarantee that I would exit the country with the bike and I had to leave a £10,000 bond with the RAC in the UK before they would issue me with the document. If I didn't return to the UK with the bike and the document I wouldn't get my money back. So I was a little concerned when emigration on the South African side of the border refused to stamp my carnet, saying it wasn't necessary. I argued with them but they were resolute that they weren't going to stamp it. There wasn't much I could do. I didn't even show it to the Swaziland side and no one asked. I had to pay $8 road tax to enter Swaziland and no one asked me if I had insurance.

Travel insurance is something I wouldn't leave home without but vehicle insurance is a different matter. I would never ride or drive at home without vehicle insurance and I know I should really have up to date cover when abroad but it isn't as easy as that. In North America I had to have, and consequentially could easily get, motorcycle insurance that meant something. Some Central American countries required me to pay on the border (and I received an official slip of paper saying I'd paid for it, although I was dubious as to how effective it would have been should I have actually tried to claim). But if they didn't ask I didn't offer. Not really because I was hoping to save a few dollars but more because I expected few people had insurance and any accident would usually be sorted out there and then by the parties involved.

Somewhere I'd read that in South Africa third party insurance is paid for via a tax on the price of petrol – so in a way I was already paying for insurance anyway. This seemed to me a very sensible way of doing things. If I got into an accident in South Africa (and indeed anywhere in Africa) the advice was to get away as quickly as possible. I felt very uncomfortable about the thought of doing this. What if it was my fault? What if I'd hurt someone? Surely I don't leave my moral responsibility at the border when travelling? However I'd read a few travel books and was aware of how quickly some situations can get out of hand. I'd also heard of stories in various parts of the world where some people cause traffic accidents on purpose when they see a foreign vehicle, in order to get as much money as possible for their family. I hated these stories, partly because it was awful to think of anyone being that desperate and partly because it's the kind of thing someone who never travels cites to justify their insular world view. I might be being naive but, if involved in an accident, my plan was to assess the situation and try to conduct myself with the same moral attitudes that I would have at home. After all I was going to have to live with myself and with the consequences of my own actions.

I didn't want to avoid paying insurance for the sake of it and I got annoyed when I met fellow Western (and therefore relatively rich) travellers cutting corners and breaking the law in order to save a little money. I guess it's a fine line between paying your way and being ripped off. I'd read of a motorcyclist who'd ridden around Central America and when he got to Tikal he refused to pay to go in as foreigners get charged a lot more than Guatemalan nationals. He said something like: "We don't have two charges in National Parks in America, one for US citizens and one for foreigners. And if we did there'd be uproar at how racist we were."

I see this as twisted logic. Foreigners are obviously much richer than Guatemalans. If the entrance ticket reflected what foreigners could afford to pay, the locals would never be able to visit their own magnificent Mayan ruins. However if the entry price reflected what the locals could afford, we would think it was incredibly cheap and the Guatemalan authorities wouldn't be able to raise the funds they need for the upkeep of the place. In cases like this it seems sensible to have a two-tier pricing system.

So, although I was riding through South Africa (and now Swaziland) without motor insurance, I hadn't planned it that way, it's just that no one had yet asked me to pay. Honest, officer.

With these thoughts banging around in my helmet I left the border and entered Swaziland on a well-paved road. Even though I was only planning to be in the country for a few days I was happy to pay the road tax if it meant all the roads were going to be well maintained, sealed and as beautiful as the one I was on. I had no idea what altitude, if any, I was at but Swaziland seemed to be a beautifully lush, green, fertile and hilly country. The road swept up and over the hills and meandered alongside a river as I came to my first settlement, rather uninspiringly called Big Bend. I'd filled up with petrol at the border so there was no need to stop and I continued northwards towards Mozambique. Just before the border, I reached the Mbuluzi Game Reserve that Tom and Pat had told me about. It didn't have any 'dangerous' animals so would let motorcycles in. The thought of being able to ride in what was essentially a private game park and camp in the middle of it was too good an opportunity to miss. Tom had waxed lyrical about the place; how they had seen giraffe and zebra and camped with monkeys and warthogs. I had to give it a go.

I turned up early in the afternoon, which was just as well as I wanted to get myself settled in the campsite with plenty of time to have a look around before sunset. I paid my camping fee and rode through the reserve towards the campsite. The park ranger, who remembered Tom and Pat from the previous week, said I was the only camper and even though it was a Saturday they weren't expecting anyone else. I was going to have a Swaziland safari all to myself!

Tom had told me that they had seen giraffes on the way down to the campsite but I didn't hold out much hope. I stood on my pegs as I rode the rough road, scanning the bush for any huge long-necked creatures just in case. I'd only been riding for about five minutes when I heard a noise off to my right and saw something rather large running parallel to me. The low African bushes suggested it wasn't a giraffe and as I glanced to my side I could just make out the distinctive black and white stripes of a zebra. I turned a corner, the bush opened out and I could see four or five zebra trotting along next to me, obviously a little spooked by the engine noise but not overly concerned by my presence. I had to keep a careful eye on the road ahead because the compacted earth track was sandy in places, but I managed to keep looking over, amazed that I was riding along next to zebra.

And then I noticed something else out of the corner of my eye. I'd been concentrating so much on what was happening off to my right that I hadn't been paying attention to what was on my left. It took a double take to realise what I was looking at, a huge animal lolloping along beside me, almost silently. I could hardly believe it was really a giraffe. And then there were three! To my right, half a dozen zebra were trotting through the bush, accompanying me, and to my left, three giraffes were also running alongside the bike. But they were so huge and their strides so long it looked as if they were running in slow motion. I didn't know where to look or what to do. For about ten or twenty seconds I just cruised along in second gear, easing off on the throttle trying to keep the bike upright as I glanced to my left and right trying to take it all in. It was an absolutely amazing experience. Never in my wildest dreams did I think I would ever ride a motorcycle through Africa alongside such majestic creatures. The zebra were cool and exciting but the giraffes were just out of this world. The nearest one was probably only about ten metres away as it lolloped alongside me; its lazy strides kicking up a cloud of dust in the late afternoon haze.

The whole thing only lasted seconds but my heart was pumping and I had a huge smile on my face as the animals disappeared off into the bush and I continued down the track toward the campsite. I was indeed the only person camping and had the whole reserve to myself that night. I went for a two-hour walk (not going too close to the river as there were, apparently, crocodiles) and although I didn't see any more zebra or giraffe I did see lots of impala and numerous colourful birds (including several toucans). When I got back to the campsite I'd been joined by some vervet monkeys and a family of warthogs. I don't know how far I was from the next human being but I couldn't hear a single manmade noise or see any unnatural light. I was, to all intents and purposes, totally alone in the African bush; just me and Heidi on a Saturday night out. It was dark by six thirty but I didn't really care as I sat outside my tent under the bright stars of an African sky.

I felt calm, serene, untroubled by all the baggage that comes with modern life. I didn't care about anything or worry about anyone. It was a little epiphany similar, I imagine, to the kind of thing people can experience when they meditate. Briefly, in my own small way, my mind shifted a little on to a different plane. I tried to hold on to that feeling of peace and oneness with nature; a feeling that I was insignificant under the huge African sky, but that it didn't matter one bit. There had been times on the trip when I had felt lonely and missed company, but not that night; that night, company would have spoiled the whole experience. I needed to be alone – only then did it all, briefly, make sense.

*

My next stop in Swaziland was the Ezulwini Valley. Swaziland's capital (Mbabane) had no attractions at all but Ezulwini was Swaziland's royal heartland and tourist centre: lush green hills, wooded game parks, the national Parliament building, a football stadium and the national museum, not to mention a brand new shopping mall and a casino. This eclectic mix seemed to sum up the country quite well. I stopped off at the national museum (I was the only visitor) and brushed up on my Swazi history and culture.

The museum was essentially a three-room building. In the main room I was drawn to a cabinet displaying a stone spear dating back 75,000 years. Nothing unusual in that I thought. I'd lost count of the number of museums I'd been to with rooms full of broken pottery and stone spears. And then I read the inscription underneath:

Many archaeologists argue that this spear point demonstrates the earliest form of abstract thinking anywhere in the world. The points are so fine and beautifully made they could never be for hunting. They were made to be beautiful and this has symbolic value and meaning. But to have symbolism we must have language and abstract thinking. Therefore these points demonstrate abstract thinking.

That was something I hadn't expected. Swaziland – home of abstract thinking.

I then headed for the Sondzela Backpackers' Lodge which was going to be home for the night. It offered me a space to camp with wonderful views, a resident warthog family and the chance to walk through the Mlilwane wildlife sanctuary in which it was situated. I went for a hike and saw deer, zebra and warthogs. Swaziland will, for me, always be the land of motorcycle and walking safaris; something I hadn't thought I'd be able to do at all as I made my way through Africa.

My short time in Swaziland was coming to a close and, as always, when leaving a country my mind tried to process what I'd seen. How could I sum up what I thought of the place? On one level if I got out of there without being struck by lightning I was going to love the country, but there had been something niggling at the back of my mind about Swaziland. And the day I left I worked out what it was: travelling through the country I don't think I saw a single person who looked older than me. Maybe it was just because I knew life expectancy was so low but it did seem that the population was very young. Filling up with petrol just before leaving, I bought a local newspaper and although it was only six pages long, two whole pages were dedicated to funeral notices. Tellingly, none of them said what the deceased had died of and I was still wondering how a country could function with such a huge HIV/AIDS rate. Then I took a closer look at the notices. Whereas in the UK it would say something like *"Dom Giles has passed away"*, here it said *"Going Home notice. We announce that Dom Giles is going home…"* I liked that. Hope over adversity. I think that is how I'd sum up Swaziland.

*

Ah, History. What would we do without it? What's a holiday without a tour of a battlefield or a traipse around a war cemetery? There hadn't been enough history so far on 'thedomwayround' and as I re-entered South Africa I knew I was about to put that right. On my way from Swaziland to Lesotho I was going to stop off at Dundee and visit some battlefield sites.

The Boer Wars, or more correctly, the Anglo-Boer Wars, took place during a period in British history about which I was very ignorant. So, it was with enthusiasm and intrigue that I started reading my guidebook and any other literature I could find as I rode Heidi into 'Battlefield' country. I also quickly became aware that there are at least three different 'Histories' depending on whom you read. As far as I could tell, the facts seemed to be as follows: the British annexed Cape Colony in 1806 and from then onwards extended their control of south eastern South Africa. The Boers, who were of Dutch origin, (*boer* simply means 'farmer' in Dutch), were unhappy with British rule and left the region in the 1830s on the famous 'Great Trek' of 1835–40. These 'Vortrekkers' or 'pioneers' took their long trains of oxcarts towards the Natal, Orange Free State and Transvaal regions where they founded a new republic, independent of British rule. This enabled them to keep their culture, religious practices and Dutch-based *Afrikaans* language. Their culture included a profound belief in the superiority of white Afrikaner Christians over heathen blacks, which partly explains why the Great Trek followed the abolition of slavery throughout the British Empire in 1833, even though very few of the Vortrekkers had ever actually owned slaves.

By the late 1870s British imperialism meant that conflict between the British Empire and the Boers was inevitable. No doubt the British also thought the result would be equally inevitable, but it wasn't. In the first Boer War (Anglo-Boer War) of 1880–81 the Boers surprised the British and over a series of battles lasting a few months, they won. (This part isn't usually mentioned in UK History books!) The British, realising they would need many more troops to beat the Boers ordered a truce which allowed Boer self-government in the Transvaal under theoretical British supervision. And this might well have been the end of it if it hadn't been for the discovery, in 1886, of gold near Pretoria. The once barren and dusty landscape now became important to the British and worth fighting over. In 1899 the second Anglo-Boer War broke out. This one is more famous in Britain because the British won. In 1902 the South African Republic (Transvaal) and the Orange Free State were both annexed by the British Empire, and would ultimately become part of the Union of South Africa in 1910.

In the second Boer War, the British distinguished themselves by inventing concentration camps and over 26,000 Boer men, women and children died in them of disease and starvation. I believe just over 7000 British and 7000 Boer soldiers actually died in the fighting. Some famous people were involved in the second Boer war: Lord Kitchener, later to play a central role at the start of The First World War, cut his teeth in Africa, first in Sudan, then in South Africa. Winston Churchill in 1899 went to South Africa as a journalist, was captured, imprisoned and then escaped, which gained him fame back in the UK. Ironically, the Afrikaner soldier who had captured Churchill was none other than Louis Botha, who went on to become not only Prime Minister of the Transvaal, but also the first prime minister of the Union of South Africa when the country was created in 1910.

Finally, Mohandas Gandhi (later known as *Mahatma*, or Great Soul) helped to create the Indian Ambulance corps during the Boer War. He had some sympathy with the Boers' grievances but felt that if Indians laid claims to rights as British subjects they had a duty to defend the Empire. He helped organise and train a group of over one thousand Indian volunteers and he and thirty-seven fellow Indian stretcher-bearers were decorated for their heroism at the famous battle of Spion Kop.

But the battlefield site I was going to visit involved the British against the Zulus. Just before the Boer Wars, the British had also been annoying the Zulus, or more accurately perhaps, the Zulus had been annoying the British. Zululand was (very roughly) a part of Southern Africa situated between Swaziland and Lesotho. In 1879 the British Army fought the Zulus. (For more details watch the 1964 film *Zulu* starring Michael Caine; available at all good Backpacker Lodges throughout South Africa.) In the Battle of Rorke's Drift, 139 British soldiers successfully defended a small mission station against some 4000 Zulu warriors. The much less commercially successful, *Zulu Dawn* (1979) recalls the Battle of Isandlwana which took place the day before, where a British force of around 1400 men was annihilated by some 12,000–25,000 Zulus. (Estimates of the numbers involved vary a lot!)

I detoured off the main road into Dundee to visit the site of the Isandlwana battle. The British (mainly the 2nd Warwickshires) were camped by the hill and ambushed by the Zulus. At the battle of Isandlwana, 1357 British soldiers died (including 52 British officers and 806 non-commissioned officers). 471 African troops died fighting for the British. Zulu casualties are estimated at between one to two thousand. Only 55 British soldiers escaped the battlefield alive. The Zulu Nation won the battle but not the war, and within ten years the British Empire had annexed Zululand. The Swazis took heed of this and negotiated a peace with Britain which is probably why Swaziland remained an independent country while Zululand was incorporated into the Union of South Africa.

Isandlwana is a memorable site. The British returned four months after the battle to bury their dead. (I'm not sure what they did with the Zulu dead.) Large white cairns were placed over the mass graves where the British had been buried. It made a striking and evocative sight. As a history teacher I'm used to death and battles and pain and suffering. And that's just the teaching part! But actually I'd got too blasé about it all. It wasn't especially because they were British, it was more the fact that each white cairn represented massive loss of life. People had fought, died and been buried on that very spot thousands of miles from their home, from their loved ones, fighting a war they quite possibly didn't even understand. But they were doing their duty.

At the small Isandlwana museum I found a list of all the British men who had died in the battle. (We Brits may not be good at winning things but we are bloody good at keeping score.) I don't really know why, but I just had to look down the list to see if my name was there. I know that Giles is only my father's, father's, father's surname and over one hundred years ago I must have had eight different grandfathers' surnames, but I looked down the list and found one: Sergeant Edward Giles of the 1st Battalion, 24th Regiment of the 2nd Warwickshires. I guess it made it personal and I was overcome with a feeling of deep sadness – and guilt. Here was I, having the time of my life, selfishly riding a motorcycle across South Africa, just for the hell of it. And yet only a hundred years ago another Brit with the same surname had fought and died on that very spot, doing his duty.

*

I tried to leave my feelings of guilt in Dundee as I headed west towards the Kingdom of Lesotho and this time I was going to stay more than two hours. I knew Lesotho was a mountain kingdom completely surrounded by South Africa but that was about all I knew. It seemed a strange, almost mythical country and when you look at it on a map one question screams out at you: Why the hell is it there? Why isn't it just part of South Africa? Geographically and historically being an enclave is not a safe state of affairs for a nation and I believe there are only two other 'countries' in the world that are completely surrounded by a larger one – the tiny Vatican City, surrounded by Rome and the not much bigger, San Marino, also surrounded by Italy, near Rimini.

A little digging online, and in my guidebook, provided some explanation, but Lesotho's independence remained puzzling. My understanding is that in the late nineteenth century the Boers and the Basotho (people of Lesotho) squabbled a lot and the King of Lesotho (Moshoeshoe) asked Britain for protection. Strictly speaking, he should first have asked the British administration in Cape Colony but he appealed directly to the imperial government in London. The British viewed continual war between the Orange Free State (Boers) and Basutoland (Lesotho) as bad for their own interests and annexed the nation, essentially protecting Lesotho. One unexpected benefit of this was that, when the Union of South Africa was created in 1910, Basutoland was a British Protectorate and was, therefore, not included; had Cape Colony retained control, Lesotho would have become part of South Africa. I think.

From Dundee I took the main road to Ladysmith, now a modern, fairly nondescript-looking city, but an important base for the British during the second Boer War. The battle of Ladysmith in October 1899 was one of the earliest battles in the war. The Boers routed the British who retreated to the walled city and the Boers then laid siege to the town for more than a hundred days. Over three thousand British soldiers died. Both Churchill and Gandhi were involved in the siege of Ladysmith. I tried to imagine a young Churchill, cigar in mouth, walking around the town watching a group of Indian Ambulance corps helping a wounded soldier. I just wondered if they ever did, inadvertently, meet. In the back of my mind I recalled that there was a story of Hitler and Lenin being in Vienna, Austria in the early part of the twentieth century. There was just the distant possibility that the two may have met each other. There is actually a painting purportedly showing Hitler playing chess with Lenin in 1909 in Vienna. I don't think it is genuine but it is possible. Indeed recent research by Charles Emerson suggests that Hitler, Stalin, Trotsky, Freud, Jung and Tito were all living in central Vienna in 1913. Amazing stuff. But Churchill as a young war correspondent meeting Ghandi – that would have been intriguing.

This was the sort of thing a history-teaching biker thinks as he passes through Ladysmith.

I stopped at a petrol station, filled up, had a coffee and a pee and moved on. I didn't give Ladysmith another thought, but I took the road towards Harrismith hoping to cross through the Golden Gate Highlands National Park and on into Lesotho.

Somewhere near Harrismith I stopped for more petrol and a break and, unusually for me, I turned my phone on. I rarely had my phone turned on but I was trying to get in touch with a friend in Lesotho and had had little luck via email. I was hoping she'd got my last message and would give me a call. My phone made a noise telling me I'd got a text and I eagerly looked down hoping it was from Lerato. It wasn't. It was from my sister back in the UK who I'd emailed a few days previously to tell her how my trip was going. This was her reply: *"You know your great-grandmother lived in Ladysmith don't you?"*

I guess the answer was no, I didn't. I did know that in 1903 my great-grandmother had travelled out to South Africa with her new husband, my great-grandfather, and had lived there for several years. Beyond that, I didn't know that anyone else knew anything. It was a really surreal feeling to think that the nondescript city I'd just passed through was actually the place my great-grandparents had lived a century ago. Just twenty-five years after Sergeant Giles had died at Isandlwana, my great-grandparents had been living in Ladysmith. I thought about turning around and going back, but why? What would I do? Where would I go? There didn't seem to be any point. So I carried on riding with a weird feeling that I was riding through a land which was no longer just a foreign country but a land I had some connection with. Somewhat spurious perhaps, at least in the case of Sergeant Giles, but suddenly everything felt and looked slightly different.

The scenery from Harrismith to the border was just wonderful as I passed through the Golden Gate Highlands National Park. The area takes its name from the huge sandstone formations which glow golden in the afternoon sun. The red rocks and scrub bush reminded me of parts of America I'd been to; a sort of mix of Mesa Verde and Monument National Park. The road was in perfect condition, apart from one section where a road gang was laying fresh tarmac and for a few metres it felt a little soft and slippery.

I reached the Lesotho border near Butha-Buthe. Border formalities were just as easy as they had been in Swaziland and I got my passport stamped and wasn't charged a thing. I didn't even mention the carnet. I walked back to my bike smiling. If only all border crossings were this easy!

And then I saw Heidi. There was something not quite right with her and it took me a moment to figure it out. Her underside was covered in a thick, black, sticky liquid. The number plate was almost unreadable and the underneath, panniers and much of the exhaust pipe were caked in South African tar. 'Ah,' I thought. 'That'll be the soft, slippery bit I rode through…'

There was nothing I could do about it at the border so I rode into Lesotho, wondering what the chances were of finding a jet-wash. The one hundred miles or so from the border to the capital of Lesotho were a joy to ride. Green rolling mountains, rural settlements and very little traffic. But the blue sky and warm sun that had accompanied me from Dundee that morning had stopped at the border. I had climbed out of South Africa into the mountain kingdom; at this altitude clouds were more common and the sky was starting to look threatening. Of course, I'd read in my Lonely Planet Guide that several lives are lost each year from lightning strikes. They suggest keeping off high ground during an electrical storm and avoid camping in the open. How, I wondered, could I keep off high ground? The lowest point in the whole country was still above 1000 metres!

As I headed for the capital, Maseru, the scenery reminded me of Switzerland, but the road was more like one of Mexico's: those dreaded *topes* speed humps had made a comeback. Wherever there was a pedestrian crossing they'd raised the walkway by a good four inches; there were no signs or warnings so I got a bit of a shock as I flew over the first one. 'Oh well,' I thought, 'With a bit of luck it might have dislodged some of the tar sticking to the back of the bike!'

CHAPTER 20

THE KINGDOM IN THE SKY

"We all live under the same sky, but we don't all have the same horizon."

(Konrad Adenauer)

It only took me two hours to get from the border to the capital but in that time the sky had gone jet black and it had started to rain. As I entered the outskirts of Maseru, I heard the first rumbles of thunder and I began to panic. I knew this was getting ridiculous but phobias are hard to control so I just had to stop, get off the bike and wait it out. But where to stop? I saw a hand-written sign pointing down a muddy track to 'The Boys Car Wash'. So I followed it.

At the end of the muddy track there was a metal hut next to a large, open-sided metal shed. I didn't see anyone around but I pulled up under the shed roof and got off the bike. By now it was teeming with rain and I could hardly hear myself think with the noise of the rain on the roof. Then I saw a flash of lightning, followed several seconds later by a loud rumble of thunder. And I was standing under a metal roof!

I turned to see someone looking at me and the bike.

"Hi, my name is Paseka. How can we help you?"

"Well, I have all this tar on the back of my bike. Do you think you can clean it off?" I asked.

"No problem!" he replied, a little too confidently for my liking. Why does the response "No problem" always sound disconcerting?

Paseka went back to the hut and a few moments later four other guys ('The boys' I assumed) came out with buckets and cloths and brushes. They proceeded to scrub and clean the bike using little more than cold water, a small amount of soap and 'elbow grease'. I got a bit concerned when they started on the panniers and had to tell them that I would do that part; I couldn't allow my stickers to get destroyed. The thunder seemed to be getting closer and at one point it was raining so hard a stream formed right through the open-sided shed we were in. I had to move the bike as it was starting to sink in into the sodden earth. One of the boys had gathered up my helmet and gloves and was lovingly polishing my flip-front lid. I don't think he put it down for the entire hour.

I knew there were a couple of things I should have been very worried about: statistically, in a thunderstorm, I would probably have been much safer riding my bike out on the streets of Maseru than standing under a metal shed, but the company made me feel safer. And I'm sure any decent motorcycle aficionado would tell you never to let someone attack your bike with bags of enthusiasm and a brush. There was probably a good chance they would dislodge something important and I'd never get the thing started again. But I was having fun. When, eventually, the rain eased off I had a chat with Paseka who, although he looked only about eighteen, was clearly in charge.

"Is this your business Paseka?"

"Yes, I own it. These guys work for me but times are really bad at the moment. Our government does not help us and there is no work. Many young people go to South Africa to find work. Maseru is not good at the moment."

"Do they find work in South Africa?"

"Some do but it is not easy. Africa is a bad place. We want to work and help our families but there is nothing to do. I started this car wash with some money from my uncle, but we are not doing well. I am a DJ at night also; let me give you my card."

And with that Paseka handed me his calling card. *'DJ Peipi Sound Hire'*

"You need a disco?" he asked with a big smile on his face.

It took over an hour for four guys to clean my bike, and even then we hadn't really managed to clean off much of the tar, but the storm had passed and I felt as if I'd had a little Lesotho adventure. This was a great opportunity, I thought, for me to use my *Pogo*. I'd bought this little device in the UK in February for just such an occasion. It connects to a digital camera and can immediately print off a small business card-sized photo. I took a photo of myself, the bike, Paseka and his boys and then printed it off and gave it to them. They were over the moon. They were all impressed to see themselves and will probably never forget the day they met a soaking wet European on a ridiculously huge and dirty motorcycle. Paseka said the photo would be stuck up in the office and I rashly promised to come back one day to check. Perhaps I will.

I spent two nights in Maseru, but not especially because it required it. I don't think I've ever been to a capital city that had less to offer. The Lonely Planet Guide had no suggested sites to see and the centre seemed to consist of just one main street which, as far as I could tell, had nothing but shops selling mobile phones. Maseru's industry seems to be built on the notion that South Africans need a conference centre 'abroad' and the few hotels were all set up as such. (I stopped at one with rooms priced at $150 a night, and moved on.) Eventually I found The Maseru Backpackers' and Conference

Centre where I got a room in a dorm for $15. There was space to camp but the site was a muddy field and I was sure the night was going to be cold, so I upgraded.

The reason I had a whole day in Maseru was to catch up with an old friend. Well, an ex-student really. I first met Lerato when I taught in Ethiopia several years previously. Her mother worked at the Lesotho embassy in Addis Ababa and Lerato was a student at the international school I worked at. Lerato has spina bifida and is confined to a wheelchair. Although she was then about eighteen years old she had hardly ever been to school as she found it hard to find any that would accept her. Mine did, and Lerato joined my form. She was a wonderfully upbeat, enthusiastic student with a wicked sense of humour and a smile that could brighten up any day. She had a great year with us until she had to leave following the sudden, sad death of her mother. All I knew when she left was that she had gone back to Lesotho and her family. We heard no more.

Then when I was back in the UK before heading to Cape Town I tried my best, through *Facebook* and email, to trace her. I managed, through the help of a few people, to get in touch with her sister who was living in South Africa. Eventually she got a message to Lerato and just the day before I arrived in Lesotho I got a text from her.

She told me to meet her at the Mediterranee Restaurant Pizzeria in Maseru. She arrived by car and as the driver helped her out I could see that Lerato had hardly changed in ten years. Her long black curly hair flowed down over her smiling face as she saw me. She was in the same old flimsy wheelchair, with a couple of pillows supporting her weak legs. Frail in body but strong in spirit, Lerato shouted at me to come over and give her a hug, and I did. She isn't a woman to argue with.

It was wonderful to catch up after so many years of no news whatsoever. Lerato filled me in on her personal story and I sat there amazed at what a tough time she'd had and yet how positive and optimistic she seemed. Her life had been turned upside down by the sudden death of her mother and she had that to deal with in addition to the daily tribulations of her disability in a country and continent where the wheelchair-bound have a hard time. Listening to Lerato I couldn't help but feel slightly ashamed and humbled – ashamed that I often complain about my comfortable, Western lifestyle and humbled by her positive attitude towards life, despite all her problems. Lerato kept thanking me for taking the time to visit her but really it was me who needed to thank her. What right did I have to whinge and moan about things when Lerato could be so positive and upbeat about life?

As a teacher I'd met a lot of young people and occasionally one comes along who, for whatever reason, you really remember. They stick in the mind and long after they are gone you think about them: where they are and what they might be doing. Lerato was, for me, one such student. I'd learnt more about life from her than I had ever managed to teach her. Over a lifetime we are lucky if we meet a few people who inspire us in this way. Lerato is an inspiration and I was so pleased I'd made the effort to seek her out. Her enthusiasm and positive outlook on life was just what I needed as I headed back into South Africa and ever onwards on my journey.

Dom with Lerato in Lesotho.

*

Graaff-Reinet. Sounds like a skin complaint but it was actually the next town on my way back to Cape Town. Set in the Great Karoo, a vast wilderness area of South Africa, and also known as 'The Place of Thirst', Graaff-Reinet is the fourth oldest town in the country and a throwback to the Dutch colonial days. It was founded in 1786 and actually named after a Dutch governor, Cornelis Jacob van de Graaf and his wife, Cornelia Reynet. (Don't ask me why the town is spelt differently from both their names!)

Afrikaans is widely spoken and the architecture is very colonial, with a higher percentage of buildings declared to be historical monuments than any other city in South Africa. The town's main church, of the Dutch Reformed faith, was designed along similar lines to Salisbury Cathedral in the UK. Its huge white steeple points to the heavens and its grey and white stonework look totally out of place in what is essentially a huge desert. Graaff-Reinet was a surprise. The central plaza where the church sat is wide and open and I couldn't get over how familiar and European the church seemed. I got off the bike and walked around for a while soaking it all up. Considering it was early afternoon and quite warm I was surprised at how many people were around and there seemed to be a lot of nuns about. I decided to spend the night but found it quite hard to find somewhere to stay. Eventually I found a motel with a spare room and enquired as to why everywhere else was full. It turned out there were six thousand Methodist nuns in town for a conference and all the cheap hostels had been booked up!

Getting closer to Cape Town I stopped at Oudtshoorn, the Ostrich capital of the world, apparently. I arrived on a Friday afternoon just in time to coincide with some sort of street festival. I later found out it was the 16th annual Afrikaans festival: 'Celebrating all things Afrikaans'. Now I must admit at first that filled me with some dread: I expected a sort of neo-Nazi parade of the AWB and a town full of fat men with long white beards. Actually I was quite shocked at how racist I was being against the Afrikaners. I walked through town and sure enough there were lots of white people about and they were all speaking in Afrikaans, and some of them were fat and did sport impressive beards, but I had no reason to believe they were any more or less racist than anyone else. And certainly no more racist than I was being, making assumptions about white people being racist. South Africa was doing this to me. It was making me feel guilty about being white.

I guess my opinion of Afrikaners had been formed by living in the UK through the 1980s. Every time white South Africans appeared on TV it was something to do with apartheid. I was also in the middle of reading Nelson Mandela's autobiography *Long Walk to Freedom*, so that may have played a part in my feelings of guilt.

As a vegetarian I didn't really have much in common with the barbecue-crazy, ostrich-eating Afrikaans festival-goers but that didn't matter. I'd not come to Oudtshoorn for the food, I'd come to take a ride up the Swartberg pass. Running through the Swartberg ('Black Mountain') range, this gravel-surfaced road snaked its way up and over the mountain. I spent a wonderful morning riding the pass, finding it much easier than the Sani Pass. I felt much more comfortable on loose surfaces now and was feeling confident that I could face whatever the rest of Southern Africa was going to throw at me. I knew Namibia was going to be mainly gravel roads and I had no idea what the roads were going to be like from there to Nairobi. So I saw the Swartberg and Sani Passes as a sort of dirt road test for myself and was pleased with how I was coping. After all, I'd now ridden nearly 25,000 miles from Alaska and I hadn't dropped the bike once!

I was heading back to Cape Town for two reasons. First of all I wanted to get new tyres on the bike and I needed to swap back the battery I had borrowed. I'd also been keeping tabs on where Tom, Pat and Chris were and I knew they were also in Cape Town resting up before heading off to Namibia. I headed for BMW Atlantic and took Heidi in for a service. They changed the oils and alternator belt and tightened up any loose nuts and bolts. I'd tried to read up on what could go wrong on a BMW R1200GS and there was some talk of alternator belts. I had no idea how old my belt was but I knew it had taken me 25,000 miles in addition to its earlier mileage with the previous owner so the sensible thing to do was to change it and carry the old one as a spare.

I was informed that the bike was in good working order although I'd lost a bolt on the centre stand which could have proved disastrous. All my spokes were fine which was good as I'd become a little obsessed with them after the revelation in Spokane, USA, that they had all worked loose. Both wheels were fitted with fresh Michelin Anakee 2 tyres, replacing the Avon Distanzias which had carried me 7,000 miles from Mexico City. The Avons had been great; the front still had a few thousand miles on it and the rear had a little tread left but it made sense to change them when I could. I didn't want to carry a spare rear and didn't feel I needed to; I expected a new Anakee 2 on the rear would last the 6,000 miles to Nairobi. Unbelievably, Shane even let me keep the battery for free! Now that is service. I bought a few spares, including a new fuel pump controller (I wasn't going to get caught out with that again). Heidi was now in the best possible condition to face what I fully expected to be the most challenging part of my whole trip.

Accommodation prices always rocket in major cities and I was expecting to have to pay over the odds to find somewhere with safe parking for Heidi in Cape Town. Fortunately Tom said I needn't worry as he and the others were 'couch surfing'. I had no idea what he meant by this so when I met up with them in the centre of Cape Town I wasn't sure what to expect.

Couch surfing is an internet-driven phenomenon whereby people who have a spare room/bed/couch offer it to travellers in the hope/belief that one day they may return the favour. People who are happy to have guests/travellers stay with them advertise on the website and all you have to do is register and ask away. What a great idea. Why hadn't I come across this before? I could have saved a fortune in America and met some really interesting people. Tom had been doing this for several years as he had travelled around South America and Europe. He had got in touch with a couple in Cape Town who were only too pleased to have us all stay. And that's saying something. Not only did they have Tom, Pat, Chris and me but the day after I arrived, Daryll and Angela turned up. Five motorcycles and six bikers!

Chris and Marlies welcomed us into their home as long lost friends. They lived in a wealthy suburb of Cape Town in a beautiful large house. In their late fifties, they had joined the couch surfing website a few years previously with the express desire to meet foreigners. Born and bred in South Africa, the couple had never travelled abroad but were keen to and this was a great way for them to meet people. Their ancestors were from northern Europe and they hoped, one day to visit Britain and Germany. For now they had to settle for us imposing ourselves on them.

I was keen to talk to a white South African couple to hear what they felt of the new South Africa. Interestingly, both Chris and Marlies had a lot of time for Nelson Mandela but were suspicious of the ruling party, the ANC (African National Congress). They appreciated that the new South Africa was moving in the right direction and that Mandela was a genuine force for good in the world. But they feared corruption, cronyism and infighting would rear their ugly heads and they worried about what would happen after Mandela passed away. I mentioned Zimbabwe and asked if they thought South Africa might end up in a similarly catastrophic condition. Chris thought that might be going too far but he was certainly less optimistic about the country's future than some people I had met.

On my second day in Cape Town Daryll and Angela turned up. It was great to finally meet them. I'd been following their blog for months and although we didn't actually meet, Daryll and I had both been at the Horizons Unlimited bike rally in Nakusp, Canada six months previously. We had so much to talk about it was like meeting old friends. Daryll was South African by birth but I think his family were originally from India. He was quite skinny, of medium height and had a quick wit and sharp sense of humour. Although he now lived in Canada and had dual citizenship, he had lived in London for several years and we shared quite a few cultural references. Angela had medium length curly blonde hairy and a soft Canadian accent. They'd met in Canada and were just about to tell me the story of how and why they had decided to sell everything and ride the world when Tom came limping into the room. He'd gone out earlier on his V-Strom to collect his *carnet de passage* which had been posted to him from Johannesburg. Tom was a portly sixty-something gentleman and was not in the greatest shape, but he seemed to be walking particularly slowly and looked very pale. With good reason: he'd just had a spill.

Taking a corner in downtown Cape Town, he'd skidded on some spilt petrol and dropped his bike. He'd crushed his right foot and grazed his knee; his toes had gone blue and his ankle was starting to swell up. We administered some first aid and bandaged up his ankle but he was adamant that it wasn't too bad and he didn't need to go to a hospital. As he had only intended to be out for a short trip he hadn't been wearing his motorcycle trousers, just three quarter length camping trousers – no protection at all. His knee was badly grazed but he was lucky; it could have been a whole lot worse. Fortunately he had worn his biker boots otherwise he almost certainly would have broken something and his trip would have been over.

It was a sobering sight. Every day on the road I had been wearing my motorcycle boots, padded black trousers, jacket and gloves. But as it was getting warm in parts of South Africa and I assumed it would only get warmer as I headed north, it had crossed my mind to be less safety-conscious and more comfortable. Tom's experience reminded me why I shouldn't. Riding a motorcycle is not like driving a car: you need to be in good health with all limbs working and no broken toes or fingers. Having got this far I didn't want a broken digit to stop me from completing my dream of riding through Southern Africa. Tom's misadventure was a salutary lesson to us all.

We spent two days with Chris and Marlies but were eager to move on. Tom said his ankle was fine, so on the third morning four of us headed north; Daryll and Angela had a few things to do in Cape Town and agreed to catch up with us in Namibia. I must admit I thought it was a little rude of us to leave Cape Town without them and I would have stayed a couple of days and waited but Tom and Pat seemed to be in a rush to get on the road. Little did I know that this theme was to repeat itself – often.

However, it was really good fun to be riding with other people for a change and it also made the accommodation so much cheaper. Amazingly (I thought anyway) Pat and Chris didn't have a tent or any camping/cooking equipment. Pat expected to be able to find cheap places to stay and couldn't be bothered to cook any of his own food. Two-up on an Africa Twin, Pat and Chris didn't have a lot of space for equipment and camping certainly means you have to carry more stuff.

However, I was looking forward to camping in Southern Africa; for me it was a major attraction of biking through the region. I expected to camp out under the wonderful African stars, sharing beers with fellow travellers around a roaring campfire. Tom had bought a tent in Johannesburg and the plan was that we would camp, when necessary, with the three of them sharing Tom's tent. But without any cooking equipment they would have to find somewhere to eat every night. I must admit to being a little apprehensive about how this would work. As we set off towards Namibia it was great to be riding with other people but in the back of my mind I had a nagging feeling that, after so long on the road on my own without having to compromise, I might find this all a little hard to deal with.

*

The west coast of South Africa was true rocky desert and as we moved north and closer to Namibia I could tell we were heading into something vast and untamed. I've wanted to go to Namibia ever since the early 1990s when I read a book about elephants in the desert. It was the first time I'd heard of Namibia and the idea that elephants lived in the desert astonished me. The book, which I still have, was full of wonderful photographs of enormous desert landscapes and sand dunes. The vast emptiness of it all captured my imagination and I had longed to see it for myself. I didn't really expect to see any of these elephants but that didn't matter. I was riding my motorcycle into Namibia; Heidi was purring with contentment, the sky was blue and all was good with the world. And what's more, Pat, Chris and Tom were ahead of me with their GPS leading the way so we wouldn't even get lost.

Somewhere on the road north of Cape Town, just before we finished riding for the day, I passed a personal milestone. I'd covered a total of 24,910 miles since setting off in Anchorage eight months previously. The distance around the equator is 24,900 so I'd actually ridden the equivalent of the world's circumference! However it wasn't the easy day's ride I'd expected. Before leaving Cape Town, Pat had keyed the day's destination, Lambert's Bay, into his GPS and had taken the lead. I assumed we'd be riding the major highway north out of the city and then veer off on the R354 towards Lambert's Bay. That's what my map said and that's what I would have been doing if I were on my own. However, a few hours into the ride, Pat indicated that he was turning left and Tom and I followed him off the lovely black smooth stuff and on to a dirt track. It was a reasonably easy road as the dirt was quite compact but occasionally we were confronted with small stretches of sand. Sand was something I feared. I knew I was heading for Namibia and it was famous for its sand and sand dunes but I had no desire to ride through it, especially if I didn't have to. I'd never ridden in sand and all I knew was the mantra: 'speed is your friend'. Easy to say when you're not standing up on a 250 kg motorcycle hundreds of miles from a hospital. What made this worse was the fact that I hadn't been expecting to do this and hadn't prepared myself mentally for what I was now being confronted with. And I knew I didn't even have to be on this dirt road! There was a perfectly decent tarmac road going where I wanted to be. Was this Pat's idea of a joke? Perhaps riding with other people wasn't going to be as much fun as I first thought.

About thirty minutes down this road I turned a corner to see that Pat had stopped at the side of the road for a break.

"Ha, ha," he laughed with a strong French Canadian accent. "That was funny."

"I wasn't expecting that," I replied, trying not to sound terrified.

"Where is Tom, did you see him?" Pat asked.

Pat had sped off down the track at about sixty miles per hour. I'd followed at a more leisurely, and I felt safer, forty. Tom had been behind me and I'd slowed down occasionally to make sure I could still see him in my mirrors. I'd not ridden much with other bikers but I knew the etiquette: always keep the person behind you in sight and slow down if you lose them. Tom was a few minutes behind me and came around the last bend rather slowly. He wasn't up on his pegs and as he got closer it was obvious that he wasn't having fun on the gravel.

"What the hell!" he spluttered as he pulled up to a stop and lifted the visor on his bright yellow helmet. "I hate this god-damned stuff." Tom had said what I had thought!

"It's not that bad," replied Pat. "You need to be up on your pegs and keep your speed up, Tom."

"Yeah, I know the drill, but I've got a bad leg."

Shit, I'd completely forgotten that Tom was still recovering from his crash and from the look on his face, so had Pat. From the way Chris looked at Pat it was also clear that she hadn't forgotten and perhaps had said something to him about this earlier. Tom's leg was bandaged up and still quite swollen, he'd even found it hard putting his boot on earlier that day. Obviously, after a spill like the one he'd experienced he'd had his confidence knocked out of him; the last thing he needed was to be riding off-road, unnecessarily.

"Why are we on this road anyway?" Tom asked as he slowly dismounted, his right leg clearly causing him trouble.

"Pat misread his GPS." Chris hadn't spoken much in the last few days, partly because her English wasn't as good as Pat's and he usually spoke for them both. She had a lovely singing French accent to her voice and to my ears she spoke with a hint of sarcasm. I'm not sure it was always meant, but I think it was just then.

"The GPS told us to come this way and Pat didn't realise that the road was not tarmacked. He has his GPS set to avoid main roads if possible!"

"So we came this way because it's off-road." Tom was clearly getting a little agitated. "What do we do now?"

"I think we have come too far to turn around. It's only another forty miles to Lambert's Bay. Let's go on."

I could see the logic in Pat's idea and I didn't really want to head back the way we had come. But I didn't feel it was up to me. Tom was the one who was suffering and I was just about to say something when Tom re-started his V-Strom and headed off.

"He does that sometimes," Pat said. "When he gets something into his head he just gets on his bike and goes. It looks like we'll have to follow."

It didn't take long to catch up with Tom. The poor guy was very nervous about riding off-road and probably his ankle was hurting too much for him to stand up. He was pottering along at about twenty miles an hour which, even I knew, was too slow for this sort of surface. At that speed the bike's front wheel digs down into the soft earth a little too much and wobbles around. You need to travel faster so the front wheel skims the surface of the road making riding easier. Also, by standing up it is easier to handle and control. You can see further ahead, and with the weight of your body now linked to the bike only through the pegs and the handlebars, you can make much quicker and finer adjustments to the balance of the whole ensemble than when you're plonked on the seat like a sack of potatoes; you can also absorb more lumps and bumps using your legs as extra suspension and nudge the tank with your knees for more 'fine tuning' if desired. (I was also convinced that I'd been told that standing on the pegs lowers the centre of gravity making it easier to control the bike. My editor has since informed me that this is 'complete bollocks'. I'm just glad I didn't know this at the time!) Nevertheless, regardless of the physics of why it works, on a loose surface, standing is safer than sitting. Tom knew all this but he couldn't do it. The next hour and a half must have been hell for him.

That night we camped in a small campground by the sea at Lambert's Bay; the three of them squashed into Tom's tent. After setting up camp we'd gone into the village and found a restaurant and had a good meal. We were all still getting to know each other and I was learning of Pat and Chris's previous motorcycling adventures around North America. They lived in eastern Canada and had been all over the country on a variety of motorcycles, including a trip to Newfoundland on a Ural and sidecar with their dog on board. Pat certainly knew a lot about motorcycles and how to fix them and even let slip that he had owned a BMW GS, so I knew I was riding through Africa with the right person!

CHAPTER 21

INTO NAMIBIA

"My map of Africa lies in Europe."

(Otto von Bismarck)

Namibia – at last. The second least densely populated country in the world (after Mongolia). Before I started my trip I knew there were two places I definitely wanted to visit – Alaska and Namibia. And in many ways Namibia was top of that list. The excitement I felt as I crossed the Orange River that forms the border between South Africa and Namibia was palpable. Exiting South Africa had been quite easy; not only was the paperwork straightforward (they signed and stamped my carnet) but the border was practically empty.

The ride north from Springbok in South Africa had taken us into a rocky desert area which seemed to go on and on. The mighty Orange River cut its way through the stark dry landscape but apart from that there was nothing but desert. This wasn't the sandy desert of the Kalahari which I knew was only a few hundred miles to the north east; it was an undulating rocky desert, inhospitable, harsh and foreboding. I had to keep an eye on my fuel levels as petrol stations, (and settlements) were rare. It was about a hundred miles from the Namibian border to the first town of Grunau and there was absolutely nothing in between. I could comfortably cover two hundred miles on a tankful, probably two fifty, whereas Pat was struggling to get two hundred on his Africa Twin so I knew I would never be the first to run out.

Also, we had no idea whether every petrol station marked on my map (or on Pat's GPS), actually existed and if it did, whether it had unleaded petrol. The wise thing to do was to fill up every time we got close to half a tank and found a station. It also meant we could stop, take a break and refuel ourselves. Not a bad plan, as even though it was now autumn, the sun was still strong and with my bike gear on I was cooking nicely as I rode along. I had to remind myself that although I was now riding in a group, which made me feel safer, I was also riding into a part of the world that was barren and poor. If something happened out here that needed hospital treatment I was going to be a long way from one.

Eighty miles into Namibia, we had a choice to make. The dirt/gravel road off to the left headed forty miles to Fish River Canyon and I was certainly keen to give it a try. However we were aware that Namibia had been suffering from some unseasonably heavy rainfall of late and we had no idea how good the roads would be. Tom was understandably concerned about riding off tarmac as his foot was still hurting a lot. He decided he wouldn't risk it and would carry on up the main road to Keetmanshoop. Both Pat and I decided we would go down the dirt road and agreed to meet Tom the following day on the road to Luderitz.

Fish River Canyon is a place you soon read about if planning a trip to Namibia. Nevertheless, I'm not sure I would have taken the gravel road if I'd been on my own. It was slightly scary to leave the highway, which itself had very little traffic on it, and to head off down an empty gravel road into the desert. It was great to have Pat and Chris with me, even if Pat did speed off at about seventy miles an hour, leaving me to eat his dust.

The road was in better condition than I could have hoped. It was a well-graded hard dirt road with some gravel. There were a few pockets of sand here and there and I gave myself a few scares but I made it safe and sound, if a little behind Pat, to the Canyon.

Fish River Canyon is one of the world's largest. At about one hundred miles long, up to fifteen miles wide and a quarter of a mile deep it's bloody impressive. The Grand Canyon is bigger, but size isn't everything. Six months earlier I'd been at the Grand Canyon in Arizona and in many ways they are very similar. In both, over millions of years, a river cut its way down through the hard ground, meandering as it went, exposing multi-coloured layers of ancient rocks. In Namibia, the result was an impressively huge canyon so deep it was actually quite hard to see the flowing river at the bottom (that we could it at all is testament to the record-breaking rainfall late on in the season, since the Fish River runs dry for much of the year).

Pat, Chris and I had ridden up the gravel track from the entrance gate to the viewing platform and were standing there in silent awe. In Arizona, I'd been on the south side of the canyon, looking across and slightly up at the northern rim. Here, we were looking down into and beyond the canyon. The flat rocky desert stretched out before us making the irregular cliffs of the gorge stand out even more. For some reason it reminded me of a huge lump of cheese: a big square flat block of cheddar with a jagged crack running through the middle of it. I think the sun was getting to me.

Pat noticed that there was a small track leading off towards the rim of the canyon. We looked at each other, smiled, and headed for the bikes. We followed what was either a rabbit run or a footpath, only metres away from the edge. This was invigorating stuff, especially for someone like me who really wasn't keen on heights. I took Heidi as close to the edge as I dared and Pat captured the moment for me on my camera. I thought 'There's no way I would have been able to do this in Arizona', as I carefully and very slowly edged the bike away from the five hundred metre drop.

I parked Heidi up and took a little walk along the ridge. As I looked out over the edge I was almost overwhelmed by the sense of personal achievement. I'd had a similar feeling when I reached the Arctic Circle, made it to the Tropic of Cancer and then again when I'd got to Panama. A tear formed in my eye and involuntarily, I started to laugh, prompting me to question my own sanity. The Grand Canyon had indeed been grand and hugely impressive. But it was easy to get to and there were thousands of other people there. Fish River was different. The solitude and quiet and knowledge that there really wasn't anyone else around made it a special place. Fish River Canyon was mine. I didn't have to share it with anyone and the silence, so lacking in Arizona, was an integral part of the whole experience. That, and being able to ride my bike to the edge, made Fish River my favourite canyon in the whole wide world.

*

I suppose it's human nature to worry about what might go wrong in any given situation. I think that might be why a lot of people don't travel. What if I'm robbed? What if I break down? What if I can't find anywhere to sleep? What if I can't wash my clothes? These were all questions mentioned to me when I talked about riding a motorcycle around the world. And if I had stopped to think about them I'm sure I would have come up with an even longer list which could have worried me so much that I might well have stayed at home and watched DVDs of other people doing stuff. That's not to say that I was blasé about problems or indeed that I didn't worry. On arriving in Africa my biggest worry was that I would be on a dirt road, in the middle of nowhere, in fading light and the bike wouldn't start. That's exactly what happened as we left Fish River Canyon.

Fortunately there were two silver linings to this rather dark cloud. First, it was Pat's bike that wouldn't start and second, he didn't seem to care. We'd been riding for perhaps an hour back towards Grunau and the main road when we stopped for a few minutes to take some photos. I jumped back on Heidi and told Pat that I would take a photo of him and Chris as they went past me. I rode twenty metres up the track, got my camera ready and waved them through. But he and Chris dismounted. Something was up.

"What's wrong?" I asked, returning to the Africa Twin. Pat was standing back from his bike and looking at it with a smile on his face.

"It won't start," he said shrugging his shoulders.

"What, nothing?" I asked, desperately trying to think of something to say that might be of some use and imply that I knew something about motorcycles.

"Nothing," Chris chipped in. "But this has happened before, remember, Pat?"

"Ah, oui. In Peru."

And with that he started to remove the seat.

"Of course, when we were in Peru, two years ago the same thing happened. The contacts had come away from the battery. I bet the same thing has happened here."

It had. The vibration of the gravel road had jolted the battery so much that the contacts had come loose. With no fuss, Pat reconnected them and she started first time. I wondered how long it would have taken me to think of that. I could have been there half the night before it occurred to me. I prayed Shane had screwed my battery in properly back in Cape Town and made a mental note to email him a huge thanks if and when I made it to Nairobi.

Just when Pat and Chris were about to remount I noticed something which didn't look quite right at the back of his bike.

"Is that supposed to look like that?" I enquired, rather nervously.

Sticking out at an angle and away from the chain was a twisted piece of metal. Pat took a look and then swore – loudly in French and then in English. Oh, the joy of being bilingual. "Merde, Shit, Shit. The chainguard. I thought I heard a noise earlier."

Pat's chainguard was hanging precariously by about a centimetre of metal and was going to be absolutely no use whatsoever. He pulled it off and stuffed it into his bag, muttering something about fixing it later. With a roar of his engine and with Chris hanging on for dear life, he took his frustration out on his throttle and roared off down the dusty track.

*

The following day we met up with Tom and headed west. Two hundred miles down what was essentially a dead end road, Luderitz really did feel as if it was at the end of the world. Riding the eight metre-wide asphalt road I looked to my left and right: rocky desert for hundreds and hundreds of miles. I was riding right through the middle of the Namib desert and I had to stay on the road because I'd be shot if I left it. That was, at least, what the sign said. The reason? Diamonds. The Namibian desert is famous for its diamonds and hundreds upon hundreds of square miles to my left were designated as a 'Diamond Area', owned by one of the world's largest diamond companies. No doubt they'd struck a mutually beneficial deal with the Namibian government allowing them to extract and export the diamonds while compensating the country and its people handsomely. Something like that anyway.

Luderitz became a diamond town at the turn of the twentieth century and for a short while it boomed. But by the 1920s the boom was over and it has been in terminal decline ever since. It was a strange place. Built during the time that the Germans occupied what they called German South West Africa, Luderitz (named after one of the founders of the colony) was a port and trading post. German art nouveau architecture dominated the centre giving it a distinctly early twentieth-century European feel. This felt very strange, having just ridden a motorcycle two hundred miles through the African desert to get to it. It did explain, however, why there seemed to be a lot of German being spoken and why the local tourist office had a huge Imperial German Flag (*Reichskriegsflagge*) in the window. A black horizontal cross on a white background in the top left corner of which there was a black, white and red horizontal tricolour with a Germanic cross in the middle. I'd always associated this flag with pre-World War One Germany; it was very weird seeing it in Southern Africa.

The 1880s saw what has become known as 'The scramble for Africa'. A rather innocent name for what was actually a brutal and bloody colonisation of a continent by a handful of European powers. Britain, France, Portugal, Spain and Belgium were largely responsible for carving up most of Africa but Bismarck, the German Chancellor, wanted little to do with the whole thing. Not, it must be said, because of any altruistic feelings towards the continent, more because Bismarck saw Europe, not Africa, as crucial to German Foreign policy. (In 1888 he said: "Your map of Africa is really quite nice. But my map of Africa lies in Europe. Here is Russia, and here… is France, and we're in the middle — that's my map of Africa.") Not all Germans, however, felt the same and in 1883 Adolf Luderitz paid 10,000 marks and 260 guns for the coastal area he humbly named after himself. Fearful that the British, who had annexed Walvis Bay further up the coast and, of course, already controlled Cape Colony, might soon declare the whole area their own, Luderitz wrote to Bismarck suggesting he claimed this particular coastline. I'm not sure what Luderitz said ("Dear Otto, please claim this barren, harsh desert for Germany. You never know when it might come in useful"?) but it worked. In 1884, Bismarck established German South West Africa. Germany held on to it until the First World War when South Africa, a member of the British Commonwealth, occupied it. South Africa was to hold on to this part of the world until 1990.

Just outside Luderitz is the amazing former diamond town of Kolmanskop. In 1908, while constructing the railway, a worker found a shiny stone. It was a diamond. The town soon developed and grew, eventually boasting a theatre, bowling alley and casino as well as accommodation for the hordes that flocked there. Fresh water was imported from Cape Town, cheese from France and the well-equipped hospital had the country's first X-ray machine. The town thrived until soon after World War One. At its height perhaps three hundred German adults and around eight hundred Namibian contract workers lived there but with the crash in the diamond market and richer diamond fields being uncovered elsewhere Kolmanskop began to decline and finally became derelict in the 1950s. Now the desert was reclaiming it, making for some great photos, especially first thing in the morning before the mid-morning mists rolled in. I was keen to visit the ghost town but was surprised to discover that none of my travelling buddies felt the same, so I went alone while they stayed in Luderitz.

My guidebook told me that the 'slightly decrepit buildings being invaded by dunes is simply too surreal to describe'. I'll give it a go. Situated a few miles out of Luderitz on the only road in and out of town, Kolmanskop consists of several buildings sitting in the middle of the desert. Some of the buildings have been left totally alone and are slowly falling apart: wallpaper peeling from the walls, broken windows and crumbling outhouses; all slowly but relentlessly being reclaimed by the sand. I went into a couple of houses, entering at first floor level as the sand had built up against the walls of the house. It was certainly weird and slightly bizarre to walk around a one hundred year old house half buried in the desert. The main town hall, which housed the bowling alley, has been restored and was clearly regularly swept clean. It now houses the tearoom and small museum. The tea was welcome – it was hot and thirsty work walking around a sandy desert at ten in the morning in motorcycle boots but it was well worth it. It was indeed, a strange and surreal little place.

When I got back to Luderitz, four had become six. Tom had already re-joined us at Keetmanshoop the previous day but now Daryll and Angela had caught up with us too. We all met up outside a café in downtown Luderitz, six bikers and five bikes. Having spent so much of the previous eight months riding solo it was an odd feeling to be in such a big group. I was glad of the company and so far was getting on well with everyone, but I wondered how the group dynamics would play out, with so many people heading the same way but with slightly different agendas. My biggest concern was over accommodation since Daryll, Angela and I were keen campers while the others were not. This wasn't an issue in Luderitz as Tom had worked his magic again and we were all 'couch surfing' with an American Peace Corps Volunteer.

I'd heard of the American Peace Corps but didn't really know much about it. I'd assumed it was a little like the UK's Voluntary Service Overseas (VSO) which Brits can sign up to for two or three years, going off to less developed areas of the world and, well, volunteering. The American Peace Corps is a government agency tracing its roots back to 1960 when Senator John F. Kennedy challenged students to serve their country in the cause of peace by living and working in developing countries. Its noble aims are to help others understand the culture of the US and to help the US to understand the culture of other countries. Volunteers sign up for an initial two-year period and are sent abroad to help with social and economic development. John, who we were staying with, had been in Luderitz for nearly two years, teaching in the local school. He'd volunteered to come to Namibia but had had no say in exactly where he was to spend his time. He was putting a brave face on it but it was clear that Luderitz didn't really have much to offer and with little money or spare time John didn't get out of town much. I've no doubt that the work he was doing, primarily teaching English, was valuable and I admired his endeavour and spirit. He was doing a good thing and the world would be a better place if there were more people like John in it.

At least, through the couch surfing network, John could meet people and, perhaps, spread the word a little. I mentioned to him that I'd done a little volunteering on my trip so far, and we talked about my experiences in Cape Town. By volunteering I didn't think I had been doing anything special but it surprised me that on my whole trip I had not met one other person who was doing anything comparable. The travellers I met were travelling and the volunteers were volunteering. No one else was doing both. To me, it just seemed like a natural thing to do, and John agreed.

Later that day I sat down with Daryll and Angela and had a long chat about our shared experiences over the previous year or so. In their early thirties, Daryll and Angela had decided to 'pack it all in and see the world' as soon as Angela passed her motorcycle test. It was really interesting and I must say quite refreshing to be talking to people who'd gone through a similar journey to me. They talked about how friends and family, while quite supportive, were also a little shocked and surprised by the notion of giving up work, selling a house and riding off into the sunset on motorcycles. I guess it's just one of those things that seem natural, compelling and the right thing to do to some people, while to others it's weird, dangerous, and even reckless.

With little previous adventure motorcycling experience, Daryll and Angela had sold their house and left Canada on two Suzuki DR 650s to see the world. The initial plan was to spend at least a year riding down from Canada to Argentina, then from South Africa up to Europe. But it nearly unravelled on the first day. Leaving their home near the Canadian/USA border they were very nearly refused entry into the United States. The border guard was suspicious of two people, with no means of supporting themselves and no ticket to leave the US. Daryll tried to explain what they were doing but the guard wasn't buying it. For some reason he thought they wanted to enter the US and work illegally for the rest of their lives. After all, who'd want to stay in Canada! It was on a warm summer's day and Daryll and Angela were getting increasingly agitated and hot standing in full bike gear pleading with the US Authorities to let them start their trip of a lifetime.

Then Daryll fainted. He just keeled over on the pavement crashing to the floor with a thud. This caused such a commotion that the border guards did the only thing they could do in such a situation. They stamped the passports and let Daryll and Angel into 'the land of the free'.

I'd followed Daryll and Angela's trip through their blog and felt as if I knew them before we'd even met. Now that we were together in Namibia (after our brief meeting in Cape Town) it was clear to me that we were going to get on. Pat, Chris and Tom were good company and it was great to be riding with them but something clicked with Daryll and Angela. We had a similar sense of humour, and a similar idea of what we wanted to get out of our trip through Africa. All three of us were in awe of Pat's riding and spannering skills. He clearly knew what he was doing and we were all pleased to be travelling with someone who could help us when needed (I never worked out what I could offer Pat in return – nothing came up!).

As for Tom, we were equally in awe of his attitude to life. Tom hadn't learnt to ride a motorcycle until he was in his early sixties yet within a few years he had ridden through South America and was now tackling Africa. He had a somewhat cavalier attitude towards riding, often overtaking me and speeding off into the distance (when not on gravel) but we had nothing but admiration for his spirit and attitude. But even at this early stage in Luderitz, I think I sensed that although we were six, we were quickly going to divide into two groups of three. I wondered how long we would stick together, but as we were all heading in the same direction for now I knew I'd be riding through Namibia and on to Victoria Falls with an American and four Canadians. That was cool. Indeed it was 'awesome'.

Yet before we even left Luderitz, six became five. While I'd been wandering around the ghost town Tom had been to see a doctor as his ankle wasn't getting better. Unbeknownst to me he'd taken it upon himself to prick a couple of blood blisters on his foot with a thorn plucked from a tree. Not surprisingly, his foot had become infected. His ankle was still swollen and he was finding it increasingly uncomfortable to wear his motorcycle boot all day. The doctor told him that his foot was seriously infected and he needed to rest it. (Apparently he shouldn't have burst his blood blisters with a thorn and then rubbed it with his dirty hands – news to Tom!) He was given penicillin and told to rest for a few days so he headed off to Windhoek on the paved road for a week's recuperation while the rest of us tackled the gravel road through the Namib Desert.

Luderitz sits at the southern end of the Namib Desert. From there, it's about two hundred miles north to Walvis Bay as the crow flies but there is no direct route through the sand. The road around is over four hundred miles of gravel, and I was sure this was going to be a highlight of my African adventure.

CHAPTER 22

SAND

"Not all who wander are lost."

(J.R.R. Tolkien)

We rode up the tarmac to a town called Aus and then turned north on to the gravel track. ('Aus' simply means 'Out' in German, but apparently the name could also come from the Khoi-Khoi for 'place of snakes'). The guidebooks talked of Namibia's excellent gravel roads but we'd heard whisperings in Luderitz that the rainy season had caused havoc on some, making them impassable in places. There were no towns on the route, just a few small farmsteads and settlements. So, as we left Aus we really didn't know if the road was open all the way to Walvis Bay and whether we could get through. It might be a sandy four-hundred-mile dead end. I wondered what I would have done if I were on my own. I hoped I would have had the spirit of adventure to take the chance. After all, what was I in Africa on a motorcycle for? But I had a nagging feeling that I might have talked myself into taking the safe route, staying on the sealed road and riding up to Windhoek. Pat seemed never to have second thoughts about anything. The more he heard about the dangers on the road and the risk of flooding the more his eyes lit up with excitement. Chris was the same – which was just as well since she was his passenger! Neither of them seemed to have an ounce of caution or fear in their bodies. I was envious of that.

The first couple of hours were remarkable. The road was in excellent condition: compacted gravel and little traffic to worry about. Pat had steamed off into the distance leaving the three of us in his dust. I rode along, standing up, occasionally prising my eyes off the road ahead to look at the surrounding countryside. The desert was more rocky than sandy here, with the occasional farmhouse but few other signs of life. The road was bordered by fencing on either side but beyond that lay scrubby desert framed in the distance by the odd mountain. I soon built up my confidence on Heidi and it wasn't long before I was imagining myself in the Dakar Rally – way behind the French Canadian couple on an Africa Twin (no doubt in a new Dakar pillion category) but holding my own ahead of the other Canadians on the DR650s. Months later I learned that the Africa Twin is based on the bike that Cyril

Neveu took to victory for Honda in the 1986 Paris-Dakar, hence its name. BMW used to make a 'Dakar' version of their air-cooled R100GS twins, in honour of the German company's four wins by Hubert Auriol and Gaston Rahier from 1981–1985, but my oil-cooled 1200 was a much more distant relation.

Two hours later we pulled in to Helmeringhausen, a hundred metre stretch of tarmac with a petrol station on one side and a hostel/campground on the other. Pat and Chris had borrowed Tom's tent so we checked in and set up camp. We were rewarded with the most glorious African sunset, reds turning to oranges and vivid purples as the sun set over the bush. The enormity and silence of the desert was awe-inspiring. This is what I'd come to Namibia for.

Just as we were setting up our tents I heard two more motorcycles. Mark and Mary were from New Zealand. They'd ridden across Asia and down through Africa on a BMW F650 and a Honda Transalp 650. Eager for news of the route we were about to take we hardly gave them time to dismount and set up camp before we started firing questions at them. It was great to hear about their exploits in Asia and Europe but the best news was that they had just come down the gravel road from Walvis Bay and had obviously made it through. Mark said that one stretch was particularly sandy but there was no sign of rain damage and they didn't think it would be a problem.

I slept well that night and awoke to a wonderful African sunrise. Every morning on this trip had been exciting, anticipating what the day might bring, but that morning in Helmeringhausen was special. I was in the middle of the Namibian desert, the sun was out, the road was in good condition and I was hoping that later that day I would visit a castle.

But first we had to get there. The road was still mainly gravel but only an hour or so out of Helmeringhausen light sandy patches started to appear in the road. This was the stretch that Mark had warned us about. As usual, Pat and Chris disappeared into the distance but I could just make out the Honda's tyre tracks as I came around a corner to be confronted with several hundred metres of sand. My instinct was to crouch down on the bike but I knew I should stand. I gripped the tank with my knees and kicked Heidi down into third gear to try to slow a little without touching the brakes.

I followed the Africa Twin's tyre tracks assuming Pat knew what he was doing and had taken the easiest route through the sand. Initially it was fine, the sand was firmer than I expected and actually felt little different from the gravel. Then it got deeper and softer and I could feel Heidi slowing down. What to do? I knew the mantra ('speed is your friend') but that's easier said than done. Nevertheless, I'd survived the Sani Pass and knew I just had to trust myself, the bike and have some confidence. I twisted the throttle as gently and smoothly as I could to speed up without jerking the bike. I was trying to keep the front wheel high on the sand because I knew that if I went too slowly the wheel would sink and I would then be in danger of losing control. My nervousness made my body tense up and I felt the back wheel wobble as it searched for a route though the sand. As I was standing up I couldn't use the mirrors so I had no idea how close Daryll and Angela were. I hoped they weren't too close as I wasn't sure I was going to make it through. My instinct was to look down at the stretch of sand immediately in front of the bike but I knew this was exactly what I shouldn't be doing (Why is it that so many instincts are wrong?) and that I should look up and ahead to see what was coming. I think I even started to talk to myself out loud. ("Look up, keep your speed up, don't touch the bloody brakes.") This must have continued for about two hundred metres. Every time I thought the sand was getting too deep and the front wheel started to wobble I would speed up a little, the bike powering me out of trouble. Suddenly the sand disappeared and the lovely, solid, reliable gravel returned. I carried on for a couple of minutes, just relieved that I'd made it through, before thinking that it might be wise to stop, take a breather, and wait for Daryll and Angela.

Finding a flat, solid stretch of road, I parked up. I was shaking a little and sweating in the morning sun. Grabbing my drinks bottle, I gulped down half a litre of water and took my bike jacket off to try to cool down. At times like this I really wished I still smoked! I took a cursory look around the bike, not sure what I was looking for but confident that it was something I should do. All the time I was listening out for the sound of a Suzuki in the distance but heard nothing at all, just the intense silence of the desert. I looked up ahead, wondering if Pat might be returning as I was sure we were a long way behind him by now. The road ahead stretched out for several hundred metres and there were no signs of anything moving along it.

As every minute passed I became more and more concerned for Daryll and Angela. They really should have caught up with me by now and I feared the worst. I was going to have to ride back down through the sand to find them! I was desperately trying to think of a really good reason why I shouldn't do exactly that when I heard the distant rumbling of a motorcycle. Daryll was on his way, but he seemed to be on his own. He was riding slowly, sitting down on his bike, clearly worried by the sand. In a way this comforted me because it meant it wasn't just me who'd found the sand tough going. But I was obviously more concerned by the fact that Angela was nowhere in sight. Daryll came to a stop next to me.

"What's happened?" I asked.

"Angela's had a spill. She's OK but she's come off her bike."

"How's the bike?"

"I think it's OK. It starts, which is the main thing. She's cracked the pannier frame and I think the panniers are bent, but it restarted OK. I thought I'd just ride on to see how bad the road got."

"What do you want to do? I don't know how far off Pat is. I haven't seen him."

"I'll go back to tell Angela that the road isn't too bad here. You just wait here."

"Tell you what. There's no sand here so once Angela makes it here she should be OK. I'll ride on to see if Pat is waiting somewhere. I'm not doing any good waiting here."

"All right. See you soon."

And with that Daryll turned around and headed off to tackle the sand once more. I felt a little guilty not following him but I didn't really see what good I could do, and I would only make matters worse if I came off my bike as well. Daryll had said Angela was OK and the bike was working, so I headed off to see if I could catch up with Pat. It only took me five minutes to find him. His bike was parked up in the shade of a tree and he and Chris were talking to some children who'd come out of the nearby farmhouse to see what all the fuss was about.

"What took you so long?" The usual grin on his face.

"Sand!" I replied.

"Where are Daryll and Angela?" asked Chris.

"Sand!" I replied. "I'm afraid Angela has come off her bike. About fifteen minutes back. I wasn't there but Daryll said she's OK."

"Do we need to help?"

"I'm not sure. Daryll said the bike was OK, so I said I would carry on to find you. I didn't see what good I could do by heading back. If we wait here I'm sure they'll turn up, it just might take some time."

"No, no. I will go and help." And with that Pat jumped onto his bike and spinning it around on the gravel, using one foot as a pivot like a true pro, he headed back up the track.

"I'm not sure what he can do, Chris?"

"Ah, Pat is Pat. He is keen to help and likes the challenge."

And that summed him up. I was annoyed with him for speeding off and leaving us but impressed with him for going back to help. Although I wasn't really sure what he could do.

"Who are these kids then?" I asked, wanting to change the conversation. We had stopped outside a farmhouse and there were ten children staring at us. They kept their distance but were obviously interested in who we were and what on earth we were doing riding motorcycles outside their home.

"They are funny. Very shy. But I managed to get one to tell me that they all live here. They are all brothers and sisters and their parents work on the farm for the big white boss who lives in Windhoek and only comes out to visit every couple of months."

I felt another *Pogo* moment coming on and rummaged around in my tank bag to find the small device. It took a few minutes to convince some of the children that I could take their photo but once they saw the result – a small snap of themselves produced out of the box I'd attached to my camera – they were ecstatic. I had to print off a second copy and the eldest one went running off to the farmhouse screaming at the top of his voice. It was nice to interact a little with the kids and to give them something that would remind them of the strange day a group of motorcyclists parked outside their homestead in the middle of the Namibian desert.

Thirty minutes later Pat, Daryll and Angela came riding around the corner. Angela's bike certainly looked the worse for wear. The front screen was cracked down the middle, leaving it dangling by the bottom screws. The rear left pannier had certainly been bent and was hanging dangerously low to the ground. More importantly, however, Angela seemed surprisingly relaxed and calm. I didn't want to overwhelm her with questions so I let her rest in the shade and had a chat with Daryll.

"How is she?"

"Not too bad. Her left arm hurts but actually she's more embarrassed than anything else."

"Well she shouldn't be. I found that sand quite scary and nearly came off a couple of times and I'm on a Ewan McGregor bike!" I joked. Ever since meeting up with them, Daryll and Angela had been poking fun at me and my huge BMW R1200GS. I'd got used to Heidi and her size and weight but when she was parked next to the Suzukis she certainly looked big. The common misperception was that anyone with a GS has it either because they have far too much money or they just want to copy Ewan and Charley, having watched 'The Long Way Round' or 'The Long Way Down'. Everyone took every possible opportunity to remind me of this.

"How did it happen, Daryll? How did she come off?"

"She was going a little too fast and the front wheel just wobbled about and she lost it. She high-sided and went down on her face. It looked pretty scary and, well, quite cool too. I'll show you later."

"What?"

"Don't tell Angela this, but I've got in all on camera!"

Daryll had a camera attached to his helmet (And he accused *me* of copying Ewan and Charley!) and, by pure chance, he'd had it running when Angela crashed. Later that evening, when she was resting in her tent, we took a look. Angela had ridden into the sand that had caught me out but had been going too fast. She made it through the first twenty metres or so but had then panicked and grabbed the front brake. The front wheel plunged into the sand and twisted the handlebars to the right. She high-sided the bike and came crashing down on her left shoulder in the sand. The bike flipped up and tumbled to the ground next to her. She was actually quite lucky she hadn't hurt herself more. It looked really quite horrific watching it on Daryll's Netbook. Very sensibly, he decided not to tell Angela that he had recorded the incident. Not yet, anyway.

Meanwhile, back at the ranch, Pat had found himself a huge four-metre long piece of piping and was using it as a lever to straighten out Angela's left pannier. It worked to an extent but Daryll was worried that the metal was now weak and wouldn't hold so he strapped the frame to the bike with some tie-downs just to make sure. The plan was to find a welder somewhere who would make a proper job of it. We never did and as far as I know Angela's pannier is still held on with that strapping to this day.

When she felt better we rode on, slowly. Fortunately we were only going to cover ninety miles in total that day and it wasn't long before we were pitching camp behind a petrol station at our designated rest stop for the night. We'd planned to make a short day of it as I wanted to visit the intriguing Duwisib Castle. After pitching the tents, Pat and I headed off to find it. It was only about fifteen miles from the campsite to the castle but I was worried about what the road would have in store for us, especially as the woman who ran the petrol station had told us that it was in poor condition, full of ruts and very wet.

We headed off up the road excited by the prospect of visiting a castle. The gravel quickly turned to sand, and although it wasn't as bad as earlier in the day, I had to concentrate to get through it. However the whole track was as dry as a bone – goes to show you can't ever rely on what you're told. Without too much trouble we finally reached Duwisib Castle.

A castle in the desert, how cool is that? I'd read about it when I first thought I might visit Namibia and had marked it as one of the places I wanted to see. A neo-baroque structure right in the middle of the barren Namib Desert, Duwisib Castle was built in 1909 by a German baron – Captain Hans Heinrich von Wolf. (What a great name!) The stone was quarried locally but pretty much everything else was imported from Germany, requiring twenty ox wagons to pull it 250 miles across the desert. Many of the builders were hired from Europe to construct the U-shaped edifice, which has twenty-two rooms. The baron and his American wife lived there for five years but in 1914 set off for Britain to buy some horses. However, while they were en route, World War One broke out and their boat was diverted to Rio de Janeiro. The baron slowly made his way back to Germany and re-enlisted in the army. Tragically, he was killed at the battle of the Somme within two weeks of joining up. His wife never returned to Namibia and spent the rest of her life in England. Pat and I were the only tourists and from the look of the visitors' book we'd arrived on a busy day! From the outside the two-storey stone structure looked completely out of place in the desert. It was the only building for miles and miles – I just couldn't get my head around the idea that a hundred years ago someone had thought this was a good idea; not just coming up with the scheme but then going to all the trouble of importing the labour and contents. Inside, the main hall resembled a stately home with plaques, pictures, swords and guns on the walls. A wooden staircase led up to a balcony and rooms led off to both left and right. Large wooden furniture, imported from Germany and dragged across the desert from Walvis Bay, adorned the rooms giving the place the feel of a nineteenth-century European stately home – which it was. It was wacky, wonderful, unique and surreal.

Pat seemed unimpressed; he was unhappy that he'd had to pay to get in and moaned that the whole place was a 'tourist trap'. He rushed around it in ten minutes and then waited for me outside. I lingered in the main room, looking at the old black and white photos of the von Wolf family. What must he and his wife have thought when they lived here? When they left to return to Europe in 1914 they knew they were going to be away from their home for a while, but they could never have dreamed of what was going to happen next. The very fact that his wife, Jayta Humphreys, never returned to Namibia says it all.

I stared at a picture of the family sat around a dinner table. They looked happy. The photo was dated 1912. It actually sent a shiver down my spine as I thought of my own life. I had no idea what was going to happen to me in the next few years. Indeed, that was part of the inspiration behind the trip in the first place. Life is for living and we really don't know what is around the corner, so we all should get on and do what we want before hitting that bend in the road that changes it all. Von Wolf and his wife had certainly lived, and I respected them for it.

I was relaxed on the way back to the main road and the campsite, knowing what the road was like and that, as long as I was careful, I wouldn't have a problem. At least that's what I thought. Only two or three miles from the campground I came around a bend to see that Pat had stopped up ahead. He was still sitting on his bike but was looking back up the road towards me. This unnerved me. What was he looking at? Had he seen an animal? Was he just waiting for me? What was going on? And then I looked at the road surface. It had got very light, a sure sign of sand, and lots of it. It hadn't been this deep on the way up to the castle, but now I was riding on the other side of the road. I was already up on my pegs, but repositioned myself to make sure everything was where it should be. I took a deep breath, slowed the engine a little and told myself it would be all right. This sandy patch was much deeper than any I'd been in before and I was going too fast. Was this the bend in the road that was going to change everything?

I tried to keep the front wheel high in the sand and hold the handlebars without gripping them too tightly. An image of Angela on her bike, from Daryll's head cam, flashed through my mind – which wasn't helpful. Initially, everything felt good and I thought I might make it through. Then something strange happened. The front wheel seemed to be gliding across the sand but the back wheel wasn't as happy. The back of the bike wobbled violently and then it felt as if the rear of the bike was going to slide so far sideways it might overtake me. There was no way it was going to come back in line and I just knew we were going down. I had a millisecond to decide how to get off in the least damaging way for both me and the bike. I was just about to throw myself to the left while trying to push the bike to the right when the rear suddenly decided to come back in line. Perhaps I could hold this bloody thing up after all. I gripped the tank with my knees and gave her a little gas. If I was going to come off I was going to do it at speed and in style. If only Daryll were here with his head cam.

Somehow Heidi stayed upright and I managed to hold on. Speeding up a little had helped and I made it through the soft sand and pulled up next to Pat. He had a huge grin on his face.

"That was tough. I got into a bit of trouble and stopped to warn you."

"Yeah, I wasn't sure why you had stopped but I guessed it wasn't good news. I really thought I'd lost it there. I was fishtailing all over the place."

"I know. I thought you were going to drop it. You did well to hold it together."

I rode back to the others proud that I'd made it through the sand and excited that I'd finally been to Duwisib and seen Baron Captain Hans Heinrich von Wolf's castle. Another great day on the bike and yet another great adventure to rack up to the memory banks. With everything I'd done since arriving in South Africa I was finding it hard to process it all. I was experiencing new things all the time, learning about the world, myself and others. It might sound daft, but I simply felt alive.

*

Although our trip from Luderitz to Walvis Bay had been a full-on adventure already, we hadn't even got to the number one tourist destination in the country – Sossusvlei. Situated in the middle of the Namib Desert, Sossusvlei is pure, unadulterated sand. The Namib Desert is at least 1,200 miles north to south and stretches at least a hundred miles inland. It's a big desert. We'd come to one tiny part of it where the enormous sand dunes are accessible and at their most stunning.

The Tsauchab river flows (very occasionally) down from the Naukluft mountains and as the river arrives in this particular section of the desert it has nowhere to go and creates a closed drainage basin. The river dries up, creating a salt pan of wonderful colours as the white salt sits on the red sand under the blue sky. It was that red sand that I'd come to see. The dunes it had created were some of the largest in the world, often over two hundred metres high and stretched further than the eye could see. An impressive sight indeed; but all the more so when you think about where that sand came from.

The sand had been washed down the Orange River, which rises in the Drakensberg Mountains in Lesotho. The river flows west towards Namibia, forming the border between Namibia and South Africa for part of its journey. It pours out into the Atlantic at Alexander Bay, half way between Cape Town and Walvis Bay. At 1,400 miles it is the longest river in South Africa. The river was given its current name by an officer in the Dutch East India Company in 1779 in tribute to William V of Orange but, in places, the name also reflects the colour of the river due to the reddish sediment, much of which is sand deposited upstream from the Kalahari. Once the sediment reaches the ocean, the Benguela current and trade winds blow it north and onshore creating the enormous sand dunes. Obviously this takes a while, millennia in fact. The Namib Desert is possibly the oldest in the world, at perhaps eighty million years of age. Scientists had recently tried to date the very sand that I would be walking on. They estimate that it could well be one million years old.

To get to this old sand, washed down the Orange River, swept up the south Atlantic and finally blown ashore, we had to ride to Sesriem. Sesriem consisted of a petrol station and several hostels and campgrounds at the entrance to the Sossusvlei Park. We checked into one of the campgrounds and enquired about the road down to the dunes. Somewhat bizarrely, amidst all this sand and hundreds of miles of gravel roads, there was a forty mile paved road from the entrance of the park down to the dunes. But even more bizarrely, they wouldn't let motorcycles use the paved road! The story goes that several years previously some bikers went down to the sand dunes and rode all over them. Now they won't let any bikes in. We begged and pleaded with the authorities. I explained that we'd all travelled from North America to get here and Pat even tried to blag it by suggesting we were from the Canadian tourist board doing research for a TV programme. Chris tried to shame them into letting us ride by putting on a really sad face and almost crying – all to no avail. We had to pay to take a minivan. So, having paid $12 park entrance fee and $16 to camp we then had to pay $35 each to get a shuttle bus to take us down the paved road to the dunes. Having ridden for three days through gravel and sand it really grated to have to pay to be driven down a sealed road.

We got picked up at 5 am the following morning so we would make it to the dunes by sunrise. It felt strange to be sitting in a vehicle, and even stranger to be on tarmac. As we headed west into the desert, the dunes stretched far into the distance on both sides but it was only when the light improved that I realised how huge they were. Our driver stopped at one of the dunes just before sunrise so we could do the touristy thing and climb one. Pat and Chris stormed off towards the nearest tall dune aiming to climb it before the sun rose – which was a bit of a shame as by walking along the rim of the dune they spoiled its wonderfully sharp edges. Daryll, Angela and I walked up a small dune and stood there trying to take it all in. We were totally surrounded by the most enormous sand dunes. As the sun slowly rose, the colours in the dunes came to life and they turned red within minutes. The sky was a glorious deep blue and all I could hear was Daryll's camera and the occasional gasps of delight. Yet another magical moment on the trip, and with the amount of sand around I was glad I wasn't anywhere near my bike.

Ten minutes later Pat and Chris came back. They hadn't got anywhere near the top of the dune. Muttering something about how hard it was to walk on sand, they headed back to the van. It's funny how people can experience the same event in a very different way. All I could think was that I was standing on million-year-old bits of red dirt washed down from the Kalahari. Pat was annoyed that he hadn't been able to get to the top.

But we weren't done with the sand yet. We moved on a mile or so to Deadvlei, a polyglot name combining 'dead' in English with *vlei,* meaning 'marsh', or 'lake' in Afrikaans (it's also known as *Dooie Vlei,* which is the all-Afrikaans moniker). As the name implies, it's an ancient, dried up lake. Hundreds of years previously the shifting dunes had blocked the path of the river and the lake had dried up. This left a white dusty coating on the ground out of which poked some dead acacia trees, some of them rumoured to be nine hundred years old. The dark wood of the trees contrasted with the white of the ground, framed by the red sand dunes and deep blue sky. The place was magical and, in my experience, unique. I had never been anywhere like Deadvlei. It was one of the most photogenic places I'd ever seen.

*

It was still two hundred miles from Sossusvlei to Walvis Bay and the paved road north to Swakopmund. We could have made that distance in a day but we were in no rush and Angela and her bike were still suffering a little. So when we got to Solitaire, a petrol station with a campground half way to Walvis Bay, we decided to stop even though it was only early afternoon. Daryll hoped that the garage might have a mechanic who could help weld Angela's pannier frame back together. While he went off to investigate I went to visit Solitaire's other attraction. We'd heard whispers and rumours from other travellers ever since entering Namibia; John in Luderitz, Mark and Mary in Helmeringhausen, even Chris and Marlies in Cape Town, but I didn't want to believe it until I saw it for myself. The word was that Solitaire had a bakery and that it sold the best apple pie in Southern Africa!

The bakery was run by a Zimbabwean/Scotsman, Moose McGregor, who lived up to his name. The size of a moose, McGregor certainly seemed to have a taste for his own handiwork and was no shrinking violet. With long flowing hair tied back and hidden underneath a large white chef's hat and a bushy grey goatee, Moose reminded me of Hagrid from the Harry Potter films. I found him in his bakery surrounded by apple pies. Everyone who stops in Solitaire to fill up on petrol also stops to fill up on pie and I had to queue behind a rather irate Afrikaans family whose noisy little children were arguing over which slice of pie to take from the tray.

"Hurry up. There are others waiting," roared Moose. I suppose when you own the only bakery for miles, customer care is a secondary thought.

"I want a bigger one," complained the small boy, who in all fairness didn't look as if he needed to add to his calorific intake. The father seemed oblivious to the fact that there was a queue behind him and was in no particular rush. One of Moose's staff, a black lady who was standing behind the till, asked for the money from the South African, who, not looking at her at all, threw a few notes down. Moose saw this, took the money and slammed the change down on the glass counter. As the family walked off Moose looked at me and in a loud voice, which, to my untrained ears, sounded half Scottish, half South African said:

"They have no respect those people. I fucking hate them."

"Quite," I muttered, not sure what to say. "Could I have a slice of your apple pie please?" I don't think I could have sounded more British if I'd tried, but in the circumstances that was probably a good thing.

I sat out in the African afternoon sun eating apple pie and cream from a plastic tray in my dirty bike gear. Travelling can just be too weird for words sometimes.

The following day, fuelled by apple pie, we made it to the tarmac. I'd really enjoyed riding across the Namib Desert on gravel roads. Mostly the roads were fine but whenever it got sandy it got tricky but I'd been pleased with the way I'd dealt with it. I'd certainly improved my dirt riding skills and I'd made it through without dropping the bike – something I didn't think would happen after the sand of the first day. Angela and Daryll were equally pleased to have made it through and when we reached the tarmac we stopped and took a photo of us kneeling down kissing the asphalt. Chris took the photo; Pat didn't join in.

Safely back on the black stuff

CHAPTER 23

WAVING AT THE LOCALS

"There had been blood pouring down my face and over my clothes – the bike was on her side by a hole in the road."

(Sam Manicom, *Into Africa*)

The coastal town of Swakopmund was a strange little place, squashed between the hot desert and the cold sea (the water never gets above 15C). Swakopmund ('mouth of the Swakop') exists in its own little bubble. We crossed the river as we approached the town and were surprised to see so many people standing on the bridge looking down and taking photos. Later we were told that the river was in flood for the first time in thirty years. I'd never associated Namibia with rain. They do have a rainy season (December to April) but this particular year had been extremely wet. Many regions in northern Namibia had had more rain in one month than they would usually get all year. Rivers like the Swakop were in flood and many gravel roads were impassable. Bearing all this in mind we had been extremely lucky to get through the previous five days of gravel roads without any rain.

Two hundred miles west of Windhoek, Swakopmund is often referred to as 'more German than Germany' and it has re-invented itself as the adventure centre of Namibia. Come here and you can go dune buggy driving, skydiving, hot air ballooning, or go on a desert safari. Or, like me, you can spend Easter Sunday doing your laundry and sitting in an internet café updating your blog. Oh, the joys of the modern adventure motorcycle traveller!

Moving on north east through Namibia we stopped in Tsumeb to catch up with Tom again. He'd rested up in Windhoek, seen another doctor and taken some more penicillin. His ankle was still a little swollen but the infection had cleared up and he was in a much more positive mood. When Angela told him what the gravel road had been like he knew he'd made the right decision to stay on the tarmac. So now the six of us were reunited and heading for the Caprivi Strip, the panhandle-shaped sliver of Namibia squeezed between Angola and Zambia to the north, and Botswana to the south, with Zimbabwe at its easternmost tip. We may have had slightly different attitudes towards our adventures but we were working well as a group. Pat/Chris and Tom were now sharing Tom's tent, aware that camping was sometimes the only option, but they still didn't have any cooking equipment.

At this point we were camping every night but as sunset was around 6 pm, night came early in southern Africa. I'd usually go to bed before eight but thanks to modern technology I didn't have to go to sleep. I had several films and TV series loaded onto my Netbook and I'd recently bought an e-reader. I had numerous books on it and had just finished Nelson Mandela's autobiography. It was a fantastic read but a huge book, which would have taken up half my tank bag in paper form. An e-reader meant I would never be short of reading material again and would still have space in my luggage.

As I went to bed quite early I usually got up at around 6 am. I'd have coffee and some South African rusks for breakfast (they are baked biscuits, great for dunking). Daryll and Angela were much better campers than me and usually managed to produce some sort of decent cooked breakfast from behind their Suzukis. I had no idea how they did it. As they weren't carrying any cooking equipment, Pat, Chris and Tom would try to find their breakfast at a café or service station. Sometimes I joined them but usually I'd make my own. This could be an issue as it meant we were all at different stages in the morning. While Tom was packing his tent away Daryll would be cooking some beans. No one was openly rushing anyone else but there was always a slight hint of tension in the air. If I went for breakfast with Pat and Tom, it was clear they wanted to get moving (Chris was a lot more laid back about the whole thing); if I stayed with Angela and Daryll they would comment that they didn't want to feel rushed but hated the idea that they were last to get ready every day.

Generally we'd set off for the day around eight. Pat insisted on riding up front. Gradually I was starting to get annoyed with always having to follow him. Sometimes it felt as if I wasn't in charge of my own trip and I was just following a tour leader. As Pat had a GPS we always knew where we were going, how far it was and when we would arrive. We also knew how fast we were riding as well. For some unknown reason Pat liked to ride at 93 kph, all the time. In return for the comfort and security of travelling with others I felt I was losing some of the spontaneity of adventure motorcycle travel.

As we moved north towards the Caprivi Strip, the scenery began to change. We'd now left the vast open desert plains of Namibia and there was more foliage as we headed towards the jungle. There were also many more people about and the road north was littered with small mud hut villages. Children were playing at the side of the road in the dirt and puddles. Men were sitting under the trees chatting, each one holding a big stick while the women were walking around in the sun with bundles of wood or buckets of washing on their heads. It was the classic southern Africa scene, almost a cliché. And just about everyone waved at us. Five big scary motorcycles zoom into your rural life for a few seconds and the natural reaction is to smile and wave. Small children would hear us coming and rush out into the road. This hadn't happened anywhere else on my trip so far but it started in Namibia and was to continue all through southern Africa. I was amazed that people seemed happy to see us just because we were on motorcycles.

When we stopped at one camp for the night on the edge of the Caprivi Strip there were two German bikers on KTMs camping there. We greeted each other like old friends and spent a few hours comparing notes on roads and swapping advice on where to go. All the 4x4s in the campground stayed in their own area and didn't talk to one another. It struck me that adventure motorcyclists seem to belong to a huge worldwide family. Many bikers use or at least know of the Horizons Unlimited website and it wasn't unusual to meet another biker and then realise that you'd been reading something they'd posted just a few days previously. Being exposed to the elements, vulnerable and with limited space for luggage, I guess bikers are more willing to share and help one another. There seems to be a camaraderie which I don't think exists among other overlanders. People in their 4x4s would almost seem to be in competition as to who had the biggest truck, or best tow rope but bikers seemed friendlier.

Leaving Rundu we continued towards the Caprivi Strip. I'd first heard about the strip while reading the excellent *Into Africa* by Sam Manicom. He had a horrific crash on the dirt road which resulted in a long hospital stay. I hasten to add that this was not why I'd come here – it was the only way to get from Namibia to Victoria Falls – but in some strange way I was worried about riding across the strip. Sam had crashed on the gravel road, waking up four days later in Rundu hospital, with several broken bones and glass from his broken spectacles in his eyes. He was extremely lucky – having been rescued by a pair of passing strangers – and pulled through eventually but it was touch and go for a while. Since arriving in South Africa I'd had that thought in the back on my mind: I was going to ride down the same road. Of course there was no logic to this way of thinking. It was twenty years since Sam had crashed and anyway, just because one person has a bad experience somewhere it doesn't mean someone else will. But the thought still lingered with me as we set off that morning. Somewhere in the back of my mind I just knew that if I was going to crash anywhere on this trip it was going to be on the Caprivi Strip.

Looking at a map it appears strange to see a thin strip of Namibia that seems to be pointing towards Victoria Falls but there is a story behind this. The German Chancellor, Leo von Caprivi, managed to negotiate with the

British and acquire the strip in the 1890s. He wanted German South West Africa to have access to the Zambezi river and thereby a viable route north east to German East Africa (now Tanzania, Rwanda, Burundi and a bit of Mozambique). In return, Germany gave up its interest in the island of Zanzibar, much to the relief of the British. The route later proved un-navigable but the deal had been done and Namibia has, ever since, been pointing towards Victoria Falls.

We spent the night at Popa Falls, a pretty little campground and lodge on the Cubango River. The Cubango's source is in the Angolan mountains and it flows not to the ocean but into the plains of Botswana, thereby creating the marshland that is the Okavango Delta. The river drops about four metres at Popa Falls, not quite as spectacular as Victoria Falls but a pleasant enough place to stay the night. The only problem was getting down to the campground.

Every day in Namibia we'd ridden on either pretty good gravel or excellent paved roads but at the end of each day, inevitably, there was some off-road riding to be done to get to the campgrounds. The track leading from the main road down to this campground was only about a kilometre long but it was sandy, and rather steep at the end. I'd taken it slow and steady on the way down the previous night but perhaps with my mind on the Caprivi Strip ahead I hadn't been concentrating the following morning as I rode back up towards the highway. Tom, Pat and Chris had left early (as usual). It doesn't take three people long to get one tent packed away and they were off to the petrol station we'd seen at the major crossroads the previous day to get a coffee. I left next, concentrating on the rocky steep incline up the hill and wondering what the day would bring.

As the track flattened out at the top it split into two sandy grooves separated by a raised grassy patch in the middle. Concentrating, I rode along the left channel, occasionally making out the tracks of either Tom or Pat's bike in the sand. I was on my pegs, looking up and feeling confident about my riding ability. It was a lovely sunny morning and, with the smell of the bush clearing my head I was hit with one of those reality checks where I suddenly remembered what I was doing. Here I was again – riding my motorcycle through Africa without a care in the world, and surprising myself at how well I was coping with the whole thing.

As I turned a corner, I saw a woman in front of me walking down the track, balancing a bucket on her head. She obviously heard me coming and stepped off the road and into the thorn bushes on the left. She turned and waved at me as I passed. Now it would have been rude of me not to wave back. I briefly raised my left hand and immediately lost control of the front of the bike. Ignoring the woman I hit the gas to raise the front wheel and get myself out of trouble, grasping for the handlebar with my left hand. It worked for a few seconds but then I started fishtailing all over the place and after about twenty metres the front wheel dug into the foot-high sand bank on the left side of the track. I don't quite remember what I did next. I would like to think that I held Heidi up as long as possible, trying to crash in a safe and elegant way but I suspect I just panicked, grabbed the front brake and made matters worse. Either way, I went down.

Dropping Heidi to the left I fell off, tumbling into a bush. Luckily I wasn't going very fast and I didn't really hurt myself. I pulled myself up out of the thorn bush and looked at the bike. The left pannier and handlebar were buried in the sand and she was more leaning over than lying down. I could hardly call it a crash really, it was more like a poorly judged dismount. I walked over, turned the engine off, took stock of the situation and took a photo. By this time the woman who had waved at me had caught up. Silently she walked along the track, bucket still on head, turning slightly to survey the scene. She looked at me as if she'd seen this a thousand times, and just carried on her way. I had to laugh.

I knew Daryll and Angela wouldn't be far behind but I wanted to get Heidi up and moving before they came along – not to try to hide my little fall but because I wanted to feel that I didn't need to rely on anyone else's help. It was my decision to ride a big heavy motorcycle through Southern Africa and I wanted to be able to get myself out of any situation I got myself into. Standing to the left of the bike I grabbed hold of Heidi's handlebar and turned it as far as it would go so that the front wheel was pointing up to the sky. I then knelt down and tried to pull her up, using the strength in my legs and trying to wedge my right knee under the tank as I heaved. Initially it worked but then the back wheel slid in the sand and we were back where we had started.

I walked around the bike and using my hands I dug the sand away from both wheels so that they would have a groove to sit in and couldn't just skim on the sand. At the second attempt I heaved her up quickly, not allowing any time for the back wheel to slide around, and got her back upright. I wanted to get her started and on to the main road before giving her a good look over. The sand was too soft to use the sidestand where I'd fallen, and I didn't want to cause another accident when Daryll and Angela arrived.

Once on the main road I stopped to inspect the damage. The front wheel looked absolutely fine, as did the left pannier. All I seemed to have done was break the front left handguard. At last, after carrying it around for months, I could finally use my duct tape!

Everyone had a good laugh at my expense when we met up at the petrol station and I told them that I'd fallen off because I'd tried to wave. Pat had a look around the bike to make sure I hadn't missed anything. I think he might have even been a little disappointed that there wasn't anything loose or broken that he could fix. He even inspected my repaired handguard and passed it 'fit for purpose'. Praise indeed. And so the day could finally begin. We were off to ride the Caprivi Strip; the one place on the whole trip I was worried about and where I just knew I was going to crash. Wait. Hold on a minute. I'd already done that!

The Strip itself was a bit of an anti-climax after that start to the day. We hit the road hoping to see some wildlife, especially elephants, but didn't see any animals of interest. The road was now fully paved which I found hard to square with my image of the hot, dusty and dangerous gravel road full of potholes that Sam Manicom had written about. Such is progress; no doubt for the locals, a paved road was a good thing, for me it was almost a disappointment.

At the eastern end of the Strip we stopped for petrol in a small, dusty village called Kongola. Five motorcycles turning up in an African village usually results in an audience but I didn't expect to meet a guy from Middlesbrough. Dan told us that the place we were heading to was flooded (that damn Namibian rain again) and we should stay with him in his lodge which was conveniently located just down the road. I must admit that I was a little suspicious of Dan. It seemed too convenient that the place we wanted to head for was flooded while his lodge was fine, and just down the road. However my North American travelling companions seemed to take to Dan and had no reservations about following him down a dusty track. And who was I to argue? After my morning's misadventure I thought it was probably wise to just shut up and do as I was told for a while.

We followed Dan eight miles down a bumpy road and then one and a half miles down a very sandy track (which he had failed to warn us about). The last thing I wanted was to finish the day by riding down another sandy track. And this one was worse than Popa Falls. Pat went first, standing on his pegs, with Chris sitting behind and he took great delight in flying through the sand without a care in the world. If I didn't know better I'd say he was showing off. Daryll and Angela went next, more gingerly and carefully. I had nothing but admiration for Angela after the tumble she'd had on the gravel. Daryll led, sitting down with his feet out to break his fall. The wrong technique, but it felt safe and he was going so slowly he was almost walking the DR through the sand. He'd go for about fifty metres then stop and wait for Angela to follow. Tom and I were waiting and watching. We knew Pat had done it properly while Daryll and Angela were following 'wimps' instincts' rather than 'recommended procedure' for riding on sand. We also knew who we'd be copying when it came to our turn. After Angela had got fifty metres ahead, Tom set off. His yellow V-Strom was low to the ground, dragged even further down by his oversized heavy black metal panniers. Tom himself, decked out in black bike gear with a bright yellow helmet, weaved his way through the bush like a lazy, drunk bumblebee looking for somewhere to rest.

And then it was my turn. I took a deep breath and set off. I tried standing up but as soon as the back wheel started to wobble I sat back down again. I didn't have the confidence anymore, not after the morning's tumble, and the self-confidence and poise I'd been so proud of the previous day seemed to have evaporated in the afternoon sun. One little tumble and I'd turned into a quivering wreck. I sat down, kicked both feet out and almost walked Heidi through the sand. Not a clever thing to do with metal panniers behind my feet waiting to crush my ankles should I stumble. It must have taken me fifteen minutes to get down the track to Dan's camp. I was swearing and cursing his name all the way. But, once we all got there, it proved to be worth it.

The scrub was more dense down by the river and the shade of the trees was a welcome break from the still harsh late afternoon sun. The long shadows gave the place a magical feel. Being close to the water there was an abundance of vegetation, with several species of tall grasses, well over six feet high. In a clearing by a bend in the river Dan had created his eco-lodge. Several small huts, with concrete bases but bamboo walls, in an idyllic setting made for the perfect hide-away. We were each shown to a clearing where we could pitch our tent and were then taken down to the river. One of Dan's staff had made tea for us and even supplied us with ginger biscuits; this place really was run by a Brit! We all settled down on camping chairs around the ashes of the previous night's fire to watch the sun set over the marshland and river.

An hour before sunset Dan took us out on a boat ride through the swamp – our own 'poor man's Okavango Delta experience' – and we got close to some hippos and an elephant. I even went for a quick swim as he assured us there probably weren't any crocodiles around. We had the campsite to ourselves when we came back and we all sat around the fire late into the evening watching a far-off electrical storm while overhead an upside down Plough (or Big Dipper) moved across the sky; another glorious African evening. This was not how I'd thought the day would pan out as I tumbled into the sand first thing that morning.

Next morning I was slightly apprehensive about riding back up the sandy path to the main road. Tom was even more worried. His ankle was certainly on the mend but he was still tentative about riding on sand. He had hardly slept during the night and set off thirty minutes before the rest of us in the morning as he just wanted to get back on the main road. He said he would wait for us at the petrol station back in Kongola.

Tom's extra early start to the day had kicked Daryll and Angela into action and they'd packed up and departed. I was last to leave, saying goodbye to Dan and gingerly heading up the track. I made it to the main road in no time and headed up to the petrol station to meet the others. When I got there Pat and Tom were crouched down looking at Tom's V-Strom. Pat was smiling as usual but Tom was not a happy camper.

"What's wrong?" I asked.

"Oh, the bike's OK, but I came off on the sand," Tom replied.

He'd fallen off on the sandy path, within sight of the main road, sliding to his right (the same side he'd hurt in his Cape Town spill). He'd trapped his leg under the pannier and it had taken him ten minutes to get himself free. But like a true adventure biker the first thing he did when he could get up was take a photo. Because he'd landed on sand he hadn't really hurt himself, but it sounded like a nasty spill none the less. Tom was in his mid-sixties, had a sore leg and had tumbled off his bike – again. He was hoping to get all the way to Europe. I was getting increasingly worried for him. He kept talking about how this trip would be the death of him and suddenly it wasn't so funny anymore.

*

To get from Namibia to Victoria Falls in Zimbabwe you either have to go north through Zambia or south through Botswana. Our route was decided when we discovered that entry to Botswana was free and what's more, relatively painless. We crossed at Ngoma Bridge and within an hour of leaving Namibia we were riding along the A33 road in Botswana's Chobe National Park. Motorcycles aren't usually allowed inside national parks in Southern Africa but this was the only sealed route through Botswana, so we were. The road cut a swathe through the bush, with the trees and high scrub making it hard to see very far. I was standing up looking out to my left and right to see if I could spot any wildlife. Occasionally I saw the odd antelope which was exciting, but I was really hoping to see something a little bigger.

Elephants were well represented in this part of the world and Chobe was famous for them. Off to my left I spotted the raised tails of a small family of warthogs running by; with their squat little bodies and erect tails they always remind me of bumper cars, bouncing along in the undergrowth. I'd heard a story about warthogs that, although I'm not sure I believe, always springs to mind when I see them. I'd been told that warthogs are really stupid animals. They are very skittish and when they sense danger they run off in a panic. But a few seconds later they totally forget what they are running away from and stop. Apparently warthogs taste good and aren't hard to catch.

As I slowed down to take a closer look at the warthogs, Tom came rocketing past me. There was little other traffic on the road and he wasn't close to hitting me but his erratic riding was starting to concern me. At least with Pat you knew where you were. Or rather where he was – out in front doing 93 kph, following his GPS. Tom would slow down, weave about and then suddenly whack open the throttle and speed up. A few times, when we'd been in traffic I'd seen him weaving in and out with what I can only describe as wanton abandon. Daryll and Angela usually stayed at the back. They had a system that worked well for them and riding with others wasn't going to alter that. Usually sticking to 80 kph Daryll and Angela were often last to get to where we were going. This wasn't a problem for me, and in a way I was glad they were a little slower than the others. Riding on my own through North and Central America I think, at times, I'd ridden too fast, especially in the USA, costing me more in fuel but more importantly, perhaps, missing a few things and putting myself in more danger than I needed to. But in Africa it was even more important that I rode conservatively. At 80 kph I could watch out for wildlife and still keep an eye on the road. Whether it be wild or domestic animals, small children running into the road enthusiastically waving at us but not appreciating how quickly we were moving, potholes, sand or gravel, there was a myriad of ways that my trip might finish sooner than planned.

I looked up and saw Tom doing a quick U-turn up ahead. Pat had also stopped at the side of the road and he and Chris were looking and pointing over to my right. Someone had spotted something and it wasn't a warthog. Pat was pointing at an elephant. I slammed the brakes on and pulled over to the side of the road, as quickly and quietly as I could so as not to scare him (the elephant, not Pat!). He was directly to my right, perhaps twenty metres away. Pat and Tom were a similar distance ahead of me. I was fumbling for my camera in my tank bag trying to keep one eye on the elephant. He was just standing there lazily pulling some leaves from a tree but I could tell that he knew we were there. Elephants have great hearing (you would with ears that big wouldn't you?) but poor vision, so I hoped that by turning my engine off he wouldn't see me as a threat. However I could hear Tom's V-Strom and Pat's Africa Twin throbbing away up the road. I took a few photos trying to get part of the bike in the shot to prove how close I'd come to an African elephant while sitting on my motorcycle. I daren't get off Heidi though, afraid that the elephant might come over for a closer look. The damage an angry bull elephant could do to a BMW didn't bear thinking about. I heard the two DRs coming up from behind; Daryll sensibly stopped a good twenty metres behind me.

Close encounter in Chobe National Park
(Photo courtesy of Daryll Naidu)

We all just sat there on our bikes for a few minutes, immersed in the wonderful African moment. Then the elephant raised his head, looked straight at me and started to shuffle his feet. His head swayed to the left and right and he took a couple of steps forward towards the road. Stamping his feet, making a little trumpet noise and swaying his head, it was clear he was getting agitated and wanted to cross. I needed to move. Hurriedly I put the camera back in the bag and turned the key on my bike. It's amazing how long it takes a BMW computerised engine to start up when you need it *right now* and in the few seconds I was waiting, the elephant shook his head once more, snorted and stamped his front foot. I pulled away, moving up to where the others were parked just in time to watch the animal cross the road between us and the two Suzukis. It was a wonderful sight and a privilege to see such an impressive animal from the seat of my bike, even if it was a little too close for comfort.

CHAPTER 24

THE SMOKE THAT THUNDERS

"No one can imagine the beauty of the view from anything witnessed in England."

(David Livingstone)

We only spent a day in Botswana; travelling a mere one hundred and fifty miles in such a vast country I can barely say I've visited Botswana at all. Nevertheless I collected a sticker for the panniers saying I'd been to Chobe. At least it was easy to get in and out of the country. I couldn't say the same for entering Zimbabwe, which was tedious in the extreme. There were no problems, as such, it just took a very long time. Standing in a queue in the heat of the day in bike gear can be excruciatingly boring and tiring. The line inched forwards and although there were only a few dozen of us it seemed to take ten minutes to process each individual. There were two officials behind the counter who seemed to be checking and rechecking all documents, filling in numerous forms and stamping just about anything they could get their bureaucratic hands on. I had been concerned that Zimbabwe might not welcome people with British passports; (after all, the BBC was still banned from the country), but once I finally made it to the desk I had no trouble – they just charged me more for the privilege. I had to pay $80 for my visa and for the first time in Africa I also had to pay bike insurance: $50.

I'd come across an article in the influential American magazine *Foreign Policy* which had ranked Zimbabwe as second on its list of failed states in the world in 2009. Somalia was top and Sudan and Chad just behind. Zimbabwe has no functioning government, at least not in the conventional sense of the word. Since 2008, in theory, there has been a power sharing agreement between Robert Mugabe's Zimbabwe African National Union – Patriotic Front (ZANU-PF) and Morgan Tsvangirai's Movement for Democratic Change (MDC). Mugabe, already in his mid-eighties, remains as President, and Tsvangirai is Prime Minister. This was never going to be a happy marriage. Tsvangirai had founded the MDC in 1999 after becoming disillusioned with ZANU-PF. He stood against Mugabe in the 2002 Presidential elections. Mugabe had him arrested several times during the next few years culminating in an arrest and detention in 2007 where Tsvangirai was severely beaten. Tsvangirai stood against Mugabe again in the 2008

Presidential elections and was faced with intimidation, threats and arrest. Following the election it took ZANU-PF over a month to count the votes. Tsvangirai scored 47.9% to Mugabe's 43.25%. As no man reached 50% a run-off was needed (the two other candidates being eliminated). This result was quite something on its own. It was Mugabe's men who had counted the vote so we can only guess at what the real result had actually been. Mugabe seems to have upped the ante for the second election and massive intimidation of MDC supporters was unleashed throughout the country; hundreds may have died. A week before the election date Tsvangirai announced that he was withdrawing his name amid fears that those who voted for him would be killed.

It might seem as if Mugabe had won, but Zimbabwe had got itself into a terrible situation. The economy had collapsed, the currency was worthless, and Mugabe didn't even have enough money to pay his army. An outbreak of cholera didn't help matters. Although South Africa, under Thabo Mbeki (to his eternal shame), continued to support Mugabe, other African nations were putting pressure on him and in what appeared to be a swift and amazing change in events, Mugabe agreed to talks with Tsvangirai. In the summer of 2008 the two sides agreed on a power sharing agreement, although I'm sure very few people thought it would last.

Nevertheless, over the next two years it seemed to, at least to an extent. Tsvangirai was sworn in as Prime Minister in February 2009, but only a month later was lucky to survive a head-on collision with a truck which killed his wife Susan, the mother of their six children and his staunchest ally. Given the number of political opponents who had died in previous mysterious car accidents, there were many rumours of foul play. Despite this terrible personal loss, Tsvangirai maintained his position and very slowly, things seemed to settle down in the country. The economy stabilised, with Zimbabwe adopting the US dollar as its currency in 2009. In late 2008 inflation had stood at 11,200,000% with prices doubling every single day. In August 2008 the central bank issued a new 100 billion dollar note; five months later they issued a new 100 *trillion* dollar banknote. Quite how a country can function under those circumstances was beyond me and this was one of the reasons I wanted to visit it.

Zimbabwe only ever hits the news in the UK when something bad has happened. I'd travelled enough to know not to believe all that I read and see about a place, but this was different. Almost a pariah state, Zimbabwe has been ostracised by much of the world for the last few decades and reports leak out of terror, oppression, land seizures and violence against the white minority who still lived in the country, not to mention Mugabe's bully tactics against the black majority. He must also be held responsible for the notorious and well-documented massacre of many thousands of civilians in Matabeleland by the North Korean-trained 5th Brigade of the Zimbabwean army in the 1980s.

I considered taking the Union Jack flag off my windshield, so as not to attract attention to myself, something that hadn't even crossed my mind in any other country I'd visited. Back in Kongola I'd asked Dan what he thought of this and on his advice I hadn't bothered. "Most Zimbabweans will welcome you with open arms," he'd said. "It's only Mugabe and his cronies who play on the whole British Empire thing."

This is what I had thought but as I lined up to get my passport stamped I was once again surprised by my own prejudice. As with Mexico, my preconceived ideas had been formed by a hostile press with its own agenda. I hoped Zimbabwe was going to be far better than I feared it might be.

It was only a short ride from the border to Victoria Falls and it wasn't long before we were putting our tents up at the Victoria Falls Rest Camp and Lodge. Well, Daryll, Angela and I were camping, Tom, Pat and Chris had booked into one of the rooms on site. I think they were getting a little tired of sleeping three in a tent and were increasingly opting not to camp whenever they could. We rode past their room and pitched our tents about as far away from them as possible. It wasn't that we weren't all still getting on; it was just that, well, we weren't all still getting on.

I'd had a clandestine chat with Angela about riding styles, during one of our breaks that day, and it was clear that she and Daryll were just as agitated by Pat and Tom's riding as I was. Angela thought Tom was downright dangerous on the road, never looking out for fellow road users and speeding up and then slowing down so you never knew where you were with him. They seemed less annoyed than me with Pat. I was increasingly getting fed up with the fact that he insisted on riding up front at all times. On a few occasions I'd tried to take the lead and he'd always overtaken me. But it wasn't just about riding styles. Like me, Daryll and Angela had already been on the road for several months, had got into a certain way of doing things and were watching their money carefully. They planned to ride all the way to Europe and were spending their life's savings on this trip. They'd sold everything back in Canada, including their house, and needed to be careful with the cash. I guess the bottom line was that we just had a slightly different agenda from Pat and Tom. The six of us had spent three weeks together now and it was inevitable that cracks would appear. We were all very polite, sociable and friendly to one another, but at Victoria Falls it became apparent to me that the full group would not stick together for much longer.

I was fine with this. I had truly enjoyed riding with other travellers, but I'd also really enjoyed being on my own. Being led by Pat and his GPS was beginning to annoy me, but conversely there was comfort in riding through Southern Africa with someone who knew what to do when or if my bike broke down, and there was no denying it was nice to have their company.

The following day we all set off to visit Victoria Falls. It was a lovely sunny warm day and we'd been told the falls were in flood at that particular time of year so we would get soaking wet. It was only a ten-minute walk to the park entrance, where we had to pay a rather pricey US $30 to get in. A little steep I thought but I wasn't going to not see the Falls having come this far. That would be madness. Who in their right mind would do that? I entered followed by Daryll and Angela. Tom and Pat were some way behind us. Chris decided she didn't want to see the falls enough to pay the $30 and went back to the campsite. Takes all sorts I guess.

The Zambezi was most certainly in flood; we couldn't see a bloody thing. Within seconds of getting close to the edge we were all soaking wet, but it was warm spray coming from the mighty river and I didn't mind a bit. Occasionally the spray would dissipate and we'd catch a brief glimpse of the river pouring over the edge and down the hundred or so metres into the gorge. Towards the western end of the park there was a huge statue of Livingstone reminding us all that he was the first white man to see the falls, back in 1855. As explorers did in those days he renamed the 'Mosi-oa-Tunya' which rather beautifully means 'the smoke that thunders', Victoria Falls, in honour of the British Queen. He later wrote, *"No one can imagine the beauty of the view from anything witnessed in England. It had never been seen before by European eyes; but scenes so lovely must have been gazed upon by angels in their flight."*

I was rather impressed with the falls too!

They looked as I'd expected, since I live in a world of photographs, TV and the internet. I have no idea at what age I first became aware of Victoria Falls, perhaps sometime at school. There are so many natural wonders in the world that I have never seen but I know what many of them look like, and at the very least, know of them. And if I didn't I could look them up in a split second on my Netbook. In some ways, there are no more 'wonders' of the world left as we don't have to wonder any more. And yet, only one hundred and fifty years ago not one single European had ever seen (let alone heard, smelt, or felt) this magnificent waterfall which had been tumbling over the plateau for at least 100,000 years. I did the maths. Europeans have known about Victoria Falls for approximately 0.15% of its existence. The privilege to witness this majesty has got to be worth $30 of anyone's money.

Back at the campground we'd been able to hear the distant rumble of the waterfall but up close we could smell it; that fresh smell of water vapour in the air, a smell I hadn't realised I'd missed. It had been a couple of weeks since it had rained on me and I'd got used to the dry dusty air of Namibia. As

I stood there breathing in the sweet smells of the lush vegetation and moist air I let the noise wash over me as I was engulfed by the whole experience. Victoria Falls was an assault on the senses and it was almost deafening. I could hardly hear what Angela was saying as we walked along the soaked pathway.

I was reminded of another famous waterfall on another continent – the Iguaçu Falls on the border of Brazil and Argentina. When I had visited them with Tracy, many years previously, I commented on how Iguaçu hadn't really existed until I'd seen it – how I hadn't *really* known about it even though I'd *superficially* known about it. Until I actually saw something with my own eyes, witnessing it first hand, it was just a theory, an idea, not something concrete. I meant it slightly tongue in cheek; it was during the early days of our relationship so I was also trying to impress her with my deep thinking (I've long since stopped trying to do that). But there was a serious point behind my musings. Previous to seeing Iguaçu I hadn't really appreciated what it was, how powerful it was and how much water was continually flowing over the edge. Knowing about something, reading about it or seeing pictures of it is not the same as witnessing it. My dictionary has three definitions of 'knowing'. The first says 'Recognising or identifying, being able to distinguish'. By this definition I knew about Victoria Falls before I had set off on my trip. But the second is deeper. 'To be acquainted with, have personal experience of, to understand'. This can only be achieved through actually being there. I knew about Victoria Falls before I saw it but I couldn't fully understand it until I'd witnessed it.

Also, once something has been witnessed it can't be 'un-witnessed'. Once we've seen a memorable place it must change us. Perhaps only in a small way, but surely we are the sum of our parts and that means we are, in part, made up of our memories. I'm not suggesting that I became a different person for seeing Victoria Falls but travelling and experiencing new things certainly changes who we are. Every single new experience was subtly changing who I was and altering my outlook on life and something as massive as Victoria Falls, brought this home to me in a powerful way. Perhaps it was just as well that Angela couldn't hear me.

The third definition of knowing – 'Have sexual intercourse with' – didn't seem relevant.

*

Victoria Falls Rest Camp and Lodges was home to several huge overland truck companies, transporting eager 'gappies' between Cape Town and Nairobi. When we were there, there were three trucks in town and this indicated that I was in the most touristy place I'd been since Cape Town. Every time I left the campground I was accosted by men trying to sell me all sorts of things: souvenirs, T-shirts, wood carvings, money. Money? The number one tourist souvenir in Zimbabwe seemed to be old Zimbabwe money. People were trying to sell me old Zimbabwe dollars in huge denominations. I bought a ten *billion* dollar note, for one US dollar.

The next best seller was the T-shirt. With so many travellers beginning or ending their overland truck trips at Vic Falls, a small business has grown up around the making and selling of bespoke, self-designed T-shirts. A guy came up to me and Daryll while we were sitting near our tents and explained. We could design our own T-shirts with details of our trip, places we'd been and a map on the back showing the route. For some strange reason I thought this was a really cool idea and sat down with him for half an hour designing my own shirt. Naturally it was going to say 'thedomwayround' on the front and on the back I was going to have a map of Southern Africa with my route from Cape Town to Nairobi marked on it – all for $20. I explained that we were leaving the following day but he said that wouldn't be a problem and he promised to have it done by 7 am. Being a trusting fellow I paid him up front. As he left, Daryll looked at me: "You're not going to see him again."

"What?" I asked.

"He's got your money and he knows you're leaving in the morning. I wouldn't have paid him up front."

"No, don't be silly," I replied. "He'll turn up. It's not as if he demanded the money, I offered it. I thought he might need it to pay for some ink or something. He'll show. Really Daryll, you Canadians are very untrusting!"

Next morning Daryll was proved right. We had planned to leave at eight and as usual, Tom and Pat were raring to go. I had a phone number for the T-shirt guy and, at eight, I rang it. He answered and said he would be thirty minutes. I told the others to leave without me and that I would find them later. We were heading for Bulawayo and I had plenty of time to catch up with them. I waited half an hour and phoned again. He didn't answer. This wasn't good. I gave him another ten minutes and then rang again. His phone was now turned off. Bugger.

Riding down the road, trying to catch up with the others, I started to wonder whether I had, in fact, been trying too hard not to appear racist. If the guy selling the T-shirts had been white I probably wouldn't have paid him until he delivered the goods. My instinct, back in Namibia, had wrongly been not to trust Dan, the lodge owner. What was a white British guy doing in Namibia? How did he run his own eco-lodge? What was he up to? This was seriously worrying me. I had always thought of myself as a liberal kind of person. It now occurred to me that I might be trying to cover up my latent prejudice by being overly trusting. Or was I over-analysing things (easy to do when your head is stuck in a motorcycle helmet all day) and really it had nothing to do with racism, overtly or covertly. Or was the guy just now turning up at the campsite with my T-shirt after a completely legitimate delay? Perhaps it was just me being an idiot. If Tracy had been with me I think I know what she would have said.

Bulawayo is Zimbabwe's second city and the main road from Victoria Falls was a beautiful tarmac one, with little traffic. I soon forgot about the T-shirt guy as Heidi and I were swept along on a twisting and slightly undulating journey south through the heartland of Zimbabwe. At about a thousand metres above sea level this was very different terrain from Namibia. Long gone were the sandy desert regions of South West Africa. The air smelt fresher, cleaner and more invigorating at this altitude than the warm scent of the desert region. It might just have been my imagination but I felt I could almost see the recent history of the country on that road south to Bulawayo. It seemed to me that this was fertile land (especially compared to Namibia and northern South Africa) but it all looked too neglected and uncultivated.

I knew that Zimbabwe had had a turbulent history and land reform had been at the heart of it. Not twenty years previously Zimbabwe had produced tobacco, cotton, coffee, peanuts, maize and wheat. The problem was that about one third of this arable land was owned by the white population of the country who constituted less than one per cent of the total. This had always been a thorn in the side of Mugabe and in 2000 he instigated his highly controversial land redistribution programme. Essentially, whites were kicked off the farms. I wasn't quite sure how I felt about this. On the one hand I could see the argument that the land belonged to the blacks and the whites were colonialist. On the other hand I'm sure those whites had lived and worked the land for generations. And either way I felt uncomfortable classifying things in such, well, black and white terms.

Whether it was right or wrong for blacks or whites, the facts were that land redistribution had proved disastrous for the economy and for the population as a whole. In 2000 Zimbabwe had been the sixth largest producer of world tobacco; ten years later it was producing less than a third by volume. The country had been known as 'the bread basket' of Southern Africa in the past. In 2010 45% of the population was considered malnourished. From bread basket to basket case…

I had a lot to think about that morning and while my mind was racing away with thoughts of land seizure, colonialism and racism, Heidi was also racing along beneath me. Unfortunately, I'd slowed down to cross a railway line, checking both ways just in case. I had no idea whether Zimbabwe had a functioning railway network or not but I didn't want to find out the hard way.

I came round a gentle curve and saw a man running out into the road waving a red flag. Travelling teaches you to expect the unexpected so I wasn't overly shocked to see this sight even though I had absolutely no idea what was going on. I gently applied the brakes as my brain kicked into gear. Realising that this was a policeman my eyes caught up with my brain and only then did I notice that it was a policeman with a speed gun.

I pulled over and dismounted. The police officer came over to me and was saying something, but I had my earplugs in and couldn't understand a word. I gesticulated to my ears, although by now I had a pretty good idea what he was saying.

"Morning sir. This is a restricted 80 km per hour zone and you were doing 89."

"Morning. Really, was I going that fast? I didn't realise."

"Yes sir, this is a built-up area. You were speeding. That is a $10 fine."

I looked around. A built-up area? All I could see were bushes, some trees and in the distance a few huts up on the hillside. I decided to try to talk my way out of the situation. This wasn't something I would even have thought about doing before I started this trip, but I had grown in confidence and decided to chance my arm. Pat had the gift of the gab and I knew he would have talked his way out of this, if he'd been stopped.

"But officer, I've had a really bad day. Just this morning I was robbed of $20 in Vic Falls."

"I am sorry sir but you were speeding. That is a mandatory $10 fine." He started writing a ticket.

"Oh, come on. I'm having a lovely time riding through this wonderful country and I didn't know this was a built-up area. I want to say I have had a great time in Zimbabwe but today has been a bad day. Is there not something you can do?"

I couldn't quite believe what I was saying. It wasn't like me at all. Was I actually trying to bribe a police officer? Is that what he would think? Is that even what I meant? I had no idea. As a habitual non-blagger I'd picked a really stupid time to start. He looked at me through his fake Ray-Bans and started to smile.

"As you were only speeding a little I will fine you a little," he said. And he proceeded to write me out a ticket for $5. I thought this was a fair compromise and paid up.

Half an hour later I caught up with the others who were having a break under the shade of a large tree. They fell about laughing when I told them what had happened.

"We saw a policeman with a speed gun," Pat said. "But we managed to slow down just in time. He must have heard you coming!"

Bloody typical, I get stopped and Pat doesn't. I went off into the bush for a pee and tried to calm myself down. It wasn't exactly his fault but it most certainly wasn't fair. Returning to the bikes I was glad, for once, that Pat's obsession with riding up front saw him speed off into the distance. At least if there were any more police down the road they were bound to hear Pat coming first.

An hour later, riding down a long straight section of road with Pat about fifty metres in front of me I saw two men out of the corner of my eye running from under the shade of a tree. One of them was waving a red flag. Pat sped past them just as they made it to the road and they both pointed at me! For a millisecond I thought of ignoring the frantic officer with the flag and riding past but with Tom, Daryll and Angela behind me I decided it wouldn't be the right thing to do. Angrily, I pulled over and flipped up my lid.

"Sir, this is an 80 zone and you were doing 86," said the out-of-breath official, still waving his flag.

"But officer. What about my friend in front. You didn't stop him?"

"He was going too fast. It would have been dangerous."

"How fast was he going?"

The officer looked down at his speed gun, "93 kilometres per hour."

I just started laughing and, amazingly, so did the policeman. I didn't need to say anything and neither did he. We both saw the absurdity of the situation. I really think the fact that I had a flip-front helmet, so he could see my face, helped. It was so ridiculous I couldn't help but laugh and he saw the funny side too. He told me to slow down and said I could go. I'm not sure I could have taken being stopped and fined by the Zimbabwe police twice in one day.

We made it to Bulawayo without further incident and found the municipal campground. The place was fairly deserted apart from one other tent and a huge overland truck, which was occupied by a family of four. This was a real African hippie family. With two adults and two young boys, all light-skinned with long blond hair. To me they looked Germanic, which in this part of the world probably meant they were Zimbabwean or South African. They were busy eating around an open fire when we arrived and although I nodded at them as I dismounted I didn't go over and say hello. As I didn't do it immediately upon arrival I later felt I'd lost the moment and I didn't speak to them at all. Days later this haunted me as I had lots of questions I would have liked to ask starting with 'What were they doing and where were they from?' I kicked myself for not being more friendly. Was this one of the negative consequences of riding in a big group? If I'd been on my own I most certainly would have introduced myself; in fact they would probably have come over to speak to me, but a group of five motorcycles turning up can be a little off-putting. Was my solo motorcycle trip through Southern Africa turning into one of those organised tours I'd always scorned?

After putting my tent up I did, however, fall into conversation with the old man who occupied the other tent on the campground. I say 'tent' but really it was a series of plastic sheets hung between trees, all set around a large campfire. Small and unkempt, with a long straggly beard, Ahmed was originally from Zimbabwe but had lived in the UK for many years. He had come back to Bulawayo to reclaim the land that his father had once owned but was having a lot of trouble with the local authorities. Ahmed told me his family was of Pakistani descent, and initially we had a friendly chat as he had lived in Leicester, not far from where I lived in the UK. I noticed that he made no effort to speak to Daryll and wondered whether that was because Daryll looked Indian. Surely not?

We spoke of life in Britain compared to Zimbabwe and it was interesting to hear his take on things. It seemed to me that he was very lonely and welcomed the attention. He spoke excellent English but the way he spoke sounded like a man who wasn't much used to conversation. I listened sympathetically as he told me his family history and the trouble he was having trying to claim what he thought was justly his in Bulawayo. After a while he excused himself and went back to his tent, returning with a battered and bruised religious pamphlet extolling the virtues of a particular sect of Islam.

"Read this, Dom," he said. "The truth is in here. And as a British person you need to open your eyes."

"Thanks," I replied in what was, I hoped, a friendly but negative way. "I'm not really into religion."

"But you must. You must open your eyes. The problem with England..." Ahmed was almost whispering now, looking around to see if anyone could hear. Tom, Pat and Chris had disappeared into town to try to find some food while Angela was cooking up something on her stove. Daryll was tinkering with his bike, not paying us the slightest attention. "The problem with England is that it's being taken over by Indians." I'm sure I saw his eyes flicker over in Daryll's direction.

"Sorry?" I wasn't sure I'd heard right.

"Indians. They are taking over your country." In the fading light I could still make out his face; his eyes had lit up and he was staring somewhat manically at me. "They are controlling your brains and sucking the life force out of you. England used to rule the world and look at it now. Most English people know this and don't look them in the eye. Have you noticed this? Most English people know and they don't make eye contact with Indians."

I wasn't sure what to say. Or rather, I knew what I wanted to say but didn't want to offend him. "Here, read this tonight. It will tell you what you need to know." And with that Ahmed gave me a booklet to read, *The truth about Jesus,* and scurried off to his tent.

*

Dawn broke around six the following morning. Not that it mattered much as I was awake long before that. Tom, Chris and Pat had decided to take their tent down early and although they had been reasonably quiet it was impossible for a V-Strom and an Africa Twin to start up and move off without waking everyone. They had muttered something about not being able to get anything to eat the previous evening and were up early to try to hunt for some breakfast. I had little sympathy with them by now; they were travelling all the way up to Europe but hadn't thought to bring a cooker with them. My understanding was wearing thin, especially at five thirty in the morning.

It was different with Daryll and Angela. I had grown really fond of them over the previous couple of weeks. They were easy travelling companions, always reliable, friendly and flexible. They knew what they wanted to get out of their trip but were willing to compromise. Daryll only knew a little more about motorcycles than me, which made me feel comfortable in his company and it was great to have people I could talk to about the places we were travelling through. They were also interested in the history, culture and sites of the places we were riding through, not just aiming for the next destination. It was all about the journey, not the destination. Pat, Chris and Tom were certainly very friendly and helpful and I had never had an argument with them but their attitude to travelling was different. They had their final destination of Europe firmly fixed in their minds and were always riding to get there. I felt they were missing out on the present with a focus on the future so they didn't always appreciate the here and now. Every morning started with the day's destination keyed into the GPS and that was it. From then on Pat was up front, riding at 93 kph with the GPS telling us where to go. He had a paper map but never once looked at it and didn't even have a guidebook of any sort. He knew exactly where we were going that day, where all the petrol stations were but no peripheral vision. A map shows you the wider context, which I found useful and interesting; a GPS just shows the road you are on. When we travelled through the Caprivi Strip, Pat had no real idea how that thin strip of Namibia fitted into the wider context of Southern Africa and how close we were to, say, the Okavango Delta in Botswana. Pat just wanted to get to Cairo. For him it seemed it was all about the destination, not the journey.

Pat's insistence on riding up front had really got to me now; it seemed to

285

be eating away at me and I was getting obsessed with it. I had spoken to him about it but he just shrugged it off and smiled. Chris had told me that Pat had always been in charge of things and found it difficult to take a back seat. He had inherited a business from his father and, as an adult, had run his own company. He'd retired before he was fifty, sold the company and had never been anything other than *The Boss*. She also found it infuriating at times but as she said: "This is Pat. You get the rough with the smooth," and had on another occasion, referred to him as her *'living Indiana Jones'*; a generous, helpful guy but also single-minded and stubborn.

Tom was more of an enigma. As a sexagenarian wealthy American I expected him to be more sensible than he was. Bursting a blood blister with a thorn in Namibia was just the tip of Tom's iceberg of folly. He was constantly moaning about how this trip would be the death of him but he rode like a teenager: too fast, erratically and without much care and attention. His bike was overloaded but he insisted on buying the odd souvenir, picking up a foot-long wooden giraffe at Victoria Falls which he tried to stuff into his pannier. He also seemed to have eternal electrical problems. Every night he would complain that his camera didn't work or his GPS wouldn't charge and often Pat would have to solve his problems for him. I think Pat liked doing this and Tom liked to be looked after. But Tom could also be generous and funny and good company. He'd led an interesting life and was clearly a giving and caring man. And after all, in his mid-sixties he was riding a motorcycle through Africa. I took my hat off to him for that alone.

By the time we were in Zimbabwe we'd been together for four weeks, twenty-four/seven. That takes its toll and even the closest of friends could get on one another's nerves by then. I'm sure I was irritating the others in ways I couldn't even contemplate. Such is life on the road.

Daryll and Angela packed up faster than me that morning in Bulawayo and headed off to meet the others. I finished loading the bike and then put Ahmed's pamphlet on the ground near his tent, not wanting to disturb him; or rather, in all honesty, not wanting to get caught up in another conversation with him. So, I was the last to leave the campground at Bulawayo. I knew it was $5 to camp but the previous night they hadn't had any change and said we could all pay in the morning. When I walked into the office to pay I was somewhat surprised to be told I owed $30.

"But, yesterday we were told it was $5."

"You must pay for your friends."

I couldn't quite believe it. There had been some talk the previous evening about leaving without paying but I had said I didn't like the idea. This had happened before, in Namibia at Sesriem where we had been forced to take a minibus down the asphalt road to Sossusvlei. The trip was supposed to cost

286

us $25 each but we were all a little annoyed that we couldn't take our bikes and were not happy to have to pay so much for a taxi ride. We did offer to pay up front (I always do!) but they said we could pay later. The taxi driver never asked for the money so when we returned we went straight to our tents, packed up and left. Pat especially was insistent on us 'doing a runner' and although I didn't feel comfortable doing it I couldn't really go and pay for just my share alone. I worried about what precedent we had set for future travellers/bikers. I heard some good advice once about paying bribes: don't do it. Otherwise it will only encourage the recipients and the next biker to come that way will be paying for your decision. I felt the same about Sesriem. After all, the reason we weren't allowed to ride our bikes down the road was because previous bikers had gone off-road and disturbed the sand. What attitude would they now have to bikers because of what we had done?

In a similar vein I'd got annoyed with Daryll at Victoria Falls. The entrance was a steep $30 for 'foreigners' but those holding a South African passport got a $10 reduction. Daryll was South African by birth but a Canadian citizen. At the entrance gate he told them he and his wife were South African and they got away with it. While not a major crime I wasn't happy with this deception. It was the one time Daryll and I had disagreed about anything, until now.

At the camp in Bulawayo it was clear that the other five had all left without paying. There was no way I was going to fork out for all of them so I put $5 on the counter, thanked them for their hospitality and walked out. I half expected the security guards to grab me as I mounted Heidi and started her up. But they didn't and I rode on to meet up with the others at the petrol station in town.

"What happened?" smiled Pat. It was just a game to him and he had won because he had left first and not paid.

"I stopped and paid. For me." I said with an air of lofty English superiority. I knew I'd done the right thing but to the others, after my Victoria Falls T-shirt debacle, I was an honest idiot, which was ironic really as I was the one who (almost) never tipped. Just as the Canadians found it hard to see my non-tipping as anything other than mean-spirited, I saw their attitude towards not paying for things as dishonest.

Not wanting to talk about it anymore I turned to the pump to see what kind of fuel I could put into Heidi. Only 'blended' was available, which was essentially leaded petrol. For the first time on my trip I had to put leaded petrol into my BMW. I had no idea how bad a thing that was. Opinion seemed to be divided on the issue when I had asked on the Horizons Unlimited forum board, but the consensus seemed to be that it would be OK short term. I would soon find out, but unfortunately I'd be on my own when

I did so. The others were keen to get to Harare and sort out their visas for Ethiopia. I didn't want to miss out on Great Zimbabwe, one of southern Africa's most amazing sites, so we'd agreed that I would catch up with them in a couple of days in the capital city. They all headed east out of Bulawayo (no doubt at 93 kph with Pat at the front) and for the first time in over a month I was on my own again.

CHAPTER 25

GREAT STONE HOUSES

"It is symbolic of a huge cock."

(Jonathan, my guide)

With mixed emotions and a tank full of leaded petrol I rode south and then east, knowing that there wasn't another biker up ahead doing 93 kph, or indeed anyone behind me either, should I break down or crash. I'd become used to the company and it felt strange riding alone even though I knew it was only going to be for two days. But I had to admit to myself that I was pleased to be in charge of my own destiny once again. I could go as fast or as slowly as I liked, stop where and when I wanted to and take full control of my trip once more. I turned south at Masvingo and was soon pulling up at the greatest medieval city in sub-Saharan Africa.

Few people I'd spoken to had even heard of Great Zimbabwe but it surely ranks as one of the great wonders of the African world. Now an archaeological site spread over several square miles, this place was once home to thousands and it was the religious and political capital of an empire that stretched from Botswana to Mozambique. I was going to give this my full attention for the rest of the day and after paying the entrance fee I checked my stuff into a *rondavel* (small round stone hut) which was going to be my bed for the night, and headed down to the main gate where my own personal guide was going to show me around.

There were two very bored looking guards at the main entrance. I handed one of them my ticket and he laboriously and meticulously copied out my name and the number on my ticket into his huge and very old book. It was just as well they didn't get many visitors, I thought. He then picked up his walkie-talkie.

"Jonathan." His languid tone sounded sleepy in the afternoon heat.

"Yah man," came the somewhat lazy, tired reply.

"Main gate."

Two minutes later my guide appeared. Jonathan was a Zimbabwean University student who was guiding in his spare time to pay for his studies. He had long dreadlocked black hair, dark skin and slightly bloodshot eyes. He wore a pair of faded jeans, blue trainers and a dirty blue T-shirt. He introduced himself and we headed off up the path towards the site.

On the way to the ruins I asked him what life was like in present-day Zimbabwe. Not surprisingly, he told me it was tough. Inflation, unemployment, little investment from outside and a regime that didn't listen, were top of his complaints, but he was quite coy about giving too much away. He seemed happy to grumble and complain but didn't want to name names when it came to laying the blame at anyone's door. I found this a few times when I stopped to talk to people in the country. They were quite open about complaining but were non-committal when it came down to saying who was at fault. I wasn't sure if this was a direct response to the current situation or a more cultural thing. Coming from a country where it's almost obligatory to moan about the government and no one gives a second thought to saying whatever they want about whomever they want, it was slightly unnerving to face a wall of silence. I didn't want to push anyone and I certainly didn't want to get anyone into trouble, so after a while we moved on to a more pressing topic; one we both had opinions on and were much happier talking about: football.

"Who do you support?" he asked.

"Spurs," I replied. "Have you heard of them?"

"Sure. They were in the Champions League. That Bale is a great player, but they lost to Real Madrid. I support Manchester United."

As we walked around Great Zimbabwe it was obvious to me that I was the only tourist there. Jonathan explained that there were hardly any tourists at all anymore. Great Zimbabwe should rank amongst the likes of Machu Picchu or the pyramids of Egypt but as it is in Zimbabwe it gets only a few thousand tourists per year, instead of per day. I had the place to myself and for a couple of hours Jonathan and I scrambled around the place alone.

"Manchester are going to win the Champions League," he told me.

The archaeological site of Great Zimbabwe is split into two sections. Dominating the site is 'The Hill Complex' – a large rocky hill with natural crevices and cuts in the rock, which were fortified by dry stone walls to make a sort of crude castle. No one really knows what it was used for but archaeologists assume it was a religious centre and the place from which the king ruled his land. Probably first settled in the eleventh century, the site was certainly occupied and developed over the next few hundred years. The problem, Jonathan told me, was that by the time Europeans arrived in the sixteenth century, in the guise of Portuguese explorers from the Mozambique coast, the original inhabitants had left. They had no writing, so there was no written history of the place. Europeans found it hard to imagine that 'native Africans' could have constructed such a place. To be fair to them it was unique in the whole of southern Africa, where there is no tradition of building in stone. European explorers often tried to depict southern African tribes as backward, undeveloped and in need of 'civilizing' but Great Zimbabwe bucked the trend and didn't fit into their simplistic theories. Its very existence countered these prejudiced assumptions.

We climbed the final few stone steps to the top of the hill complex and looked down at the area known as 'The Great Enclosure'. I took a deep breath (it was a steep climb) and looked out across the complex. I could see for miles in every direction, across cultivated fields to tree-covered hills. Greenery everywhere. I tried to imagine what it must have looked like four hundred years previously; how the king would have felt surveying his empire and what his subjects must have thought of it all. I was reminded of the Mayan temples that Tracy and I had visited in Mexico and although Great Zimbabwe wasn't as huge, or as developed or as impressive, it was, for Africa, unique and special and moving. I tried to drink it all in, the silence of the place adding to the atmosphere.

"Manchester are playing tonight. We are going to win."

As he had broken the silence I tried to wean Jonathan off football and asked him about the history of Great Zimbabwe. He explained that Zimbabwe means 'Great Stone Houses' and the great enclosure was the very essence of this. He told me that I was standing in a royal compound and the hill complex was where the king had lived and from where he ruled his kingdom. I nodded in polite agreement but I knew that this was just the best guess. One of the things I liked about Great Zimbabwe was that no one really knew how it had worked.

"I think we will play Barcelona in the final."

"Good, good. Eh, Jonathan, can you tell me about The Great Enclosure?"

As we walked down from the hill complex its true size became evident. The Great Enclosure was nearly one hundred metres across and two hundred and fifty metres in circumference. From the hilltop it looked like a huge circular walled arena almost large enough to hold a football pitch. The walls were up to eleven metres high and five metres thick. I was looking at the largest ancient structure in sub-Saharan Africa; that fact alone was impressive. They say it was where the king's wives lived but I don't think anyone really knows what the structure was for. Entering it from the northern gate I was confronted by lots of rubble and low walls making it hard to picture what it would have been like. But there was one striking structure. At the south western end, standing ten metres tall, was a conical tower which dominated the interior of the enclosure. It looked like a smaller version of the huge cooling towers you see at power stations. Was it a symbol of the king's grain store? A defensive tower that hid the royal treasury? Or an astronomical tower?

"It is symbolic of a huge cock." Jonathan was smiling. I wondered if this really would be why someone had commissioned a large tower to be built several hundred years ago.

To get from the northern gate to Jonathan's 'phallic tower' I could have walked straight across the enclosure but intriguingly, there was a second way, one which the builders of the enclosure had seemingly intended. Immediately to my left was a second inner wall built a few feet away from the outer wall to create a narrow, curved seventy-metre passage which would take me from the entrance to near the base of the tower without being seen from within the enclosure – a private way for men/guards/soldiers to reach the tower without being seen by the women inside the great enclosure? I had no idea (and neither did Jonathan – he was still telling me about the huge cock) but I had never come across anything like this before. Iron Age forts in Scotland, called brochs, have hollowed-out walls which are similar, but this structure was tapered, getting narrower as you walked around it. In the middle of southern Africa here was a unique fortified compound built centuries before the Europeans arrived and tantalisingly deserted by the time they found it.

Great Zimbabwe left a lasting impression on me. I hadn't really known what to expect and I was blown away by it. It just amazed me that such a place could exist and very few tourists ever visited. It truly did deserve to be up there with the pyramids; perhaps not quite as visually stunning and grand but Great Zimbabwe was certainly unique, mystical and evocative. And of course, it provided the new name for the former British colony previously called Rhodesia after Cecil Rhodes, the nineteenth-century English 'Imperialist'. I loved the fact that I left there with more questions than answers and that I'd had the whole place to myself. Jonathan had been a great guide. A little obsessed with the Champions League perhaps but he'd given me an insight into the complex and into life in Zimbabwe and I left him a tip to help him with his studies. Typical; the one time I leave a tip the Canadians aren't there to see it.

My next stop was Harare. This was going to be my first African capital city and I didn't have a GPS. I enjoyed looking at my 746 National Michelin map and I enjoyed having to think about where I was going, how to get there, how long it would take, where I could get petrol from, where I could stop along the way and what to do if any of that went wrong. It also meant that occasionally, just occasionally, I would have to talk to locals. It is quite amazing how easy it is to travel through a land and hardly ever talk to anyone. Of course you talk to people at shops, petrol stations and lodges but beyond that I could ride for days without having a meaningful conversation with anyone. That was until I got lost. Then I would have to stop and ask directions. Usually this resulted in people telling me the way to go (or often, telling me what they thought I might want to hear, regardless of whether it was the right way or not) but occasionally it would also result in me having a proper conversation. I'd struck up conversations all through my trip which had started with a simple request for directions which I wouldn't have had if I'd had a GPS. Of course, sometimes conversations start for other reasons.

One of these chance encounters happened on the road to Harare. I was on the main road from Masvingo to Harare which was also the main road from Pretoria in South Africa to Harare. It was a busy two-lane tarmac road. (After the roads I'd been on from Namibia, through Botswana to Zimbabwe, any traffic would have made the road feel 'busy'.) This route was used by lorries and trucks plying their trade between South Africa and Zimbabwe. It's never fun to be on a motorcycle behind a slow-moving, smoking lorry on a twisty road but here, overtaking was particularly risky because I couldn't be confident that there wouldn't be potholes up ahead, or that the traffic coming the other way wouldn't simply plough straight into me; I'd heard that this road was a 'black spot' for accidents. The rutted but traffic-free gravel roads of Namibia now seemed like heaven by comparison.

As I overtook a large and heavily over-laden truck, listing to its side and spewing out enough smoke and pollution to make me cough inside my helmet, I spotted something out of the corner of my eye: a service station. There was a pull-off to the left, several small buildings advertising food and about half a dozen coaches parked up in a big car park. I was surprised to see this as I hadn't seen anything remotely like it since leaving Cape Town three weeks and three thousand miles ago.

I didn't need any petrol but I pulled in anyway to have a break and some food. There was a little supermarket that sold all sorts of South African food, including rusks, which I stocked up on. I could even have bought some Marmite. It was very strange to see so many South African foodstuffs in Zimbabwe, but although it had taken me a few weeks to get here from Cape Town my map told me that the border with South Africa was only about three hundred miles south of here and the people milling around the shop had probably woken up that morning in Pretoria or Johannesburg. Of course if I hadn't had a map and had just relied on a GPS I would have known my exact grid reference, the altitude and temperature but it wouldn't have been so obvious where South Africa was. Context is everything. I found myself perusing the fruit stall in the supermarket when I heard a voice behind me.

"Hi, there."

I turned to see an attractive woman standing next to me. She was tall and slim and wore a bright-red long flowing shawl over her dark black skin. She had tightly-beaded long black hair, dark eyes and full bright red lips. Her white teeth dazzled in the midday sun. But most striking of all, she seemed to be talking to me!

"Er, hello," I replied. Travelling around the world on a motorcycle had certainly not improved my conversational skills.

"Are you from England?" she asked.

"Yes, I am. How can you tell?"

"Oh, I saw you get off your bike, and you have a Union Jack on the front."

My prejudice and suspicion was immediately aroused. Perhaps in any other country I would have simply replied that I was indeed from England, but in Zimbabwe I still had a fear of admitting that I came from the colonial land of the hated white man. I was nervous to say yes but also disturbed by own bigotry. Was I about to get beaten to death with some South African fruit by an overzealous Zimbabwean woman, angered by the colonialism of Britain? Didn't Mugabe once say, *"The only white man you can trust is a dead white man."*? Was this it? Was it all going to end here? 'Thedomwayround', starts: Alaska, ends: side of the road near Harare. No, I was being ridiculous.

"Yes, yes I am. Are you from Zim?" I asked. Apparently I thought that it sounded friendlier to say 'Zim', rather than Zimbabwe.

"Originally, yes. But I live in London now. I've just flown into Jo'burg and am heading to Harare to see family. It's great to see another Brit here. But how did you get here?"

"Oh," I sighed with relief. "I started in Cape Town a few weeks ago. I'm heading to Kenya eventually." I couldn't remember what I said next, I was just so angry with myself for thinking the worst. Had this trip taught me nothing? Wasn't my reaction that of a suspicious xenophobe who never travelled? Surely I should have known better. My preconceived ideas of Zimbabwe had had more of an effect on me than I would care to admit. Our conversation came to a close and I crawled back to Heidi, ashamed of myself, again.

I'd spent the previous evening drawing out a route on paper to get me through Harare and to the Small World Backpackers Lodge. (OK I admit, there's a downside to my Luddite approach to travel.) I knew that was where the others were heading; after all, there weren't many places to stay in Harare. My Lonely Planet Guide to Southern Africa usually had a page or so of places to stay in major towns and cities; not so in Zimbabwe. Bulawayo showed three places and even in Harare there were only six listed. Six places for a capital city; that tells its own story. (Later, when I was back in the UK I dug out an old Lonely Planet Guide dating from 1995. It had more than four pages of accommodation in Harare, including at least a dozen backpacker lodges.)

I'd marked Avondale Shopping Centre on my map and knew the lodge was near there. I rode into Harare, following my pencil-drawn map, which I could just make out on the tankbag. (Note to self – pencil-drawn maps aren't easy to see through a shiny plastic cover on a bright African sunny day!) The centre of the city looked and felt as if it could be anywhere in South Africa. I was surprised to ride down the main street and see Jaguar and BMW forecourts alongside some large building housing major banks and insurance companies. Evidently some people in Zimbabwe weren't doing too badly. At every set of traffic lights, (or 'robots' as they are called in this part of the world) I peered down at my map checking I was on the right road. Just once I had to pull over to ask for help. A friendly newspaper seller reassured me I was going the right way for Avondale Shopping Centre and sure enough, five minutes later I was pulling into the Avondale car park.

I was just about to turn the page on my hand-drawn map to get the final directions to the lodge when I saw Pat and Chris walking down the road. I'd only been on my own for two days so I was surprised at how pleased I was to see them. They were just off to do some shopping and pointed me in the direction of the lodge saying they would be back there in ten minutes. Small World Backpackers Lodge was really someone's house set in a large walled garden in a wealthy suburb of Harare. They had a few rooms and plenty of space to pitch tents in the garden by a small pool. Tom's large three-man tent and Daryll's smaller tent were already erected along with three or four others. I found a space and settled in. In the small parking area, next to the motorcycles, there were two fully-loaded adventure quad bikes. Interesting…

CHAPTER 26

FROM HARARE TO MALAWI

"Cowardice asks the question – is it safe?
Expedience asks the question – is it politic?
Vanity asks the question – is it popular?
But conscience asks the question – is it right?'
There comes a time when one must take a position that is neither safe,
nor politic, nor popular but one must take it because it is right."

(Dr Martin Luther King)

The Quad Squad were two young Aussies who had set out from Turkey to break the world record for long distance quadricycle riding. And in fact they had broken that record just a couple of days before they made it to Harare. Kristopher and Jamie had started from Istanbul, ridden around Europe and then down through Africa getting through Tunisia, Libya and Egypt just before the 'Arab Spring' erupted. The world record had been 17,000 miles and they had passed that in Zimbabwe, somewhere on the road to Harare. The plan was to head on to Namibia and then South Africa before finishing their route by traversing Australia. They should have been over the moon but their achievement was tinged with immense sadness. Just a few weeks previously, in Malawi, a stolen car, being chased by police, had careered into their party killing the third rider, Valerio de Simoni.

I spent the evening talking with Kristopher and Jamie. They were very positive about the whole experience and were determined to finish what they had started. They told me that Valerio had said, before they started, that if any of them had a serious accident, or even died, the others should still finish. They had just never expected it to happen. Initially I thought this was almost callous but thinking about it, what other option did they have? Giving up and going home wouldn't bring Val back, and continuing with the trip (they were sponsored and raising lots of money for charity) would probably help them deal with the tragedy. Chatting with them reminded me how fragile life is, how much of a lottery it is and how much I needed to have my wits about me as I headed north through East Africa. But it also reminded me how short life is. Whether it's twenty years or eighty years we're not on this planet for very long and it really is a crime if we don't all live life to the full and seize every opportunity. That can take many different forms for each of us but it reminded me that I was absolutely right to have done what I was doing; giving up my job to see some of the world from the seat of a motorcycle. I could almost sense Kenya creeping up on me, it was one more fold on my map, and soon I was going to have to give some serious thought to the next stage of my life.

Despite their awful tragedy, Kristopher and Jamie were determined to follow their dream, see the world and raise money for charity in the process. They had a zest for life and a wonderfully optimistic view of things. They reminded me of how I had felt when I had started my trip. I still had that zest but occasionally I needed to remind myself of it. In some ways travelling had become a chore and a routine and the Quad Squad reminded me that I was lucky enough to be doing what I had always wanted to do. What did it matter if Pat always rode up front at 93 kph and Tom buzzed round like a crazy bumblebee? I was on the road, on Heidi, in Africa. If I wasn't careful, the remaining time on my trip would pass me by and I needed to drink in every minute, savour every event and enjoy every experience.

The record-breaking 'Quad Squad', Harare

When I got back to the UK, I followed the Quad Squad on their website and was delighted to see that later that year Kristopher and Jamie made it to Sydney, Australia. They set a new quadricycle world record: 35,000 miles and 38 countries.

We spent four days in Harare, partly just to relax after being on the go for so long but also because the Canadians needed to get Ethiopian visas. It appeared that Kenya was not issuing visas for Ethiopia anymore and Harare was the best place to get them. When they received them they were over the moon as there was no way around Ethiopia. Now they felt confident that they would be able to get Sudanese visas in Kenya and there was nothing stopping them from getting all the way to Europe. Even Tom started to think that he might make it to Europe and not die by the side of the road somewhere along the way. The mood seemed to lift among us, as if we all now knew that bureaucracy wasn't going to stop us fulfilling our dreams.

I had spent some of my time in Harare looking at my own options. All along my idea had been to ride to Kenya and then fly back to the UK. My carnet didn't allow me to get in to Egypt, and there was no easy way of getting around that country. Ethiopia is an amazing place, but as I'd spent some time living there, I didn't feel the need to return on a motorcycle. So the logical thing was to end the trip in Nairobi. I had always been absolutely fine with that but as the final destination approached and I became increasingly aware that my time was coming to an end, I didn't want to stop. I was having such a great time that I just wanted to continue. Perhaps I could try to sneak into Egypt without a carnet? Perhaps I could ship from Kenya to Singapore and carry on into Asia? Perhaps I could head up to Nairobi and then turn around and go back down to South Africa? I had no one telling me what to do and although I certainly didn't have unlimited funds I had a few thousand pounds I could call upon if needed. I had no job to get home for, so as I sat in Harare talking to the Aussies who were breaking a world record, Canadians who were eagerly discussing North Africa and an American who, at last, was talking about 'getting there' rather than 'dying while trying to get there' I found it really hard to make a rational and sensible decision. But in the end, I did.

I emailed Tracy to tell her that I would be arranging to fly the bike home from Nairobi and that I should be back in Britain within the month. The rationale was that I should stick to my plan and end the trip while I was still having a great time. Going on from Nairobi would be expensive if I shipped somewhere, or risky if I tried to move north towards Egypt without a carnet. I wasn't the sort of person who could try to blag their way into a country. My carnet said I wasn't permitted to enter Egypt and I wasn't going to try.

Pat was. His Canadian carnet also said it was not valid for Egypt but only on the back (mine said it on every page). He was convinced no one would ever look and if they did, a little *baksheesh* would oil the wheels of bureaucracy. For some reason this really annoyed me and a side of me, that I'm not especially proud of, half wished he wouldn't be allowed in.

Relations with Pat, Chris and Tom were fine while we were in Harare but we were spending increasingly less time with each other and my solo diversion to Great Zimbabwe had convinced me that I didn't really want to travel with them anymore. I knew Daryll and Angela felt the same and we hatched a plot to escape. However, there was only one major route north from Harare to Nairobi so it was going to be difficult to go our separate ways. We wanted to split but didn't want to offend. We were going to have to pick our time carefully. I had just had a chat with Angela about how we were going to get away from Pat when he came over and made me feel really bad about myself. "Why don't we change your oil?" he said.

I'd mentioned to Pat that I'd never actually changed the oil on my bike. I knew the theory but had never done it, preferring instead to pay someone else to do it. I knew this was lazy and for someone who was about to complete his trip and say he'd ridden a motorcycle half way around the world I really should change the oil at least once. With Pat there to oversee my attempt to do something mechanical with Heidi I felt I really shouldn't turn my nose up at the chance to become a real biker. Heidi had only done about three and a half thousand miles since Cape Town where she had last had fresh oil but it was probably going to be another two thousand to Nairobi. I'd been really good at getting the oil changed at least every four thousand miles and this was going to be Heidi's sixth oil change since Alaska.

Thirty minutes later I was sitting on the ground next to an oily bike wondering what all the fuss was about. Changing the oil on a BMW was easy. Why hadn't I done it sooner? All I needed to do now was to get rid of four litres of engine oil. But this was Africa so that wasn't a problem; someone would always take it and re-use it. I thanked Pat for overseeing the operation but felt guilty that I was secretly planning my escape from him. But that was the enigma that was Pat: annoying and controlling, yet wonderfully generous and helpful. That night I logged onto the internet and tried to sum up my feelings on Zimbabwe:

So, how do I sum up my time in Zimbabwe? Well, considering all you hear about the place in the UK is riots, inflation, riots, elections, riots and riots, it's remarkably peaceful. The people are very friendly, (perhaps the friendliest so far?) but it's also certainly the poorest country so far. The supermarkets have food but some shelves are empty. Most of the food is stock cooking foods like millet or rice and there aren't many vegetables. Petrol stations don't have shops of any kind and sometimes they don't even have petrol. Twice, I've had to fill up with leaded as there was no unleaded, the first time I've had to do that anywhere on this whole trip. The money (US dollars) is the dirtiest I've ever seen and people very rarely have change.

It will be no surprise to anyone who has travelled a lot (but it's always a surprise to those who haven't) that the people in Zimbabwe are really friendly. People who are poor and especially people who have just come through war or troubled times are often the most generous, friendly people on the planet. When I went to a supermarket on my own the other day several people came to look at the bike and chat and they were all super friendly and very polite. Two even thanked me for talking to them. When the woman on the till asked where I was from she said, "Oh, England. I've always wanted to go there. Will you take me?!" She had a huge smile on her face. Back home, Tesco's check-out people just ask me if I've got a loyalty card. You don't need fifty different types of breakfast cereal to be happy! Sorry, but whenever I come home it always amazes me how much stuff is on sale in supermarkets. How you can always buy everything all year round and how unhappy everyone looks buying it all.

No doubt the whole trip was changing who I was a little but for some reason I was feeling it most in Zimbabwe. Perhaps it was the history of the place and the fact that I had so many pre-conceived ideas about the country, more so than any other land I'd passed through. Zimbabwe's recent history had been awful and yet the people were so friendly. The place looked and felt as if it was struggling along, aware that things had been bad but slowly overcoming them but I knew that just under the surface there was still a lot of oppression, violence and injustice at play. Being a member of Amnesty International I was aware that Zimbabwe is not a safe place for people who disagree with the authorities; what I didn't know was that this had come to a head at the very time I was in the country.

Women of Zimbabwe Arise (WOZA) is an organisation aimed at providing women with a united voice against social, economic and human rights conditions in Zimbabwe – no small undertaking. (It's also a pun on the word 'woza', which means 'come forward' in the Ndebele language.) Unbeknownst to me, on the day I rode out of Harare heading for Mozambique, 2,000 members of WOZA marched on the Zimbabwe Electricity Transmission Company to protest about poor services and excessive bills. Riot police intervened and indiscriminately beat them. Later in the year, on another march, several were arrested and the two leaders charged with 'kidnapping and theft'. The continued harassment of WOZA by the authorities beggars belief. Almost every time they protest about something they are arrested.

Occasionally on my bike trip I would get a ridiculous notion or feeling that I was being brave, or doing something wonderful. I wasn't. I was indulging myself in a personal act of selfishness. Organisations like WOZA across the globe are the brave ones, campaigning for freedom, justice and equality. I think if I had known what was happening on the day I left Harare I would have ridden out of the country feeling sickened, saddened and overall, guilty. I'm glad I didn't know.

But the persecution of WOZA goes on. In February 2012, on their 10th Anniversary, at a peaceful demonstration in Bulawayo, the leaders were arrested again. The following February 181 WOZA members were arrested at another demonstration in the same city. In May 2013, 14 WOZA members were arrested for calling on Zimbabwe's neighbours to help bring an end to state-sponsored violence in the context of the 2008 election. WOZA leaders Jenni Williams and Magodonga Mahlangu were detained for 37 days. Their courage and bravery is a lesson to us all. For what it's worth, this section of my book is dedicated to WOZA.

*

The scenery changed subtly but noticeably as we left Zimbabwe and entered Mozambique, moving down from the 1400 metre plateau into the hot valley of the Tete corridor. The deforestation that had blighted Zimbabwe was replaced by thicker foliage and different species of trees. The boab tree, sometimes known as 'the upside-down tree', which we had last seen on the Namibia/Botswana border, reappeared. This tree is almost symbolic of hotter regions and I assumed Zimbabwe was too high, cold and wet for it but down in the Tete Corridor it was certainly hot enough. The people had also changed. Mozambicans are taller and darker and the women had longer hair than their Zimbabwean neighbours.

So, we were riding through the Tete corridor, a thin slice of Mozambique squeezed between Zimbabwe and Malawi. The great Zambezi river, which starts somewhere in Zambia and flows over Victoria Falls, continues on its two thousand mile meander towards the Indian Ocean – Africa's fourth longest river (after the Nile, Congo and Niger). As we rode across the suspension bridge the mighty Zambezi stretched off into the distance to our left and right.

We camped for the night in Tete on the north side of the river, within view of the impressive bridge, at the *Campismo Jesus e Bom* or *'Jesus is good campsite'* to translate its name from the Portuguese. We'd dropped to 200 metres above sea level and it was now hot and humid by day and the mosquitoes were out at night. Tete didn't seem to have much going for it and while Pat and Chris headed off on their XRV750 to find a restaurant, the rest of us stayed at camp and cooked. This was the kind of African camping that I had hoped to avoid: warm and sticky. I didn't really feel like eating but knew I needed to keep healthy. The mosquitoes were quite fierce and of course they were attracted by my torch as I tried to cook. I heated up some pasta and threw in a tin of vegetables. Eating it just made me sweat even more.

Daryll and Angela weren't having much more fun than me, and we moaned and cursed together, wishing we were still on the plateau up in Zimbabwe enjoying the cool air. When Angela read out of her guide book that Tete was reputed to be the hottest place in Mozambique we weren't surprised. Tom, meanwhile, had gone to bed without any food. I had offered, for the umpteenth time, to loan him my cooking equipment. But he didn't have anything to cook. I was also glad Pat and Chris had gone off into town. I was worried that the stress, heat and mosquitoes might have got the better of one of us and resulted in a full-blown argument. Pat had managed to annoy me again that day, although his intentions were honourable.

When we had arrived at the little campground in Tete, which was basically a fenced-in patch of dirt by the river, the friendly family who ran it had been very helpful. They lit a fire so we could have hot water from rudimentary outdoor showers and had even pointed out a hippo floating down the river for us. Pat had delved into his pannier and produced a couple of sweets to give to the children. This is what had annoyed me.

I knew he had the best of intentions and I appreciated why people do this but I felt strongly that they need to think through the consequences of their actions. There are certainly places blighted by aggressive begging, where children run up to tourists demanding gifts. I was once in a car behind an overland truck in Ethiopia and I couldn't believe what I was seeing. European tourists were actually throwing sweets out of the windows of a moving truck to children standing at the side of the road. These children were rushing into the road trying to gather up the sweets. We had to take evasive action to avoid hitting them.

If you want to help, take pencils, with rubbers on the end; they make a great gift that will last, and one that is universally welcomed by children and parents alike. Or consult www.stuffyourucksack.com where you can find out what sort of things you can take to the country you are going to visit and just as important, how best to donate it. Many years ago Tracy and I went to Cuba and we took some pencils, rulers and rubbers to donate to a school there. While travelling around the country we stopped at random at a primary school and, in poor Spanish, tried to explain that we were teachers on holiday in Cuba and we had brought some materials for them. They were over the moon, making us go into one of the classrooms and present the pencils and rulers officially to the school in front of one of the classes. The head teacher meticulously wrote down the details of everything we gave them and added our names and passport numbers. I assume so she could justify the sudden boost in numbers the next time an official came knocking on the door. I had been worried that the whole experience might seem patronising but in fact our gifts were warmly received.

Give pencils not sweets

The following morning we left Tete as soon as it was light and already getting warm and headed for the border. This was going to be my ninth African border crossing and I was by now totally relaxed and chilled about the whole experience; in fact I almost looked forward to it. The three hour waits and ridiculous photocopying of Central America was a distant memory; Southern African crossings seemed orderly and professional and most importantly, quick.

Leaving Mozambique was the easy bit; entering Malawi was a bit of a hassle. We had to get motor insurance and needed to work out whether the guy selling it to us was genuine or not. This was always a problem at borders. Not being quite sure what you need to do and whether or not to trust what you are told. If we had to get motorcycle insurance to ride in Malawi you might expect that there would be some sort of official way to tell us. Either a sign or piece of paper or perhaps an official in an official uniform with an official sign and official piece of paper. But this isn't how Africa works. The law might say something but it's up to the individual to find out and obey it. After all, the police will be waiting a few miles down the road to put you straight should you not have the right papers.

While I was dealing with the (free) visa and carnet Daryll and Angela were outside looking after the bikes. They were surrounded by over a dozen men, several of whom were telling them that they needed to get bike insurance. When we swapped over and they went to do the paperwork I was accosted by these gentlemen who were quite convinced that I needed insurance. One had a piece of paper saying something about traffic insurance on it and, he told me, we had to follow him to his office to get the paperwork done. He told us our friends had already gone there. I discussed with Daryll and Angela what we should do and we decided that we would go with him; after all, there were three of us.

We followed our official about a hundred metres down the road from the last border checkpoint and then left on to a mud track. We rode our bikes slowly while he ran ahead of us. His office was a converted ship container, and outside were two other motorcycles. Tom and Pat had just got their insurance and told us that they thought it was probably all legitimate and we would be wise to get some. Ten minutes later and $25 poorer I came out with a piece of paper saying I had road insurance. I still have no idea if it was genuine.

Meanwhile, Pat had been changing money. He said he'd negotiated a good price and had got 160 *kwacha* to a dollar. I was usually on the ball when it came to money but as we had moved from Zimbabwe to Mozambique and then on to Malawi so quickly I didn't really know what a good rate was anymore. When it came to money Pat was no mug either and I just hoped he'd got his numbers right. I changed a hundred dollars. Just as I was counting my last kwacha Tom appeared and said he'd got a rate of 185! Pat's face was a picture. He didn't like to lose at anything.

It was about eighty miles to Blantyre, our destination for that day. On the way both Tom and Daryll got stopped by the traffic police. Daryll was doing 56 kph in a 50 zone, Tom was obviously going a little faster. They were both fined $30. I couldn't help but laugh and saw it all as karma for them laughing at my traffic violation in Zimbabwe. The only injustice was that Pat hadn't yet got stopped and we all knew what speed he was doing: 93 kph.

CHAPTER 27

SPLITTING UP

"Tourists don't know where they've been, travelers don't know where they're going."

(Paul Theroux)

Malawi is all about the lake – there's 30,000 square kilometres of it, following the fault line of the Great Rift Valley for nearly 600 kilometres, 75 kms across – so after a night in Blantyre we headed for Monkey Bay on Lake Malawi. The Quad Squad had told us of a ferry that plied the route north up the long expanse of water, and we thought it might be an interesting alternative to riding (especially as petrol in Malawi was the most expensive I'd found anywhere at just under $2 a litre and we'd heard rumours that it was in very short supply anyway). Once we got there and checked out the details, Tom, Pat and Chris booked themselves in for the trip up the lake. I was quite keen to take the ferry as well but Daryll and Angela decided it wasn't for them and that they would stay in Cape Maclear for a few days. Was this going to be the end of the group? It was a long time coming and we really needed to break up while we were all still (just about) talking to each other.

Angela hadn't really been talking to Tom since Namibia. Daryll was equally annoyed with Tom, and Pat and Tom had been having a dig at each other occasionally as well. Chris and I seemed to get on well – her English was limited and I spoke no French, so perhaps that helped. We had spent five intense weeks together and for a bunch of people who'd essentially just met up on the road it was quite amazing that we got on as well as we did for as long as we did.

However, from my point of view the group seemed to be breaking up the wrong way. I decided to ride on with Daryll and Angela a few miles up the coast to Cape Maclear beach and stay with them at Fat Monkey's campsite for the night to say goodbye. I told Pat I would be back in the morning to catch the ferry and with that we headed off. I'm not sure if Pat believed me but at the time I meant it. I really did.

I had thought that the road to Fat Monkey's would be short and paved. It was neither. It was a mixture of dirt and sand and horrible corrugation. It took us over an hour to get there and when we did I knew I wasn't going to get up at dawn the next day to ride back to the ferry. I felt really bad about the way I had ditched the others and promised myself that when I next had wi-fi I would email them and explain. It wasn't how I wanted the split to happen. All three of them had been helpful, friendly and kind. They'd been a huge part of my life over the previous few weeks and although Pat and Tom did get on my nerves, that was bound to happen and there had been no animosity. I was fairly sure I would never see them again and slept uneasily that night. But Fat Monkey's was situated on the crystal blue Lake Malawi, the camping was $3 a night and the beer $1.50. We were going to be here for a few days.

Sitting by the water, reading, sunbathing and chatting to people I soon got over my guilt and thoroughly enjoyed my holiday at the lakeside. It was tempting to swim in the clear water but Lake Malawi has bilharzia. Larvae, released by freshwater snails penetrate the skin and mature into adults. Untreated this can threaten the urinary system and cause liver damage. The water looked refreshing and inviting but not that much. Cape Maclear had been what I had expected from Lake Malawi: decent camping at the beach side campground; guys trying to sell us everything from fruit to wooden necklaces to fish, but only half-heartedly in the heat of the day; great sunsets and wonderful night skies. Bed by 8 pm, up at 6 am.

Whilst there, we inevitably chatted about our options heading north. The road led up alongside the lake and on to Tanzania and it didn't take a GPS to tell us that this was the way to go. We decided we were in absolutely no rush whatsoever and planned to take our time enjoying the relaxing holiday feeling that being alongside a huge lake gave us. We didn't have to ride at 93 kph so we wouldn't. Also, from my point of view, I knew that my trip was coming to an end and it was now a matter of weeks, not months, before I'd be in Nairobi confronting the bureaucratic nightmare that getting Heidi back to the UK was bound to be.

Moving up Malawi we stopped at Mzuzu to get provisions for ourselves and the bikes. The first petrol station we found was empty but the second had fuel so we filled up even though I only needed half a tank. We then stopped at a supermarket to stock up on groceries. We all agreed that Malawi had the worst-stocked supermarkets in southern Africa. I assumed it was because everything had to come up from South Africa and the further away we got from SA, the less stuff there was available. It was pleasing to know, however, that I could still get Heinz baked beans and Marmite, even here.

While I was packing my food into my pannier, a young guy came up to me. He was standing a few feet away looking at the bike.

"Hello, how are you?" I said.

"I'm good. How are you? Where are you from?" He spoke good English but with quite a thick African accent. I thought it best to keep my answer simple. "London, England."

Suddenly his accent changed. "Oh, you a right geezer innit!"

"What? How come you speak like that?"

"My cousin. He live in London innit, and he learn me English."

I just had to smile. We had a long chat about England, football (obviously) and especially how good Wayne Rooney was. He'd never been to the UK but knew more about English football than I did and certainly more than Jonathan (at Great Zimbabwe) had. He kept saying things like:

"I fink Abramovich is rubbish, innit, He's well bad. Apple and stairs. Know what I mean."

He hadn't quite grasped the niceties of Cockney rhyming slang but it was one of those weird and wonderful conversations you have in the middle of another continent with a complete stranger. The sort of thing that never happens at home and, I think, happens all the more often because of the motorcycle.

We managed a leisurely hundred miles before stopping at Chitimba Camp. This was a real find. I have to admit that sometimes Daryll's GPS came up trumps. It was marked on his *Tracks4Africa* GPS map and without it I would have gone straight past the faded sign leading off down another sandy track. By now we'd become quite accustomed to our little end-of-the-day off-road experiences. I'd not dropped Heidi since the Caprivi Strip incident and Angela hadn't eaten sand since Namibia either. Daryll seemed to be the only one without a story to tell, until one night, lubricated with local beer, he admitted to me that he'd rear-ended a van in Mexico several months previously. Riding up ahead of Angela he'd looked in his rear view mirror to see where she was as they were caught in traffic and failed to notice that a taxi van ahead had stopped suddenly. He'd gone straight into the back of it. He'd only superficially damaged himself but his front wheel had dented the back of the van. Two angry Mexicans jumped out to confront him. "What did you do?" I asked.

I'd been over and over this kind of scenario in my head hundreds of times. Obviously the right thing to do would be to call the police and deal with it properly. Or was it? Many travellers' advice in this sort of situation is to deal with it quickly and leave. The last thing you want to do is get the police involved. That would just cause more problems down the line and delay the trip.

"I paid them and we left. There was no way we were going to get the Mexican police involved. It was my fault after all, so we agreed on a price and I paid it."

No doubt this was the right thing to do but Daryll never told me how much. $100? $1000? At least he had Angela with him and they could discuss it. This was the sort of situation that I just didn't want to get into on my own. So, we totted up our accidents and speeding fines and drank a toast to motorcycle travel. But it was another reminder of how dangerous motorcycle travel can be. We'd both heard of bikers who'd died on the road since we'd left on our trips and spared a thought for them as we drank another beer around our campfire on the shores of Lake Malawi.

Chitimba Camp was run extremely well by a Dutch couple who I got talking to when I went to the bar to get more beers. They'd only owned the place a few years and had clearly put their heart and soul into it. We were the only people staying there that night but they said they were often very busy. In fact we'd just missed an overland truck which had left that morning heading south. I was glad of that. The beauty, for me, of staying at a lodge on the lake was in its peace and tranquillity. Perhaps at the beginning of my trip, in Alaska, I had craved company but now it was the other way around. Sure, I had Daryll and Angela with me but we were all very comfortable with each other by now and I could easily go off on my own and not speak to them for hours at a time. I think we were all in the 'zone' that long distance travellers get into. The rhythm of my life had slowed right down and the simple things were giving me so much more pleasure than I could ever have imagined. I couldn't even remember, let alone care about all the kinds of things that would usually occupy my thoughts in my 'normal' world. I didn't care what I was supposed to smell like, wear, buy, eat or do. I didn't feel insecure around, belittled by, or inferior to my peers. I couldn't care less what the latest gadget, mobile phone or i-stuff was. I was what all those things are supposed to make you feel but never really do. I was content with my life.

Carmen handed over three beers and asked if we wanted to order any food; they had chicken stir-fry on the menu.

"No thanks."

Ed, her husband, then came around the corner with a huge dog.

"Is anyone in your group by chance a vegetarian?" Like most Dutch people, Ed spoke excellent English but with a slight drool, as each word slurred into the next. Or perhaps he'd just had as much to drink as I had that night and was finding it hard to control his tongue.

"Yes, actually I am," I replied, unsure why he had asked, but thinking he might be offering to rustle up a vegetable stir fry.

"Oh good. It's my dog. He's drinking but he won't eat."

This was followed by a very long and uncomfortable silence.

My alcohol-riddled brain slowly tried to make sense of the conversation. Was this some kind of Dutch joke? I didn't get it. Then, slowly, very slowly, as Ed stood there, looking hopeful and waiting for an answer, it dawned on me.

"Ah, you said *veterinarian* didn't you?"

I might have been in the 'travel zone', but it was also comforting to know that I could still be a complete twat at times.

*

All too soon Malawi came to an end and we were in the familiar surroundings of an African border crossing again. Leaving Malawi should have been straightforward – the passport guy stamped the passport and the carnet guy cancelled the carnet, and like all the borders I'd crossed (except getting into Zimbabwe) there had been no queue and no waiting. However we had money to change. I had about thirty dollars' worth of Malawi kwatcha and Daryll had two hundred dollars' worth. We'd stopped at the last big town before the border but the banks weren't interested. I had one bizarre conversation with the man sitting at the 'Foreign Exchange' desk of the Malawi National Bank:

"I'd like to change some kwatcha into Tanzanian shillings please." A reasonable request I thought.

"Oh no, not possible. We don't do that," came the reply.

"Can I get US dollars then?"

"No we don't do that either. Change with the men at the border."

"Can you tell me what the official exchange rate is?"

"Oh, it changes. Ask the men at the border. You know it's all down to supply and demand."

I really couldn't believe it. I was in the country's National Bank at the foreign exchange desk and I was having a chat with someone about supply and demand economics of the black market.

At the border it was quite hard to find someone who wanted to change money but eventually word got out and someone turned up with a calculator. But as it was highly illegal I had to leave the border area and enter a small shanty town which had built up behind the border sheds. I went off with a guy who'd promised 7.8 shillings to the kwacha. We went up a narrow, dark alley and past a few butchers. (When changing money illegally, at the border, it's always good to see that the locals have huge meat cleavers and know how to use them!) We changed money in a small shop. However, for the first time ever (and I'd crossed a few borders and changed a lot of money by then), I was scammed. While doing the calculation on his phone he typed in 7.08 instead of 7.8 as the rate. I caught him doing it and he said it was a slip! Later Daryll changed money with him too (there really wasn't anyone else to go to) and he tried a bigger rip-off, giving Daryll 600 instead of 6000. Not a great way to leave what was otherwise a lovely, friendly and beautiful country but it should have been a reminder that you need to remain on guard.

On the Tanzanian side the immigration and customs guys were efficient, friendly and helpful. We got our paperwork done in no time. Then we had to get insurance for the bike. Again, it was a walk down a back alley to an office but it all seemed legal enough. I got insurance just for Tanzania and Daryll got a COMESA which covered him and Angela for all countries heading north.

I also decided to change a little more money into Tanzanian shillings while Daryll sorted out his insurance. Although I was wary after my experience on the other side of the border it can be really difficult to change money in towns in East Africa and as I was waiting around for Daryll it seemed to make sense to get a few more shillings if I could get a good rate. Back at the bike I was surrounded by money changers. It was close to midday and I was baking under the hot sun. I still had my bike jacket on, not wanting to take it off in case it went missing. In hindsight it wasn't perhaps the best place to change money and after our experiences on the Malawian side I really should have known better. Perhaps, after so many border crossings and so many months on the road, I was getting a little big headed, thinking I could deal with every possible situation.

I started negotiations with the guy nearest me and although the others accepted this (perhaps they all belonged to the illegal money changing border union and would share all profits) they stayed to watch, which was a little intimidating. Perhaps that was the plan.

First he offered me 1500 shillings to the dollar which did indeed seem to be the going rate. I wanted to change $200. My maths suggested that this should be 300,000 shillings – a lot of zeros to be dealing with in the heat of the day. He gave me 100,000 in 10 x 10,000 shilling notes, then another 100,000 the same way. I was sweating in my bike gear, very thirsty and starting to get a little confused by all the zeros. This had all the ingredients of a major disaster, but still I carried on, convinced I could cope. My money changer then gave me lots of 500 shilling notes. As I was trying to count it, he kept talking to me and putting me off. The bike, where this illegal transaction was going on, was surrounded by his mates and onlookers all telling me it was the right amount. But something was telling me to recheck. I was starting to get a little agitated as I tried three or four times to count the money but just couldn't get through it all. Either I lost count half way through or he would count over the top of me and put me off. Was he being over eager and helpful or was I missing something? Perhaps he just wanted to get the illegal transaction completed before the border guard took an interest (and a cut?).

Luckily my brain was alert enough to know something was wrong and I asked Daryll, who had just returned from the insurance office, to double check for me. He counted out the 500 shilling notes. My money changer didn't look happy about it and sure enough it was another scam. He'd given me 200,000 but the last bundle was only 10,000 not 100,000. In essence he was giving me $140 instead of $200. I thrust the whole lot back in his hands (Clearly I'd learnt from my Victoria Falls experience and at least I hadn't already handed over the $200) and told him, in no uncertain terms, to go away. He stood there arguing that this was the right amount. He looked so indignant that I even questioned Daryll's maths; but he was right, this was a scam.

I should have ended it there and then, got on Heidi and ridden off, but another guy offered to change money with me and although he suggested a rate of 1450, we settled on 1500 and he gave me the full 300,000. I handed over my US$200. Daryll and Angela went back to their bikes and started to mount. I made sure my wallet, papers and passport were where they should be and put my helmet on ready to leave when yet another guy came over and started shouting at me. It appeared that he had the US$200 that I'd exchanged in his hand and he wasn't a happy bunny. He was telling me I owed him 10,000 shillings as the rate was 1450 not 1500. This was obviously the big boss and the guy I'd done the deal with had got into trouble for giving me a 1500 rate instead of a 1450 one.

Things were starting to get a little ugly now. We'd attracted a lot of attention (there were no other tourists crossing the border at all) and I just wanted to get out of there. I felt extremely uncomfortable having an argument about money changing literally ten metres from the border surrounded by about a dozen men. I was extremely angry that twice at one border money changers had tried to rip me off and I was angry at myself for getting into this situation. I knew that under the baking midday sun, if I didn't get out of there quickly I might do something I would later regret.

I told Angela and Daryll to get on their bikes and head off. I'd follow but I assumed they'd all chase me down the street and I wanted a clear road in front of me so I could accelerate away; I felt it was the only way to get out of the situation. The guy with my original $200 just kept waving it in my face and demanding his 10,000 (about $6). He stood right in front of the bike but by now I was mounted and ready to go. I'd stopped arguing with him as that clearly wasn't getting us anywhere. I was pleased I'd locked all my valuables away either in my jacket pocket or in my tank bag and I focused on starting Heidi up. Perhaps the roar of the engine would scare them away.

I turned the ignition key. Now was not the time for the BMW computer to fail me and tell me the bike wouldn't start. It didn't. As I hit the starter button the noise of the engine made many of the group take a step backwards and even the guy in front of me moved slightly to his side. I took this as a sign of weakness and turning my handlebars slightly to the right I pulled my flip-front down, kicked Heidi into first and made it obvious that I was leaving. If this was going to work I was going to have to be quick, decisive, and lucky. If any of them held onto any of the bike we could all end up on the tarmac. I let the clutch out and the engine bit as first gear was engaged. I swerved to my right and without looking back or thinking about all the bad things that could happen, I sped off up the road towards Tanzania and freedom. I took a quick glance in my rear view mirror, but all I could see was a dozen or so men standing in the road where I had left them, waving and shouting at me. I'd got away.

It wasn't long before I caught up with the others and we were riding north into Tanzania, heading for Mbeya. All that grief over changing money and in the end it all came down to an argument over $6. I felt angry, annoyed and frustrated all at once; not a great way to feel when riding a motorcycle in a brand new country. I needed to forget about the border and concentrate on riding through Tanzania. I focused on the glorious lush scenery that we were riding through and quite quickly my heart rate slowed, my grip loosened on the 'bars and I started to calm down. We were soon climbing away from the hot basin of Lake Malawi into the Tanzanian mountains. Passing banana and tea plantations, we climbed to over 2200 metres before dropping down again. Motorcycles were replacing bicycles as the main form of transport, although there was still very little traffic on the roads. The altitude and scenery calmed my nerves as I started to enjoy the experience of my ninth African country.

CHAPTER 28

THE END OF THE ROAD

"It is good to have an end to journey towards; but it is the journey that matters in the end."

(Ursula le Guin)

Mbeya was a hot, dusty town, clearly popular with truckers if the traffic was anything to go by. With limited options for the night we headed to a church mission. *Tracks4Africa* had suggested this was just about the only place to stay and we hoped we could camp in their compound. We found it quite easily thanks to Daryll's GPS, and the mission people were more than happy for us to pitch our tents on their lawn (which doubled as a volleyball court). We paid a few dollars for the privilege and as we handed over the money the security guard smiled at us and said: "Just watch out for the guard dogs, my friends. You will be fine in your tents. But at night we have guard dogs loose in the compound. If you leave your tents they will attack. If you need to go somewhere just shout for the night guard and he will come to help."

I didn't fancy risking it so I woke up the following morning with a very full bladder. Heading east towards the coast and Dar es Salaam, the traffic increased and we had to share the road with big, slow and very smoky trucks. Up to this point there had been surprisingly little traffic on the roads of southern Africa, at least outside the large towns, but in Tanzania that changed. Overtaking one of those trucks I ran into a Tanzanian traffic policeman and his speed gun. I was doing 54 kph in a 50 zone. I argued that this was only just over the limit and he laughed and told me to enjoy my trip. I was beginning to like Tanzania.

A day short of Dar es Salaam it began to rain. This was the first time it had done so since I'd left Lesotho. We rode on past boab forests and on towards Dar and the rain got quite heavy, making it impossible to overtake trucks. For a while riding became miserable. Rain mixed with dust on the roads meant that the trucks were kicking up walls of muddy spray. Low cloud cover made the African bush less inviting and for half a day riding just became a dull, wet experience.

But by early afternoon the rain had disappeared and as we approached Dar it was hot again. Unfortunately we arrived on the outskirts of this huge port at around at 3 pm on a Friday. Bad move. I blamed Daryll's GPS. Surely it could have warned us? The heat and traffic were crazy and in a strange way it actually reminded me of my arrival in Las Vegas. Hot, sweaty and confusing and I had no idea why I was there. It took us almost two hours to get to the port and the ferry that Daryll told us would take us across the water to where the campsites were. (Dar itself didn't have a campsite.) We queued up for the ferry. Us and hundreds of locals going home for the weekend.

The ferry was predictably chaotic. As soon as we could board, passengers, cars and tuk-tuks were all edging their way forward towards the roll-on roll-off boat. It had been a long, hard day in the saddle and although it had started out wet by now it was sweat rather than rain that was making me feel uncomfortable. All I wanted was to get across the water, to find a campsite and take a long cold shower. My jacket and trousers were caked in dry mud from the trucks' spray that morning and I was tired, grumpy and had a sore arse. There were no officials anywhere coordinating the loading of the ferry; people and vehicles were just edging forward and piling on. If we didn't join in we'd be left behind. Angela's bike boarded first followed by Daryll and I just made it on before the ferry was full. My back wheel was a few metres from the back of the boat and only a metre above the waterline. There were half a dozen cars on board and hundreds of passengers. I couldn't have got off the bike even if I'd wanted to as I was surrounded by people standing next to me just staring at Heidi. Daryll had said it should only take about ten minutes to cross the estuary but, sitting there, squashed in like sardines, sweating, dirty and tired, even ten minutes was going to feel far too long.

I sat on the bike and stared into the middle distance. I was in no mood to chat with anyone. All day long I'd had a vision of a beach-side campground in the back on my mind and that thought had propelled me through the dust and rain and past truck after truck. We'd ridden two hundred and fifty miles but it had taken ten hours and I wanted it to end. I wanted to be lying on the beach staring out at the Indian Ocean with a nice cool beer. We were nearly there; nothing could go wrong now.

When the ferry docked on the other side I let all the other traffic and pedestrians get off before wearily riding off myself, up the slope and over to where the two DRs were parked next to a tuk-tuk. On the ferry Daryll had got talking to a local woman, Alisha. She wanted to hear our stories of biking through Africa and insisted that we went to her house for the night. This was unbelievably kind of her, and very brave to invite three bikers to your house on a whim.

So instead of finding a campsite we followed Alisha in her tuk-tuk taxi to her brand new house. In fact it was so new she didn't have any running water and the electricity wasn't working. I wasn't going to get that cool shower or, indeed, that cold beer. It was hard to take but Alisha had been so kind to invite us to her house that I couldn't really complain. She wanted to hear all about our trip and we spent a lovely evening telling her our tales and in return she told us what life was like in Tanzania. But I ended up going to bed smelly, sticky and very tired.

However I didn't get to sleep easily. The three of us were sharing a room, sleeping on a couple of old mattresses. It was incredibly hot and humid on the coast and as there was no electricity there was no air-conditioning or even a fan, and it was a muggy night. We'd sprayed the room with mosquito repellent but that only seemed to agitate the little buggers and the whole night was spent tossing and turning, unsure whether to cover up with a sleeping sheet and get hot or uncover and get bitten. It was, without doubt, the worst night's sleep I had on the entire trip.

In the morning I counted fifteen mosquito bites on myself. Daryll was counting the bites on Angela and stopped at seventy! Itchy, sleepy and feeling encrusted in two-day-old sweat, I went outside to get some fresh early morning air.

"Morning Dom. Sleep well?" asked Alisha.

"Yes, great thanks."

It was deeply ironic that the worst night's sleep had been at the hands of the kindest gesture. Alisha had been so friendly; it would have been ungrateful to let her know we hadn't slept well. She has a job and a family and responsibility and would never, in her wildest dreams be able to do the sort of travelling that I was doing. And there was I, moaning about the mosquitoes and complaining about the state of the ferry. Alisha had to use that ferry twice a day, every day and was back off to work now. We needed to find a campsite, so after the briefest of breakfasts we thanked Alisha for her kindness and moved on. Daryll's GPS told us where the nearest campsite was and we headed off in the early morning air to finally find the Indian Ocean.

*

We stopped at Mikadi Beach Camp and had a relaxing two days on the beach. We had the place to ourselves by night and I got talking to the couple who owned the site. Jo was from Zimbabwe and Lucho from Chile. They had found the place for sale on the internet and bought it three years earlier. I loved their free spirit and sense of adventure. I'm not sure where or how they met but they were undoubtedly travellers at heart and had decided to risk everything and try to create a traveller-friendly lodge on the beach in Tanzania. Talking to Jo and Lucho reminded me again of all the friendly, helpful and open people I'd met in the last year. Travelling can be hard, sometimes. The very nature of moving on makes it hard to form anything

315

other than very superficial relationships with people. I must have spoken to hundreds and hundreds of peoples since Alaska but it scared me to think how few real conversations I'd had.

I was just beginning to wonder whether there was something negative about riding a motorcycle, and that perhaps travelling with others in a vehicle would bring so much more by way of conversation and companionship, when a truck turned up at the beach camp with a dozen British overlanders on board. It had crossed my mind on more than one occasion that this would be a very cheap way to travel through Africa, but the more I saw of overland trucks the more I was convinced that they just weren't for me. Perhaps because of the low cost, they seem to attract youngsters who see the trip as one huge party. Often they didn't seem all that interested in where they actually were and their evenings revolved around drinking competitions and one-upmanship games as the lads competed with each other to impress the girls. I was too old for all that and much preferred riding a bike, alone.

I was lying in a hammock by the bar reading a book and listening to the lapping of the Indian Ocean on the white sand when the overlanders came in. They ordered two beers each and started playing drinking games. They were all British and their conversation revolved around British celebrity culture. Hearing it all, for the first time in months, reminded me of what I was about to return to in the UK. Which famous footballer was shagging which famous model? Which phone was the latest and greatest must-have and what I should be wearing. We were in Africa for God's sake! This sort of superfluous, mindless nonsense was what I was trying to get away from. I couldn't stand it and I had to leave the hammock and go for a walk.

Walking along the beach gave me time to think and instead of worrying about what I'd just heard I mulled over what I'd just accomplished. I sat on the sand looking out at the Indian Ocean thinking, 'I rode Heidi from Alaska to get here.' On the one hand it seemed surreal, almost impossible; on the other, it was quite straightforward. I was two days' ride away from Nairobi and the end of my trip. I didn't want to tempt fate, but sitting on the beach in Dar I knew I'd got away with it. I couldn't help but feel a little sad that my dream was finishing. The conversation in the bar persuaded me that while my trip might well have changed me, the world I would soon be going back to hadn't changed at all.

Daryll and Angela had decided to go to the island archipelago and former independent state of Zanzibar for a few days and asked me if I wanted to join them. I couldn't think of a good reason not to, so we left the bikes with Jo and Lucho and caught the ferry to the Spice Island where I went scuba diving.

I had considered doing some marine volunteering somewhere on my trip.

I love diving and am aware that our coral reefs are in imminent danger. Many scientists think that by 2050 there will be no functioning, healthy coral systems left anywhere in the world. A recent report I'd read suggested that coral reefs in the Indo-Pacific region are disappearing at an alarming rate. At 1% a year the reefs are actually disappearing faster than the rainforests. The UN says that a third of the world's coral reefs have already died and by 2030, that figure is predicted to be closer to two thirds. We need to understand why this is happening if we are to do anything about it and that is where conservation and volunteering projects come in. Although the reefs in Zanzibar looked quite good, I knew that I was seeing an increasingly endangered environment as threatened and unique as the rainforests of Brazil and as important. I enjoyed my diving but felt hugely guilty that I wasn't doing anything to help.

Back at Mikadi Beach Camp our bikes had been joined by two others. These were the first bikers we'd seen since Namibia. David and Claudio had started in Johannesburg and were heading up to Ethiopia. David was on a Suzuki DR 650, Claudio on a BMW F650 Dakar. Both bikes were overloaded with gear strapped on with nets and bungees but what was impressive about David's bike were his panniers. They were home-made, out of old plastic toilet cisterns. Before I started my trip I had assumed that by the time I finished I would have learnt a lot about motorcycles and would be able to hold my own in a conversation about engines and stuff. I couldn't. Claudio asked me about my GS and I struggled with the answers. Except the one about how heavy it was. There is no doubt that a BMW R1200GS is a big bike. It looks big and it is big, (although not as heavy as its predecessor, the R1150GS). He asked me if it was too big. He had one of the big twins at home but had chosen the smaller 650 Dakar single for his African adventure. I had been extremely impressed with the way Heidi had dealt with Africa. It certainly wasn't the skill of the rider which had got us this far. Yes, she is big and heavy but it never ceased to amaze me how well she handled. On tarmac she was manoeuvrable, flexible and had the power to get out of the way of trouble. On sand she was certainly more of a tank but not as bad as people who haven't ridden one might imagine. I'd only had the one tumble and that was certainly my fault and it would have happened whatever bike I was on. 'The weakest part of a motorcycle is the nut that holds the handlebars to the seat.' Nevil had taught me that in Canada.

I can honestly say that I have been very happy with my choice of bike. If I had only been riding through Africa, solo, then perhaps I would have chosen a smaller bike. I don't really need the twin's hundred brake horsepower and she's certainly heavy to pick up. However, it hadn't been a problem and bearing in mind that I did a lot of miles two-up in Central

America with Tracy on the back, Heidi had been wonderful. There really isn't a 'best' bike, it all depends what you want to do with it, your riding style and personal preference. Too many people get caught up in arguments over which bike is or isn't the right one for a certain trip. I'd met so many bikers on my trip on all sorts of things and every bike had been the right choice for them.

I'd got a lot of friendly stick from the Canadians as I was the one on a BMW. Pat had ribbed me about having more money than sense because I was riding an expensive BMW while he was two-up on a twenty-year-old Honda Africa Twin. Of course he had a point. I could have gone for a cheaper, smaller bike. Whether it was right or wrong, however, one of the reasons I'd chosen a GS was because I knew nothing about motorcycle maintenance. I was of the opinion that I needed a newish, reliable motorcycle that wouldn't break down (or at least if it did break down it would be some computer-related issue that I wouldn't be able to fix however good my mechanical skills were). It would have been foolish for me to have ridden Pat's bike as I didn't have the skills or confidence to repair it. Horses for courses.

Our evening talking with the South Africans was soon over and the following morning we packed up and headed off towards Arusha. It took us two short days to ride from Dar to Arusha; I was going slowly because I didn't want my trip to end.

As we entered Arusha we pulled over to the side of the road to stop for a few minutes while we decided what to do. We had a look at the guidebook for a cheap but friendly campground and lodge within walking distance of the town centre. Daryll and Angela wanted to go on safari to the Serengeti National Park and although I hadn't made my mind up whether or not to join them I was in no particular rush to get to Nairobi, so finding a nice place to stop for a few days in Arusha seemed like a good plan.

As we were conferring, a couple of armed police spotted us and came over to see the bikes. By now we were used to people coming over and had well prepared answers to the usual questions. In Southern Africa these questions usually revolved around how much the bike cost. I had a theory that the type of questions I was asked about the bike and my trip reflected the culture I was travelling through. In North America people were just amazed that I had given up my job and was travelling for so long. How could I get the time off work? Why would I voluntarily give up a job to travel? Why was I travelling alone? (as it's dangerous) and where was my gun? In Central America most questions revolved around the top speed of the bike; a particularly tricky question to answer when it was asked by the police. They always seemed a little disappointed when I said that I kept to below the speed limit. In Africa money was on everyone's mind. How much did the bike cost? Again, difficult to answer. If I gave the correct answer it was such a huge amount to most people I feared they might decide to rob me. But if I lowered the price, which I sometimes did, I was confronted with a look of disappointment. It was always hard to please the punters.

So, I was ready with the stock answers as the police turned up. In fact, they didn't fit the usual stereotype and were just keen to take a look at the bikes and chat to us about our trips. They were so friendly that I decided this was a *Pogo* moment and I took photos of the police, proudly displaying their guns next to the bikes. I gave them a copy of the picture which they were thrilled with. We were going to be in Arusha for a few days, you never know when a friendly policeman might come in handy.

We stayed at the Masai Rest Camp. Angela talked me into going on a safari trip with them so we headed off to the Serengeti to see some animals. We hooked up with a Dutch couple, Martijn and Ivon, so there were five of us in our Land Cruiser for four days. It took eight hours to ride from Arusha to the campground in the Serengeti. We stopped off at the Mary Leakey Museum on the way. Mary Leakey is famous for discovering 'the footsteps' – footprints in volcanic ash which are three to five million years old and the first recorded evidence of *homo sapiens erectus*. (Crucially these people walked upright like us, the proof being the way the big toe is aligned with the heel, not off-set like an ape's.) Incidentally, this epic discovery was made (in 1978 I think) when two of the party were messing about throwing elephant dung at each other. One fell to the ground and literally stumbled upon the prints. What a great way to make such an immense discovery.

Returning from a fantastic safari in the Serengeti we stopped off at the Ngorongoro crater. Geographically the crater is a large volcanic caldera, which means it's a huge bowl-like depression caused by the collapse of the land following an eruption. The volcanic mountain, perhaps originally as high as Kilimanjaro, erupted and collapsed over two million years ago creating a six hundred metre deep bowl some one hundred square miles in size. This creates a rather unique ecosystem. Few of the animals migrate out of the crater, resulting in a sort of inbred ghetto. The lions especially, breed within a small gene pool and because of the abundance of food for them they are significantly larger than other lions and can easily repel the odd outsider who comes in. I had a comical image in my head of large, inbred lions chasing zebra up the steep edge of the crater until the zebra can't climb any higher and fall back to be caught and eaten. It wasn't quite like that.

We camped on the rim (which, at 2,400 metres, was cold) and got up at 6 am so we could get into the crater before sunrise – and before most of the other dozen or so groups who had been camping with us. Although I'd read about the animals I would find in the crater I was also interested to read that even though indigenous tribes had lived in and around the crater for thousands of years the first Europeans didn't set foot in there until 1892. Again, I found this amazing. I'd taken it for granted that I could visit the Ngorongoro crater if I wanted to. All I had to do was find a tour company and pay them some money. We get so used to the idea that we can do whatever we want, wherever we want if we have money. And yet, be it Victoria Falls or the Ngorongoro crater, it was only in relatively recent times that Europeans had even known about them. I was humbled, again, to realise that I was so fortunate to be living in a time when, with a British passport, I could travel freely around so much of the planet. All I needed was time and money, and in relation to my ancestors, not really very much of either of these two commodities. I could visit the Ngorongoro crater and the Serengeti on a two-week holiday from Europe and it might cost me a month's wages. My grandparents couldn't do that.

Go a little further back and my forebears wouldn't even know these places existed. Living now and knowing all this, it seems criminal to be alive in this day and age, living in the rich industrial west and not to go and see some of the wider world. But equally, I felt guilty that it was certainly in large part due to the comfortable, wasteful lifestyle that we have created for ourselves in the West that so much of this natural world was under threat. It is ironic that in creating the conditions by which we can appreciate the world, we are also destroying that very same environment. In the forty-four years I have been alive we have discovered so much about the planet on which we exist, and yet at the same time we have done more than any other generation to destroy it. When I was born there were three and a half billion people sharing Earth; that figure has now doubled.

In all we had five hours in the crater spotting numerous lions and even a solitary black rhino. There are only about twenty black rhino left in the Ngorongoro crater and they are all radio-tagged and monitored. Apparently there are only fourteen in the Serengeti. In the whole of Africa there are possibly only three and a half thousand. To put that in context, a hundred years ago there were probably several hundred thousand. Going on a safari can be life-affirming and wonderful, but it can also be quite depressing.

After a few quiet days back in Arusha it was time to move on. Reluctantly, one day in the early morning mist I packed my tent up, loaded the bike and headed off, for the last time. By the end of the day I planned to be in Nairobi and to all intents and purposes it would be the end of my trip. Daryll and Angela rode up front, I wanted to take it super slow that day and savour every last minute. As we rode around the foothills of Kilimanjaro and on towards the Kenyan border I couldn't help but think back over the year and all the amazing things I'd done. It could have been the wind blowing through my open visor but my eyes were getting watery and I was actually choking back a few tears as I reached my final frontier. This one was different. It was the last one. I'd crossed nineteen borders, visiting eighteen countries and Kenya wasn't just another one, it was the last one.

As soon as I arrived two or three guys came over to 'help' me. One offered to sell me motor insurance for Kenya (we were still in Tanzania). Another wanted to change money and the third wanted to help me through the process of leaving one country and entering another. Again, the perennial problems travellers face at a border. Should I trust the guy selling insurance? What's a good exchange rate? Is it worth being helped through the process? I'd have to give him a few dollars but it might save a lot of time.

After a chat with the insurance guy I decided that I'd trust him and he went off with my details to get me one month's motor insurance for $37. I told the guy who wanted to help me that I didn't need any help and went into the building to get stamped out of Tanzania. I didn't change any money (his rate was 80 shillings to a dollar). I was getting good at this border thing. One of the things this sort of travel develops is the ability to make quick decisions about who you can and who you cannot trust. I didn't always get it right but I'd certainly got better at it and I wondered whether this would be useful back in the real world. The real world? What the hell was that? I couldn't imagine myself back in the real world. But I knew it was going to happen.

Back on the bike I moved a few hundred metres into Kenya behind the two DRs. Same process. I didn't need insurance as I already had it (it looked official, I just had to hope that if I got stopped by Kenyan police it was). I was offered 81 shillings to a dollar but when I pointed out that there was a bank in the customs building offering 83 we settled for 83.5 and I changed $200. I had to pay $25 for a Kenyan visa and $20 road tax (or something similar) for the bike. My carnet was stamped and that was that.

We headed out into Kenya and the final hundred or so miles to Nairobi. I was looking forward to a pleasant, leisurely ride into the capital; I didn't get it. Like most of Africa the worst roads were to be found where they are constructing good roads. Huge stretches of the road north to Nairobi were being worked on and we were diverted off on to poorly maintained, dusty and occasionally muddy by-passes (if that's not too grand a word for what was in fact just a rough track by the side of the road). So much of my last day's riding involved dealing with corrugated earth roads, dusty trucks and crazy matutus (minibuses). I thought of all those fantastic roads I'd been on: Dalton Highway in Alaska, Stewart-Cassiar Highway in Canada, Route 101 coast road in the United States, parts of Baja California, the Sani Pass in South Africa, Namibia's gravel roads.

As we entered Nairobi, Daryll's GPS took over and with the traffic bumper to bumper, we slowly made our way to Jungle Junction. Well known to overland travellers, 'JJ' is the place to stay in Nairobi. It had camping and rooms but more importantly a garage where people could work on their bikes, Land Rovers or trucks. Anyone who's been overland through East Africa will have stayed there. It had always been in the back of my mind that JJ, Nairobi would be my final destination and as I got closer I have to admit that I was getting a little emotional. I tried not to, it was silly really, but all the way into Nairobi images of things I'd done and seen over the year flashed through my mind. Not a good idea really as the road was terrible, the traffic little better and I needed to focus on what I was doing.

Finally, we turned a corner and entered Jungle Junction through the large gates. I rode the bike over the gravel pathway towards the office, stopped and reversed a little to get a better angle at a parking spot. Daryll told me to move the bike forward and he would take a photo of me finishing my trip. I let the clutch out to inch forward.

Heidi stalled.

My journey had ended.

EPILOGUE

WHY NOT?

"Wandering re-establishes the original harmony which once existed between man and the universe."

(Anatole France)

Two years later, I'm sitting at home in the UK trying to sum up my journey. Heidi the R1200GS is parked outside, having made it back to the UK by plane and through the tortuous import procedures. Her Alaska licence plate now has pride of place on my mantelpiece. Every time I ride her I get a thrill from thinking that I rode this very bike half way around the world.

Coming home was a bitter-sweet experience. Of course it was great to have made it back and to be home with Tracy again. But I had been on this wonderful adventure and it was hard to readjust to domestic life having been on the move for so long. For nearly a year, all I thought about was the bike and moving and what I wanted to do and see. Now I have essays to mark, household chores to do, bills to pay and every morning I wake up in the same place. This is perhaps the hardest aspect of travelling: returning home.

On my trip I had been with other people who were doing the same thing; I felt at home. Now I was at home but it felt unnatural. I had a lot to say about what I'd done but nobody wanted to hear about it. People were, quite rightly, getting on with their lives and didn't want to hear about my 'holiday'. They asked, out of politeness, but they didn't really want the details. And more importantly, I found it hard to explain; hard to sum up in a few sentences what it had been like to travel 30,000 miles through 18 countries on two continents by motorcycle.

Frustratingly most questions focused on the dangers of travelling and I tried to explain that the world isn't a dangerous place, that I'd met kind, friendly and helpful people wherever I went. I hadn't felt in danger (apart from those bloody bears) and didn't want to talk about any of the so-called 'bad stuff' as it would be the only message people would take away. But people like a good scare story and almost seemed disappointed when I just said I'd gone riding.

I *had* had a wonderful time and I wanted to share *that* with people. I wanted people to appreciate that the world we hear about in the news and read about in the papers or see on package holidays is not the real world; or at least it's not the full story. The generosity, help and friendship I had been shown, from Alaska onwards didn't surprise me but it did humble me. It reminded me how lucky I was and renewed my faith in humanity. Living in the rich west and watching TV it's all too easy to see the rest of the world as corrupt, dangerous and immoral. American media coverage of Mexico and British media coverage of Zimbabwe are examples of this. But go and explore and you will find a very different planet.

I wanted to explain that the world has some wonderful natural sights worth seeing. Whether it be the enormity of the Yukon, the amazing National Parks of the United States, the Mayan settlements in the Central American jungle, the vastness of Namibia or Great Zimbabwe. I was well aware that I was incredibly fortunate to be in a financial and social position to do what I had done. But I wanted to encourage others to take that vital first step and embark on a life-enhancing if not life-changing experience.

I'd also learnt so much about myself. I'd stepped out of my comfort zone, dealt with situations I wasn't used to and tried to help a little by volunteering along the way. I'm not sure if I'd managed to pick up any new skills which would help me in life but I'd taken a break from my normal life and it felt good. I hadn't come back a changed man and my trip hadn't changed my life. That was fortunate really as I didn't feel I needed my life to change. But I'd grown as an individual and thoroughly enjoyed myself. What better way to spend a year of one's life? Getting promoted? Buying more stuff? There's always time for that.

I'd also made friends. I've kept in touch with Daryll and Angela, who ended their trip in Kenya having detoured to Uganda and Burundi. I hope to visit them in Canada one day. Pat, Chris and Tom made it to Europe, though not together. It appears they split up in Ethiopia and Tom rode north, through Sudan in the summer months on his own. I don't know how lucky he was to survive in that heat but I have nothing but respect for him in accomplishing such a feat at his age. He came to visit me in the UK and it was great to see him again. We'd spent four weeks travelling together through Southern Africa, and although we may not have been the best of buddies towards the end we had got on well most of the time. Travelling puts an enormous strain on relationships and it says a lot for the six of us that we put up with each other for as long as we did. I'd like to see Pat and Chris again. I hope they feel the same.

Recently I heard from Lerato in Lesotho. She's managed to get a place in the National University to study Adult Education. Her life is on the up. I'm still in contact with Jim and Nevil, two people whom I travelled with only briefly but who will nevertheless forever remain good friends. I often wonder what happened to the other bikers and travellers whom I met en route. I hope they are still out there in the world, living the dream.

On a sadder note, unfortunately neither Sebastian nor Viola, the twin sloths, made it to their first birthday.

Back in the UK, I was not only finding it difficult to reintegrate I was also feeling guilty. Guilty that I lived in a comfortable, rich country where the supermarkets never run out of food, the electricity always works and I am free to say whatever I want about whomever I want. I'd tried to give a little bit back with my volunteering but it was a drop in the ocean.

I spent the first few weeks after returning in a sort of weird, post-trip 'bubble'. I'd completed my journey but had nothing to show for it. I had so much I wanted to say to people but no way of saying it.

And then, in one of those coincidences that happen every so often in life, I came across The Ted Simon Foundation. It seemed the perfect way for me to try to communicate what I had learnt, and I hope what I have written will encourage others to venture forth into the world. It doesn't have to be on a motorcycle and it doesn't have to take a year. I sincerely believe that our Earth, which, let's face it, is the only one we have, will be a better place if more people who are privileged enough to be able to, get out there and explore it. Travelling helps break down barriers, dispel myths about other peoples and broadens the mind. Wouldn't the world be a better place if every world leader had to take a GAP year and travel before taking up their post?

Writing this book helped me to think through the trip I had been on, reliving the highs and lows and taking time to appreciate all that happened. It also helped me to finally answer that one question that I had never really answered. Why leave everything behind to travel? Well, I now know the answer and I hope that after reading this book you do too. 'Why?' is the wrong question. We shouldn't need a reason to explore our world. This is *our* planet, *our* life, *our* time. The question shouldn't be 'why?'; it should be 'why not?'

What next? Well, I want to experience as much of the planet as I can, while I can, with Tracy. So, when time and money allows, we plan to continue to wander around it. I hope you will too.

Dom

"Perhaps travel cannot prevent bigotry, but by demonstrating that all peoples cry, laugh, eat, worry and die, it can introduce the idea that if we try to understand each other we may even become friends."

Maya Angelou

JUPITER'S TRAVELLERS — THE TED SIMON FOUNDATION

The Ted Simon Foundation is a non-profit organisation based in Northern California. It aims to encourage and assist independent adventure travellers in their exploration and comprehension of the world and the communication of what they discover – whatever their medium of expression might be.

"Travellers survive and flourish by adapting to the world around them. As a result they learn a particular truth about the societies they move through. What they learn can be of great value in explaining the peculiarities of foreign cultures and in reaffirming what is common to all of us; generosity to strangers and a desire to live in peace. The purpose of the Foundation is to bring those truths to the general public, to counter the generalisations of the media, and to remind us all that life is lived family by family, mile by mile, regardless of the great issues which may be dominating the news.

We believe that all travellers have it in them to be reporters of truth in the world, and we want to encourage them to broadcast that truth by whatever means may be appropriate. The honest personal experiences of perceptive observers have great power to remind us that we all share this world. Our ultimate aim is to promote understanding, reduce tension and to favour the chances of peace in our world." Ted Simon

For more information go to:

jupiterstravellers.org